Sexual Orientation and Identity

Heterosexual, Lesbian, Gay, and Bisexual Journeys

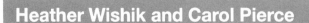
Heather Wishik and Carol Pierce

New Dynamics Publications, Laconia, New Hampshire

Library of Congress Catalogue Card Number 94–69743
ISBN 0–929767–03–9 pbk

© 1995
Printed in The United States of America

NEW DYNAMICS Publications
P.O. Box 595
Laconia, New Hampshire 03247–0595

Graphic Design: Todd Smith

To Susan and Sydney

CONTENTS

Sexual Orientation and Identity

Heterosexual, Lesbian, Gay, and Bisexual Journeys

PREFACE

This book provides some stories, some strategies, and a diagram. They are a guidebook, if you will, for heterosexual, lesbian, gay, and bisexual people and organizations interested in moving forward to repair what is dividing and hurting us about sexual orientation. Our goal is for each of us to have the opportunity to become the best self, colleague, friend, family member, lover, and member of the community possible. We want to help build healthy organizations and communities that are creative, productive settings able to invite each member to contribute her or his best. If such goals are worth pursuing, it is time we all pay attention to and take responsibility for changing the troubled ways in which human sexual diversity is understood and treated in contemporary society. This work is also a necessary aspect of dealing with issues between women and men in society, and is related in important ways to understanding and making progress in dealing with race prejudice and racism.

Much of what people write and say today about sexual orientation focuses on gay, lesbian, and bisexual people's actions and experiences. However, heterosexual people also act out of and experience negative consequences of learned fears, confusions, and behaviors related to sexual orientation. This is not to say that the trouble in contemporary culture which surrounds sexual orientation doesn't affect gay men, bisexual people, and lesbians differently than it affects heterosexual people. What we are saying is that our society and organizations will not keep moving forward on this issue as long as it is framed as an issue belonging to a small percentage of the population. Heterosexual people also are negatively affected by—and have a positive stake in changing—the ways in which contemporary cultures construct the concept of sexual orientation in general, and heterosexuality in particular. Everyone also benefits when heterosexually identified people can move beyond phobias, presumptions, and obliviousness, as well as beyond behaviors involving violence, discrimination, and prejudice related to sexual orientation.

It is time heterosexual people started doing their own work of awareness about heterosexuality as a journey, as a consciously developed and publicly sustained and privileged aspect of identity. It is time to learn more about how excluding, silencing, and rejecting gay, bisexual, and lesbian people function socially and personally to sustain and enforce heterosexual identity. It is also time lesbian, gay, and bisexual people had tools for a deeper understanding of the ways their experiences are related to heterosexually dominant culture and more personally to the stages of development at which they, themselves, as well as the heterosexual people who matter in their lives, are situated. Gay people need to find more autonomous, grounded, and positive ways of interacting with heterosexual culture and heterosexual colleagues so they can maintain health, career, and a sense of integrated wholeness not simply within gay/lesbian institutions and settings, but in all the family, work, religious, and community settings important to their lives.

The facts are simple. Some people have wanted, and have created, primary, intimate relationships, sexual or not, with persons of their own sex, and other people have done this with persons of another sex, or with both sexes, in every culture and time from which we have any historical or anthropological records. Cultures have understood these varied desires and behaviors in many different ways, and have invented many ways of incorporating people having these types of desire into society. In several cultures male heterosexual maturity is believed to require homoerotic experiences first. Sometimes heterosexual union, or marriage, was expected to coexist with one's romantic inclinations and passions toward a person of one's own sex, usually a younger person for whom the male partner served as mentor in the case of males, or a co-wife in the case of females. Sometimes homoerotic desire was evidence of special spiritual powers; sometimes it was thought to mean the person was of a third gender. In other cultures, homoerotic relationships, usually between an adult and an adolescent, were part of expected human development and training for adulthood. Some cultures saw persons who wanted to be with those of their own sex as unusual but normal, or sick, or evil. Many cultures combined several of these approaches. Sometimes those who desired closeness with their own sex lived among everyone else, and such desires and behaviors were viewed as consistent with heterosexual marriage. Sometimes the homoerotically inclined people became a special spiritual cult, or outcasts, or hidden members of the rest of society. More recently there have developed in Western countries a variety of homoerotic and ambierotic (or bisexual) subcultures within dominant heterosexual cultures.

We in contemporary Western cultures, in some Asian cultures, a few African cultures, and traditional American Indian cultures, live in a time of transition. For example, no longer are Western cultures characterized by widespread denial of the existence of sexual diversity or when its existence is acknowledged, by exclusively negative judgments about nonheterosexual orientations. Instead in many settings, people, organizations, and institutions are reacting in an increasingly welcoming manner to the visible presence of gay men, lesbians, and bisexual people.

Despite these changing attitudes, people in many parts of the world live in societies where segments of the population face both violent and more subtle forms of harassment, discrimination, and ostracism because of sexual orientation or identity. Harassment, discrimination, and ostracism, whether actual, threatened, or feared, hurt organizations and their members, reducing productivity and disrupting or creating barriers to collegial communication. Anyone can be the object of such attitudes and behaviors regardless of actual sexual orientation, since much reaction is based on stereotypes about appearance and behavior rather than knowledge about a person's actual sexual identity.

This reactive turmoil often includes attempts to enforce narrow ranges of acceptable male and female behavior, and thus affects us all. In the United States seventh-grade children are affected by the fear of being called "queer" or other words. Some boys report that such fears limit the colors of clothing they wear and their involvement in activities such as dance. Girls report that similar fears affect their choices of jewelry and clothing, their involvement in sports, and their participation in class. At its worst this adolescent form of homophobia involves violent gay bashing, including assaults against heterosexual teens who don't fit closely enough the increasingly rigid ideas of maleness and femaleness. For adolescents of all orientations who are uncertain about their own sexual identity, the consequences of our culture's trouble with sexual orientation all too often involve suicide. The possibility of being gay feels like a fate worse than death.

Fear about homoerotic feelings keeps many persons, especially heterosexual people, from the fullest friendships and colleagueships they could experience with others of their own gender. These fears also interfere with family relationships and are a factor in premature adolescent heterosexual behavior. In the United States cultural constructs about sexual orientation teach and encourage heterosexual people to mistreat and dehumanize colleagues, family members, and friends. All these are consequences of the cultural morass surrounding sexual orientation and structuring heterosexuality, in addition to the stigmatization experienced by gay, lesbian, and bisexual people. That stigmatization results in loss of creativity, productivity, and participation as well as discrimination, violence, and waste in human lives.

We believe none of us want our children dead, beaten, or arrested for beating someone else. We believe most people and organizations want fear, ostracism, discrimination, and harassment to stop and want to find ways of interacting respectfully with one another. To do so, we must find ways of talking with one another across the barriers many of us have been taught to make of sexual orientation.

If all of us are going to feel safe enough with each other to work toward respecting sexual diversity and managing it well in our organizations, it is crucial to understand that such work involves for everyone, regardless of sexual orientation, experiential journeys that can be acknowledged and described. This book, through both narrative and graphics, describes a variety of these journeys along a continuum of attitudinal and behavioral change.

Several theorists have designed models which describe racial and sexual identity development as experienced by people of color, gay men, and lesbians. We believe the portion of our work that describes lesbian and gay journeys taken by people of color and by white people is consistent with such models, and we have found them helpful. Our work has a broader focus, however. We try to map and describe the development of attitudes, understandings, and sexual identity by gay men, lesbians, and bisexual people; the journeys of attitude, understanding, and reaffirmed identity which can be traveled by heterosexual people; and the relationships between these journeys.

We've discovered that people are often able to move farther in their own journey when they see a picture or diagram of journeys on which they can nonjudgmentally place themselves. Others feel sustained and acknowledged for the work they have already done in moving along the journey as well as supported in moving farther. The sexual orientation and identity continuum diagram (following p. 272), the model we introduce through workshops and this book, also provides individuals the opportunity to see privately, without embarrassment, where they are in relation to a diverse group of others, encouraging changes in attitudes and behavior with minimal resistance.

In working toward respecting sexual diversity, we have an immediate need for common language. Readers may be used to, though not always comfortable with, the word *sexism*, which raises questions about the assumption of superiority and institutionalization of dominance of one gender over another, and *racism*, which raises questions about the assumption of superiority and institutionalization of dominance of one race over another. Now the word *heterosexism* will involve us in looking at assumptions that one sexual orientation is superior to another. A term related to heterosexism is *homophobia*, that is, an irrational fear of and hostility toward lesbians, gay men, and homosexuality, including one's own capacity, if any, for same-sex feelings. Another related term is *biphobia*, that is, an irrational fear of and hostility toward bisexual people and bisexuality.

What This Book Is and What It Is Not

This book is based on many people's stories, including those of lesbian, gay, bisexual, and heterosexual people of color and white people, children and adults. It is about how people experience living in heterosexually dominated cultures.

This book is about how information, attitudes, and values about sexual orientation, sexual identity, and gender emerge, are internalized, and affect individual and community development and behavior. (See Appendix A for definitions of and distinctions between key terms such as *gender*, *sexual orientation*, *sexual identity*, and *sexual behavior*.) It is a book which suggests that each of us is on a journey of discovery and awareness about sexual orientation and on a journey of construction of gender and sexual identities. During this journey we may learn, in the context of our culture, how to understand, recognize, and act on our own orientation, how to understand and react to people of orientations different from our own, and how to construct both a sexual identity and a gender identity that feel right to each of us.

This book is about how heterosexual dominance makes it difficult, occasionally even impossible, for lesbian, gay, and bisexual individuals to discover and develop a healthy selfhood. Many gay, bisexual, and lesbian people do nonetheless succeed in healthy, proud development of sexual identities consistent with their sexual orientations. This book is about how heterosexual people often are not aware consciously of their own process of sexual orientation recognition and, therefore, often fail to develop fully as persons because unconscious heterosexuality places limitations on who they can be as heterosexual men or women.

This book explores the heterosexual privilege of functioning oblivious to the existence and needs of people with other sexual orientations, and the hurt such oblivious dominant behavior can cause to collegial, familial, and community relations. It is a book about how we all can move along journeys and in the process develop our capacities to work together across lines of sexual orientation diversity, and to work in ways that value our diversity and enable deeper, more trusting, more productive relationships.

This is not a book which sets out to settle the many political and scholarly debates about human sexual diversity's causation, history, or variety. We are more interested in the sense people make of their sexual feelings, desires, and actions than in the causes of sexual orientation. However, in order to describe and structure the attitudinal journeys represented by the continuum model we have created, we have found it necessary at times to make working assumptions about some of the issues in those scholarly debates. (For a discussion of these issues and our assumptions see chapter 2 and Appendices A and C.)

How This Book Is Organized

This book adopts two overlapping approaches to its subjects—one mostly theoretical, one largely descriptive of experiences. Chapter 2 gives the assumptions, context, and frameworks on which the continuum and this book are built. (The continuum diagram is bound into the back cover of the book.) Appendices A and C constitute the often theoretical parts of the book. For readers interested in understanding at the outset our definitions, Appendix A explains the key definitions we have used or developed in creating the continuum model. Appendix C summarizes ideas from some of the theorists engaged in the scholarly dialogues and debates about human sexuality and gay, lesbian, and bisexual identity development.

Chapters 1 and 3 through 8 constitute the more experiential parts of the book. The authors' and consulting colleagues' own journeys are set forth in chapter 1. For readers who prefer to begin with or only wish to read about the adult experiential journeys depicted by the continuum diagram following page 272, these include chapters 1 and 3 to 8. In chapters 3 to 8 phrases on the continuum diagram appear in bold type at the place in the text where each is discussed. Childhood journeys are found in Appendix B.

This book on Sexual Orientation and Identity is a part of a series, which includes *The Male/Female Continuum: Paths to Colleagueship*, by Carol Pierce, David Wagner, and Bill Page, and *The Black/White Continuum in White Culture: Paths to Diversity*, by Linda Thomas and Carol Pierce. This series addresses those identities, other than class, that culturally carry the heaviest burden of emotional resistance to change from the dominants: gender, race, and sexual orientation.

Who We Are and How We Coauthored the Book

We are a lesbian and a heterosexual woman, both white, both living in New England, one Jewish and one Protestant. Heather Wishik wrote Appendix A, Definitions and Categories, chapters 4 and 5 dealing with gay, lesbian, and homosexually identified bisexual peoples' experiences of subordinance and transition, chapter 6 about bisexually identified people's experiences of transition, Appendix B, "Childhood," and Appendix C, "Scholarship about Sexual Orientation." Carol Pierce wrote chapter 3 about heterosexual and heterosexually identified bisexual peoples' experiences of dominance and chapter 7, dealing with transition away from dominance for heterosexual and heterosexually identified bisexual people. The preface, chapter 2, "A Journeyer's Guide," and chapter 8, "Where the Journeys Lead," were jointly written, though Heather took the lead on chapters 2 and 8. Chapter 1 consists of stories written by us and a multicultural group of colleagues and workshop participants.

ACKNOWLEDGMENTS

We thank our many friends and colleagues who have supported us in the writing of this book.

Our first sexual orientation workshop based on this idea of journeys and this continuum was held in the summer of 1990. We are grateful to the participants, whose response validated our work, giving us support to complete the writing: Richard Cornwall, Chris Forbes, Keith Goslant, Al Halverstadt, Richard Hasty, Ron Henderson, Pamela Holliman, Lennox Joseph, Bunty Ketcham, Erna O'Shea, Beverly Reddick, Alexsandra Stewart, and Lynda Stolzman, also an early reader of the manuscript.

Participants in several 1992 and 1993 workshops and presentations about this continuum also added immeasurably to our understanding through their responses and disclosures.

We thank our colleagues and New Dynamics partners who have been in dialogue with us and commented on our work—Keith Goslant, David Wagner, Lennox Joseph, Rick Huntley, Sharon Bueno Washington, Linda Thomas, Bill Page, Karen Terninko, Barbara Berry, Ron Gibson, and Richard Orange.

We also thank others who read the manuscript: Kathryn Ragsdale, Susan Sasser, Will Sherwood, Blaine Bershad, Sarah Litchfield, Marcia Hill, Nicola Morris, Linell Yugawa, Rianna Merrill Stone, and Karen Sandhaas. Their comments are appreciated and added immeasurably to the content.

Kathryn Gohl's editorial skills were essential. Melanie Heinis's tireless word processing of the many drafts was also essential.

Heather wishes to thank Susan L. Donegan for their many clarifying conversations during the writing of this book.

Carol particularly thanks Heather for her patience and clarity in facilitating a "straight woman's journey" in order to coauthor this book; David Wagner for his "straight-male" insight into men's issues used as a basis for her writing, and for steadfast support; and Keith Goslant for his forbearance and generosity of spirit in their work together on these issues.

PART I

Real Lives:
Stories for Understanding Our Journeys

Journeying

*Eight Sexual Orientation and Identity Journeys
and an Invitation to Your Own Journey*

In this society it is difficult to obtain accurate information about how people discover their own sexual orientation and go about making meaning of it in their particular cultural context, that is, go about constructing their sexual identities. Although gay, lesbian, and bisexual people sometimes tell their "coming out stories" to each other, and more rarely to heterosexual people, real-life stories that describe the process of sexual orientation discovery and sexual identity construction aren't told often, least of all by heterosexual people, who are rarely asked to think about their lives in these terms. We believe that such retrospective life stories, and the patterns and themes of stories from heterosexual, gay, lesbian, and bisexual people, are some of the most useful, easily available data from which to look at how we learn about sexual orientation, how we construct sexual identity, and how we can grow and change in our understandings and attitudes about sexual orientation and identity.[1] Some researchers also have begun collecting data from gay- and lesbian-identified adolescents with the hope that prospective, longitudinal studies may tell us even more accurately how individuals in particular age and cultural groups construct sexual identities or engage in "life course construction."[2]

In our consulting work, we lead several types of workshops. One type involves an in-depth, three-day format working with a small group whose participants are willing to disclose their sexual orientations and identities within the confidentiality of the workshop's confines. In that format we ask every participant to prepare a ten- to twelve-minute oral response to the following three questions:

1. How do you know you are (your sexual orientation)?
2. Describe your process of figuring out your sexual orientation and constructing your sexual identity, starting with when your process first began.
3. What has it meant and what does it mean now in your life to be the sexual orientation and sexual identity you are?

Additional questions, particularly for heterosexual people to respond to, are:

1. What has moved you to reassess your assumptions, values, and beliefs about homosexuality and bisexuality?
2. What has it felt like to open these issues up?
3. What has held you to your journey?

Within the workshops, the group of facilitators spends a great deal of time with participants, who are sometimes separated into gender, culture, or sexual orientation groups, figuring out how to make the workshop feel safe enough for people to speak to the group in response to these three questions. Eventually, all participants are given ten to twelve minutes to tell their journey. Most of a day of workshop time is occupied with hearing these journeys, one after another. These stories are the data from which workshop participants then work with us to make meaning both of individual experiences and of the cultural, historical, political, and institutional contexts which frame and affect those experiences. Then participants can start talking about how to effect needed systemic changes within the particular setting or settings from which they come. It is in the context of the data provided by the group of stories, and the themes that emerged in them, that we as facilitators talk through the sexual identity journey diagram contained at the back of this book and explained in detail in chapters 3 through 8.

As a reader of this book, you do not have the benefit of a day's worth of individual stories as data. In an effort to provide you with some comparable data, we invited our two most-frequent workshop cofacilitators and several other colleagues and workshop participants to join us in writing for this chapter the sorts of responses we each make when we are in a workshop setting and speak for our ten minutes about our individual journeys.* In addition to reading our stories which follow, we encourage you to take some time to answer the questions for yourself, to set forth on tape, or in writing, or just in thought, your journey. Then you will have, at a minimum, nine journeys to reflect on as you read the rest of this book. We hope the book will help you make meaning of your own journey and of ours, and of the larger historical and cultural contexts in which we live such journeys. It can also help you examine where you are and where you want to go next in your own journey as well as suggesting what next steps might be useful to you or your institutional setting.

---

*Each of us has responded to the workshop questions differently at different times. This is to be expected. We each make sense of our lives anew in new situations or at new life stages. Thus, a person's understandings change over time and so the reconstructed journey changes.

The book may also help you understand where colleagues, friends, relations, or organizations may be on their journeys, what responses from you may be most helpful to them, and what you can most appropriately expect from them.

Carol's Story

I know I am straight because I am attracted to maleness. I enjoyed partnership in a marriage with a man. It gave me great comfort to be loved and cared about intimately by a man.

I don't remember having to figure out I was straight, though I did have to figure out being sexual. I have always been aware of special interest and attraction to maleness. However, calling this interest heterosexual was not in my vocabulary as a child. In early childhood I assumed I was to get married to a man but I didn't understand how that would happen for me. It wasn't until junior high that I thought of myself being in a relationship and, of course, it would be with a boy. I did not think of this as being heterosexual, but rather just what one did as a girl.

My earliest memories are of loving to be included in groups of children playing together. I was fascinated with the boys. I preferred groups where there were both boys and girls. The boys made it exciting and the girls made it safe. I lived across the street from my elementary school and could watch older kids playing, particularly boys. I could observe them safely from the curb. Groups of girls playing made me want to be included but were of lesser interest or, I should say, excitement.

Boys were a mystery and a bit scary. I was afraid to talk to them very much, so I avoided them and watched them from a distance. White culture supported me early in thinking about my feelings, rather than acting on them. As I grew older, I wanted to be liked by certain boys, but if I was I didn't know what to say or do. There was never any question in my mind that I was attracted to the other sex. I enjoyed girls' company as comfortable and safe, but I didn't pay attention to them in the way I did to boys.

I remember one boy in grade school who was a terrific artist. He could draw anything and was very funny. He was different from other boys. I was not afraid of him, but I did notice that he only talked with girls. The boys would not include him in groups. I wondered about him but was pleased that there was a boy who didn't scare me.

By adolescence my attraction to boys was known to me through my daydreams and fantasies, through the novels I read and the pop music I listened to secretly late at night on the radio, and through my fears. In junior high it was clear that my crushes were on boys—about one each year (I am very loyal)—and on several male teachers.

I remember needing to know about sex. I wormed the "truth" out of a girlfriend who was a year or two older. Once she described the male/female sexual act to me, I said, "Fine. That's all I want to know." I kind of laughed to myself; it felt so logical and right. I found a sex manual in a church bookstore when I was away from home. I was bold enough to buy it. It may have referred to homosexuality, but I wasn't interested. Heterosexuality fit me, though I didn't call it that.

Because of my straight identification, I did not have to figure out my sexual orientation. I was expected to be attracted to boys and was supported in this choice by everyone around me. However, one of the main ways I was supported was in the form of warnings not to go "too far."

In senior high my church youth group meant a great deal to me. I appreciated my girlfriends in the group—all of them. However, I liked the fact that we stayed as a group with the boys. It was a safe and wonderful way to get over some of my fears of maleness and to have boys who were friends. I learned I could be a leader, but I secretly assumed that such assertiveness kept certain boys from liking me. (It was just as likely my awkwardness.) Upon entering college, my heterosexuality felt a strong need for recognition. I consciously turned off my leadership abilities until I had met and married my husband. He never needed me to do this. I thought I had to.

In my college days of the early 1950s, I was unaware of homosexuality or bisexuality as orientations. I was so wound up in my heterosexuality—dating a man and thinking of marriage—that I now see I didn't want to hear about gay, lesbian, or bisexual people. There was a security in my heterosexual world, a belonging and doing "the right thing" that matched my sexual orientation. Being white and heterosexual gave me this sense of security so that I could choose when to push my issues of being a strong girl or woman and when to let them go. The combination of my whiteness and heterosexuality supported a feeling of being in control of my life, particularly since I had not experienced physical abuse or overt discrimination as a girl growing up.

I never considered any other orientation as a young woman because I didn't consciously know of the possibility of being lesbian or bisexual. Not until I actively entered the women's movement in the early 1970s did I stop to think about my, and others', sexual orientation.

My early days in the women's movement brought me friends who were just coming out as lesbians. To be accepted as oneself in a women's group required accepting everyone else for who they were. My need to be included was high because I was sometimes given the impression that I fell short of what the "new" woman should be. I made a commitment to myself that my seeming exclusion at times would not be my way with other women—all would be included. Therefore, lesbians would be counted among my friends and in my work on women's issues (including my work as a consultant and as chair of a state commission on women). My habit of thinking things through and then acting reflects my white, intellectual way of handling deep emotional issues.

My first reaction then to homosexuality was Why not the possibility of woman-to-woman orientation? It seemed logical that homosexuality would occur. It shouldn't be a big deal. However, another more emotional reaction came as I listened to the stories lesbians told. I was overcome with the pain, alienation, and fear that comprised everyday life for them. I resolved not to be a part of the world that was unaccepting of homosexuality.

I "jumped" into my journey in understanding the possible diversity of relationships and sexualities with an intellectual acceptance and tolerance of homosexuality, based on my general wish for civil rights and justice for everyone. My emotional involvement, though real, tended to be intellectualized—my white cultural training. My oblivious heterosexism was just beginning to crack. Until then, at an emotional level I had avoided all cues about any orientation different from mine. There is no doubt they were there, but I assiduously avoided them.

The difficulty for my lesbian friends was that my justice/tolerance stand was not enough. This was confusing to me, so I kept a low profile with them. There were times I felt excluded from their groups. There were whispered conversations barely outside my hearing, where I picked up snatches of sentences about the pain of lesbianism. I knew I wasn't being talked about, but wondered at my lack of inclusion. I now know they were getting support from other lesbians—doing their own work; plus, my heterosexual demeanor lacked acceptance of them. I was very straight in how I looked and acted. I couldn't imagine sharing my feelings of exclusion with anyone. It was confusing to be left out for being heterosexual. I wanted the focus to be on all of us together as women, with some who were different and apparently needing special understanding.

In New Hampshire in the early 1970s, I was part of a group of women who organized consciousness-raising weekends to explore our concerns. As word of what we were doing spread, several radical lesbians from Boston came to one of our sessions. (Today I would not see them as radical, but that's what they were called in the 1970s for being out and politically active.) We had been experimenting with designs and content, and were just becoming comfortable with what we were doing. I had a personal development tape that my brother had given me which featured a man talking about (men's?!) development, using *man* generically in the title. The Boston lesbians let us know in no uncertain terms that we were naive to use the tape on a women's weekend. We salvaged what we could from the learning experience at the time. However, the major impact for me was learning how angry women can be at men (justifiably) and how easy it is to accept unquestioningly a male worldview and not challenge assumptions about women. It made me wonder why I hadn't perceived the implications of what the man was saying on the tape. I felt very heterosexual and got a glimpse of how strongly I bond with heterosexual people (men) when I am unaware of a lack of attention to women's experiences. I still often think about how blind my heterosexuality can make me to women's issues.

There have been two times when my heterosexuality was raised to me in interpersonal relationships with women. Generally I find a common bond with those women who have developed awareness about themselves as women. Such self-understanding is mutually recognizable and forms an instant bond (more quickly with white women, because we also share a culture). However, my heterosexual woman's expression of feeling a bond was taken on these two occasions to be sexual interest.

Within a year these two incidents happened. S. and I had occasion to work together. We had a good time laughing and talking about our work. I was becoming comfortable with more generous hugs with everyone in my life and we had some wonderful hugs. She invited me to stay with her one evening when I needed to work in her area. I arrived to find a white tablecloth and candles, dinner just for us. Others in her household were gone. It suddenly hit me as we were dining and I was talking on and on, and she was quiet and staring, what this was all about. We never said anything about what happened. I left the next morning with mixed feelings, a sense of wonderment that a woman had been "interested" in me, a sense of her hurt at my lack of response, and confusion on my part about what I was supposed to have done.

M. was and is a good friend of mine. She was not yet out to me. On one occasion when visiting her, after a long conversation I got up to leave the room momentarily and she reached out to hug me in a way that surprised me. I walked past her without response because I wasn't feeling a connection at the moment, but I knew something more was there for her. I felt I had let her down.

I had not considered the possibility that these two women were lesbians. I had to think about my part in their assuming I was sexually attracted to them. I could see that my actions could be interpreted that way. One of the comforts I had come to assume with women was that I could be expressive, spontaneous, and free. It was a welcome relief from being misinterpreted by men as giving sexual messages. (I had not had enough experience with gay men to know I needed to refer specifically to heterosexual men here.) I learned I needed to be more thoughtful about such assumptions.

The women's reactions caused me to raise questions about who I was. Was I lesbian? What was my relationship to women? Was I erotically attracted to women myself? Had I missed something by never considering lesbianism or bisexuality? How did I know I was heterosexual? For the next year or so I tried to be aware of my feelings and actions with women I liked and felt close to. I found I enjoyed my friendships with women but in no way was I erotically drawn to them. However, I did find I had been missing much emotional connection and appreciation for women's culture by being so exclusively heterosexually focused all my life.

As l look back on this time, I did not have to work hard to decide on my orientation. It could be thoughtfully explored without much hassle, because my erotic attraction to maleness had been clear all my life. The question I was really asking myself was Was I bisexual? At this point I really hoped I might find this true; but alas, so far I have not identified as such.

As a straight married women, I received respect and support for being married and acknowledgment for being paired. I loved the feeling, though I took care to be seen individually also. In public I could hold hands and kiss my husband fondly when meeting and parting. Friends ask about my husband (who recently died) and my family. I often show pictures of them.

My belongingness is affirmed. My heterosexuality is so "normal" that it has been an assumption on my part, resulting in an undeveloped appreciation for the process of knowing my sexual orientation and being comfortable with who I am. The process I have gone through to confirm my heterosexuality has brought an understanding and comfort with my orientation but also an appreciation for the self-discovery of others' orientation.

My comfort with my own orientation has made it considerably more easy to be comfortable with lesbians, bisexual people, and gay males. It has helped me separate myself, that is, set my boundaries in relation to homosexuality and bisexuality. My boundaries were set based on my comfort and awareness of my personal needs.

Early in my journey I gained a sense of balance toward homosexuality by intellectualizing the issues as justice for all, with little emotional involvement. Later my emotional involvement grew as some bisexual people, lesbians, and gay men became more comfortable and open in my presence so that their love and caring for each other was expressed in such ways as holding hands, kissing, and dancing together. My initial feelings of distaste were based on what it would feel like if *I* had to do this. Since I was clear about my orientation, my heterosexual boundaries differentiated me from homosexual people. They were who they were and I was who I was; a simple statement, but I could begin to see the emotional disorder that had been caused by being unclear about my sexual identity. I could relax and get more used to same-sex expressions of fondness and love.

I also remember wondering a lot about "how do they do it." As one or two lesbian friends answered a few questions, I laughed and said, "That's enough, I understand." I am aware now of how things unknown or defined as unnatural support voyeurism. I don't want that to be a part of my life.

Sexual energy is erotic energy but also creative and spiritual energy. I am aware of this in the creative process of working with others. As I understand this part of myself, I have taken time to understand women's culture and my tie into the spiritual side of it. My sense of myself as a sexual being affects the intensity and depth of my creativity, and thus the sense of the spiritual. These are bound together for me.

The process of becoming clear about my straight orientation has brought growing awareness of women's culture as exemplified by lesbian culture. I pay more attention to those like myself—women. As I listen to, observe, and occasionally participate in lesbian events, I catch a glimpse of connection and support between women that is new to me. Though I do not participate in the depth of sexual attachment, there is a sense of broadening my emotional connection with women—all women. My experiences with lesbian, gay, and bisexual friends also bring insight to the limitations of being heterosexual. I do not experience these limitations as a deficit, but as reality, as my lesbian, gay, and bisexual friends do with their orientation.

As I struggle to understand my white identity, my female identity, and my heterosexual identity, these identities-of-difference give me more ways to connect, both within them as well as across them. I know myself better and have more to share.

I have been held to my journey in several ways. My sense of justice for everyone will always be basic. My professional work as a consultant and trainer demands that I continue to expand my learning. However, the two most important reasons are my love for those close to me living in the midst of homophobia and biphobia and the excitement I will always have of knowing more about myself as I understand the diversity of others.

Heather's Story

In the deepest center of my being I know my sexual, erotic, and emotional/affectional desires, interests, and energy are for women. I identify as a lesbian, rather than as queer, gay, bisexual, dyke, ambisexual, autoerotic, sexually diverse, in the life, or some other way because, among the identities available at this time in history, and as a white woman, the word *lesbian* best describes my locus of desire and best describes my sexual, emotional sense of self as well as my political commitments. It wasn't until I was twenty, however, that I understood anyone might feel so centrally other than heterosexual. It was even later that I first identified myself as lesbian. Almost twenty years after my first lesbian identification, lesbian identity for me carries complex meanings.

In fact, my sense of being a lesbian is one of ongoing transformations of identity, as what is possible and comprehensible in this culture shifts, and as what is meaningful and necessary politically and personally changes. Sometimes I feel pressured, both by my cultural and political contexts and by my personal relationships, to speak about my lesbianism in a way that confirms a greater continuity of sexual identity and sexual desire, and a greater exclusivity of inmost erotic capacity, than seems accurate in terms of my own experiences. In order to be honest about the actual discontinuities in my journey I need to recount some of my sexual and relational history.

I was sexually active in childhood, but my early experiences did not suggest any particular or fixed sexual orientation. Behaviorally and in terms of fantasy I was exclusively autoerotic as a child; that is, I was from an early age secretly involved with my own body genitally and oblivious to the idea that such physical pleasures might include feelings toward or sexual activities with others.

My memories of intense feelings, fantasies, or fascinations about and longing for closeness with other people during early childhood include people of both genders. First was my passionate emotional attachment to a best female friend, H., with whom I spent huge amounts of time—overnights, afternoons, weekends—and about whom I often felt very possessive, from the age of two until she moved away when I was twelve.

After H. there was a series of one-at-a-time best girlfriends to whom I was emotionally attached. Sometimes I watched them and found them beautiful, but I was never conscious of erotic feelings or fantasies toward them except once. When staying overnight at A.'s house she started teasing me that she'd show me her breasts if I showed her mine; she started flashing her undershirt up and down so I got split-second glimpses of the buds underneath (we were eleven or so). I did not wish to reciprocate because I had a large heart surgery scar across one breast, but I knew I really wanted to see more of what she was offering to show me and that it was very exciting. Also, from age three there was R. He was the eldest son of family friends, seven years older than I, that is, old enough when I was three to carry me piggyback. I think at that stage he thought I was cute, and I adored him for being a big kid who would pay me attention. This affection was quickly noticed by adults, who declared that this meant I was in love with him. I took their word for it that the feelings I had for him were what "being in love" meant. I felt shy around him. When I made a secret birthday wish, for years it included marrying R. He left for prep school when I was about seven and we saw each other rarely from then on, but he remained a safely distant object of romantic fantasy until my early teens.

As a white child, my early experiences of being "other" had to do with my parent's religiously mixed marriage, and with my father's McCarthy era problems, both of which affected how adults treated me at times. I never had a conscious sense of being different or other in terms of my gender or sexuality, although I certainly went through feeling awkward, shy, and unsure of myself socially, and was labeled a tomboy often before my teens. I also doted on my share of teachers, mostly female but occasionally male. If I had even known the words and had been asked about my sexual orientation, I would have labeled myself heterosexual.

In high school I was involved in religious youth-group social activities. There was little pairing off. I had intense "best" friendships with girls. I also had many crushes on boys and one boyfriend, M., whom I adored and about whom I felt romantic and erotic. He wanted to be fully sexual and I didn't, and I won that struggle. We both went to college, me at age sixteen, him at eighteen, which ended our relationship. It was 1966 and I had never heard the word *lesbian*. I didn't know that there were people who felt erotic about people of their own sex, let alone that such people could lead productive lives, have relationships, develop cultures and communities. My entire store of information about behavior other than heterosexual consisted of hearing my mother warn my brother that there were men who might try to undress or touch boys in public rest rooms at the ball park.

Then I met S. She and I started college together and immediately became best friends. She was, to me, gorgeous. I loved to look at her. When S. dropped out in the spring and rented an apartment, I spent lots of time with her. She was very nonchalant about undressing and dressing in front of me. I was able to look at her often. She was lithe, blond, freckled, very different from my dark solid body. One day she was changing her clothes, we were talking, and I was looking at her small breasts. I realized consciously that I felt turned on by her. I didn't say anything but she saw me staring and said, "In high school a lesbian approached me once and I didn't like it." I didn't know what a lesbian was, didn't know what S. meant by "approached," but I didn't ask any questions. "Oh," I said, and left it at that. It was 1967, I was seventeen years old, and I didn't know what any of the feelings I was having for S. might possibly mean. They also did not feel central or urgent enough for me to overcome my fear and go looking for answers. I simply went on exploring sexuality with men.

In the fall S. moved to New York City and I moved to Ithaca. When I went to visit her, S. took me to a lesbian bar, although she didn't call it that. She just said, "I know a place we can go where we won't get hassled." I spent the hour we were there trying to figure out if the very butch bartender was a woman or a man.

I don't recall the question of my feelings for women surfacing again for about three years. Meanwhile I had gone into therapy for mild depression with a male psychiatrist with whom it never occurred to me to discuss feeling erotic toward women. I went to therapy after a period of promiscuous heterosexuality. I was concerned that I had not "succeeded" in having a love relationship with a man. In therapy I dealt with problems about my father, and the therapist confirmed that I would be "better" when I was in a sustained sexual relationship with a man.

Shortly before terminating therapy I moved in with the man I later married. During the same therapy year I became a member of a women's consciousness-raising group, made a new best woman friend, began developing my feminist politics, and for the first time met a woman who said she was a lesbian. This woman was married and told us she had recently left her husband because she was a lesbian. She seemed to me unhappy and physically unattractive. I was twenty and remember feeling both frightened of her and smugly glad I was heterosexual. I think it was the first time I ever consciously identified as a particular sexual orientation.

Several years later the man I'd been living with and I married and had a child. Three years into the marriage, after some attempts at joint counseling, we called it quits. I lived alone with our son, then age two. This time I found a woman counselor to help me through the transition. Shortly thereafter I admitted to myself that I was in love with a best woman friend and that this was not the first time I'd felt this way. I used the word *lesbian*, quietly, privately, to myself, for the first time. I was twenty-six years old. The word, the identity lesbian, felt like a way of loving myself and honoring the deeply affectionate and erotic feelings I'd been having for women for so long.

This time my woman friend and I talked with each other. The sexual/ emotional feelings were mutual. However, she had been in a relationship with a woman after her marriage ended, which had provoked her husband to threaten to fight for custody of her son because of her lesbianism. She wasn't willing to risk that again.

It hadn't occurred to me that custody was an issue until she said this, but I too was terrified of losing my son. We kept things platonic. My friend felt her primary erotic feelings were toward women, but she told me she wasn't brave enough to live as a lesbian. We did go to a lesbian bar together, and she introduced me to other lesbians. It was suddenly easy to find other white lesbians. After all the years of thinking I'd never met any, I suddenly was given access through my friend and my new awareness to bars, coffeehouses, parties, concerts—all the aspects of community and culture that white lesbians were developing in southern California. I recall that despite the location, I never met a Chicana lesbian, that the lesbian settings were almost completely white. As soon as I finished graduate school I moved away. That same summer I had what turned out to be my last affair with a man. My woman friend married again the following fall.

About two and a half years of celibacy ensued while I read everything I could get my hands on about lesbians and toyed with the possibility of sexual relations with several women but did nothing. I was still scared, still unsure. My custody fears about my son served as a convenient excuse. I fell in love with another woman friend and she with me during this time. I told her how I was feeling toward her but said I wasn't sure I was a lesbian and didn't want to act on my feelings yet. I also continued occasionally to go out with new men, but a single date was usually enough to confirm that I wasn't interested anymore. I did not identify publicly as a lesbian during this time, although I told individual women friends and colleagues I thought I was a lesbian.

When I finally began my first lesbian relationship I immediately felt I had found myself sexually. I had come home. I couldn't believe it had taken me so long to do this. I couldn't stop smiling for weeks. That relationship settled into a friendship fairly soon, but I was finally, at age twenty-eight and a half, clearly and completely out to myself as a lesbian and happy about it.

I came out to my son around this time and then began the process of coming out by talking, not by behavior, to friends and family. This impulse to name my identity and to speak about it rather than simply to show up at an event with a girlfriend or to leave some other behavioral clue was very much part of my white, middle-class culture. I was used to labeling verbally and judging things, and to using language instrumentally to help me know what I felt, to make things feel real by saying them out loud.

What has lesbian identity meant to me? I grew up without language, stories, role models, or information about anything but heterosexuality, with a physiology that made it very easy for me to feel genital sexual pleasure by myself or with other people regardless of gender, and with what is probably a slightly ambisexual sexual orientation that leans strongly toward women. Given all this, I identified as heterosexual until my mid-twenties.

Having found an identity, lesbian, which honored the emerging primacy of my feelings for women and my commitment to being sexual exclusively with women, I sometimes felt pressured by heterosexual family and friends to identify as bisexual, because to them that identity seemed more acceptable. I never did so, however, having felt clear from the first relationship with a woman about the primacy and exclusivity of my commitment to women from that point forward in my life. I also recognized with that first relationship that my deepest and strongest and core sexual feelings were for women. Within lesbian circles and relationships I sometimes felt pressure to deny or minimize my prior heterosexual history. In some settings today I feel comfortable using Julia Penelope's language for myself: I am an "ex-het" lesbian, as distinguished from a "never-het" lesbian. In other settings this language is used to call me less a real lesbian than the "never-het" lesbian. My fierce response to all this obsession with defining identity from heterosexual, lesbian/gay, and bisexual quarters is to remember my goals. One aim is to help create a world in which we can expand the available identity concepts so the complex truths of each of our lives can be valued, supported, and comprehended.

Lesbianism has also meant for me as a white woman relatively easy access to woman-identified culture, politics, social networks, rituals, and symbols that have mirrored me and enriched my understanding of the world, other people, and myself. It has also meant experiencing social, political, legal, and civil ostracism in ways from which I was insulated as a white, middle-class, and able-bodied female until I came out. These lessons have provided me with reasons to learn more about, and from, other experiences of oppression and to attempt to interact with a wider range of individuals and groups than I might otherwise have done. In particular it has been an impetus to learn about and work on my white dominance. My last decade of political work toward civil rights for gay and lesbian people, people with HIV, and with AIDS, and my educational work about homophobia and heterosexism also have enabled me to meet people all over this country and have stimulated me to keep elaborating my healthy, prideful sense of lesbian identity.

Lesbian identity has both strained relationships and intensified relationship changes with family and friends. My lesbianism has proven to be a doorway to more openness with one aunt and a cause of distance from a stepfather. Often I have felt socially isolated from straight people who, but for my lesbianism, probably would have included me as a part of certain social circles. Such social isolation had consequences for my son when he was younger. He wasn't included in many gatherings because I didn't socialize with the parents of the children in our home or school community. As a result it took extra effort to keep him interacting socially with his peers.

My lesbianism has also meant positive things for myself as a mother and for my son. Isolation and secrecy, but also honesty, brought us closer together. At the same time my woman-identifiedness sometimes helped me remember to take care of myself while mothering a son, helped me know my limits, helped me teach my son about prejudice, about how to explore consciously his own gender and sexuality, how to value and nurture his friendships with men, and not to expect women to do his feeling for him.

For years my lesbianism involved considerable professional isolation from many colleagues, who kept their distance due to my lesbianism or from whom I kept my distance out of fear of rejection. Sometimes we simply had little in common. It has meant, in the past, not getting certain jobs, inability to progress in others, and the need to leave others because the isolation or homophobia was too great.

My lesbianism kept me for a long time estranged from any group practice of religion. More recently I stopped accepting that limitation too. I am now a practicing Jew within the Conservative tradition, having gone through a formal conversion and adult Bat Mitzvah. This process has felt like another coming home to my core self.

The continuing ambivalence of Conservative Judaism toward gay and lesbian people is a source of pain but also is an opportunity for me to give back something to the synagogue community that has been so giving to me during my adult conversion process. I am so far the only out lesbian in their midst who is willing to be in dialogue about these issues. So right now I take great joy in working to be a good Jew while having a role in the Jewish struggle to interpret tradition in a manner that honors human sexual diversity.

I also have come to value what my experiences of being a lesbian, with the associated experiences of otherness, contribute to my work-life skills. For example, being other and developing a sort of biculturalism to survive have given me both the need and the chance to develop skills that have made me a better administrative hearing officer, attorney, and teacher than I might otherwise have been as a white, middle-class female. I have learned to watch for the impact of behavior and processes on people, rather than always focusing on the intent. I have learned to read nonverbal cues better. I have learned to keep secrets very well. From closeting I learned to translate, and I used that skill when holding hearings with litigants who were not lawyers and who had no lawyer representing them. My lesbianism has enabled me to have some collegial and affectionate relationships with gay men. More importantly, my lesbianism has meant the opportunity to have healthy intimacy in my life. My twelve-year-long relationship with a woman has been a locus of joy, nurturance, laughter, silliness, adventure, passion, friendship—and has challenged me to become my best self in ways I would not and could not have done alone. Finally, the creative courage necessary to live as a healthy lesbian in these times has found expression in poems I would otherwise have been incapable of writing.

David's Story

I know I am straight because my sexual interest is in women. Women in person, in fiction, and in movies arouse my interest in quite a different way than do men. With some women I have a sensual, sexual response. With men there is an absence of erotic response. When I think back, it is clear to me that I knew this early in life but did not have words to describe it—that this was how I approached sexual identity. Given the world I grew up in, I assumed a straight identity without affirming it.

What comes to mind about first starting to figure out this identity is that when I was around eight or nine my boyfriends and I had contests to see who could pee the farthest. A girl on the block joined in one of our events. In addition to being surprised at how far she could pee, I had interest and feelings toward her that were different from those I had for the boys. About that same time I started seeing girls as different and being a little afraid of them, afraid of my own feelings.

I have been introspective and relatively gentle from an early age. This led other boys to tease and harass me for being different, that is, for seeming effeminate or homosexual. I handled this harassment at first by withdrawing into myself and into education, but I had occasional violent reactions. As I grew, I used my natural athletic abilities to match and outdo other boys. In my teens I worried about my gentleness and introspective ways. I was upset by rejection and played harder to prove myself. In high school I became the school's best long-distance runner, a journeyman basketball player, captain of the football team, and one of the better students. I believe that my early experiences of being singled out and socially and physically harassed for being nice, sissy, and "gay" shaped me in various ways. In addition to intensifying my drive, it stopped me from joining in teasing, harassing, and baiting activities. Through my academic, athletic, and adult-fostered leadership achievement, and through strategic violent retaliation, I established myself as someone to be left alone and respected even though I walked my own path. For example, in tenth grade a classmate teased me constantly about being the prime candidate for the teachers' model student award (the winner was seen as chief sissy by most of the boys). One day he pushed me too far. I threw him out of the classroom window, landing on top of him as he hit the ground. That action blew my chances of winning the award, but I was never teased again. Looking back, I see that while not actively homophobic, I was, through silence and inaction, heterosexist. I saw it then as self-protection.

The messages of tolerance and love of others I heard at school, in church, and in the community as I grew up seemed dissonant with the subliminal and overt hatred of homosexuals that surrounded me. On reflection, I know those messages influenced how I acted. I also know that the messages of love and justice were strong and at times dominated the judgmental messages I received in my active leadership at school and in a Protestant youth movement. I remember writing newspaper columns first for a church newsletter and then for the local newspaper which argued for tolerance and acceptance in a democratic spirit.

I am backing into the question of when I started figuring out issues of sexual orientation. My perspective fit generally with the patterns reinforced at school and in my family, among other places. However, I was aware that my internal sense of how I related to my peers was quite different from the more objectified way I was being told was the proper way to relate. I readily compartmentalized this part of me that was different, which fit well with my training as a young man to keep things in separate boxes. Sexual maturing brought feelings I didn't understand and the physical response of erection. My response was entirely cross-gender.

16

At college I grew close to two men. In one relationship we dealt with our caring for each other through intellectual and physical competition. We wrestled a lot and one time fought until neither of us could get up. Looking back, we were both clear in our heterosexuality and showed our affection for each other through ways acceptable for men at that time. My relationship with the other man was less straightforward. He was clearly my intellectual superior (he got straight A's with little effort). Physically he was no match for my strength. A handshake was our only physical contact. We appreciated each other's achievements and thought nothing of contacting one another day or night to share creative work or new insights. We continued our intellectual and creative exchange post-college through letters and an occasional time together. Deep in an intellectual correspondence stimulated by reading James Baldwin's *Giovanni's Room*, I realized that his love for me was different from mine for him. This was frightening for me, and I did not raise it with him but rather started distancing myself from him and for awhile increased activities that made me feel straight. I know the latter only in hindsight. If I had been more conscious then, I would have described my activities as masculine, not straight. He and I gradually drifted apart, with neither of us acknowledging what was happening or with me sharing my insights. It was not until twenty years later, after considerable personal growth on my part, that we were able to spend time with each other looking back. But the pain I caused by withdrawing from him was, and is, too strong a reality for him to allow us to revisit those early years except superficially. Today we are distant friends. We connect easily but infrequently.

It was in my thirties, through personal growth concerning gender, that I started consciously reassessing my assumptions, values, and beliefs about homosexuality. As I came to understand my separation from other men and my dependency on women, I started exploring new ways to relate to other men. Fear, projection, and concern for how I would be seen by other men surfaced. My internalized heterosexism was an invisible barrier to connecting meaningfully with other men. In a series of mixed- and single-gender learning communities, I came to accept feelings and push through fears which allowed me to relate more directly to other men. Much of my learning came as the result of direct action. I pushed myself to nonathletic contact with men, doing such things as hugging and dancing, taking turns leading each other around by imaginary strings, and then sitting down and talking about reactions.

I remember a particular weekend in Maine with nineteen other men. There I was able to comfort and accept comforting from other men for the first time in any sustained way. In acknowledging each other's pain and comforting each other, I learned that sexual orientation was not an issue, given that safe setting. That weekend was a marker on my personal journey, which had started several years before with talking about reactions and attempting to share my feelings with other men early in our gender journeys. As I looked at issues I had in common with other men, particularly dominance with respect to women, my relationship with men changed. I claimed fully my sexual orientation. As a result I am less controlled by external and internalized societal definitions. Better relationships with men and with women, as well as the excitement of my self-actualization process have kept me on this journey.

I remember attending the Second Annual National Men's Conference when I was in my thirties. In a small group with men of mixed sexual orientation, I talked about my fear of gay men. In the conversation I realized I was afraid that a gay man would approach me. I learned that I needed to be clear about my sexual orientation and also that I needed to say rather than posture it. This became more distinct for me as I looked at how I needed to figure out with men and with women what I wanted, and learn to negotiate rather than react.

Another issue was my fear of gay men's sexual aggressiveness, based on my expectation that all gay men exhibited the worst of male sexual aggressiveness, and on my concern about how I would react. I feared that if a man were attracted to me, then I must be a homosexual. I learned that in not being clear about myself, I gave mixed messages that confused gay men. As I developed clarity about my heterosexuality, I learned to respond directly without hostility or embarrassment to men who approached me. I also learned how much I left definition of my sexual orientation up to the general marketplace.

During the conversation at the Second Annual Men's Conference, a gay man said to me, "You're afraid of me? Do you realize that if I approach you, I don't know whether or not you will be offended and punch me right in the nose? Given my experience, you are a lot more dangerous to approach than I am." Mark, and I do remember his name, helped me to look at how much violence and fear of violence were a part of my relationships with men and how they befogged for me issues of straight, gay, and bisexual identity.

I was held to my journey of exploration and understanding of sexual orientation by my need for clarity and self-understanding. Mixed with these was a need to have some sense of what was me and what was society. I sorted out my value system. As I moved further on, friends on journeys of self-discovery helped sustain me in developing competencies to work and relate across and within my sexual orientation. Somewhere along the way, sexual orientation lost its fearful edge and became something that just is.

Heterosexism is prevalent in the systems I seek to work with as an agent of change. My comfort with diversity shapes who wants to hire me and who I want to have as clients. Writing this essay increases peoples' exposure to my views and means they can make judgments about me without ever meeting me or seeing my work.

Abuse by males (for the most part, white) is at the heart of enforcing heterosexist dominance. Violence against women, children, and gay (bi, out, closeted, suspected) men maintains the system. Acknowledgment that I know and will tell, that I will push through the illusions of words that hide this reality, makes me vulnerable to shunning and possibly to violence. Traitors to this system are given a special hell by those who maintain it. Part of the power of this repressive system is that after writing this essay, I start to think and feel that what I have said is untrue. Yet I know it is true. I have experienced its violence and, in my adult years, its shunning.

I am a person who resides in the space between the gay, lesbian, bisexual communities, and the unexamined straight community. It is a place of marginality. I must constantly remind myself that I need to work actively with people who are bridges between communities, people who can understand what it is to live learning constantly, and people who do not place unacceptable requirements on me. From my history as an agent of change and as an educator, I know I find excitement in being on the edge of what I don't understand.

Keith's Story

I have always known I was gay. I may not have had the words to describe it, but I knew the deep sense of intimacy I felt toward other men. I also somehow knew this intimacy was something I wasn't supposed to talk about, that somehow I had to keep it a secret. It then became a question of how do I survive.

I grew up in a small Vermont town with a population of less than fifteen hundred people. Both of my parents had grown up in this town, and both my maternal and paternal grandparents lived there. I have three brothers, all of whom identify as heterosexual in their adult lives. My father worked in law enforcement, first with the state police and later with the Department of Motor Vehicles. My mother worked for the postal system. We were the nice family who went to church every Sunday and were good to our neighbors.

I stood out in this community. I had what are traditionally described as effeminate mannerisms; I was a queen in a rural town. This meant I was the last person who was picked for teams or the person who was usually not included. The Boy Scouts certainly didn't know what to do with me. My peers found it difficult to be friends with me openly. It might mean they were sissies too. My brothers were asked if it was true I wore dresses at home and played with dolls. I was often referred to as their sister. I was an easy target for someone, anyone, to bully. I remember being called names as I walked down the street or the corridors of my school. Names like pansy, sissy, queer, faggot, and dirty cocksucker. There were occasions when I had snowballs with rocks inside thrown at me for no apparent reason. No one, adult or other authority figure, challenged any of these actions. It left me with the impression these actions were justified, that I deserved this treatment. The one instance when a peer tried to defend me, after comments were made about me in a locker room, resulted in his being hit. Although I saw his black eye, I didn't know what had really happened for several days. When I was finally told, it made me frightened for those who were my friends. If you were near me, you got hurt too and it was my fault.

During my adolescence my peers often coerced me into sexual activity with them. Usually this took the form of a threat: if I didn't blow them I'd get hit. It made little difference what I did because later I would still be publicly harassed and embarrassed by these same people. Everyone knew what I would and could do. It left me with conflicting messages about what it meant to be intimate and sexual. I had no adult role models. Any age peer who felt the same as I did wasn't admitting it. I had no one of whom I could ask questions and discuss the confusion I felt. It left me with a distorted sense of relationships and little hope for a meaningful future.

I came out to my parents when I was seventeen. I had been involved for five months with a man I had met doing community theater. It was clear this relationship was more than a mere friendship. One afternoon when my mother and I were alone in our home I told her about my emotional involvement with this man. She cried and said both she and my father already knew but hadn't said anything because they really didn't know what to say. She said they had always known about my sexual orientation. However, they really knew nothing about homosexuality, so rather than doing something truly harmful they had decided to let me find my own role models and support system. She also said she felt she had done something wrong as a woman, causing me to be attracted to a man rather than a woman. I told her actually I thought she had done well as mother and friend, that I wanted her in my life—all of it—instead of trying to hide parts of it from her. My father's response was to bring me books to read so I could make informed decisions, which was the same way he had previously approached the subject of sex with me. My brothers' responses varied. One brother merely accepted it as part of who I was. One brother really didn't want to know details or my friends. He just wanted to deal with me as an individual, the brother he had always known. The other brother initially responded with anger, leaving hostile notes in my room. Later we were able to talk about who we were as people, how if we had not been brothers we never would have met and both would have missed a great deal. My family did not make me feel rejected. Being gay was a secret we were finally allowed to talk about.

In my adult life I went in search of my community of sexual peers which in a rural area was not an easy task. The tradition was to grow up, move away (usually to Boston), and then come out. However, I found a hidden social network of gay men in Vermont. Most of them were not out in their public lives or to their families. None were involved in public politics. As I was already fairly open about my sexual orientation, I wasn't always welcomed into these social groups. There were occasions when other gay men would deliberately avoid me in public due to fear of disclosure. After being beaten at a local bar I became more cautious, carefully choosing which restaurants, bars, stores, and even towns were safe for me. I went to work in public mental health at the state psychiatric hospital. It was rumored the nursing administrator hired gay men because she thought they were more compassionate. There was also something affirming about caring for people who needed me and what I could offer. I accepted these limitations without much question. It was the unspoken rule, the price for being gay in a rural area. It wasn't until AIDS became part of my life that this really changed.

I stopped accepting limitations in 1982 when my lover was diagnosed with Kaposi's sarcoma. Initially he had been hospitalized for an atypical panic disorder. Our relationship had been difficult, with much unspoken anger and insecurities. Although I thought this was probably contributing to his sense of panic, I could not say it to anyone, as both the medical and social service staff totally ignored my relationship to this man. His chart identified him as a single, sexually active, homosexual man. No one talked with me about what was happening. When I walked into his room, the nursing staff, and on one occasion his doctor, would walk out. When I was visiting, no one would come in. While he was there, the medical staff discovered an unusual discolored lesion and decided to biopsy it. No one told either of us the results of this biopsy before he was discharged. He was discharged with the expectation that he would be returning to my apartment. But still no one had spoken with me. No one really knew if there was a home for him to return to and certainly no one had asked me if I knew how to do the follow-up care needed for his biopsy site. He did come back to my apartment. Our relationship did not improve, however, and with a great deal of anger it ended. Shortly after, I was told by a mutual friend who worked at the hospital that the lesion was diagnosed as KS. The friend also said the reason no one came into the room while I was visiting was because they were afraid of what they might find. They thought if two homosexuals were in a room together with a bed, of course they would be having sex; an insult to my professional and personal ethics. Their behavior intensified the difficulties in our relationship so that I did not say good-bye to a lover who had always been afraid of dying ugly and alone.

I am now very open and proud to be a gay man. I have become actively involved in public policy and politics. This has made me highly visible and still not terribly popular with some of the social networks; if I'm with them, people will know. Along with a small group of friends, I helped found Vermont's first AIDS service organization. I have worked on and advocated for antidiscrimination laws protecting persons living with HIV. For eight years I have served as co-liaison to the office of the governor, representing the Vermont gay men's community (there is a co-liaison representing the lesbian community). I lobbied for, and proudly stood behind, our governor as first the hate crimes bill and then the sexual orientation antidiscrimination (gay rights) bill were signed into law; my mother was standing there as well. I have lectured at high schools, colleges, churches, civic groups, health care facilities, and the state police academy on both homophobia/heterosexism and AIDS. I still have names yelled at me and get late night obscene phone calls. But I now have a strong support system of both biological and extended family members. I make the choices about what is right for me and when. And I am still learning what it means to be intimate with another man.

Sharon's Story

I never gave it much thought growing up, whether or not I was heterosexual. It was always assumed, by me and others around me. I was oblivious to any other reality until, as a teenager, a series of experiences got me thinking about things.

During the early part of my high school years, my family moved from New York City to a small New England town where I experienced feeling different and unattractive. I was the only Latina and one of only a few people of color in a largely white community. I wondered about my sexuality because my appearance and behavior did not match the standard view of what was beautiful and feminine in the Anglo culture. I was a brown-skinned, curly haired girl with a non-Twiggy-like figure who had opinions and spoke her mind. I knew I liked boys, but they didn't seem to like me. I knew I wasn't attractive to them. The lack of acceptance affected my confidence and self-image.

During my first year at a women's Catholic college, I experienced an incident that got me to thinking about what it meant to be a heterosexual woman. In my dorm room, the beds were the only furniture, aside from our desks. One day a friend and I were sitting close together on my bed when the door opened and my room-mate and her friends saw us, which resulted in snickers and jokes about us being "homos." The incident probably was forgotten by everyone except me moments after it happened, but it resulted in a change in my behavior. From that point on I refrained from any physical contact with this friend which would be deemed too intimate and made sure my door was left open whenever this friend was in the room. As I think back on the incident, I remember feeling ashamed and conscious of being considered a weirdo. I also felt confused, for until it was pointed out to me, I had not known that some behavior could be considered too intimate between two straight women. The incident left me with a deep discomfort and distrust of my own intuition about girlfriends and how we should behave.

During my junior year in college I had the opportunity to travel to Spain to explore my heritage and experience life. What a shock! I began to enjoy the attention of men, really for the first time. I consistently received, from a variety of men, very clear signals that I was attractive. It wasn't a fluke! The experience gave me profound confidence. The attention was affirming. It proved that there was nothing "wrong" with me. I was all female and sexually attractive. What a relief! It was a year of getting to know and value myself.

The next significant experience happened during the summer after my senior year. While visiting a friend in another city, we happened upon a gay club while looking for some fun on a Friday night. Since there didn't seem to be much going on anywhere else we decided to visit this club, even though both of us knew ourselves to be straight women. The club was crowded, there were people dancing everywhere, and the music was good. There were many more male than female couples. While standing at the bar having a drink, my friend and I said virtually nothing. Instead we stood there, enjoying the music, drinking our drinks, and taking in the "sights." I was aware that I was gawking and hoped I wasn't being too obvious. I had never seen so many gay people in one place at one time and I was amazed. I was conscious of two things. Of the couples who were dancing I systematically tried to figure out who was the "man" and who the "woman" by looking for feminine and masculine traits. Second, I was conscious that I was misrepresenting myself by being there. Wasn't I saying to everyone there that I'm like you—I'm a homosexual, a woman who likes women? That concerned me. At one point a woman who seemed attracted to my friend came over to ask her to dance. Since the woman was persistent and my friend was obviously uncomfortable, I decided to come to her rescue. Without really thinking, I reacted by slapping the woman's hand from my friend's and locking my arm through hers while proclaiming, "Go away, she's mine." The woman retreated. It worked as I suspected it would. I had succeeded in fooling her. But it felt risky. I didn't think I could go on fooling everyone too much longer, and I felt ashamed for having lied to these people I didn't even know. I felt like I was invading a sacred place or a members-only club. I knew I didn't belong. We downed our drinks and left. As we drove away, I felt excited, excited about having gotten away with something and excited about having seen something I knew I should not have had access to. My friend and I never talked about the incident, which I thought was strange, because this friend and I talked about everything.

Later that same weekend, while at my friend's apartment, an acquaintance of ours came to visit with two female friends. We hadn't known his friends before that day. Almost immediately I was aware of a difference in the relationship between these two women. They seemed affectionate in a way that was unusual between two straight women. I suspected within the first fifteen minutes that they were lovers. I couldn't keep my eyes off of them. I began to wonder what their relationship was like. I experienced mixed emotions, disgusted at viewing their affection while at the same time ashamed for feeling that way. They seemed normal enough, I thought. I moved from gawking at them to ignoring them during their brief visit. It was a strange experience for me. I never talked with anyone about it; I just kept all my feelings and thoughts and questions inside. That was approximately thirteen years ago.

Over the next three years or so, although I didn't talk with anyone about it, I began working through some of my thoughts, beliefs, discomfort, and fears about homosexuality and my own sexuality. Although I liked men, I wasn't sure if I was repressing my attraction to women and thus denying my bisexuality. I felt confused. How was I supposed to know? I felt I needed to test myself by looking at pictures of all kinds of women to see if I was attracted to them. It was important for me to know definitively. For awhile the question lingered with me.

During the last ten years I have had the opportunity to have among my close friends gay and bisexual men, and lesbian women from whom I've learned about myself through my reactions and inaction around them. I have learned about their respective cultures and about the assumptions, stereotypes, and prejudices I've carried about what it means to be something other than heterosexual.

I attribute a great deal of my most important growth to the relationship I've shared with one friend in particular. Through his openness and willingness to answer my questions and share with me information about his journey as a gay/ bisexual man, I have been exposed to and had access to a rich and complex culture. Before getting to know this friend well, I thought of the issue strictly in terms of who one chooses to be sexually intimate with. It was in trying to understand this friend through conversation with my husband that I began to see things differently. My husband put it in terms that really clicked with me. He said, "It's more than who you go to bed with; it's about relationships, a whole culture of who you are and how you see the world." That really opened me up to understanding in a way I was unaware of before.

What have I learned from my gay, lesbian, and bisexual friends and colleagues? I know how to communicate by what I say and do that it's okay to come out to me. That if a part of who you are is gay, lesbian, or bisexual, I'm receptive to knowing that. It's safe to let yourself be known to me, if you choose to. I've done enough of my own work to be conscious of not letting my own insecurities get in the way of our relationship (most of the time, that is).

I've also learned about the damage, pain, and hurt the assumption-laden words I've chosen to use in the past can cause a gay, lesbian, or bisexual person. So I take responsibility for using language that is more inclusive or neutral and that doesn't make assumptions about people's sexual orientation. This process is an ongoing one about which I accept feedback, but mostly I take responsibility for the learning and keeping myself in check.

Most importantly, as the mother of two small children, I have committed myself to talking abut sexual identity with them in a way that is meaningful and understandable. So when my son, who was six at the time, and I went to visit a female friend in her new home, I talked with him before and during the visit about my friend's partner and how they were more than just roommates. We talked about how, even though they were both women, they love each other in the way daddy and I love each other. How they are special and best friends and make each other very happy like nobody else can. And yes, they kiss and get mushy, mushy like daddy and I do, and no, it's not weird.

Through these friends, and as a result of my relationship with them, I feel like I've done a lot of my most important work in a very short period of time.

At thirty-four years old, I know I am heterosexual. I know because I am attracted to maleness and aroused by the masculine form. Even before I had relationships with men or before I was intimately involved with a man, I could envision being with a man and it was something I strongly desired and still do. My fantasies are of being with men. Having enjoyed a relationship with one man for the last eleven years, I am as sure now as I have ever been that this is right for me. I realized that this is not a thinking choice but a feeling choice. I do not feel for women what I feel for men. In my gut I've always known it. So it seems that the original assumption was accurate for me.

But what does it mean for me to be heterosexual? It means not having to explain myself, which frankly is quite a relief because as a woman and a person of color, I spend enough of my time and energy having to explain myself. In this one significant dimension I am what society expects me to be, so I don't have to deal with society's disappointment and disapproval of my sexual orientation. It also means that because I happen to be heterosexual, I am free from the threat of violence that is real and very present for gays, lesbians, and bisexuals. I conform to the majority expectation; I'm normal by society's standard. Lastly, it means for me that I have responsibility to own up to my prejudices about gay, lesbian, and bisexual folks, because I don't need to contribute to an environment already flourishing with hate and contempt for people who are not heterosexual.

As I reflect on where I am in my journey, I am aware of several things. I talk about the issues on a regular basis with all kinds of people. I state my opinions whether or not I'm asked about them. And although I know that as a heterosexual person I can choose to have the conversation when it's convenient for me or not at all, I choose not to table the discussion as frequently as I used to.

In recent years I have moved from considering my sexual identity work as separate from race/ethnicity and gender, to integrating it. It feels more whole and makes more sense to me.

Lastly, I am aware of how naive I still am about some of the issues relating to being gay, lesbian, or bisexual, which makes me acutely aware of how as a heterosexual person I will never fully understand.

Susan's Story

I am a thirty-nine-year-old Italian-Irish native New Yorker and lifelong lesbian. I'm also a lawyer, golfer, and reluctantly retired rugby player who is the life partner of one of the authors.

I know I am a lesbian because throughout my entire life I have been physically, emotionally, and sexually attracted to females. Thinking back to my childhood, I now understand that I had feelings of desire for women from the age of two onward. My first feeling of closeness to a woman was with my mother's sister, who used to play with me, hold me, and cuddle me. I can remember her having really smooth skin and dark features. I liked to be close to her. I wanted her attention.

I remember very early feeling curious about, and loving to look at, women's bodies. I always wanted to look down their shirts or up their skirts. These desires were about women, not kids. This included my kindergarten teacher.

The first time I knew I was "different" was when I was in third grade. For me, that was ages seven and eight. Our teacher was somewhat younger than the other teachers in our school. She was very alive and appealing. She had the smoothest legs. I was pretty short so I used to stare at her legs a lot. I always wanted to just touch and feel them. I remember loving how silky they looked in her stockings. I remember wanting to feel close to her and imagining she would hold me, but I knew I shouldn't tell anyone I felt that way because it would be seen as weird. I knew from that moment on I had a big secret because I was different.

I never was interested in playing any of the typical boy-girl games. I had just as many friends who were boys as girls, but I tended to be a typical tomboy—fairly athletic—and not a traditional female in any sense of the word.

The next time sexuality emerged was in the form of curiosity and exploration with the boy down the street when I was in fifth grade. It was popular to go steady then, which we did, but it was nothing romantic or highly sexual. It was more of an elementary school status thing, but we never did anything together and it just died a natural death.

In seventh grade I had my first sexual experiences with another girl. We had slumber parties with just the two of us. Slumber parties were in fashion, and you could get away with a lot in the guise of a slumber party. We didn't slumber much; we listened to Simon and Garfunkel and kissed and fondled each other's breasts. There was another friend that year with whom I did similar things. We never spoke about this, even among ourselves. We just did it; we didn't talk about it. We didn't think it was bad. We just knew it was sexual and you didn't talk about those things. I then went off to a girl's junior high school, which was like dying and going to heaven.

From junior high school through high school, it was clear that I was sexually attracted to my female peers, my female teachers, and my female friends, both older and younger. As is true for many junior high school kids whose hormones are raging and whose sexuality feels constantly on the surface, I was in a constant state of semiarousal through eighth grade. But heterosexual kids get to talk and joke about it, feel shy about it, experiment with relationships, get recognized and rewarded for their emerging grown-upness. I had to keep it under wraps, but there were moments when it surfaced anyway. The best had to be the school play in which I acted the leading male role and had to kiss one of my classmates. I kept wanting to practice that part over and over again.

It wasn't until ninth grade that I had another sexual episode. Because this one was with a classmate whose father was running for state office, we knew getting caught would mean nothing short of "death" for us both. Again in the guise of slumber parties when her parents were on the campaign trail, I used to be invited to her house. We'd sleep in her double bed and wind up in each other's arms. One night we kissed and somehow our braces locked together. So there we were attached at the teeth, scared to death we'd be found this way in the morning and it would be headline news. We decided to untangle by ripping apart part of our braces and blaming the coincidence of both having broken braces on eating peanuts, a real no-no with the orthodontist.

No one suspected anything, but we knew in our hearts we had tempted fate in some way. From my friend's point of view, this activity had to stop. She withdrew from me and didn't want to hang out anymore. In fact, she transferred to a large public high school nearby because she said she had to find a boyfriend. I felt sad. I just knew she was going to go marry the first boy she met and not be herself because it was so important she be a certain way for her family. What the episode did for me was make me go underground even more. I was clear from that moment that I wanted someday to be fully sexual with women—a complete get in bed, clothes off, do whatever we were going to do. I knew I could never take that risk while I was under my parent's roof and attending a small private school where someone would find out and I would get caught.

I made myself a vow that I would wait until I got to college. I knew that distance from family and home community meant I would finally be able to do what I knew was right for me. I directed my sexual energy toward other activities—being very involved in school, having lots of close friends, being athletic. But my dreams at night were dreams of making love to women.

Two weeks after going to college I finally got in bed completely naked with another woman and had sex with her. There were several women I had affairs with my freshman year, but still I had no words for it. I didn't know what the word *lesbian* was; I was too involved living it to think about what it was, but I knew by then there were a lot of people like me in the world.

During my sophomore year of college I fell in love with a woman who was a senior. Attending an all women's college meant I found a large group of women who were sleeping with each other, but they were all practicing varying degrees of closeting. My lover and I were definitely out and knew we were going to live our lives this way no matter the consequences. Back then the consequences sometimes included expulsion from school, which I sort of knew but didn't really think about. As the first open and out couple we proceeded to go on a journey of discovery about what it was like to be lesbian in the world. We went to our first gay bars in Philadelphia during the era when, to get in, you had to knock and then were eyeballed through a peephole. We found several different kinds of bars—bars for working-class lesbians, bars where everyone was butch or femme in appearance. Some of this scared us; some of it intrigued us. There were no such things as support groups or coming out groups. There was some literature, which we found and read. Still it was the early seventies, when gay liberation was young, so we had to search to find out more about how we could live as lesbians.

After my lover graduated and got a job in the New York area, I transferred to a New York college to be near her. We were still a couple. We were trying to figure out how to be true to ourselves and fit into the world at the same time.

Being a lesbian has meant being hated, despised, feared, cherished, loved—all with an incredible intensity that I suspect most heterosexual people, particularly white people, don't experience. For example, I don't think most heterosexual people are told by a parent that because of who they love they are no better than a murderer on death row and should be killed too. My father told me that. My father was the first person I'd ever heard use the world *lesbian*. He used it with such a vile tone it was as if he was vomiting. It sounded like such a dirty, disgusting word that it took me years to be able to use it, to call myself lesbian, not just say I was gay.

The summer after my freshman year of college my parents found out, by reading my personal mail, that I had had an affair with a female friend. My father confronted me and I didn't lie. I told him yes I had. He flew into a rage and told me I was sick, that I needed a psychiatrist; he wanted to know "who did this to me" because of course no daughter of his could figure out such a thing on her own. He then told me the solution: I would be yanked out of that liberal college I was attending and put into a convent school in the next town because those nuns would teach me a thing or two. It sort of sounded good to me, but the reality was he and I were beginning what has been a lifetime of conflict over my lesbianism. During the rest of my college years he and I were estranged. I was virtually exiled from the house and kept from my younger brother and sister so I wouldn't "recruit them to my lifestyle."

My father and I didn't talk to each other throughout my college years. He paid my tuition but gave me no money to live on, and I stayed away. When I graduated he decided I was to come back home to live. He wanted me to choose between the family and my "lifestyle." It didn't seem like a choice to me. He wanted me to come home and make believe I was something I wasn't. It was as if he was asking me to change my race. He didn't understand there was no choice for me. I had no alternative but to move out completely, which I was going to do anyway because I was already living with my lover of three years.

As I physically got ready to leave the house, my father was so mad at me that this relatively docile guy flew into a rage and came at me, grabbed me and threw me against the refrigerator in the kitchen, yelling at me the whole time that I was sick and needed him to help me get better. He just kept throwing me against the refrigerator until I turned around and grabbed his collar and screamed at him that he was never to lay a hand on me again or I'd kill him. He was so shocked he just stood there as I got my jacket and walked out the front door, leaving my entire family on different levels of the house crying and sobbing as I walked down the road and away from what had been my life. My brothers, sisters, and mother were completely hysterical. I didn't talk to my father for five years after that.

I also don't think the average straight person ever has the experience of that moment in life when all the pieces of your personality and sexuality and purpose come together in a huge light bulb, when all those mysteries about who you think you are come clear. The answer for me was, holy shit, I am a lesbian. There were no more monsters under the bed, no more dirty secrets, no more fear. The first time the woman I'd fallen in love with said, "I love you," meaning me, Susan, the lesbian, was the moment all the heartache disappeared.

Being a lesbian has meant some other, more trivial things, like loss of job promotions, lack of spousal benefits, and having to prove my competence when straight people don't. It's meant harassment and homophobia thrown at me. But what it means to me now is that I know who I am. I wouldn't change my orientation if I had the choice because I see and experience the world in a way that feels like a gift to me. I am the best person I can be because I am a lesbian.

It has also meant I've had the good fortune of experiencing two long-term loving relationships. All my life I heard that I was going to grow up and fall in love with that one special man who was going to love me and I would love him in a special way. I knew it wouldn't be a man for me but I have, nonetheless, lived that romantic life story. I've grown up and I've fallen in love with my princess charming, twice. It all happened the way it was supposed to happen, just with different players. The first of these relationships lasted five years. The second relationship is almost thirteen years old now and still ongoing.

Being a lesbian now means I am a fierce, unflappable, mouthy dyke. That's the story.

Rick's Story

I was reared in a family of two elder brothers five and four years my senior. My father died when I was five years old, and my mother remarried two years later. As I recall the early years in my family, I was chronologically and emotionally the youngest boy of the three sons. I always knew on some level that I was different. Of course I had no language for this nor did I know what this difference was about. As the years progressed, however, I slowly became more aware of it.

My older brother was my role model. I wanted to do and try to feel whatever he did and whatever I thought he might feel. As the years progressed, I noticed my difference through the many things in which he developed an interest but in which I found I had none. This was especially true about sports.

Religion was a mainstay in our home. Traditionally, religion has played a significant role in the African-American family, and in my family it was truly pervasive. Because of this I developed an overwhelming sense of what was wrong and right. As a young African-American male, the message said, "Your sexual orientation is wrong." So I lived with the shame of what was reality for me. In as much as the church was the root of our home and community, I saw no venue to question aloud what was authentic within me.

Not until junior high school did I start to know more clearly my sexual feelings, mainly by interacting with peers, mostly males. I vaguely recall that in school, particularly gym, I experienced strong sexual attraction to males. I never did anything with these feelings, but I was very much aware of them.

During this period my friendships were important. As I reflect, I remember I always had close ties with other males. It was as though these were dating relationships, similar to those my peers had with girlfriends. I too had girlfriends, that is,

29

girls I dated. But for me this dating was never very serious. There was never a feeling of wanting to be with these young girls sexually. Sexual arousal for me came largely from seeing other males in the shower after gym class. Often these emotions made me feel strange and certainly very awkward because I didn't know what to do with them, nor did I know exactly where they originated.

Coupled with this were my mother's attempts to encourage me to participate in what she considered more masculine activities. These were activities in which my brothers were largely interested, particularly my older brother.

When I reached high school, my sexual fantasies about men continued and if anything became stronger, though I had no sexual activity with other males. I always got a lot of fulfillment from my relationship with my best friend, a male with whom I did many things. We talked on the phone often and shared school experiences and interests. I recall that often friends were interested in doing things, particularly attending sporting events, in which I had no interest. But that seemed not to have interfered with the relationship. By the time high school ended, I realized within myself that I was gay; though I certainly had not stated it aloud, I knew that someday my gayness would be expressed.

By this time I had given language to my gayness. In the early 1970s, homosexuality was discussed, though infrequently and usually in negative terms. Despite these negative terms, I had heard the word *gay* used often enough so that I associated it with myself, with having an attraction to men, and I knew in my heart that this was something I would someday pursue.

During this time, the thought of going to college was always on my mind. Talking with friends about college and where I would go excited me. I never associated it with wanting to explore my sexuality, though being away from home would give me an opportunity to do so. I think somewhere in my heart I knew that to be the case. My best friend throughout high school, for whom I always felt a sexual attraction, strongly encouraged me to attend the same college he planned to attend. For reasons important for myself, I chose not to do so. Instead I traveled to a school not far from home, yet far enough away where I could have anonymity and develop my individuality.

When I left for college in 1973, I discovered I had a gay roommate. Not only was he gay but he openly expressed his gayness. This was challenging for me, knowing within myself I was gay but not yet saying it. I recall that semester well. As it turned out, his friends became my friends, and some have remained lifelong relationships.

As my matriculation continued, I did come out but only partially. While my social life was rooted largely in the gay community, my gayness still remained unspoken in other important areas of my life, including my family. I believe by keeping the secret I unknowingly disabled myself from living my life in its fullness.

There were challenges as an undergraduate. For example, I was active in fraternity life. Once a small group of members confronted me with their suspicion that I was gay. This was devastating! Even then I could not allow myself to deny it. I just did not confirm it.

After graduation I worked and traveled, continuing not to talk about sexuality issues. This was easy to do because my community of gay friends supported it. Not until the mid-1980s, with the AIDS epidemic starting to devastate our community, did I want to speak about who I was as a gay person. With close friends dying and testing HIV positive, it felt shameful not to tell persons whom I loved and who I know loved me that I was gay. It seemed unacceptable.

This journey of telling loved ones came about by doing some intense intrapersonal work and coming to terms with myself. As a result, I am now talking to loved ones about my gayness and what that means for me. Talking about my gayness is a journey within my journey. It is one I can say I proudly travel. It is a journey where I welcome the obstacles before me and gain strength from my friends and from within myself. I truly believe, for me, this is important as I travel toward wholeness.

Jim's Story

When I was young, I knew I was interested in men's physical strengths, and I was particularly fascinated by Popeye's fanciful muscles. In grade school I had my share of crushes on female teachers. But grades seven through twelve were horrible: not only was I into academics in a sports-interested school, but someone had started a rumor that I had performed oral sex with another boy in gym class.

The taunting, ridicule, and roughing up were endless. To survive, I built an emotional shell around myself. I never ate lunch, because the lunchroom area was unsupervised. Sometimes I'd wake up at night and hear a drive-by carload of youths yelling obscenities toward my house.

There was no one to talk with, and certainly no bodyguard (as in the movie *My Bodyguard*).[3] During all this time, I was very confused because I had done nothing to warrant such labeling. I dated two girls, but was afraid to get close.

When I went to college, I braced myself again for how I thought all people would treat me, but there were no taunts, no shadows that followed me, no tormenting. I was free!

In my early twenties I was lonely and allowed situations on two separate occasions to develop where a gay man, in a teacher/coach role, befriended me over a long time span and paid attention to me. I allowed them to do sexual things to me and always felt terrible afterward. From ages twenty-two to thirty-five I had a series of four serious, wonderful sexual relationships with women, but each time the relationship broke up after about two years, as the intimacy increased.

I am on the fence, a barbed-wire fence. On one side is the attracted-to-women part of me, on the other, the attracted-to-men part. I've spent my life trying to survey my feelings and chart my emotional and sexual maps, but I still cannot figure out the topology. Sometimes I feel like I'm distracting myself from intimacy by trying to match one of society's labels to the way I feel.

Most of the time, I dig myself into the barbs on the fence because I'm not completely comfortable when I'm in a relationship with a woman (I see men I want to be close to). And when my mate is a man, I miss ever so much being emotionally and sexually close with a woman. I want both, but I am too shy or conservative to embark on a journey that would lead to a relationship trio.

I used to think I was supposed to make a life decision about my sexual orientation. I thought I was undisciplined and even procrastinating about making a commitment. When I found out I had Adult Attention (Hyperactive) Deficit Disorder, my first thought was that my life-as-a-candy-store approach of wanting to try a little of everything was preventing me from committing to one gender.

Now I see that most people have trouble settling down to make a commitment with one person. I know my hesitation is not about the person, but the gender. I've always had trouble identifying with either gay or straight labels. I don't feel I fit either, but if I had to choose one, I would choose bisexual. When I've been in multiyear relationships with women, they assure me I'm heterosexual until I bring up my unsettled fence questions. I don't feel complete in a relationship with a woman or with a man, and I feel an added fear of being gay because of my horrible experiences of ridicule and torment during my teen years. Thus I cloud my search for sexual orientation balance with negative self-images and memories.

At age thirty-five, I met a gay man; friendship developed and we became partners (I dislike the term *lover*). At this writing I am forty-one and, even though I'm in love with and committed to him, I continue to try to sort out my feelings and attractions to both genders. I really miss a relationship, including sex, with a woman, and I grieve that I probably will never sleep with a woman again.

A Journeyer's Guide

Assumptions, Context, and Frameworks

During the twentieth century, most people in Western countries have lived in cultures which label heterosexuality the norm, and other forms of human sexual orientation and identity anathema or nonexistent. (Words and phrases such as sexual orientation, sexual identity, and ambisexual as we use them in this chapter and throughout this book are defined in Appendix A.) Modern heterosexually dominated cultures also define heterosexuality and homosexuality as polar opposites and tend to deny the existence of bisexuality or other sexual orientations or identities. Such cultures compel heterosexuality and stigmatize homosexuality and bisexuality by attaching to homosexuality negative social, economic, and religious consequences. Thus, heterosexuality is, in addition to being a human sexual variant, a contemporary political institution.[1]

Many recent sociocultural changes have pushed institutions and individuals to reassess beliefs, behaviors, and rules about sexual orientation. These changes include shifts in attitudes about gender and sexuality; the insights of contemporary women's organizing and theorizing and their impacts on attitudes about gender and sexuality; the increasing political activism, social visibility, and sexual-identity-based cultural development of lesbians, gay men, and bisexual people since the 1950s; and the recent AIDS epidemic. Nonetheless, most Western-culture adults alive today were raised in households, cultural communities, religious institutions, and schools, as well as in a larger society, which taught that everyone was heterosexual or that the few who were not were sick, sinful, criminal, or all three. This is less true for younger people.

Since 1969 there has been increased public visibility of gay and lesbian people and institutions in the United States. During the last decade, outreach services to adolescents have emerged. The first generations of people who developed their gay/lesbian identities with social support are now young adults, and more adolescents are on the way. This largely urban phenomenon is helping to press institutions, families, and people of prior generations to address the reality of, and complexity of, human sexual diversity in new ways. It is now possible, probably for the first time in human history, for a fourteen-year-old to come out proudly and positively as gay to a peer support network sponsored by his school and led by out gay/lesbian teachers, to have support services available to help his family respond to his declaration of gay identity, and to have social events in which same-sex dating, dancing, and flirtation comparable to that available to heterosexual adolescents are possible.

However, many children and young adults continue to be raised in families and social contexts that are overwhelmingly heterosexist and homophobic. Also, a majority of gay/lesbian/bisexual youth do not yet have such access. They will emerge into adulthood needing to travel the adult journey away from internalized stereotypes about gay/lesbian orientation and identity, as will most of their heterosexual peers. The journey from negative or homophobic attitudes toward valuing the actual diversity of human relationships and sexualities is a complex one for everyone. The diagram in this book depicting the journeys does not describe fully all lesbian, gay male, and bisexual people's experiences of the various gay/lesbian or the emergent bisexual communities and cultures. Instead, it focuses on the experiences of gay men, lesbians, and bisexual people, particularly in the United States, as they try to give positive meaning to their orientations in the face of compulsory heterosexuality.[2] It also maps the experiences of heterosexual people as they attempt to understand the possibilities for and actual diversity of sexual orientations and identities that heterosexual dominance attempts to render invisible and to punish.

An Overview of Heterosexual, Lesbian, Gay, and Bisexual Journeys

The top lines of the sexual orientation and identity diagram (see p. 274), often referred to in this text as "the continuum," show the movement of heterosexual and heterosexually identified bisexual women and men as dominants. The bottom lines of the diagram show the journeys for lesbians, gay men, and homosexually identified bisexual women and men as subordinants. The middle lines show the journeys for bisexually identified women and men from the point of most likely primary identification as bisexual people.

The journeys differ for women and men and by culture, and therefore are shown on the continuum as two interspiraling lines. The text addresses these differences. Because most bisexual people today live large parts of their journeys primarily heterosexually or lesbian/gay-identified, the bisexual journeys are represented on the continuum and discussed in the text in both contexts, until the point along the continuum (in the blue section) where we understand it to be typical for self-identification as a bisexual person to occur. From that point on, bisexual experience is depicted and discussed as a separate strand for some people and for other people as a journey continuing within a primary identification as heterosexual or gay/lesbian.

Motivation to Change and Risks of the Journey

Intellectual curiosity can begin the process of increased understanding for some people, but for many an emotional imperative is the more likely catalyst for real movement on their journeys.

The motivation to change is always stronger for the subordinant,* since unexamined subordinance is so confining, even damaging, to the self. For gay men, lesbians, and bisexual people, the need for change is inherent in the self-hatred (internalized homophobia and biphobia) taught by compulsory heterosexuality and in the need to learn ways to be healthy despite cultural ostracism. For heterosexual people the impetus for change is often the discovery that someone of personal importance is lesbian, gay, or bisexual. That person may encourage change directly, or the simple fact of discovering the gay, lesbian, and bisexual identity of such a person may constitute a sufficient challenge to prior assumptions or create enough discomfort to stimulate change. In addition, a homoerotic experience or desire or a resurfaced memory of such experiences or desires may cause heterosexual people to question their own orientation or identity.

Such experiences often provoke decisions to learn more, although they may first cause a period of fear, regression, and increased homophobia. For bisexual people, their dominant orientation, if any, or the way they self-identify may affect their motivation to learn. If they have a strongly ambisexual orientation they may be traveling, at least internally, a version of the gay/lesbian or subordinant journey because it is their same-sex feelings that are likely to be negatively internalized and externally rejected in this culture. On the other hand, some strongly ambisexual

---

Subordinant is used here as parallel to *dominant*. It describes a state, not just a place in relation to a dominant, as the use of *subordinate* would imply. It does not, however, suggest that the state of being a subordinant in a culture is the equivalent of, or the same as, the state of being a dominant in a culture. These two states are particularly not the same in terms of power and autonomy, constraints on selfhood, and the risks to survival involved. Nonetheless, both states can be examined consciously and can be experienced as journeys in which choices may be exercised; choices that facilitate movement away from gender-, culture-, or sexual orientation-based domination and subordination and toward the capacity to live in ways that value diversity. Men's and women's journeys are discussed in Carol Pierce, David Wagner, and Bill Page, *The Male/Fale Continuum: Paths to Colleagueship* (Laconia, NH: New Dynamics Publications, 1994). The journeys of white people and people of African origin in white culture are depicted in *A Black/White Continuum, In White Culture: Paths to Valuing Diversity,* Linda Thomas and Carol Pierce, Laconia, NH: New Dynamics Publications, 1988. (Currently in graphic form only.)

people spend large parts of their lives identifying as heterosexual and travel the heterosexual journey, including sometimes feeling actively hostile toward lesbian and gay people.

The journeys of heterosexual people and those of bisexual people, lesbians, and gay men not only begin differently, but they proceed differently as well. When one is gay, lesbian, or bisexual, every new life setting presents risks of rejection if one is recognized, or for those people who are not easily recognizable, a new setting requires a new decision about whether to hide or reveal one's sexual identity. Every gesture identifying the self as lesbian, gay, bisexual, or in the life entails not only a risk of rejection but sometimes a risk of injury. The journey toward positive self-definition as gay, lesbian, or bisexual and participation in lesbian/gay communities or emerging bisexual communities offer amelioration of some of the damage of compulsory heterosexuality. To come out—to allow family to know either implicitly or explicitly, or to attempt relationships with heterosexual people while being visible about one's bisexuality or lesbian/gay identity—involves ongoing choices about identity management that are fraught with risk as well as opportunity. Bisexual people face dual coming out issues. The consequence of coming out as a bisexual person in heterosexual culture is often social ostracism for the lesbian/gay aspect, yet within gay and lesbian communities a bisexual person's heterosexual relationships may be what must be kept secret or what causes rejection.

For heterosexual people there are simply not comparable dangers in taking this journey toward valuing sexual diversity, since in most settings heterosexual privilege continues to operate. However, heterosexual men's fear of this journey may be based in part on the fact that they often pick on or beat up one of their own who acts gender inappropriately or who, as a result of defending or befriending someone gay, is viewed as possibly gay himself (that is, guilt by association). For heterosexual women, the pervasive fear of physical and sexual abuse by men, including the fear of such abuse if they act gender inappropriately or in ways that are viewed as "disloyal" to heterosexual men, may make this journey feel particularly dangerous.

For all persons who begin the journey self-identified as heterosexual there also exists the risk of coming to know the self better and recognizing that one is lesbian, gay, or bisexual as well as the fear of violence from homophobic heterosexual people as one associates openly with gay and lesbian people. There is also the possibility of losing relationships with bisexual, lesbian, or gay family and friends if one refuses to learn. The continuum tries to depict these issues of safety and of changing awareness about one's own orientation in two ways. Arrows dropping down from the top line to the middle and bottom and, though less frequently, reaching up from the bottom toward the middle and top, show changes in self-identification that occur for some people as they move through the journeys. In addition, along the bottom of the continuum a straight line for coming out and another for dual life represent the ongoing issue of closeting with which lesbians, gay men, and bisexual people live. Along the top of the continuum a straight line for dealing with guilt-by-association fears represents that issue, which heterosexual people face on this journey.

Bisexuality

Heterosexist cultures divide people into polarized categories of sexual orientation, heterosexual and homosexual, and stigmatize the homosexual. In the process the culture denies the frequency of so-called bisexual behavior documented by Alfred Kinsey[3] and denies the possibility of a sexual orientation consisting of variously balanced erotic and emotional attractions toward both men and women. Although we believe the term *bisexual* is imprecise, we use it as an identity label in part out of respect for the current linguistic preferences of people identifying as such. By *ambisexual* we mean those persons whose sexual orientation is bisexual, that is, whose orientation consists of sufficiently strong erotic attraction toward persons of both genders to lead them to having and/or desiring sexual relations and intimacy with both genders during adult life. Some but not all ambisexually oriented people choose *bisexual person* as their sexual identity.

We believe that many people whose sexual orientation is heterosexual, lesbian, or gay have at times desired sexual relations with both genders and, in fact, have had sexual relations with both genders at some time during their lives. It is in part because of our belief that exclusivity of erotic capacity and/or behavior is rare, although predominance of heterosexual or homosexual orientation is probably quite common, that we find the term *bisexual* imprecise. We do not apply it to persons who are primarily homoerotic or heteroerotic but who have had occasional exploratory sexual encounters with both genders at some point in their sexual development as adults. We also do not use it to refer to persons who spent years acting heterosexual and later recognized or admitted to themselves their gay or lesbian orientation and then adopted a gay or lesbian sexual identity.

We intend the term to include some of the persons who ostensibly live heterosexual, lesbian, or gay male identities while also desiring and/or seeking sexual interactions outside of those constraints, since we are aware that in current culture most bisexual people live much of life closeted either as heterosexual or gay/lesbian. However, not all married people who live such dual lives are bisexual. Some are gay or lesbian and are simply unable or unwilling to come out or are inhibited from leaving their marriages by continuing love for their spouse, the threatened loss of their children, or their economic stability, or by other family and social pressures. Obviously the term also includes people who are, in increasing numbers today, self-identifying and/or publicly identifying as bisexual people.

The sexual orientation diagram does not have a separate line for a bisexual journey until part way through the blue section. People who engage in bisexual behaviors are depicted early on the continuum as situated in the journey in which their behavior and sense of identity place them. Part way through the blue stage, a separate line for self-identified bisexuality emerges at the point in the journeys where we understand it to be most likely for people to develop a positive separate bisexual identity. In the green section of the continuum, where the dualism of the separate lines yields to a circling around and intertwining, the assumption is that possible self-defined sexualities include the exclusively heteroerotic, the exclusively male homoerotic and lesbian, and a variety of other possibilities including bisexuality. Such possibilities may not leave what we think of today as heterosexual and homosexual exclusivity at the poles of the new range, but rather may require a more flexible concept of human sexual orientation and its variations. This more flexible concept may include recognition that gradations of ambisexuality play a much greater role in human sexuality than is usually acknowledged today. The understanding at this stage may also involve recognition of orientations not yet named—including, for example, the autoerotic—with all the orientations envisioned as arrayed around a circle, or around two axes, thus avoiding the linearity typical of many sexual orientation scales.[4]

Gender Issues

Cultural constructions about biological sex and definitions of gender significantly govern the distribution of power in most, if not all, contemporary cultures. (See Appendix A for additional discussion about our use of such terms as *gender identity*.)

We understand contemporary compulsory heterosexuality to be in large part an artifact of modern Western, male-dominant, or patriarchal cultures.* In order to maintain polarized notions about gender and the hierarchy of valuation which puts men on top and women underneath, male-dominant societies must fiercely reinforce rigid definitions of maleness and femaleness. Male dominance grants men the right to desire and have sexual access to women. It also defines men as people with such desires and access. Women are defined as beings desiring and granting sexual access to men.

Definitional reinforcement is accomplished in part by the rules constituting compulsory heterosexuality. Assertive women and gentle men are terrorized into greater gender conformity with the accusation that they are not real men or women, that they are lesbian or gay. Such accusations are often accompanied by the threat or enactment of violence and social approbation for failing to act in gender-appropriate ways. Attachment to rigid definitions of male and female and anxiety about one's own adequacy within such definitions also produce phobic responses to lesbian and gay men who actually break the gender definitions by

---

*It may also be an artifact of older and/or non-Western and/or less patriarchal cultures. However, many such cultures also made a place for same sex sexual behavior so long as it was constructed in ways consistent with the gender system, that is, involving dominance and subordinance such as an adult male and adolescent male, or involving male- and female-type roles, such as the American Indian two spirit or berdache traditions. For more about this see Appendix C.

desiring sexual, emotional, and/or social intimacy primarily or exclusively with persons of their own gender. Some lesbians and gay men also react to and challenge the dominant culture's assumption of male/female polarity through behaviors and appearance which "blend" traditional notions of gender, including, among other things, cross-dressing.[5]

In addition, lesbian and gay male identities have distinct meanings in "heteropatriarchy."[6] The disobedience of being a lesbian in such cultures has to do importantly with placing oneself beyond or outside the spheres of male control and access. Gay men, on the other hand, break the heteropatriarchal rules of contemporary maleness by acting "like women" in desiring to be sexual with men.

The frequent assumption that homosexuality means gay male experience has rendered relatively invisible lesbianism and the ways in which lesbian identity, orientation, and experience differ from that of gay males. We have drawn the journeys of subordinance as interspiraling lines to emphasize that the lesbian journey is not the same as the gay male journey. In describing the journeys of lesbians and gay men, we have also tried to make clear some of the important ways in which lesbianism as an identity differs from gay male identity.

Multicultural and Racial Issues

One's cultural background and racial identity profoundly affect how one lives and experiences issues of gender and sexual orientation. As two white women, we represent the Midwest and Northeast of the United States, Protestant and Jewish, and eastern and western European cultural and religious origins. We have sought out, listened to, and learned from people of other white cultures and from people of color who attended workshops and provided feedback about this volume while it was in manuscript form. We have also read the work of many persons of color writing about sexual orientation issues, as part of our efforts to become more familiar with these issues in racial and cultural contexts other than our own, as well as to deepen our understanding about the ways in which our experiences of these issues are part of our whiteness. We have raised issues of sexual orientation in workshops about multiculturalism in which we have participated while working on this book and have learned much from the resulting interactions and responses.

Insights from many of these sources are included in the text and always attributed to the source because we do not believe we can speak for people of color. We want the voices and experiences of people of color, lesbians, gay men, and bisexual and heterosexual people to be heard and to be part of this book, not simply as illuminators of experiences specific to their own cultures but as sources of illumination for us all. We also try to note in the text when something we are describing is to us clearly specific to whiteness.

The continuum uses broad categories that reflect how sexual orientation is framed in the dominant contemporary culture that is white and heterosexual. This is particularly true in the orange section. We use these categories in part because it is that dominant frame against which and within which we are all reacting at least some of the time. These dominant categories are not the only ones operating for people of some cultures.

For example, the categories gay/straight/bisexual and heterosexual/homosexual are categories which have limited presence inside many Mexican-American and other Latin American communities where the sex/gender systems still use divisions between active and passive, with active closely associated with masculine and passive with feminine, as the more important distinctions. Thus a man who is the active partner in sexual activity with another man can still be viewed as appropriately masculine, and the categories heterosexual/homosexual do not apply to him based on that activity. The passive male in the relationship is demeaned for being feminized: the language in Nicaraguan culture is *cochon*, a derivative of the word for mattress, *colchon*.[7] As Cherrié Moraga has written, a Chicana or Chicano growing up in the United States deals with both this Latin representation of sexual orientation and the white culture's categories.[8]

In African-American communities, gay/lesbian/bisexual people often refer to themselves as "in the life" rather than taking on one of the category labels.[9] The resistance to categories may be in part based in a culturally grounded realism about a history of fluidity of sexual object choice in African-American people's lives. This includes a tradition among women of relying on each other for intimacy, support, and sexual relations, which coexists with their relations with and childbearing with men, a tradition grounded in West African antecedents as well as survival strategies necessitated by slavery and postslavery conditions.[10]

We have included in the diagram some specifics in the journeys of understanding which people of various cultures travel, given the context of the dominant white framework and the coexistence of other cultural frameworks. The text of the book tries to go further, by grounding significant moments of these journeys in specific examples from lives—our own and those of colleagues, friends, and workshop participants from whom we have gained insights.

We are aware that the specificity of culture defines the meaning and shapes the experience of each moment depicted on the continuum. For example, the language "coming out" is language from white gay/lesbian culture, but the issue of whether to be hidden or visible, whether by behavior or words, is one faced in many ways by people of many cultures involved in homoerotic identities and lives. For African-Americans there is sometimes room to be known and visible within a community, but speaking about it is not acceptable. In other African-American communities, secrecy and silence are enforced by religious norms and views of racial solidarity which label homosexuality "a white thing."[11]

In contemporary Latin American communities, a man who identifies as gay, rather than simply having sex with men without talking about it or identifying as other in any way, is often viewed as anglicized or an *internationales*.[12] In white culture, to speak about being gay, to expect family to acknowledge one's lesbianism, or to want to be visible at work is viewed as "flaunting" something which belongs in one's bedroom if it has to exist at all. Clearly cultural variability about acknowledging the existence of people living homoerotically involved and identified lives exists. Yet these examples help confirm that the issue of silencing, secretiveness, visibility, of whether or not we can have "tongues untied,"[13] is present in many if not all cultures.

Many lesbians and gay men leave home communities ostensibly to seek education or jobs, but also to enjoy greater access to lesbian and gay communities and greater room to explore their own identities as gay or lesbian. Such a decision becomes a choice to risk never seeing your long-time partner if you are a Filipina lesbian whose "wife" is unable independently to obtain immigration papers from Canada and Canada will not admit her as a spouse in the same way a male marriage partner would be admitted.[14]

Everything about the journeys depicted here is particularized by cultural and racial context and by whether one is, in those contexts, a dominant or subordinant. The language for sexual orientations, the explanations of the causes of homosexuality and bisexuality, the reasons they are said to be wrong, the contexts in which lesbians, gay men, and bisexual people are tolerated, the punishments meted out for variance from heterosexual norms, the definitions of gender-appropriate behavior, the presence or absence of gathering places and published literature about lesbian and gay life experiences, the cultural history and variations through time of gender and sexual orientation-related norms, the lesbian and gay cultural motifs and political agendas—all these and more vary depending on whether you are white, Asian (and the particular Asian culture matters), Pacific Islander, American Indian*/First Nation (and the particular tribe matters), African-American, Afro-Caribbean, East Indian, Latino, or Hispanic. The specificities of race, culture, and religion matter so profoundly in these journeys in part because it is early in childhood—in one's home community, family, and religion—that the journeys begin. In childhood the first and very powerfully internalized lessons about sexual orientation are taught, taught by the adults upon whom we rely as children for survival and by the peers with whom we create ourselves, taught out loud and through silences, through emotional rewards and punishments, through glances, raised eyebrows, taunts, beatings, rapes, sermons, and stories. These childhood years are also the years when we are most likely, although not always, to be embedded in our original culture and cultural community.

A white gay or lesbian person who has not examined his or her whiteness may find it difficult to deal with some of the issues inherent in the journeys depicted here. Lack of awareness about one's own dominance makes it difficult to travel very far in understanding one's experiences of subordinance. Such blindness

---

*We note that many, if not most American Indians have always referred to themselves as American Indian not Native American. Our colleagues who identify as American Indian also note that anyone born in the United States can be considered native American.

also tends to breed resistance from white gay men and lesbians when the issues of racial dominance and subordinance within the gay and lesbian communities must be addressed as we work toward valuing diversity.

An African-American heterosexual woman or man may find it difficult to acknowledge dominance on this continuum because she or he has identified with subordinance in racial terms in white-dominated culture. These journeys thus push all of us to expand prior learnings about dominance and subordinance developed in the context of race, culture, and gender and require each of us to acknowledge and learn about the ways in which our various positions of dominance and subordinance coexist, combining to produce diverse journeys, all aspects of which require attention as we address the journeys on the sexual orientation continuum.

How to Read This Book

This book assumes that everyone lives in, and has matured in, heterosexually dominant cultures. No blame is attached to any individual's location in the past or present on this journey. Each person begins with the information and resources available from childhood and his or her own life experiences. This book and the sexual orientation and identity diagram are designed to assist individuals, and people in groups, on the journey

— away from the dominance and subordinance of compulsory heterosexuality,
— through the transition of learning about one's effect on others,
— to valuing one's own sexuality and a diversity of sexualities.

The sexual orientation and identity diagram does not necessarily describe what everyone experiences. However, the orange section does describe the often unnamed cultural assumptions that form the bases for stereotypes and prejudices. We do not all start at the earliest end of the orange section of dominance and subordinance, though we probably perceive in hindsight that we entered the journey earlier than we often would like to admit. The continuum diagram shows a full range of possible experience, not what every individual goes through.

This book does not profess to describe everything that could be said. Rather, the intent is to define the idea that we are all on journeys away from dominance and subordinance and to outline a range of interactions between heterosexual, gay/lesbian, and bisexual people, from the most violent to comfortable openness. We have tried to highlight the markers on the way which, when noticed and understood, may facilitate our journeys and affirm and support the work we have done and wish to do. Readers are asked to fill in gaps they perceive from their experience, to particularize the general statements and give them personal meaning, and to put our terminology in their own words. We hope the book and continuum diagram will support and encourage dialogue between those of differing orientations and within orientations. Neither the book nor the continuum is prescriptive. They are descriptive of what many in hindsight acknowledge they have learned. They are intended as stimulants for change.

The sexual orientation and identity diagram is linear. It cannot portray the recurrent or spiraling nature of life experience, of how we cycle back and forth through the different stages of our journeys. We often find ourselves at many places on the continuum simultaneously. A heterosexual person may be trusted by a gay or lesbian friend not to identify him or her in public (the late blue section), yet be surprised and jolted when a family member comes out, and may resist the idea (early blue section). The same person while at the office may express judgmental attitudes about someone's nonconforming gender behavior (mid-orange section). One can be different persons in differing situations. It is important to assume that everyone is doing the best they can based on their own life experiences.

PART II
The Journeys

Rejecting, Denying, Tolerating

Early Journeys of Heterosexual and Heterosexually Identified Bisexual People

CAROL PIERCE

Being homophobic is the predictable result of growing up and living in a homophobic world.

—*Cooper Thompson, "On Being Heterosexual in a Homophobic World"*

It is a waste of energy for anyone to assume that their condemnation will ensure that people do not express varied sexual [orientations].

—*bell hooks, talking back*

It takes an experience that delivers a strong emotional impact for us as heterosexual people to have a reason to look at ourselves, rather than see the issues of homosexuality as something only gay men and lesbians need to deal with. In many ways the orange section of heterosexual journeys is best read and understood in hindsight.

Heterosexual people do not consciously enter the adult journeys depicted in the orange section of the continuum diagram. The major headings in the orange section, **Ostracism**, **Denial**, and **Oblivious Heterosexism**,* implicitly infer a lack of awareness. Bisexual people are dismissed as confused. For many heterosexual people it isn't until the early blue section, when someone close comes out as lesbian or gay, that this continuum suddenly gains meaning.

As described in my story, I was in college before I was much aware of the possibility of same-sex attraction. Having grown up in the 1930s and 40s, I was aware of secrets in my extended family, but when I asked about them no answers were given. There was complete silence about homosexuality in my home, school, and church. Due to the subsequent deaths of family members, I cannot confirm what is quite possible—that there were lesbian and gay people in my extended family. Because I grew up in an atmosphere socially tolerant in other ways for that time, as I came to the women's movement in the late 1960s and early 1970s I had a basis for intellectual acceptance of my friends who came out as lesbian in

---

*Starting with this chapter, words in boldface are taken directly from the sexual orientation continuum graphic following page 272.

feminist surroundings. I watched, listened, and learned. They gave me a slight jolt to move on my journey. However, I could quietly bask in the silence of oblivious heterosexism. There was nothing to do as far as I was concerned. I was tolerant and saw nothing else to do.

As we developed this continuum starting in the late 1980s, I began to look back and admit to myself that there was a time much earlier in my life when I thought homosexuality might be deviant or something curable, but that I didn't have enough information to decide for myself. I knew then that I was uncomfortable around "them," thankful that I didn't know "any"! So my journey through **Dominance of Compulsory Heterosexuality** on the continuum is real for me, and perhaps a typical experience for other blue-collar or middle-class white heterosexual women who grew up in a socially liberal atmosphere and learned tolerance of homosexuality through work in the women's movement. My homophobia was, and is, more covert than overt; nevertheless it is very real.

Writing about heterosexuality in relationship to homosexuality and bisexuality is not easy. A wide array of books exists about homosexuality and a growing number exists about bisexuality. Almost nothing has been written about developing as a heterosexual person, though almost all books are written from a heterosexual point of view. Books reflect our culture. As a result of this silence and lack of attention to heterosexuality, the implicit dominance and assumed normalcy of heterosexuality have not been examined. The effect on the individual of identifying as heterosexual and the process of describing how heterosexuality develops remain unexplored.

Martin Hoffman tells us that "virtually all the literature on homosexuality is marred by the failure of its authors to take account of the fact that heterosexuality is just as much a problematic situation for the student of human behavior as is homosexuality. The only reason it does not seem to us a problem is because we take its existence for granted."[1]

Heterosexual people talk a great deal about growing up sexually but not about growing up *hetero*sexually, that is, the development of their sexual *identity*. Such a discussion feels not just boring, but ludicrous. What would one talk about? Of course, if heterosexuality is not a subject of interest, then heterosexism, homophobia, and biphobia are also unrecognized and unexplored. If homophobia *is* discussed, it is mistakenly thought of as something that is wrong with homosexual people, *not as a phobic condition of heterosexual people. Biphobia* is not even a recognized word, because bisexuality is thought of as an unclear psychological or physiological condition, not as an orientation. When anything so basic as our sexual orientation is unexamined, the result can only be insecurities, fears, and projections, though it takes admitting discomfort and embarrassment before we have the patience and desire to understand that this is so.

The focus of homophobic fears varies in different cultures. In white culture the fear is focused on the gay, lesbian, or bisexual person. This reflects the individualistic nature of white culture. Ron Simmons speaks of a different emphasis in the African-American community: "In the African American community, 'homophobia' is not so much a fear of 'homosexuals' but a fear that homosexuality will become pervasive in the community. Thus, a homophobic person can accept a homosexual as an individual friend or family member, yet not accept homosexuality. This is the attitude that predominates in the African American community."[2]

Because heterosexuality is so taken for granted in almost all cultures, our first step in addressing our heterosexism is to want to focus on the victim, that is, the homosexual or bisexual person. One reason for this focus is our culturally reinforced habits of voyeurism and titillation toward the unknown of homosexuality and that which is labeled immoral. Another reason is that it is easier to talk about people with the problems of subordinance than to speak about ourselves as dominants who create and participate in a climate of homophobia. We face our insecurities and the effects of our behavior on others when we focus on ourselves as heterosexual *and* dominant. *When dominants start recognizing and including themselves as dominant in the process under discussion, their effect on subordinants must be taken into account by them and their control over subordinants starts to erode.* In this way our power of dominance begins to fade and we can move on to the comfort and security of self-knowledge.

It is hard even to focus on how dominance is associated with identifying as heterosexual. Heterosexuality is so normal that having to think through how we acquired attributes of heterosexuality, much less that it is allied with dominance, seems like nit-picking, ridiculous, and a waste of time. Our resistance is so deep that the topic seems a nonsubject. We are more used to identifying dominant or subordinant in terms of male/female issues and people of color/white people concerns. It is easy to assume that these are the really important concerns (and they certainly are important). Our resistance to identifying as heterosexual in order to understand our dominance in relation to those with other sexual orientations and identities is intense. We often use the importance of dealing with racism and sexism as an excuse not to deal with heterosexism. Homophobia and biphobia infect us all regardless of gender, race, color, or creed, although the particulars of attitudes toward language and mythology about gay men, lesbians, and bisexual people vary with one's ethnic, racial, class, and religious background as well as by gender within such groups.

Jewelle Gomez and Barbara Smith speak of the challenges in the black community:

> **Smith:**   . . . So I think that one of the challenges we face in trying to raise the issue of lesbian and gay identity within the Black community is to try to get our people to understand that they can indeed oppress someone after having spent a life of being oppressed. That's a very hard transition to make, but it's one we have to make if we want our whole community to be liberated.

Gomez: . . . At this point, it seems almost impossible because the issue of sexism has become such a major stumbling block for the Black community.[3]

Pramila [sic] speaks of the Indian community: "sometimes I really feel isolated . . . and because of my lifestyle I could never live in an Indian neighbourhood. Because I feel that I could not live as a lesbian there. There would be too many restrictions and who needs more hassles."[4]

Our endless assumptions about sexuality come from inculcated **religious beliefs and family values which define acceptable sexuality**. Whether or not our own religious experience was profoundly homophobic, as a culture we are caught up in the powerful influence of those religions that claim homosexuality is evil and sinful. They have been allowed to set the standard for sexual identity as exclusively heterosexual, making it almost impossible for straight people to see a presumption of dominance in heterosexual identity. Such a standard for normalcy creates holes in our understanding of ourselves and others.

Our journey, then, as heterosexually identified people* in the orange section of compulsory heterosexuality is to understand our fears of homosexuality and bisexuality.

Compulsory Heterosexuality

Compulsory heterosexuality, which ascribes dominance to heterosexual people and subordinance to lesbians, gay males, and bisexual people, has been so thorough and relentless that we do not perceive heterosexuality as compulsory. Rather, we assume it is the right or only way to be. Those who may later identify as heterosexually oriented bisexual people cling tightly to their heterosexual self in the orange section.

Compulsory heterosexuality is sustained by a rigid hierarchy between heterosexuality and homosexuality and a denial of the existence of bisexuality. Dominants always decide who subordinants are, defining what is permissible for them as a way of life. Through hostile, negative definitions, heterosexually identified people have created such outright fears of homosexuality that hatred and fear of homosexuality and bisexuality have become the logical response.

We must understand how we participate in a homophobic and biphobic society. A good place to begin is to become aware of the **silence** around homosexuality in the polite company of **oblivious heterosexism**. This is currently the

---

*Because the compulsory heterosexuality of society denies the diversity of sexual orientations, the term *heterosexually or straight-identified people* includes those who will always identify as heterosexual as well as those who do so at this stage of the journey out of fear and repression. They may in time identify as bisexual, lesbian, or gay persons. The term *straight-identified* is often intended as derogatory by gay people; when used by straight people it is often intended to enforce the "normalcy" standard. It is used here as parallel to gay, lesbian, and bisexual, *without* such baggage.

standard for groups which shun overt violence. Many enter the journey at this later point in the orange section, growing up in liberal, permissive families. Straight-identified people are not ready here to acknowledge homosexuality and, even less so, bisexuality—their own or others. Bisexual people are just homosexual people with a fancier name.

Since utter silence about homosexuality was demanded for so long, we are only beginning to perceive the frequency of homosexuality and bisexuality and to hear what homosexual and bisexual people have to say. Our fears and defensiveness create a wall of resistance against which only silence about homosexuality, and therefore bisexuality, feels safe to *us*.

The pronoun *we* is used to talk about dominance and heterosexism in the orange part of the journey, because even though many of us may privately question cultural assumptions about homosexuality, few straight people stand up publicly in defense of gay rights. *We* remain quiet as a group, thus supporting all the ways the silences around homosexuality are built into our culture. This silence is like a cultural mask behind which no one must speak openly about homosexuality. Therefore, since straight-identified people as a group are silent and unquestioning, issues of heterosexism are addressed with *we* throughout the compulsory heterosexuality (orange) section in order to emphasize how *we*, as members of this group, are perceived by homosexual and bisexual people. Our learning in the orange section, then, comes from *identifying with heterosexuals as a group*.

Those of us in the later parts of the orange section try to disconnect ourselves from responsibility for the early parts. However, the silence of oblivious heterosexism in the late orange section supports and condones the violence of those in the early orange section. Silent heterosexist people create and perpetuate a homophobic and biphobic society. If we are not part of the solution, *we* are part of the problem. With this understanding, we are ready for a description of the overall themes of the dominance of compulsory heterosexuality on the upper line of the orange section of the continuum graphic.

A recurring theme throughout the orange section is that **"real" men and women are heterosexual**. In most cultures our femaleness and maleness are questioned if we do not identify as heterosexual. Much of male identity is formed as a reaction against being perceived as feminine. Richard Isay says that men's real fear is of the feminine. Men are more anxious about this than are women. He says that "it is in societies in which femininity is seen as 'pollution' that feminine characteristic traits in males will be most feared. . . . The roots of homophobia . . . lie in the hatred of what is perceived and labeled as feminine in men."[5]

In black culture, the effects of racism have much influence on what it means to be a real man. Isaac Julian and Kobena Mercer describe the need to be macho as a part of black male heterosexual identity in the United States:

> Our social definitions of what it is to be a "man," about what constitutes "manliness," are not natural, but are historically constructed and culturally

variable. The dominant definitions of masculinity, accepted as the social norm, are products of a false consciousness imposed by patriarchal ideology. Patriarchal systems of male power and privilege constantly have to negotiate the meaning of gender roles with a variety of economic, social, and political factors such as class, divisions of labor, and the work/home nexus. So, it's not as if we could strip away the negative stereotypes of black men created by Western patriarchy and discover some natural black masculinity that is good, pure, and wholesome.

The present repertoire of images of black masculinity—from docile Uncle Tom to Superspade heroes like Shaft—have been forged in and through the histories of slavery, colonialism, and imperialism. A central strand of the "racial power" exercised by the white male slave master was the denial of certain masculine attributes to black males, such as authority, dignity, and familial responsibility. Through these collective historical experiences, black men have adopted and used certain patriarchal values such as physical strength, sexual prowess, and being in control to create a system of black male gender roles in which macho tactics are used to cope with the repressive and destructive power of the plantocracy and the state.[6]

Men of all cultures resort to macho behavior to a greater or lesser degree to ward off accusations and perceptions that they are feminine. Men's fear of the feminine in themselves is fear of loss of power and exclusion from male society. Such exclusion exposes men to an unprotected status in which abuse is condoned and supported. In those cultures where men's comfort comes to depend on the feminine as powerless, we sometimes see an abhorrence of the feminine in men coupled with a fear of power in women. This is often a characteristic of white culture, producing hatred of lesbians who seem beyond male control and too powerful, and of gay men who seem unmasculine. The fear can move to violence all too quickly. Straight-identified men and women can both show their homophobia toward gay men through physical violence. Women often urge men on to brutal behavior and can be violent towards "unmanly" sons.

Because of gender dominance and subordinance in many cultures, women learn to fear their own power. This may be least true in American Indian and African-heritage culture, where deference by women toward men is not the rule. Much of straight-identified women's homophobia toward gay men comes from absorbing discomfort with feminine characteristics in men. Women's discomfort with men who seem feminine generally takes the form of gossip, avoidance, and encouragement of more masculine behavior (as when mothers push sons to act more masculine, that is, aggressive).

Another overriding theme in the orange section is the **religious beliefs and family values that have defined acceptable sexuality**. We have been conditioned not just to fear and condemn same-sex sexuality, but to feel profound emotions of disgust and repulsion toward it. Our most intimate sexual self is engaged. We dread the idea that others might think we are homosexual or bisexual because of our behavior, appearance, or association. To be thought gay, lesbian, or bisexual is to be reviled and excluded. Therefore, we are *straight* with a vengeance, that is, no one must question *our* orientation. In fact, if we are asked whether *we* are heterosexual, we are offended by the question.

We have not yet learned that these attitudes reflect our own fears, which we transfer into projections on gay, lesbian, and bisexual people. Projection as defined by *Webster's New World Dictionary* (3d ed., 1980) is the "unconscious act or process of ascribing to others one's own ideas, impulses or emotions, especially when they are considered undesirable or cause anxiety." *Our* fears of same-sex attraction and sexuality cause us to feel disgust and horror toward homosexual and bisexual people. We feel anxious around "them." Our fears are projections which influence our actions and beliefs about homosexuality and bisexuality, though they have nothing to do with the reality of homosexuality and bisexuality. They only reveal our ignorance of sexuality and our limitations in defining and envisioning maleness and femaleness.

The history of the last hundred years of Western sexuality, stemming from white Victorian mores, has been a history of repression, to say the least. Though sexual expression was freer in the 1960s and 1970s, allowing many homosexual and bisexual people to find support in communities, we returned in the 1980s to a degree of repression. Birth control and abortion, which are primarily heterosexual concerns, and AIDS, which, in the United States, first surfaced as an epidemic among gay men and is, in a heterosexist's view, still identified as a gay disease, became political footballs. Fundamentalists and conservatives still view sexuality as something to exploit for political purposes.

Heterosexists simplistically tie together homosexuality and AIDS. The fact that far more heterosexual people worldwide have AIDS than do homosexual people, and that the number of heterosexual people in this country with AIDS is fast growing, is overlooked. Religious fundamentalists intensify fears of homosexual people and of AIDS by suggesting that the disease is punishment from God, thus heightening religious intolerance and creating a new realm of homophobia.

Homosexuality has long been mistakenly feared as contagious. Homophobic demagogues take the contagion of AIDS and link it to the assumed contagion of homosexuality and bisexuality, reinforcing and enlarging our fears. Such bigots create conditions of isolation, punishment, and nonsupport for all who suffer from AIDS and for lesbian, gay, and bisexual people in general.

The repression of homosexuality in the last century and the current interpretation of AIDS as punishment from God make it difficult to discuss a range of responsible sexual behaviors and sexualities. Not only do we fear being labeled a "lover" of homosexuality and bisexuality; we also fear the same violent reaction that gay men, lesbians, and bisexual people often experience. Homophobic men, in particular, are often violent men. The license for violence toward gay and bisexual people is enormous. Antigay violence is encouraged in heterosexist culture when public morality and sex education do not support a variety of sexual orientations as normal and healthy. Straight-identified teenage boys and men caught beating up gay men often report no remorse. To them, gay men are inhuman and undeserving of respect. Tormenting them is justifiable.[7] Such repression, violence, and condemnation of homosexuality make heterosexuality compulsory.

The range of compulsory heterosexual behavior (orange section) from ostracism of gay men, lesbians, and bisexual people to oblivious heterosexism is detailed on the sexual orientation and identity continuum diagram following page 272. Let us look at the journeys in more detail, starting at the beginning of the orange section where ostracism and violence are found.

Ostracism and Violence

Ostracism and **anti-gay violence** characterize the earliest parts of the orange section on the continuum. It is particularly in the last one hundred years that in western cultures the inflexible boundaries have emerged around sexual diversity which help to produce such behavior. (See Appendix C.) When psychiatry and religious dogma created the rigid distinction between heterosexuality and homosexuality, ignoring bisexuality altogether, a hierarchy of values also was created validating compulsory heterosexuality and rigidly condemning homosexuality and bisexuality. This created an environment of ostracism of gay men, lesbians, and bisexual people. By tying together religious and psychological condemnation of homosexuality and bisexuality, the worst kind of abhorrence permeated society, giving license to heterosexual and heterosexually identified bisexual people to act out violently their terror of gay men, lesbians, and bisexual people. Also, denial of same-sex attraction by those who will later identify as gay, lesbian, or bisexual people ranges in the orange section from the most overt public condemnation of homosexuality and violence toward lesbians, gay males, and bisexual people to the quiet suppression of attraction to others of the same gender.

In 1987 The National Gay and Lesbian Task Force began compiling statistics on *reported* antigay episodes, which they update each year.[8] Figure 1 shows a comparison of their statistics for 1987 and 1988. In 1992, the NGLTF reported 1,898 antigay incidents, twelve known homicides, and 350 incidents of physical menacing—up 139 percent from 1991 (see fig. 2). Though most antigay crimes go unreported, enough are finally beginning to be reported that we can realize their extent.

The following are typical hate crimes and acts of physical violence described in the 1988 report.

> In **San Mateo, California,** two parents who attacked their gay son and his
> friend, Dennis May, with an ax and golfclubs were ordered to pay $16,000
> in damages to May. The attack, which was accompanied by antigay epithets,
> severely injured May and damaged his car. (P. 27)

54

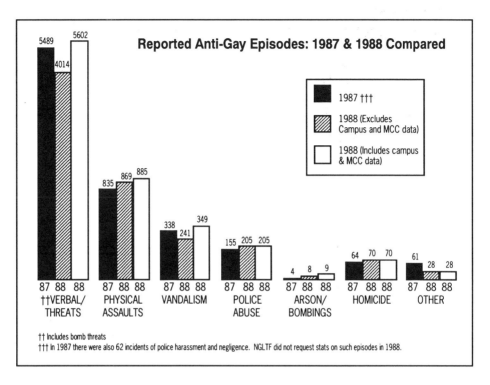

Fig. 1
Source: National Gay and Lesbian Task Force,
"Anti-Gay Violence, Victimization, and Defamation in 1988," p. 10.

In **Portland, Maine,** on World AIDS day, Vincent Boulanger, a gay man with AIDS, and his mother, Shirley, were assaulted by a tow-truck driver hired to bring them from the local church where they were working on the Names Project AIDS Memorial Quilt to a lot where their car had been towed. When they got in the tow truck, the driver started screaming and striking at both of them. As the two scrambled out of the truck, the driver punched the man with AIDS in the back, chest, and head and then drove away. (P. 17-18)

Arson and other attacks against churches affiliated with the **Universal Fellowship of Metropolitan Community Churches,** a Christian denomination with a special outreach to lesbian and gay people, are a longstanding problem. Since the founding of the denomination in the early 1970s, MCC places of worship have been the targets of arson at least twenty times. One firebombing incident in New Orleans in June 1973 claimed thirty-two lives. MCC churches have also experienced hundreds of incidents of harassment, vandalism, and intimidation. (P. 16)

As reported in the *Arizona Daily Star,* **Tucson, Arizona,** an employee at a gay bar was attacked by skinheads who wielded a ball and chain as a mace.

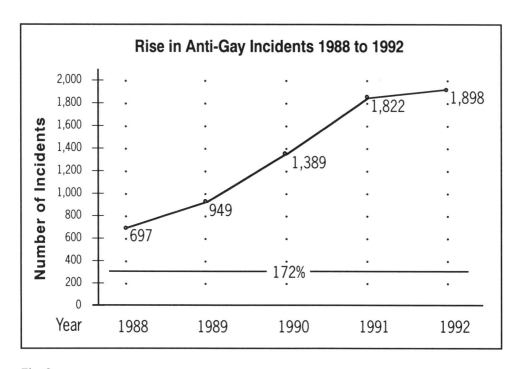

Fig. 2
Source: National Gay and Lesbian Task Force,
"Anti-Gay Violence, Victimization, and Defamation in 1992," p. 12.

The victim was struck with the spiked ball, opening a six-inch gash in his forehead and nose. When the victim fell to the ground, his assailants continued to beat him with the ball and chain and a wooden pole, bruising and lacerating his body. Wounds to the victim's head and face required sixty stitches. (P. 19)

In **Adams County, Pennsylvania,** two lesbians—Claudia Brenner and Rebecca Wight—who had been hiking along the Appalachian Trail, were shot at by a lone assailant who had stalked them for a day. The women were camped in a secluded area near a stream when the assailant, who hid in the woods eighty feet away, opened fire on them. Wight was shot in the head and the back and died at the campsite. Although Brenner was shot in the head, face, and upper arm and twice in the neck, she managed to walk nearly four miles to a road where she was able to get help. (P. 20)

An inmate in the **Tarrant County, Texas,** jail reported having been subjected to repeated harassment, threats, beatings, and rape because of his sexual orientation. According to the victim, perpetrators included other inmates and jail personnel. Appeals by the victim for a stop to the violence were ignored by jail officials. (P. 23)

56

In **Miami,** radio station WGTR ran several commercials for a nightclub that offered a variety of "special" activities, including "beating up queers." The disc jockey cut into the ad stating that "beating up queers" was something he agreed with and enjoyed doing. (P. 29)

Today, the levels and types of violence against lesbians, gay men, and bisexual people are no different than they were in 1988, although an intensity is present that reflects the broader political context. This context includes: initiatives against gay rights on the ballots in Colorado, Oregon, and many other states and localities; President Clinton's raising the issue of gays in the military, then backing down in ways that left gay, lesbian, and bisexual people at risk; and hateful Republican party ideology, expressed in speeches at the 1992 national convention.

The 1992 National Gay and Lesbian Task Force report describes the following incidents.

Indianapolis, IN: On February 16, a man was arrested for the murder of a gay man whom he shot to keep from testifying against him in an earlier gay bashing. In the previous incident he choked, bound, and robbed the victim after having sex with him. The perpetrator told police he committed the acts because he dislikes gays. (P. 25)

Kenton, OH: On September 16, a man lured a gay man to a quarry for sex. Two friends then helped him rob the gay man, beat him to death, and throw his body into the quarry. (P. 25)

Washington, DC: In July, two men leaving a popular African-American gay club were shot by two teenagers. The victims were left on the street and nearly bled to death. (P. 25)

Dallas, TX: On September 18, three teenagers yelling "faggot" and "queer" attacked and beat two gay men as they left a gay bar. Afterward, the gay men flagged down a taxi, whose driver refused to help and drove away when he realized what had happened. They then went back to the gay bar, where the security guard told them it was the third attack by the same perpetrators that night. (P. 26)

El Paso, TX: In August, a gay teenager was physically assaulted by his father after he was caught talking to another boy about being gay. The youth, who reported being struck in the face, causing a "pretty bad bruise," now fears returning home. (P. 26)

Hillsboro, OR: On October 11, vandals and arsonists broke into St. Matthew's Roman Catholic Church and painted antigay, anti-Semitic, and anti-Catholic graffiti on the walls. The church walls were painted with hate messages such as "Yes on 9," "We kill Catholics," and "We hate gays." A fire was set in the rectory of the church, nearly killing the assistant pastor. After services the following morning, an advocate for the Oregon antigay initiative attempted to hand out a campaign flyer. (P. 27)

Denver, CO: On October 30, a man accused of making $18,000 worth of harassing long-distance phone calls to groups around the country, including lesbian and gay community centers, was arrested. (P. 28)

Douglas County, OR: Beginning on July 18, a Nazi skinhead group targeted seven lesbians living in a farmhouse. The skinheads sent death threats with swastikas to the women, damaged the women's mailbox, and smashed headlights on the women's cars. A group of the men surrounded the house one night, yelling antilesbian slurs at the women. When one of the women went outside to investigate, she was fired upon by three men. She fired a single shotgun blast in return, which provided her enough cover to return safely to the house. (P. 28)

Albuquerque, NM: In December, owners of gay-owned businesses reported struggling with police in a dispute over traffic and parking near the businesses in a two-block area. Gay business owners claimed their customers were being singled out to be ticketed and towed by police. One police officer told a customer he would "clean up the business area of gays and lesbians." (P. 29)

Cook County, IL: On March 3, a gay man who attempted to enter a jail building to bail out his brother was attacked by a county sheriff's guard, who arrested him, handcuffed him, and beat him while yelling antigay epithets. The man suffered numerous bruises and required four stitches in his head, and was not allowed to press criminal charges against the guard. (P. 29)

Madera County, CA: In May and June, the family of a gay man with AIDS was terrorized by their next-door neighbor, a former California Highway Patrol officer. The former officer left antigay and anti-AIDS messages on the family's answering machine, killed several of the family's farm animals, and fired a rifle at the family's house. When the gay man's sister-in-law asked a family friend to take her son for a walk, the assailant beat the friend and held a gun to the head of the sister-in-law's son. (P. 30)

Denver, CO: On December 1, a gay man riding a bus was harassed by another man who yelled, "This guy has AIDS," and "You queers, you deserve it." As the gay man exited the bus, the perpetrator kneed him in the groin. (P. 30)

Salem, OR: In early September, Brian Mock, a disabled gay man, was severely beaten by skinheads yelling antigay slurs. The skinheads tracked

Mock to his Salem, Oregon, boardinghouse and taunted him from the sidewalk as he recuperated. One of Mock's housemates, Hattie Mae Cohen, confronted the gang repeatedly in an attempt to protect him. The skinheads then turned on Cohen, an African-American lesbian, with jeers of "nigger dyke." In the early morning of September 26, after yet another confrontation between Cohen and the skinheads, the sounds of breaking glass and the roar of flames awakened the boardinghouse residents. Mock and Cohen's skinhead antagonists had thrown a firebomb into Cohen's window. Cohen died in the flames and Mock died of his burns within hours. (P. 31)

Portland OR: Several gay and lesbian employees of Cascade AIDS Project received death threats by telephone and by fax in May. The messages, believed to come from three male callers, made references to murder, castration, dismemberment, and a "holy war" against gays and lesbians. "We will do away with all of you," claimed the voice on one message. (P. 31)

Eugene, OR: On October 27, a heterosexual man holding a sign supporting Oregon's antigay ballot initiative was beaten by two men who believed he was gay. (P. 31)

Colorado Springs, CO: A mental health counselor who supported a local group opposing Amendment 2 was attacked at her office in December. After being knocked unconscious, the woman was doused with scalding coffee and had crosses cut into her clothes and hand with a knife. The attackers vandalized her office and spray painted "Seek God," "Stop Evil," and "Repent" on the walls. (P. 32)

Sasebo, Japan: On October 27, shipmates of Seaman Allen Schindler beat him to death in a public restroom. Schindler was awaiting an administrative discharge for being gay. He had complained to his superiors about being harassed. However, the Navy denies receiving such a complaint. Despite that fact, a shipmate who was also harassed and beaten for being bisexual was taken off their ship, the USS *Belleau Wood*, the day after Schindler died because of the incident. Schindler was beaten so severely about the face, arms, and torso that his mother and sister were able to identify his body only after seeing his tattoos. (P. 32)

Honolulu, HI: On January 17, four army soldiers beat and kicked a man, calling him "faggot" and "queer." The man suffered cracked ribs and bruises. Two of the men were caught by a security guard, but when local and military police were called and discovered the nature of the crime, they released the assailants. The victim said an officer justified the release by claiming, "Well, you said yourself that you told them you were gay." (P. 32)

Mobile, AL: A bisexual man was asleep on February 7, 1993, when three of his former shipmates beat him up in his own bedroom. The veteran, who left the navy in December, stated that his shipmates claimed he turned his back on them when he left the navy and came out as a bisexual man. (P. 33)

August 1992: "Family Rights Forever/Gay Rights Never" was the slogan on very visible signs frequently displayed on the floor of the Republican National Convention in Houston. (P. 35)

What a painful list to read! It may seem long, but it by no means covers the majority of incidents given in the NGLTF report. Heterosexist people not only believe such violence does not occur but that if it did it would be justified!

What is the origin of these irrational fears of homosexuality and bisexuality, that they should generate such violent, destructive behavior? Various themes emerge from the incidents listed here, although all seem based on hate and fear. The themes include premeditated acts of violence; violence when a family member or acquaintance is found to be homosexual or bisexual; the perpetrator of the violence first having sex with the victim; the youthfulness of many instigators; the religious justification for violence; and the unwillingness of police or citizens to come to the aid of victims. When one considers that most threats and violence go unreported, the depth of the constant fear and intimidation that gay, lesbian, and bisexual people live with becomes clear. Newspapers daily report incidents of torture, **murder, rape**, harassment, vandalism, assault, and arson of lesbians and gays, though often they do not write clearly about this violence—that is, its homophobic basis— and articles are often ambiguous about whose fault the violence was.

In the heterosexist orange section of the continuum, such multiple stories of violence toward gay, lesbian, and bisexual people are read by straight-identified people with a voyeuristic feeling that confirms "their" inhumanity—"they" must have deserved it. Heterosexist people do not read or hear the news stories in terms of the injustice of the violence, nor do they gain a feeling of the prevalence of the violence, that is, the large number of such stories.

The question needs to be asked again and again: Where do such rage and fear come from that other human beings must be destroyed because of their sexual identity? Each of us must answer for himself or herself questions about the origins of such violence and intolerance and the form it takes—overt or covert. An obvious answer is that society plays a role in perpetuating intolerant beliefs and attitudes, such as the religious beliefs that homosexuality and bisexuality are sinful, evil, or a disease; the notion that we must all fit certain stereotypes of maleness and femaleness; and attitudes and behavior that objectify sex. In the end, however, it is not society but each of us who is responsible for our behavior.

Straight-identified men's and women's fears of homosexuality and, therefore, bisexuality are expressed in various ways. Stereotyping based on the norms of white culture, where maleness is tied to dominance, entitlement, and the need to feel in control, and femaleness is tied to subordinance and the need to defer, greatly influences how homosexual people are viewed. Every culture gives us two questions that are constantly with us. The first tests for one's gender "appropriateness"—"Am I male?" or "Am I female?" The second asks, "What can I do to make me feel male or female?" The answers differ for men and women.

Men's reactions to fears of being labeled gay call forth more physical challenge and the need to prove physical prowess and strength. Men's equation of homosexuality and, therefore, bisexuality, with subordinance and weakness brings with it a feeling that "if I am homosexual, I am less than even a woman and will be despised and banished from the realm of men." Rumors of gayness have destroyed many a straight man's reputation. Straight men know the lengths to which they go to guard against such an accusation or rumor.

Straight-identified homophobic women have much fear of being identified lesbian or bisexual. Our reactions are apt to be quiet avoidance, or shunning, where we exclude a gay person from interactions with straight people; or we use verbal harassment or gossip to "out" the lesbian, gay, or bisexual person, destroying his or her reputation in heterosexually dominated settings.

Some women punish homosexuals with physical cruelty, such as hitting, slapping, or beating. Most likely such violence is acted out on someone close—a suspected gay son or lesbian daughter. Women may also goad men on to violence for which the women then take no responsibility. As girls are encouraged to become more physically competent, the number of reported beatings by straight high school girls of known or suspected lesbians among their peers has increased. High school girls and boys must work out their sexual identity under pressure from both homophobic peers and adults.

When straight women are suspected of lesbianism, we often attempt a more feminine and seductive demeanor to prove how straight we are. We accentuate our role as wife or girlfriend. We increase our deference and attachment to men if we live in cultures where these are important characteristics for women. We fear that straight men's violence will spill over toward us if we are associated with lesbians or gay men.

Such behavior has its own effect on women. For one thing, it keeps us in our own victim behavior in relation to men, with all the attendant stress of physical self-abuse, depression, loss of self-esteem, and stress illnesses. If we are denying our own lesbianism (or gay maleness) by identifying as straight at this point, we are likely experiencing the same kinds of consequences. All the hurts of self-limitation are supported and condoned by us, though we cannot see this when we adopt behavior in the orange section. As straight-identified women, then, we tend to use covert, psychological violence on known lesbians, bisexual people, and gay men rather than physical violence. Of course such covert violence and silence on the issues of homosexuality and bisexuality support our own victimization as women. When we participate in the denigration of femaleness in any way, we detract from our power and acceptance as feminine and as women.

61

Because male identity in the orange section is tied to physical strength and power over others, physical acts are the traditional measure of manliness. The use of brutal violence against gay men, lesbians, and bisexual people becomes a way for heterosexist men to prove their manhood. Physical violence sometimes occurs as a reaction to accusations of being unmanly, that is, a sissy. Such men strive to be more athletic if they fear others perceive them as "less than a man," or they prove their manliness by bashing, that is, brutalizing, a gay or straight effeminate-seeming man. Within organizations, psychological weapons such as intimidation and avoidance may be more the norm, since institutions generally do not tolerate brute violence.

One of the most violent places for young gay men of all cultures is high school (see Appendix B on childhood). This is an intense time for boys to explore the meaning of maleness. Here the basic question of "Am I a man?" is first faced. High school boys, desperate to define their sense of masculinity, use physical and verbal abuse against any boy they perceive as gentle or odd and, therefore, presumptively gay. (Note the stories by the men in chapter 1.) Participation in this abuse is often a way to clear oneself of suspicion or for a leader to set the boundary for group membership. Many male coaches and teachers create and condone a homophobic environment by looking the other way when boys tease and make fun of other boys who seem gentle, nurturing, or emotionally connective, or by imitating such teasing themselves.

The snapped wet towel at a "sissy" in the locker room, the exclusion of boys who seem nonathletic in order to establish one's own sense of maleness, and **gay-bashing** and **gay-baiting** excursions into known gay neighborhoods are all terrorizing techniques used to build a sense of superiority vis-à-vis other boys and men who seem less masculine, that is, feminine. Men's need to feel superior to women is often so strong that it makes an effeminate-appearing man particularly contemptible even if he is straight. His very being threatens the myth of masculinity.

Carmen Vazquez describes an incident in San Francisco:

> The 24 bus line brings people into and out of the Castro. . . . The very gay Castro is in the middle of its route. Every day, boys in pairs or gangs from either end of the city board the bus for a ride through the Castro and a bit of fun. . . . Sometimes, their fun is brutal. . . . Brian boarded the 24 Divisadero. . . . Epithets were fired at him the moment he turned for a seat. . . . Brian stuffed his hands into the pockets of his worn brown bomber jacket and stared. . . . He heard the flip of a skateboard in the back. The taunting shouts grew louder. "Faggot!" . . . He saw a beer bottle hurtling past the window and crash on the street. A man . . . yelled at the driver to stop the bus and get the hoodlums off. The bus driver ignored him and pulled out. Brian dug his hands deeper into his pockets. . . . It was just five stops to the top of the hill. When he got up to move toward the exit, the skate board slammed into his gut and one kick followed another until every

boy had got his kick in. Despite the pleas of the passengers, the driver never called the police. Brian spent a week in a hospital bed, afraid that he would never walk again. . . . [The] lawsuit . . . states, "As claimant lay crumpled and bleeding on the floor of the bus, the bus driver tried to force claimant off the bus so that the driver could get off work and go home."[9]

Brian was a *straight* man.

Abuse of women thought to be lesbians is often tied to sexual harassment. Straight-identified men use harassment and lesbian baiting to keep women "in line." Michelle Benecke and Kirstin Dodge discuss lesbian baiting in their report on women in the military.

> Lesbian baiting is the practice of pressuring and harassing women through calling, or threatening to call them, lesbians. . . . Lesbian baiting is tied to sexual harassment of military women in that it is often triggered by a servicewoman's refusal of sexual advances. For example, one officer told of sexual advances made by a male peer toward her and two women colleagues. All three made it clear that they were not interested in pursuing a sexual relationship. Soon after, they learned that the spurned officer was suggesting to other men in the unit that the three were lesbians and were engaging in sexual acts together.[10]

Dominant sexist men find support for their male entitlement and superiority over women through violent homophobic reactions to gay-appearing men and women in nontraditional roles.* The prevalence of "all-or-nothing" competition between men, an important component of sexism, implies and approves of physical violence. Heterosexist men's need to feel superior to women is reinforced by violent sanctions against men who exhibit feminine characteristics. This need gets translated into bashing and rape of gay and lesbian people.

The fear of being raped by homophobic straight men is enormous for gay men and lesbians. A common reaction to a lesbian coming out is to say, "All you need is a good lay to straighten you out." A straight parent may even say this to a lesbian daughter. A lesbian friend told of a call for help from her girlfriend who needed to leave her home immediately because her mother was going to have her boyfriend rape her that evening. Individual or group rape is all too real a possibility. It is homophobic people's way—our way—to control and enforce heterosexuality.

Such violence is a socially approved outlet for proving straight men's masculinity and straight women's acceptance of heterosexist men's definition of sexuality. There has been a 300 percent increase in violence toward gay and lesbian people since the AIDS epidemic brought increased visibility to gay males in

---

*Dominance and subordinance between heterosexual men and women are the foundation for heterosexism. Therefore, for heterosexism to be addressed, straight men and women need to deal with the dynamics of dominance and subordinance between themselves. See Pierce, Wagner, and Page, *A Male/Female Continuum: Paths to Colleagueship*.

the United States.[11] The number of people murdered solely because they identified as gay, lesbian, or bisexual skyrocketed in the 1980s and is intensifying in the 1990s. In a Boston survey taken in the early 1980s of sixteen hundred gay and lesbian people, 24 percent had been physically assaulted, 20 percent had experienced discrimination in employment, 21 percent had been subjected to vandalism, 13 percent had lost housing, and 76 percent had been verbally assaulted at some time in their lives—because of their homosexuality.[12] Such statistics on homosexuality need to be put into the perspective that only a small proportion of gay and lesbian people are known for survey purposes.*

Straight male violence toward gay, lesbian, and bisexual people is not just a matter of proving manhood and protecting womanhood. Mixed up with the need to defend a sense of maleness and femaleness is the belief that homosexuality and, therefore, bisexuality are **evil**. Political conservatives, particularly those with fundamentalist religious beliefs and "traditional" family values, define acceptable sexuality through compulsory heterosexism. Orthodox Christian and Jewish precepts are used by many to prove the immorality of homosexuality and, therefore, bisexuality. Such beliefs are being challenged in surprising quarters, however. Letha Scanzoni and Virginia Mollenkott, conservative, evangelical Christian theologians, write convincingly in favor of acceptance of homosexuality as normal in *Is the Homosexual My Neighbor?*[13] Instead of questioning kinds of sexual orientation, they focus on moral sexuality, which they define as a committed relationship, regardless of sexual orientation.

An interesting analogy can be made between religious rejection of homosexuality and left-handedness. It is hard to believe the strong negative reactions that left-handedness has generated in many cultures. For instance, Jesus was thought to give preference to right-handedness by his reference to sitting at the right hand of God; there was a time when left-handed people actually had their left hands cut off for minor offenses. For centuries many cultures have believed the use of the left hand for anything of importance to be evil and sacrilegious. Many adults in Western culture still remember having their hands tied behind their backs or their knuckles rapped for using the left hand. Such drastic action, to change the natural inclination of the body—often causing stuttering—frustrates and warps what is innate and true for the person. Today, it is unthinkable to punish such a natural tendency—at least when it comes to left-handed people.[14]

Deviance

The **violent antigay climate** created by homophobic, heterosexist people produces in straight people a need to ostracize gay, lesbian, and bisexual people. Such ostracism is based on a belief that homosexuals are unclean, **sinful,** and **sick**. Later in the transition, as we listen thoughtfully to coming out stories of lesbians,

---

*This perspective includes recognition that these numbers are probably understatements and that the statistics are based on nonrandom samples which yield, nonetheless, important descriptive data.

gay men, and bisexual people, we hear the deep pain created when we label homosexuality **deviant** and unnatural. We shun gay men, lesbians, and bisexual people out of fear for who *we* might be. We need an "otherness" or opposite against which to clarify our own masculinity or femininity—for our own self-assuredness.

When homosexuality is considered deviant, the gay man's and lesbian's private life is assumed to be in the public domain. We feel we have a right to intervene, as if they were children, that is, bad children, and to define what is suitable and unsuitable. We feel we may deny them such things as jobs, housing, friendships, public displays of affection, and parenthood. We write laws about what is sexually permissible. We decide they are sick and evil. No such measurements of acceptability are even dreamed of for straight people. In fact, until recently a straight couple could have a violent, debilitating relationship and no one thought it anyone else's business. The husband/father was expected to be in charge. So long as the partners were heterosexual, no one would intervene within a family. Family behavior has been private territory for straight people (except, of course, for birth control and abortion). A man could beat his wife and yet present himself as charming, intellectually stimulating, and God-fearing in public life, without censure or loss of esteem. Suspected wife beating, abusive physical discipline of children, and incest were not to be checked on or interfered with by those outside the family. There is still much resistance to interference in these matters.

Heterosexist men often associate sexual excitement with secrecy and the forbidden. In the early part of the continuum, heterosexist sexuality is built on domination, submission, the risqué, hostility, deriding humor, perversion, and violence. Homosexual relationships are the target of much of this behavior, which puts them outside cultural protection; so gay, lesbian, and bisexual people are not only defined as deviant but treated as fair game for the worst kind of abuse. They are ripe for **exploitation,** scapegoating, and extortion. One of the most notorious examples is that of the exploitation and extortion of J. Edgar Hoover, director of the FBI from 1924 to 1972, by the Mafia.* The more we cloak homosexuality and bisexuality in secrecy and the illicit and risqué, the more vulnerable are lesbian, gay, and bisexual people to illegal acts perpetrated on them. Straight people have long kept homosexual and bisexual people under control through such abusive behavior because we know other straight people will not come to their defense. We treat bisexual people, gay men, and lesbians as outside the protection of the law. A good example is the actions of the bus driver who refused to respond to the beating of Brian, reported earlier.

---

*Since his death in 1972, investigators from the U.S. Department of Justice and others have pieced together the story of Hoover's extravagant gambling habits and his ties to organized crime leaders, especially Meyer Lansky and Frank Costello, who rigged horse races for Hoover in exchange for immunity from FBI investigation from the late 1930s until his death in 1972. The hold the Mafia had over Hoover was his "known" homosexuality. See PBS Frontline, "The Secret File on J. Edgar Hoover," February 9, 1993, written and directed by William Cran, PBS Video, 1320 Braddock Place, Alexandria, VA 22314.

A common form of exploitation of homosexual people is **voyeurism.** What is seen as illicit and perverted is titillating. One type of voyeurism in which straight men participate is looking at images of eroticism between women and fantasizing about them for sexual arousal. Such pornographic voyeurism treats lesbians as sexual objects and has been a staple of heterosexist pornography since the early days of film.

Another form of voyeurism occurs when a straight person is suddenly aware that he or she is speaking with a bisexual, lesbian, or gay person. Images immediately come forward of the person being sexual. In this instance, talking with the lesbian, bisexual, or gay person is never just speaking about an everyday or work subject; pictures of imagined sexual acts are an overlay.

Voyeurism also shows up in the demagogic sermons of fundamentalist ministers. Giving lurid detail and distortion when describing the "fornication" of homosexuals is a form of voyeurism. If it is so sinful, why give all the details in a voice full of excitement and intensity?

Though voyeurism is unhealthy, it gives some people permission to reflect on their sexual identity and to consider same-sex sexuality as an option. It is here on the continuum that some straight-identified people, mainly men, may quietly reconsider their own sexual orientation. Note on the continuum diagram a line dropping down from voyeurism to the homosexual journey. Because of where he leaves the heterosexual journey, this man's entry into the homosexual journey most likely occurs very early in the orange section, at the rejection of self and self-hatred areas. Deciding or suspecting one is gay from the milieu of ostracism and denial, one often experiences self-abusive reactions. The man may later identify as gay, or as a gay-identified or straight-identified bisexual person. However, at this point he moves to the gay journey to explore this orientation. Bisexuality probably seems too complicated and confusing to consider.

Although homosexuality is shunned as a way of life by heterosexual people, **male-to-male sex acts** in the teen and adult years are common occurrences. In fact, Kinsey reported in 1948 that 37 percent of adult white men, at some point since puberty, had at least some overt homoerotic experience. Fifty percent who remained single until age thirty-five had had homosexual experience to the point of orgasm.[15] This percentage far exceeds the ten percent figure that has been commonly accepted as the number of predominantly homosexually behaving persons in the general population, which means many straight-identified men do not define themselves as homosexually or bisexually oriented, though they have had same-sex experiences. This does not mean they *should* define themselves as homosexual or bisexual, but to express denial of homosexuality as healthy and normal while participating or having participated in same-sex experiences implies fear and self-hatred for having been involved in what are seen as risqué or perverted acts.

The extreme **distaste** that many seemingly straight men and women have of homosexuality sometimes covers up their own bisexuality or homosexuality or their fear that they may be so oriented. Some of the most homophobic and biphobic public statements come from men, and some women, who later admit to being gay, lesbian, or bisexual themselves. Their public railings against homosexuality as sick and deviant are efforts to keep hidden from others and perhaps from themselves their own homosexuality or bisexuality. Though J. Edgar Hoover never publicly came out (he was outed by others), he and Roy Cohn (also known to be a gay man),[16] attorney and aide to Senator Joseph McCarthy, were responsible for much of the homophobic hysteria of the early 1950s when the House Committee on Un-American Activities searched for homosexuals and Communists in the U.S. State Department.

Many discussions about sexual orientation end with rabid exhortations and accusations about the homosexuality of others by people who hold rigidly defined dualist views of male and female, heterosexual and homosexual, and are so terrified of the possible implications of their own same-sex feelings that they cover up their denial with homophobic finger-pointing. Heterosexist people believe that anyone who ever has any same-sex erotic feelings or who ever wants to act in ways at odds with traditional maleness or femaleness *must* be gay or lesbian, and they find their own homoerotic feelings and desires terrifying. These feelings are particularly common in those cultures where there is little casual hugging or touching of one's own gender.

It is not only the thought of touching or being intimate with someone of the same gender that is repugnant, but once again the fear of being thought less than a "real" man or woman. Because we are terrified to imagine such sexual intimacy, it is bad and wrong for everyone. To allow others to act on their natural inclinations is threatening to us personally.

A gay man described his treatment by a waitress in a restaurant where he went to celebrate his birthday. His partner arrived early, engaged a table, and asked for flowers to be brought to the table. When the gay man arrived, he gave his partner's name as waiting for him. The waitress was so shocked that she stalked to the table, grabbed the flowers, and insisted that the men follow her to an unoccupied bare room to eat. She left them in shocked silence.[17] There was a time I would have wondered what the men had done to deserve such a reaction. Now I think about the distaste and fear the waitress embodies. Is it toward herself?

Labeling Homosexuality a Sickness

Another way to deny that homosexuality and bisexuality are normal is to put them into the category of **curable mental illness**. A step on the journey away from physical violence to acceptance of homosexuality is to believe that homosexuality is a curable illness. This is a small step to someone well into the transition but large to someone giving up overt violence. At this point we assume homosexuality is similar to alcoholism: it is something we may be susceptible to, but with patience it can be cured. Homosexuality is no longer thought of as sinful and evil. Now, instead of wishing "they" were arrested and locked up, or even killed, we expect anyone identifying wholly or partially as lesbian, gay, or bisexual to enter therapy. If "they" would search their childhoods for the traumatic experiences that caused them to prefer same-sex relationships and, therefore, arrested their development, or if "they" would try aversion therapy to learn to associate homosexuality with nausea and pain, or if "they" would get a "good heterosexual lay" or get married, "they" would be cured. The therapist is expected to do what we as parent, relative, or friend have failed to do—change someone's orientation to "normal." This view holds that time and willpower conquer "misplaced" sexuality.

If homosexuality is considered an illness, then it is easy to believe that a gay or lesbian lifestyle is **contagious** (even though not all illnesses are contagious). We shun lesbian- and gay-identified people because we fear their ways and habits will rub off on us. We do not understand that specific sex acts do not make us either straight, gay, lesbian, or bisexual. Adopting a sexual identity is a developmental process we each pursue for ourselves through self-discovery, not something we are seduced into. Sexual orientation is probably a combination of a matter of birth and hormones as well as cultural socialization. Other people cannot change us into anything different or decide for us who we are.

It is scary to imagine homosexual people being close to us (either physically or emotionally) if we have never had to think about our own sexual orientation or identity. Because there was never a time when we specifically thought through our own sexual orientation and made a decision about our own heterosexual identity, how can we be confident we really are heterosexual? We never consciously said, "I am heterosexual because . . ." When we do not understand what sexual orientation and identity are and have not acknowledged that we have the autonomy to decide what is true for us, then we fear others can "change" us by their homosexual advances. As we move toward the transition on our journeys, we tend to think more about our own sexual orientation and identity and gain confidence and comfort with who we are. When we have thought through our own identity, we are more comfortable with and understand how others have arrived at their identification. We are apt to be judgmental and homophobic toward others when we lack appreciation and understanding for the work it takes to arrive at a fully elaborated and self-affirmed sexual identity.

In the denial stage of the continuum, however, we are too afraid to do this work. We assume that homosexuality and bisexuality are a sickness and that all who identify as homosexual are prowling around trying to convert others to their ways. We do not understand how we emotionally isolate gay men, lesbians, and bisexual people, making it difficult and painful for them to find friendships and people with whom to share their problems of dealing with homophobia. When they do reach out, we see it as an attempt to convert others to homosexuality. In fact, we interpret anything beyond silence or total closeting on the part of gays, lesbians, and gay-identified bisexual people as prowling and flaunting one's sexuality. Of course most married heterosexual men and women flaunt their hetero-sexuality by wearing wedding bands.

Our **fear of exposing children** to known homosexuals is overwhelming. "Keep them away from our children!" is a common expression. Behind the statement is the fear that children will be sexually abused as well as have their orientation influenced. Children are thought to be particularly vulnerable to being influenced by homosexual people. We fail to realize that most child sexual abuse is committed by men who lead heterosexual lives. We also do not, based on this pattern, exclude heterosexual men, as a group, from elementary and high school classrooms.

We distrust expressions of all childhood sexuality, same-sex as well as female/male. Children should be sexless until maturity. As long as heterosexual people believe that homosexuality is acquired through contact, neither heterosexual nor homosexual children can be trusted to know themselves and decide who they are. Some lesbians or gay men say that even as children, they knew same-sex attraction was part of their makeup. Others say it was a revelation that slowly unfolded (see Appendix B). Psychologists who have studied children raised by gay and lesbian parents report that the children are psychologically healthy and turn out hetero-sexual, bisexual, and homosexual in about the same proportion as those raised by heterosexual parents.[18] We can discover this on our own by meeting and talking with gay and lesbian parents.

As we move from denial to oblivious heterosexism on the continuum, our **hostility** becomes less focused on overt violence and more on the use of **jokes and pejorative words**. Words such as *fag*, *wimp*, *dyke*, *queer*, and *fairy* continue to be used, but now these derogatory words alone, without physical violence, are relied on to express our hostile feelings. We have become so used to saying and hearing such words that we are rarely aware that we use them, much less of their impact. If we have been using them, they are so ingrained in our slang that we don't stop to think of their meaning. Since we assume everyone around us is always straight, we are oblivious to the offensiveness and impact of these words. They are "fun" to say and "smart" to use. Earlier on the continuum, in the ostracism area, pejorative words and jokes were chosen intentionally for their hurtful impact. Here it is often just habit and the unacknowledged need to feel "in" by excluding others who are assumed not to be present.

Though our language is sloppy and our fears are still present, our homo-phobia starts to decline about here on the continuum. Our resistance to the *idea* of homosexuality has been lowered. We are a bit more accepting of homosexuality: "If 'they' will just go about their business away from my life, well, let 'them' be."

Bisexuality has yet to be acknowledged as an orientation or identity, even if we are aware of people attracted to both genders or have ourselves had sexual experiences with both genders. The concept of bisexuality is still too threatening to think about, much less acknowledge as a possible way of being.

Oblivious Heterosexism

Our **oblivious heterosexism** is in full bloom. **Silence** is the name of the game. It is impolite to mention homosexuality and bisexuality; ladies and gentlemen never mention the subject. It is rude to gossip, which everything concerning this subject is. Gossip puts those in the spotlight who may someday be sorry they were ever so naive to think they were gay or lesbian, and we would not want to embarrass anyone in that way. We are nice people. After all, we must protect "them" from themselves. Such attitudes are examples of debilitating paternalism and maternalism.* Of course those being protected are ourselves. We are still terrified of the subject, therefore we assume lesbians, gay men, and bisexual people must also be terrified. We do not grasp that *our terror* is what is terrifying for bisexual people, gay men, and lesbians. We **avoid known and suspected homosexual and bisexual people**. We are uncomfortable in their presence because we see them only through their sexual nature. We feel something is expected of us and are afraid of what that is. We assume if we associate with a gay man, lesbian, or bisexual person that he or she will want to be sexual with us. For our own comfort we avoid all contact and feel **nervous around "them."**

Growing up in a good liberal white family meant for me entering this continuum at oblivious heterosexism. I find this is also true in many liberal families of color. It may be wrong to be violent toward others, and we shouldn't say unkind things such as those found in the early part of the orange section, but "we just can't be permissive about sexual orientation." Children are not just assumed to be heterosexual but pressured to be, whether or not there is any question. We don't think of our heterosexuality unless we feel threatened by children or others close to us who show signs of what we perceive as homosexuality or bisexuality. We want to act as if **"everyone" is heterosexual**.

We **reject nonconforming gender behavior**. Boys and men should look certain ways, and girls and women should be traditionally identifiable. Males with feminine characteristics and mannerisms and females who seem too masculine are unhealthy and make us uncomfortable. They always have, but now we talk about the propriety of male and female characteristics and mannerisms in men and women, because it feels like an acceptable way to express discomfort with those who identify as homosexual. It is more refined to talk about homosexuality this way than to say it is sinful or a sickness.

In sexist societies, boys and men have always seemed funnier dressed up as women than do girls and women dressed as men. Men in women's clothes are hilarious as long as they are making fun of being feminine. As soon as men in women's clothes take themselves seriously, they are suddenly not funny and we are uncomfortable. Cross-dressing, of course, is identified with male homosex-

---

Maternalism is used here as a parallel term to *paternalism*, holding women accountable for "protective" behavior that maintains dominance.

uality, which may or may not be true. A woman in male clothes is more normal, even chic, particularly if she is wearing unisex clothing. She will need to be in a business suit with pants and a tie, men's dress shoes, no makeup, and short-cropped hair before she provokes a negative reaction. Then she likely will be seen as pathetic and unhappy.

Women in nontraditional jobs such as the armed services, public utility work, and engineering are often assumed to be lesbian. They are vulnerable to accusations by straight women and men, as when women in professional sports are accused of seducing younger players.

When women's jobs are associated with physical force and strength, hetero-sexist men and women assume that the women who perform them are not real women, that they are more like men. If women can prove they are feminine by being passive, deferring to men, and dressing at times in soft, feminine ways, such women are more likely to be accepted—ignored perhaps, but accepted. However, women in nontraditional jobs, such as construction and machine-shop work, who act in such feminine ways would court rejection as unreliable colleagues. Straight women in these jobs are often assumed to be lesbian, which is stressful.

Here is another place on the continuum where some people who have hidden their homosexuality decide to identify with the lesbian, gay, or bisexual journey. The movement into oblivious heterosexism brings a surface calm to the journey. We no longer view homosexuality as a sickness, and some of our buried feelings about our sexual identity can be acknowledged more easily to ourselves. Women and men who have assumed they were heterosexual have more leeway now to identify with the lesbian, gay, and bisexual journeys. They can watch others and consider options that have not been open to them before. They may still be close enough to thinking of homosexuality as a sickness and feeling the sadistic hostility of others so that their fears are overpowering. Unless they meet someone who is bisexual, gay, or lesbian who gives them support for their choice, they likely enter the homosexual journey on the continuum in the rejection-of-self and self-hatred areas of the early orange section; they are not likely to trans-plant themselves parallel to where they were on the upper line of the continuum or move forward into the transition right away.

Pressure Builds for Reconsidering Our Beliefs

The straight-identified person is beginning to feel **pressure building to examine issues of gender**. Avoiding known lesbian, gay male, and bisexual people in one's family, in friendships, and at work is becoming more difficult because so much more is said publicly in the media about homosexuality. More individual gay and lesbian, and perhaps bisexual, people risk coming out to us. We are confused about what to consider appropriate gender behavior. We feel **defensive** when we realize established roles for men and women are being challenged. We may loudly condemn others, but quietly we raise questions about our own gender identity as well as our sexual identity development. We are unsure. We can't talk about homosexuality or bisexuality, but our curiosity is piqued and we question previous assumptions we have made. We are surprisingly defensive if others accuse us of homophobia and biphobia. Since we do not openly harass gays or lesbians, we assume we have done all there is to do. We define homophobia and biphobia as open harassment. Since we don't do that, we can't be perceived as homophobic. We do not understand what it takes to reach out past our fears to feel comfortable with a full range of sexual diversity and to be inclusive.

We are becoming more aware of the number of gay men, lesbians, and bisexual people in our daily lives, though we still avoid acknowledging their sexual orientation as well as understanding the implications of our own. We **blank out everyone's sexual orientation**, our own and others, whether it is like ours or not. We say there is nothing to talk about. We think it is polite and helpful to "forget" what we know about people. There is no reason to pay attention to differences in sexual orientation. When we do this we **set the rules** of heterosexuality as those by which lesbians, bisexual people, and gay men must live.

We speak or respond to bisexual, gay, and lesbian people as little as possible. We **minimize the person** we discover is gay, lesbian, or bisexual. If we work in a group with a person we know or suspect is gay, we quietly distance ourselves from that person. We are nervous talking to her or him and don't know what to talk about. We self-censor our behavior. We still see the gay man, lesbian, or bisexual person through his or her sexual behaviors rather than as a whole person. We need to ask ourselves, "Do we approach every heterosexual person with visions of what he or she does in bed?" Why then, when interacting with lesbians, gay men, or bisexual people, do we limit ourselves to viewing them through their presumed sexual behaviors?

We have come to the point on our journey of saying, "Well, maybe some people could legitimately be gay, lesbian, or bisexual, but they should be absolutely sure, because it is a frightening way of life." Some of us are even ready to say that "it could be **'natural' but, if so, one should be celibate**." Currently this is a strong stance within much of the Christian community; for many it is considered as "far as one can go and still be Christian." "Love the sinner, not the sin" is the common admonition. Nevertheless, the judgment and stigma of sinner have been pronounced. That is, of course, an act of spiritual violence. The non-religious version of this stance is, "Be gay, but don't talk about it. Keep it quiet. Don't throw it in our faces." We **require gay, lesbian, and bisexual people to be silent** about themselves and their sexual orientation.

We have not yet confronted the thought of same-sex intimacy and cannot equate it with sexual expression. Our own fears of intimacy with the same gender prevent us from feeling comfortable with imagining same-sex loving, let alone sexual expression. We ask of others what we would never ourselves accept: do not fall in love with someone, but if you do, do not touch or hold them in any way.

Our defensive behavior includes loud denial of being homophobic, biphobic, or heterosexist. However, by no longer thinking of homosexuality or bisexuality as evil or a sickness, we have lost most of our arguments against accepting homosexuality and bisexuality as normal. We are becoming aware that what stands in our way are our own fears of same-gender sexuality, which are related to our fears about shifting the meaning of maleness and femaleness.

Tolerance

We are **polite** and **tolerant**. Our own comfort is at stake. However, the thought of two men kissing good-bye in an airport is beyond our comprehension. Two women holding hands in public is seen not as a loving gesture, but as a pitiful sight, though again we would do nothing. We would feel embarrassed for them that they would do such a thing, but we wouldn't react publicly. We tolerate the behavior, though with discomfort.

We project our discomfort onto gay men, lesbians, and bisexual people for whom this behavior seems normal and natural. Since we are uncomfortable, we think they must be uncomfortable and feel ill when they touch. We cannot fathom such relaxed, open, public affection. We have not considered how painful it must be never to exchange loving gestures in public, nor have we imagined their pain from watching us be affectionate in public and knowing they cannot. Nor do we understand how important it is to the two people being affectionate to have a response of good will from others. Our tolerance gives a level of permission, but acceptance and pleasure for another's love relationship are missing.

As we think back to homosexuality and bisexuality in our families and neighborhoods as we grew up, we may remember a number of men and women who either lived with us in our families, as bachelors or old maids, or with "friends" of the same gender. In my family, no one would say why the maiden aunt was taken from independent living to be sheltered the rest of her life or why the bachelor uncle preferred his own place, alone. Many have had relatives who were teased or treated in ways that isolated them, yet at the same time they were included in family gatherings. No one would discuss "them" or answer questions of childhood curiosity. They were just different. People avoided them and left them alone, or if they were included in family and community gatherings, they learned to act normal, that is, they set aside all behavior that made heterosexual people uncomfortable. The question remains: Were they gay or lesbian people? We can only wonder. All unmarried people are not homosexual, but if a certain percentage of the population is homosexual and bisexual, where are they? As we think about how friends and relatives were treated as we grew up, we need to ask, "How would we treat them today?"

Our quiet reflection brings an **intellectual acceptance** based on treating people fairly. Perhaps lesbian, gay, and bisexual people have not been treated well.

Everyone deserves a chance. That's the American way. Our quandaries may turn us to important sources of information such as books, television programs, and movies. Our reflections as well as our reading, viewing, and still unanswered questions make us ready for the transition. We are willing to **read** and to listen to others speak of their experiences, though we hesitate being seen buying books about differing sexual orientations or reading them in front of other people. The reader may want to choose several books from the bibliography at the end of this volume and discover what it feels like to buy books on homosexuality or bisexuality or to check them out of the library.

We are moving away from oblivious heterosexism by granting a tolerance and intellectual acceptance to homosexuality and bisexuality. It is a way to quiet our emotions and give us a breather as we prepare for the transition. The problem has been, and is, that this acceptance is thought of as the culmination of a journey, that we have done all there is to do. It reflects the rational norms of our dominant culture, that if we have thought through justice and fairness, we have done it all. It discounts the need to get our emotions, feelings, and behavior in line with what we say we believe and the need to redress the lack of community for those perceived as other.

Tolerance manifests itself in different ways in different cultures. For instance, at this point on the journeys, in the African-American community, tolerance of the individual within the family or church is experienced by the gay man or lesbian, but the expectation is that he or she "won't talk about it too much." About here on the continuum, some "straight" African-American men and women (as well as people of other cultures and races) are engaged in secret same-sex relationships. It is also expected by straight African-Americans that the issues of race will be the dominant priority and concern of lesbian, gay, and bisexual people in the African-American community. One's homosexuality is tolerated, but it is expected that one's racial identity will be the "driving force." In this way, straight African-Americans intensify black lesbian, gay, and bisexual people's struggle to find or create a supportive African-American gay, lesbian, or bisexual network along with a broader network of multicultural gay, lesbian, or bisexual people including white people who are consciously on their race awareness journey.[19]

This time of intellectual acceptance is another place on the continuum where some who have identified as straight may feel comfortable enough to question whether that is who they are. Their own tolerant attitude and willingness to read about differing sexual orientations support them in reconsidering who they are. At this point the double lines on the continuum show a reaching forward into the lesbian or gay male journey or toward an earlier place on that journey. Where the gay male or lesbian journey is entered depends on the attitudes of those close to a person and on the person's own unresolved fears. If connection and support are found in gay or lesbian communities, one is less apt to move to an early part of the lesbian or gay journey.

Secret same-sex relationships are often found at this point on the continuum—sometimes while concurrently participating in a heterosexual relationship, sometimes not. Such relationships are found for men and women of all races. At this stage the risk of openly acknowledging such a relationship feels far too high, not only because of cultural sanctions against same-sex sexuality, but because of one's own fears and uncertainty. Participating in such a secret relationship as one enters the transition is very different from the secretiveness found earlier in the orange section. There, surreptitious interactions are just that: same-sex sexual encounters without questioning deeply one's orientation. Here, near the end of the orange section, the relationship is more likely to have a commitment and a thoughtfulness about it that includes an awareness that one may be gay or lesbian, or possibly bisexual.

For those who are not questioning their heterosexuality, it would be great to say that the transition is entered because of a personal commitment and dedication to justice. Mostly we just slide into or are driven into the transition because of the shock of someone close coming out. We are stunned by the revelation, whether we suspected it or not.

Subordinants as a group, and individually, always move into the transition first. The dominant and subordinant journeys are never parallel on the continuum. It is when gay, lesbian, and gay/lesbian-identified bisexual people move along their journey of deciding to come out that we are jolted.

Heterosexual people are as jolted by homosexually identified bisexual people as they are by lesbians and gay men. Heterosexually identified bisexual people still seem confusing. Why would anyone bother to be a heterosexually identified bisexual person? If one could be heterosexual, just forget the bisexual part and "be normal!"

It is the tension of subordinants being "down the road" that draws us as dominants into the transition. Therefore, the lesbian, gay man, and lesbian- or gay-identified bisexual person's experience of subordinance and their move into the transition are described next.

Struggles for Survival and Identity

Early Journeys of Lesbians, Gay Men, and Lesbian/Gay-Identified Bisexual People

HEATHER WISHIK

I loved my friend.
—*Langston Hughes, "I Loved My Friend"*

Say the least said and tell the least told.
—*Cheryl Clarke, "Saying the Least Said"*

Many lesbians, gay men, and lesbian/gay-identified bisexual people consciously enter the journeys depicted on this continuum at the point where we begin the process of **coming out to the self**.* This is the moment when I not only recognize the same-sex attractions and feelings I've been having, but I admit to myself that these attractions and feelings are important. I may not yet have enough information to put labels on all this. I may not use words to myself like *sexual orientation* or *sexual identity* or *lesbian* or *gay*, and I am even less likely to know about bisexuality as a possibility. On the other hand, at the same moment I may both admit the reality and centrality of my same-sex feelings, consciously label what I believe is my sexual orientation, and adopt a sexual identity. I may call myself lesbian or dyke, or gay or queer, or in-the-life or maricón, and what I call myself may change as I move forward into figuring out what it means to be who I now recognize myself to be. Coming out to the self is a complex process often involving some reframing of, or separation from, a prior presumption of heterosexuality. The process is necessary if any recognition of one's orientation and later construction of a sexual identity consistent with that orientation are to occur.†

---

*I have written this chapter using at times the pronouns *I* and *we,* and the words *us* and *our.* As the lesbian author of this chapter, I use these words to refer to my own experience and to the experiences of lesbians and gay men with whom I have talked, worked, and lived. I also sometimes use these pronouns to illustrate in the most direct manner what a particular moment on the orange stage of the continuum may feel like to some lesbians, gay men, and lesbian/gay-identified bisexual people, whether or not that has been my own experience. I also use such words when a person in the orange section would tend to generalize his or her own experiences as that of many gay or lesbian people.

77

For me, coming out to myself took two years between the ages of twenty-six and twenty-eight, after the birth of a son and a failed marriage. My process began when I admitted to myself I was feeling sexually attracted to a woman friend at law school. She felt attracted to me but, when we talked about our feelings, said she was too scared of a lesbian custody battle to have a sexual relationship. Coming out to myself continued as I tried my last affair with a man, moved with my son across the country, and fell in love with another woman friend with whom I was sharing a house. This time both of us were too scared to act on our feelings. I again moved away. In a new place in a new house I told myself a new version of my life story, one that helped support the sexual identity I was ready to adopt as my own. I told myself these weren't just feelings I'd been having at random. I'd been doing this since age three, loving my female friends, loving them too intensely, masking my feelings poorly enough at age sixteen to have provoked my freshman college friend S., with whom I was head over heels in love, to warn me that she had been "approached by a lesbian once in high school" and that "the lesbian had been scary." As I related in my story, that was the first time I had ever heard a word for a woman who wanted to love another woman. At home alone at age twenty-eight, I sat with myself and let it sink in. After two years of toying with and running from and coming back to it, I recognized that this sexual, emotional, erotic woman-identifiedness was important; it counted for something. I told myself I was a lesbian. It was another six months before I found my first woman lover.

For adults, coming out to the self happens under many different circumstances and at a wide variety of ages. It is depicted on the continuum diagram late in the orange section. Soon after coming out to the self or later on the journey, many of us, as I did, look back at childhood, adolescent, and adult events prior to that coming-out moment with a new frame of reference, probing for how sexual orientation issues may have been involved in our lives much earlier, including sometimes recognizing in our own stories experiences of the deep **sexual denial**, invisibility, and/or pain depicted earlier in the orange section. Others of us knew consciously as we grew up that we were struggling with what it meant to be a person with a sexual orientation the world rejected. Sometimes our behavior was viewed as so unacceptable that others told us we were "queer" before we even understood the meaning of the word. Sometimes we just knew inside from the age of two, when the touch of a favorite aunt's cheek felt exciting in a way nothing else did, or from age five when men's bodies were what all the dreams were about.

Some of us consciously live through many of the struggles represented at the beginning of the orange section of the continuum—in youth, in early adulthood, in late adulthood. Some of us skip these and go directly from registering same-sex feelings to coming out to ourselves. Some of us never get past denial, or bargaining

---

†Stages of coming out to the self have been described by several researchers. These stages share some common ground with descriptions of the development of racial identification.

with ourselves to persuade ourselves we aren't really "that way." Some of us don't survive suicide attempts or the alcohol and drugs with which we try to shore up our denial. Some of us live whole lives resignedly labeling ourselves homosexual and never develop a healthy, positive sense of gay or lesbian sexual identity. The orange section of the lesbian/gay and lesbian/gay-identified bisexual journey and the text of this chapter tell about all this.

I told a lesbian friend I was writing about how some bisexual adolescents and adults, gay men, and lesbians become very depressed, even suicidal, when they realize or suspect they are bisexual, lesbian, or gay. She said, "You know, I've never met a lesbian who felt that way. Are you sure that isn't just what straight society wants everyone to believe about what it's like to discover you're lesbian or gay?" She had a point. Heterosexually dominant society teaches it is a tragedy to discover you are gay, lesbian, or bisexual, but this is not a true description of all lesbian, gay, or bisexual experiences of coming out to the self, and it is less likely to be true of people who come out to themselves in adulthood than during adolescence. Contrary to heterosexual society's stereotypes, many adolescents and adults discover their bisexual or homosexual orientation joyfully and experience the adoption of a lesbian or gay sexual identity as a kind of "coming home" to themselves at long last after years of incomprehensible unease. As Adrienne Rich tells it,

> I have an indestructible memory of walking along a particular block in New York City, the hour after I had acknowledged to myself that I loved a woman, feeling invincible. For the first time in my life I experienced sexuality as clarifying my mind instead of hazing it over; that passion, once named, flung a long, imperative beam of light into my future. I knew my life was decisively and forever different; and that change felt to me like power.[1]

> Becoming a lesbian is not a "personal solution." It's a freedom to explore my feelings, my thoughts, my politics. I feel a sense of relief, a sense of joy. I'm an outlaw that just escaped the posse! I became a lesbian tonight.[2]

For many people, knowledge of the realities of living with the deep social disapproval gay men and lesbians must face daily comes later, after initial periods of relief, self-recognition, and happiness.[3] Even experiencing the phobic responses of family, friends, home or cultural community, colleagues, and society in general does not prevent development of deep satisfaction with one's bisexual, gay, or lesbian identity for many men and women.

Life in the Closet

The fact that sexual orientation is rarely obvious from the outside, as race and gender usually are, deeply affects how the journey of awareness and attitude about sexual orientation and identity is shaped for heterosexual, bisexual, and lesbian and gay people.* The ability of most lesbians and gay men to hide sexual orientation is both a blessing and a curse.

The lack of external markers permits many of us as gay men and lesbians to explore internally without at the same time having to suffer directly all the aspects of social prejudice; it allows time to experiment and permits a modicum of privacy for a very complex and personal journey. Lack of markers also makes it possible for heterosexual society to insist that we as bisexual people, gay men, and lesbians keep our orientations secret, or at least silent, to call anything other than secretiveness and/or silence "flaunting it," and to label bisexual people, lesbians, and gay men untrustworthy because of the lies the required secretiveness and silence inevitably breed.

Refusals to keep bisexual, lesbian, or gay orientation secret can be and are punished with everything from job loss to murder. The keeping of such secrets and the presumed vulnerability to blackmail which such secrets create have been used until very recently as reason to bar lesbians and gay men from many occupations, including, for example, law enforcement positions and most federal jobs requiring security clearances.

The secretiveness heterosexual society requires then permits most heterosexual people to believe gay and bisexual people don't exist, are rarer than is true, or are only effeminate men and masculine women, and prevents the majority of heterosexual people from knowing who among them is gay, lesbian, or bisexual. Secretiveness aids the perpetuation of negative stereotypes, which would be impossible were everyone's actual sexual orientation as obvious as is their gender or race. Thus the capacity to hide sexual orientation becomes the requirement to do so.

The lack of obvious markers for sexual orientation, combined with the silence, imposed secrecy, and negativity of compulsory heterosexual cultures toward gay, lesbian, and bisexual existence, makes it difficult for lesbian, gay, and bisexual people to become visible, to come out, even to themselves. This issue of invisibility to self has been particularly acute for lesbians and bisexual people of all cultures, and gay men of color. Lesbian and bisexual existence, and the existence of lesbians, bisexual people and gay men of color, have been even more unmentionable in heterosexual cultures than the existence of white gay men. Accessible

---

*Some children early in life act in ways viewed by their peers and/or families as so gender inappropriate that they are labeled "queer" or "dyke" early on and are harassed, beaten, and sexually abused for presumptively being gay or lesbian. The stereotypes about gay men being feminine and lesbians being masculine contribute to this sort of harassment of both straight and lesbian/gay people who don't act gender appropriate enough. Stereotypes also make it difficult for gay men and lesbians who fit them to keep their orientations hidden. Thus, not all people are able to hide their sexual orientations. Society jumps to conclusions based on the rules about gender, and adults as well as children who do not fit gender expectations are treated as if they were lesbian or gay whether or not this is true. "Butch" women and "effeminate" men often experience constant and severe harassment and abuse from people on the street, family members, law enforcement personnel, and co-workers, simply due to their inability to fit gender norms.

gay/lesbian culture has often been almost all white. Whatever one's cultural identity, emerging as a lesbian, bisexual or gay person, in a total "informational vacuum,"[4] is difficult. Often if there is any information, it is negative. A.N., a Japanese-American gay man, said he could find no evidence of the existence of Japanese gay men among his family, friends, or culture community, none in literature, and none in the gay bars he finally found. Until he read some personal ads in which white gay men sought Asian gay men, he thought he was the only one and that no man would ever want to be with him or find him attractive. Despite the racist fetishism inherent in such ads, he said it was a relief finally to know people like him must exist and be found attractive by someone.[5] "Without any external validation of who you are, who can you be? This is 'invisibility.' It is real."[6] "Where is my reflection? I am most often rendered invisible, perceived as a threat to the family, or I am tolerated if I am silent and inconspicuous."[7]

Once a person has begun to come out to the self, the issue of "closeting" and "coming out," that is, the decision whether or not to disclose one's sexual orientation and identity in every new setting and with every new person, becomes a continuing motif in the life of most gay men, lesbians, and bisexual people. Coming out can be verbal but it can also be behavioral, making no secret of who you care about or live with or like or spend time with, but not necessarily talking about it. The open-secret strategy is sometimes accompanied by avoidance of situations where one might have to talk about it. Among some African-American and Chicano communities, "talking about it" is viewed as white behavior. Regardless of the form of coming out, verbal or otherwise, this theme of the **dual life/ coming out** continues throughout the entire journey. Yet early in the journey most lesbians and gay men assume they must keep their sexual orientation and identity secret to practically everyone except their lovers, and that coming out is not worth risking loss of family, friends, jobs, or cultural community.

This often feels especially true for lesbians and gay men of color, who have not found as respectful or nurturing a welcome from the white lesbian and gay communities as is found by white people coming out into such communities. For people of color there is no guarantee of welcome and support from the white-dominated gay, lesbian, and bisexual community; urban areas offer the greatest likelihood of finding gay, lesbian, and bisexual groups specifically for people of color. The risk of coming out for people of color thus includes lack of a gay, lesbian, or bisexual community to come out into and loss of "home," one's own cultural community, which leaves only the "hostile white world."[8]

Issues of closeting have differed at different historical moments as well as by cultural origin, and the reasons heterosexual people have given for demanding that gay and lesbian people stay closeted have varied as well. Speaking of her experiences in New York City in the 1950s, Audre Lorde has written:

Most Black lesbians were closeted, correctly recognizing the Black community's lack of interest in our position, as well as the many more immediate threats to our survival as Black people in a racist society. It was hard enough to be Black, to be Black and female, to be Black, female and gay. To be Black, female, gay and out of the closet in a white environment . . . was considered by many Black lesbians to be suicidal.[9]

Discussing the black gay male writers of the Harlem Renaissance, Essex Hemphill has written:

> For the homosexuals of the Harlem Renaissance engaged in the creation of literature, it would have been inappropriate to "come out" of whatever closets they had constructed for personal survival. The effort to uplift the race and prove the Negro worthy of respect precluded issues of sexuality, reducing such concerns to the sentiment of the popular urban blues song- "Ain't Nobody's Business if I Do." The defeat of racism was far too important to risk compromising such a struggle by raising issues of homosexuality."[10]

At some moments in history, it has been possible to come out as bisexual but not as homosexual, lesbian, or gay. For example, during the Harlem Renaissance, many prominent women artists, singers, and community leaders including Bessie Smith, Ma Rainey, Alberta Hunter, and A'Lelia Walker were quite publicly bisexual, engaging in relationships with women while married to or going out with men. Historian Lillian Faderman has suggested that bisexuality may have been viewed as urbane, that "although unalloyed homosexuality may still have connoted in the 1920s Harlem the abnormality of a man trapped in a woman's body, bisexuality seems to have suggested that a woman was super-sexy."[11]

Issues of closeting for bisexual people are different from those faced by people who identify as gay or lesbian because bisexual people may live in two settings that encourage or require them to remain secretive: gay and lesbian culture has often been as biphobic as has heterosexual culture, although for very different reasons and without the same kind of power held by dominant culture. Lesbian and gay communities have witnessed the heterosexual privileges that many bisexual people at times have some access to. The availability of retreat to that heterosexual realm has been a factor which both distinguished experientially bisexual people from gay and lesbian people and contributed to economic, familial, cultural, and political divisions between the groups. In addition, many gay and lesbian people have experienced bisexual people as untrustworthy or lacking commitment because, when relationships became difficult or the consequences of standing with gay or lesbian people became costly, some bisexual people left and reentered the realm of heterosexual privilege. However tenuous acceptance in that realm may actually have been for individual bisexual people, from the gay or lesbian perspective the presence of the option was enough to raise serious issues about whether or not it was safe to include bisexual people in lesbian or gay communities. This power to exclude from small communities is a much more limited power than that held by heterosexual culture to affect negatively a bisexual person's employment, family, and all the other contexts of a person's life. Nonetheless, as a result of these dual pressures, bisexual people often spend much of their lives identifying as and being presumed to be gay when in relationship with a person of the same sex and identifying as and being presumed to be straight when in relationship with a person of the other sex. If they hold to a bisexual identity when in a relationship with someone who isn't, bisexual people are often accused of lacking commitment to the relationship.[12]

Dual closets also mean dual settings in which to come out where the risk of rejection exists, although gay and lesbian culture is beginning to act more inclusive of bisexual people, mostly as a result of the insistence of and organizing by bisexual people themselves within gay and lesbian organizations. In part because it is their same-sex desires which are rejected by the dominant culture, a culture which also says that having such desires must mean one is homosexual, many bisexual people self-identify as gay or lesbian early in their process of coming out to themselves and others. Other bisexual people know inside they are bisexual but identify as gay or lesbian because of a primary intimate relationship with someone of the same sex, and/or because of a desire and need to participate in and belong to gay or lesbian communities in the absence of organized bisexual communities. In either case such people often travel the lesbian and gay journey described and depicted in this chapter and in the orange section of the continuum.

Am I Male? Am I Female?

Cultural definitions of woman and man, male and female, in the contemporary West include heterosexuality. A man is, by definition, a person who desires women sexually. A woman is, by definition, a person who desires men sexually. To have feelings for a person of one's own sex is to call into question one's gender identity and one's sex identity. (See Appendix A for definitions of these two terms.) Questioning one's own gender identity and questioning the gender definitions present in one's particular culture continue throughout the journeys of gay men, lesbians, and bisexual people as well as those of heterosexual people. Initially, for some bisexual people, gay men, and lesbians, the inconsistency between internalized gender definitions and same-sex erotic desires serves as a reason for rejecting the self who feels such desires. For others this inconsistency produces a conviction that there has been a "mistake" of biological or karmic proportions:

> During this time I constructed various theories to explain my desire for
> women in a world that clearly told me that only men loved women, that
> only men could have sex with women, that only men could marry women.
> The theory I regarded as most satisfying combined my belief in
> reincarnation with the recently announced sex-change operation of
> Christine Jorgenson. . . . I decided that something I'd done in a past life (my

karma) had dictated that I would spend my life as a male soul "trapped" in a female body, as punishment for some transgression. This theory helped explain my feelings in early childhood when I believed that some mistake had been made along the way, that I'd certainly been meant to be a boy and someone had slipped up when the bodies were being passed out. I believed I was "really" a man.[13]

At the culmination of the journey, an expanded understanding of maleness and femaleness will help solidify positive gender and sexual identity. In between, the meaning of gender needs to be reexamined many times and in many ways.

Rejection of Self

Not everyone who discovers erotic feelings for persons of the same sex on which he or she wishes to act—the aspect of sexual orientation which garners the greatest disapproval from contemporary heterosexually dominated culture—greets such self-discovery with ease. How someone experiences discovering a bisexual, lesbian, or gay orientation depends to a great extent on a person's preexisting information and attitudes about homosexuality. Also important are a person's degree of self-esteem, culture and race, family configuration, and degrees of support available, especially from siblings and close friends. Access at the time of discovery to information about or to people who can serve as positive models of adult gay, lesbian, or bisexual identity or who can provide counseling that recognizes such positive possibilities is also important.

Typical experiences of people who begin their journey into their bisexual, gay, or lesbian identity with extremely negative internalized views about homosexuality and little access to accurate information are depicted by the beginning of the orange section of the continuum diagram. The people most at risk of negatively experiencing the initial awareness of their own possible gay, lesbian, or bisexual orientation (other than teens, who often but not always lack sufficient real autonomy and sense of self to come out safely at home and in school; see Appendix B) are people who hold very polarized and hierarchical views of appropriate gender roles and behaviors; who hold conservative religious beliefs; whose families share these views and beliefs; who work, live in, and are members of cultural communities that also strongly hold such beliefs; and who have no access to any positive information about gay and lesbian existence.

Most people in contemporary culture know gay or lesbian people around them or have at least seen such people on television. This is just as true for people beginning to register their own same-sex feelings as it is for heterosexual people. The initial internal surfacing of same-sex interest or desire takes place for many bisexual people, gay men, and lesbians during childhood or early adolescence, although for some it does not take place until well into adulthood.

84

Regardless of the age at which this internal surfacing occurs, there is sometimes a fairly long lag time between that consciousness and the first sought-out interaction, sexual or otherwise, with other bisexual people, gay men, and lesbians. This is true except for interactions with the specific individual, if any, toward whom the desires are first felt and with whom such desires are sometimes explored. In the interim a person often vacillates between longing to know more about these feelings, to do something about them, to meet other people who have them, and attempting to change or erase the feelings and the memory of having them.

This is not to say that the first sought-out same-sex adult sexual experiences are necessarily the first such experiences in a person's life. Nonetheless, youthful same-sex sexual experiences often do not operate in a person's consciousness to facilitate recognition of same-sex or bisexual orientation except retroactively. The exception is the child who knows early that she or he is strongly or exclusively attracted erotically to her or his own gender. For these children, initial exploration of their sexual orientation typically takes place during junior high or high school; their coming out process is well along by the time they become adults. Increasing numbers of contemporary teens enter the adult continuum at age eighteen, somewhere between the post-coming-out-to-self point in the orange zone and the mid-transition cultural immersion/decision-to-learn stage of the blue zone of the continuum; others are still in the self-destructive early orange zone.[14]

Assuming a person begins the adult internal inquiry about sexual orientation from a context of strong negativity toward homosexuality, for example, at the beginning of the orange zone, the first response to feeling same-sex sexual desires may involve massive deep **rejection of the self**. The rejection comes because of the bombardment by homophobic cultural messages, including negative information and attitudes about gay men and lesbians and the invisibility of bisexuality. Charles Harpe tells us, "I grew up and entered adulthood with practically no self-esteem, a desperate need to love and be loved, and an ingrained sense that I was unlovable."[15] Some people attempt to deny all sexuality in an attempt to rid themselves of same-sex feelings. Sometimes this takes the form of joining a celibate religious order.

When someone has same-sex feelings, they often ask themselves, **"Am I evil?"** Heterosexual cultures teach, among other things, that gay men and lesbians are predatory people who seduce children and cannot control their sexual urges—the modern equivalent of a vampire. The evil imagined may be that to be gay feels like one is a traitor to one's race or a shame to one's family. "Don't say that because I am gay, I am not Chinese anymore; and don't accuse me of trying to become white."[16] If someone comes out of a religious tradition, the question may be, **"Am I sinful?"** Mainline religious groups, such as Catholics, Episcopalians, and Conservative Jews, in the past have said little or nothing about sexual orientation. Such silence, combined with the many religious references to heterosexual models of maritally based sexuality, provided clear messages that heterosexuality was what was acceptable. Today, fundamentalist or evangelical religious organizations tend to view homosexual orientation itself as sinful or to deny that orientation rather than behavior exists. Mainline denominations tend to teach that all sexuality is a divine gift, although many continue to require various limitations on acting upon one's sexuality. These limitations often include telling gay and lesbian people there can be no sin-free enactment of their sexuality nor any recognition of their partnerships. More conservative religious training still teaches that homosexual desires are sinful and that homosexual people are, in a biblical sense, "sodomites." One twenty-year-old gay man left a suicide note that began, "How could you have done this to me God?"[17]

Often the values taught by our families, churches, and cultures have been internalized. If persons believe themselves both evil and sinful, then they feel **terror** and **guilt** about their same-sex desires and about themselves for having such desires. Culture's rejection, while still internalized as self-rejection, can effectively block the capacity to know the self sexually, or can block the development of a positive sense of sexual identity.

Sometimes admitting to same-sex sexual desire precipitates behaviors that constitute **self-abuse**, such as inappropriate use of alcohol or the use and misuse of illegal **drugs.** Many people attempt **suicide** or become depressed. Some people ask themselves at this point, **"Am I sick?"** for having homosexual feelings, and sometimes the answer seems to be yes, because they are feeling depressed and anxious about their same-sex feelings and their implications. What usually isn't recognized at this stage is that homosexuality is not an illness, but that coping with the culture's rejection of it and/or an individual's difficulties in constructing a positive sexual identity can cause illness.

The AIDS epidemic has produced additional difficulties for men first feeling same-sex sexual feelings. Fear of AIDS and linkages made in the media and by religious and other leaders between gay male sexuality and AIDS may add to the already existing familial, religious, and cultural bases for believing the gay self is sick or perverse, and may result in social isolation or sexual inhibition.[18] On the other hand, partly as a consequence of AIDS, gay men, especially white gay men, have access to more organizations, books, sources of information, and social and health services created and operated by other gay men than ever before.

Early in the journey, men in particular may lash out verbally and/or physically at other gay men and lesbians in the immediate environment, while at the same time exploring sexual desires through **same-sex sex acts**. A gay man, not yet ready to acknowledge his gayness, at this stage may go to a gay bar, solicit sexual contact from a stranger, and then project his rejection of his gay self by beating up the other person. This is **horizontal violence.** As a lesbian at this stage, I am more likely to keep my distance from any women in my environment whom I know or suspect are lesbian, and may collude with heterosexual people in telling jokes about or putting down gay and lesbian people as a way of keeping my closet securely shut, to keep out both my own awareness and that of other people.*

At some point people coming out as bisexual, lesbian, or gay will be involved in **same-sex sex acts** separate from an ongoing intimate relationship and/or enter into an ongoing adult **same-sex relationship.** Accounts of contemporary gay male stages of coming out suggest that many men seek out sexual contact, or have sexual interactions with male acquaintances or friends without an ongoing intimate relationship, before they self-identify as gay. Some accounts of lesbian coming-out processes suggest that many lesbians live through one or more same-sex romantic and emotionally intense relationships that have erotic aspects before becoming sexual with another woman and that such a relationship sometimes becomes sexual before the women self-identify as lesbians.[19] These reported differences may be manifestations of gender socialization, including possible developmental differences between lesbians and gay men which may be the result of childhood behavior and parental responses to it. Longitudinal (prospective) studies now under way with gay- and lesbian-identified adolescents may provide more accurate information about differences in the journeys of gay men and lesbians. Gay/lesbian-identified bisexual people may continue, after initial same-sex experiences, to be aware of heteroerotic desires, which may or may not be acted on and or spoken about for a long time after beginning to have same-sex sexual relationships.

Self-Hatred

Whether trying a same-sex relationship or not, many people at this stage are still preoccupied with internalized negative feelings about lesbians and gay men and about the parts of themselves which do not feel gender appropriate. At this stage many gay men and lesbians may attempt to reject the parts of the self which fit with notions of the traditionally feminine; others may reject the parts of the self which seem traditionally masculine. All these feelings may operate as **self-hatred**.

One way of coping with such emotional crises is to deny the feelings, bury them, repress them, forget them, or run away from them. Some people **try to change** sexual orientation, to convince themselves they are really heterosexual. Some may do this by seeking **therapy** for a "cure." In the past more than today, some therapists were willing to pursue such an agenda.[20] Some people turn to a pastoral counselor for help through **prayer**. A gay man may try to change his body

---

*At this early stage of awareness, the relative invisibility of bisexuality as a human sexual orientation and identity causes particular isolation and confusion for many people who feel sexual toward persons of both sexes. For some bisexual people, recognition of same sex feelings leads to the conclusion "I must be gay." On the other hand, for other people, both gay and bisexual, identifying as bisexual feels less frightening than identifying as gay or lesbian because it maintains bridges to one's heterosexual past or continuing feelings and doesn't imply stark rejection of heterosexuality. Initial identification as gay or lesbian or bisexual at this stage may later give way to another identification.

in an attempt to change his sexual orientation, becoming, for example, obsessed with reshaping himself into classic "masculinity" through **bodybuilding**.

After I fell in love with my law school woman friend, I tested the reality of my emerging lesbian identity by checking out whether things could work for me with a man. I had a brief affair with one man and went out on initial dates with three other men. I discovered that, having recognized my feelings for women, romantic interactions with men felt, at best, flat. I simply wasn't able to develop or sustain interest in them sexually or emotionally, and most of the time I felt actively turned off.

Some bisexual people, lesbians, and gay men **marry** a **heterosexual** person at this point and/or have children. For some, this is part of denial. "I can't be a lesbian or gay man if I'm married or a parent, can I?" For some people this move toward heterosexuality or marriage plus side relations lasts a lifetime. However, such moves made at this stage may send a person into the orange section of the heterosexual journey at a point where hostility toward or denial of homosexuality is manifested.

At the same time that this whirlwind of internal terror is occurring, there is also a pull to find out more about what this same-sex erotic desire means, but internalized homophobia can prevent us from noticing or seeking positive information. At this point I'll read every negative news story about someone gay, notice every church leader's condemnation, but my fear of facing a librarian or bookstore cashier with a book about homosexuality or bisexuality can prevent me from gaining access to accurate information. On the other hand, I may seek out information in a library, the most anonymous way to look, only to find nothing helpful, nothing reflecting my existence as a gay man or lesbian of color or as a married or formerly married gay man or lesbian with a child.

Relationships that form when a person is still at the stage of internalized hatred of his or her bisexuality or gay/lesbian self sometimes end up involving violence, as the person's self-hatred is enacted upon the partner. Lesbians are more likely than are gay men to be in ongoing relationships at this point, and **lesbian horizontal violence**, or lesbian battering, occurs. Even if there is no violence, relationships that occur when people are internally rejecting their same-sex orientation are fraught with ambivalence and psychic violence, often exacerbated by the isolation caused by both partners' hiding their intimacy from family and the world at large. In addition, the habits of secrecy, lying, and duality about the innermost self, adopted as survival skills to maintain closets and safety in the world, may get carried into intimate relationships, with negative consequences.[21]

Avoiding externally initiated violence is also difficult when the only way to find others who have same-sex feelings is to go to gay or lesbian bars. This way of meeting other gay or lesbian people was most common until as late as ten or twenty years ago and is still important for many people today. Bars are often located in neighborhoods unfamiliar to the newcomer; the newcomer alone must interact with the people inside, who are strangers, if any contact is to occur, and he or she must travel through streets frequently haunted by straight men there to bash or rape a "fag" or "dyke." Also, many bars cater to particular subgroups within lesbian and gay communities. There are white bars, black bars, S&M bars, working-class and middle-class bars, and so forth. The emerging gay man or lesbian may be misled or frightened by a bar's patrons if they are the first group of gay men or lesbians he or she has found and they do not match the person's own sense of gay or lesbian identity.

Even if a man or woman trying to figure out his or her sexuality is lucky enough to find a student group or support group, friends, or a counselor where conversation and information can be shared, the initial stages of admitting to having same-sex erotic desires still may involve intense terror and self-blame or doubt, if not self-hatred. Thus, initially, people who begin their journeys having internalized strongly negative attitudes about homosexuality and bisexuality may feel a social isolation combined with internal denial, terror, and bargaining.

Whether or not we begin this journey of recognition by going through the internal crises described above or instead greet our discovery with joy, at some point each person **comes out to the self**. This is the moment when the actions and feelings and experiences stop being rationalized. We stop bargaining, **stop trying to change**. This moment may come from inside, joyfully or resignedly, or may be precipitated from outside; it may be caused by one of the events we most **fear, exposure by others.**

If a man has been having sex with men but continues to believe inside that he is heterosexual, and his sexual activities become known to family or friends or colleagues, their labeling of his behavior may precipitate internal resignation or recognition. If a woman has been in love with another woman and living with her for a while, but inside keeps saying "I'm not a lesbian, I just happened to fall in love with a woman," her sister's confrontation of her and use of the label *lesbian* may push her to stop avoiding acknowledgment of the identity or may precipitate coming to bisexual identity. Persons who are "brought out" to themselves through such public or familial exposure may, because keeping their orientation secret in the most important settings in their life is now impossible, skip to the end of the orange section, where the question becomes how to like oneself as lesbian, gay, or bisexual and how to live in the world as a lesbian, gay, or bisexually identified person.

Other events can precipitate coming out to the self. If a person is married, increasingly strong same-sex desires may result in recognition of homosexual or bisexual identity and sometimes a decision to end the marriage. Even a speech given by a public figure may precipitate self-recognition.[22] For a moment, everything that has been confusing may make sense and the secrets fly away. Or this moment may be one of terror. If it comes joyfully or as a relief, we may skip forward to the late orange section's central propelling questions of Can I like myself and How can I live as a gay man, lesbian, or bisexual person? If coming out to myself feels scary, ominous, or just plain true but not what I dreamed my life would be about, I may move into resignation and grief.

Resignation/Grief

Once a person comes out to the self, the internal bargaining stops, but at this early stage, he or she may not yet feel happy or at ease with the orientation, may still lack information about bisexuality, homosexuality, and gay and lesbian cultures and communities, and may be without known bisexual or gay and lesbian friends or acquaintances. All this makes it difficult for many people to construct a positive gay or lesbian identity. Coming out alone to oneself in this way, from a context of internalized homophobia and prior attempts to deny or change one's feelings, tends to involve a sense of resignation or grief rather than joy. I may **feel like a failure** for being unable to change my orientation.

I may also need to grieve the loss of my own fantasy future as a presumptively heterosexual person, that imagined life. Part of what frightens me now is the fear that being gay could mean changing everything about my life so far. I'm not sure what all the real implications are, but I'm afraid about how enormous and negative they may be. I don't know much about my options, about how to live as a gay or lesbian person. I don't have much sense of future; I don't have a clear life story with which to replace my old imaginings.

I may feel limited to the stereotypes I have internalized about how I can act and look if I am gay or lesbian. These stereotypes operate virulently in heterosexual culture and are often the only information I have about what it means to be lesbian or gay. They also have been used by lesbians and gay men as a form of resistance, as defiant insistence on our queerness kept visible to a hostile world. For example, African-American and white lesbians earlier in this century in the United States elaborated a whole culture of butch and femme. These were the lesbians who could not pass, or refused to hide and pass as straight; they were also women who passed as men in order to lead lives that were freer, more assertive, and less subject to abuse; the couples who held hands in public in the 1950s and got beaten or arrested for it.[23] Rebellion and resistance also bred gay and lesbian cultural norms, which sometimes operated as constraints on how one could live as a gay or lesbian. Some white gay men, for example, told by culture that their desires were "crimes against nature," adopted artifice as their province. Richard Rodriguez reminds us, "So many [male] homosexuals retired into the small effect, the ineffectual career, the stereotype, the card shop, the florist."[24] The issue for us at this stage of the journey is that I need more information beyond the stereotypes and public gay and lesbian norms, more examples of how to live, how to be gay, but I'm afraid to go out and find them.

Coming Out: Dual Life

If internal bargaining has stopped, bargaining with the world may now begin. We are not ready to construct an identity consistent with our orientation. Since internal change didn't work, what's left for safety's sake is making sure we are as perfect as we can be in all ways other than sexual orientation. Having come out to ourselves, many of us now begin in earnest figuring out how to live the dual life of knowing privately that we are gay, lesbian, or bisexual while maintaining the world's assumption that we are heterosexual.

In our families we will often be aided in a version of this dual life by our parents and adult siblings. **Parents** of gay and lesbian people often practice elaborate **denial and silence** despite all sorts of clues about their adult children's sexual identity. I recently found out that a first cousin, distanced from contact with the family but close to my age, is gay. Although he is presumed to be gay by his brother and sister-in-law and surviving aunt, no one has talked with him directly about this. His parents, both recently dead, apparently never acknowledged what has been clear to many in the family for years, nor did these other family members discuss my cousin's sexual identity with the parents. The collusion here is in his taking care of the sensibilities of the family by not being explicit about his gayness, and the heterosexual family members' expectation, even requirement, that he will keep quiet just as they keep quiet. All this denial and silencing permits a family fiction to operate to this day in which my cousin is spoken of as "keeping to his own lane." What is sacrificed in the name of propriety or preserving family ties is all possibility of real relationship between my cousin and any family member.

My cousin's decision to maintain a distant and dual life, hiding his gayness from family, may well have originated because he rightly expected his very conservative father would have required a complete break if his gayness became explicitly known. In fact, after coming out to ourselves, one of our major fears is how this bisexual, gay, or lesbian orientation is going to affect preexisting relationships. We **fear exposure** because we **fear** that if our lesbian or gay identity is known, we will be criticized or rejected by or actually **lose our jobs, family, cultural community, and/or friends.** The particular reactions and losses we most fear depend on our particular culture. For example,

> Gay and bisexual Indian men and women are no different from anyone else in their fear of criticism. But I think it is more intense within a tribal structure, because our traditional way of correcting behavior is public chastisement and ridicule. And today, the view of the gay Indian man or woman has been twisted to fit the mix of Christian and Indian beliefs in contemporary tribal culture.[25]

For married bisexual people, gay men, or lesbians, the fear and the bargaining with the world may have to do with trying to avoid loss of what may still be a deeply loving relationship with the spouse, loss of custody or visitation with children, and loss of the economic security of marriage.

When we are terribly frightened of loss, some of us take great pains to avoid it. We may try in our relations with family and the heterosexual world to **be a helper**, to be good, to **be polite**. We volunteer to babysit heterosexual friends' babies or help them redecorate their homes. Many of us keep our orientation firmly shut in a closet. We may live our lives this way, discretely carrying on a relationship for years with someone of the same sex with whom we do or do not live, publicly known as a "spinster" or "bachelor," holding on tightly to our place within our corner of our particular straight community. My gay second cousin lived his retirement years alone in a small Cape Cod town, everyone's favorite adopted uncle, premier donor to the volunteer fire department, completely closeted. As Essex Hemphill tells us, "We constitute the invisible brothers in our communities, those of us who live 'in the life'; the choirboys harboring secrets, the uncle living in an impeccable flat with a roommate who sleeps down the hall when family visits; men of power and humble peasantry, reduced to silence and invisibility for the safety they procure."[26]

We may **bond with straight friends for camouflage**, finding a straight woman whose husband is stationed overseas with whom we can attend the office party, thus avoiding the need to have a date. We may make up the existence of an out-of-town girlfriend. A lesbian may wear traditionally feminine clothing and never pants to work, may **act and dress straight.** In conversation we keep the sex of the "significant other" unknown or use the other-sex pronoun.

The "closet" is being constructed, and subordinate forms of collaboration with the dominant culture are taking place. This posture is reactive: approval from heterosexual people feels crucial, especially from family, members of our cultural community, and other people with whom we have been emotionally connected.

The married bisexual person, lesbian, or gay man may try for a period to keep his or her same-sex desires secret from the spouse and separate from a married life, may try simply not to act on those desires at all, or may for a time carry on dual lives. The unmarried man or woman may also try to keep same-sex relations isolated from the rest of his or her life. Examples include a gay congressman who, after coming out, admitted that for a long time he only sought out sexual relations with men who advertised in gay publications because he did not dare to be seen in a gay bar.

If a person comes out to the self through an initial same-sex relationship at a time in life when coming out carries great risks, such as during a marriage and after having had children, the person may believe that the new same-sex relationship is forever, that it is more meaningful and stable than in fact it is. Such overinvestment in the initial same-sex relationship is a way of making it feel safer to have risked everything relied on from the heterosexual world. Even though initial gay or lesbian relationships often do not last, but are rather part of beginning a lived identity as a bisexual person, gay man, or lesbian, some people may need to believe the relationship is forever in order to feel comfortable about engaging in it.

For some gay men in particular, whose sexual exploration may be inhibited out of fear of exposure to the HIV virus, the AIDS epidemic has accentuated the need to believe that the first relationship they finally dare to have is going to be monogamous and forever. All these feelings are in some ways similar to heterosexual people persuading themselves they are in love in order to feel moral about having premarital sexual relations or leaving a marriage. For many lesbians and gay men these feelings may also be the consequence of delaying the experiences of romance and intimacy until late adolescence or adulthood. That is, many lesbians and gay men miss preadolescent and adolescent opportunities for "going steady" and youthful dating. As a senior in college or as a twenty-something adult, it may seem more difficult to keep relationships short-term or casual than it might have been as a seventh grader. "I am thirty-nine years old and I need to grow up," said one long-closeted gay man who had recently come out enough to meet other gay and lesbian people.[27]

For a married woman, a relationship with another woman may actually be a transition out of a failing marriage. Friendships with women are the only friendships really permitted to married women, and such friendships sometimes shift into sexual intimacy as the married woman readies herself to leave her marriage. Whether the married woman is actually straight or in the process of discovering her lesbian or bisexual identity, she may temporarily persuade herself both that she is in fact lesbian and that her newfound woman lover is the love of her life. This gives her the psychological permission and safety necessary to leave the marriage and either risk or leave her parental role. When coming out is thus twisted together with ending a marriage, it is only after the transition out of the marriage is complete that any accurate assessment of the new relationship and of sexual orientation and sexual identity can take place. The terror involved in leaving the marriage, trying to avoid being alone, and losing one's prior sense of identity as spouse and/or parent blocks such an assessment for a while. After living in a same-sex relationship for a certain period, the person begins to understand the meaning of living as a gay man or lesbian in society, begins to resurface as a separate persona, and then either returns to a heterosexual identity or moves into the transition toward discovering more about gayness, lesbianism, or bisexuality.

As the closet grows more elaborate, the chasm between inner life and outer persona widens, producing tension, stress, and anger which helps pull us into the transition. Regardless of how we feel about our coming out to self, as we grow clearer about our lesbian, gay, or bisexual orientation and begin to construct or feel the need to construct a gay or lesbian identity, we tend to experience **increasing isolation from family and straight friends**. We do not usually share our discovery about ourselves with such people for a long time. The subterfuges and silences born of all the secrets we are keeping cause distance. As Richard Rodriguez tells us, "In no other place are those secrets more closely guarded than within the family home. The grammar of the gay [community] borrows metaphors from the nineteenth-century house. Coming out of the closet is predicated upon family laundry, dirty linen, skeletons."[28]

Heterosexual culture requires such quiet duality by its punitive and life-threatening responses to gay men and lesbians who don't stay closeted. The same culture rewards such external obedience by treating as invisible the issue of sexual orientation, holding to the assumption of heterosexuality, so long as a lesbian or gay man maintains the public fiction of being single or married and asks for no recognition of her or his own needs. Keeping this sort of closet means "passing" for heterosexual and it carries high costs: "the 'passing' person must accept the twin albatross of silence and invisibility. Invisibility may be defined as the ability or will of the power group not to acknowledge the presence or influence of the 'other' . . . Silence may be defined as the act of subordinating the expression of the other's needs to the will of the power group."[29]

Many people live their whole lives in this stage of "high closet" dual life. Some become angry when other gay men and lesbians are vocal and public, viewing such people as threatening their own continued quiet double lives. In one Vermont town, three female elementary school teachers, who for years have been known in their community, each reside with a "friend" of the same gender. These teachers' willingness never to call attention to the quality of those home relationships permitted their school district simply never to "see" their homosexuality. They became particularly terrified when an openly lesbian college student came to work as a classroom aide at the school. They were correct in believing that the school district would fire them if their lesbianism were made public. Their invisibility was fragile, and if the classroom aide's actions made parents or school board members notice it was possible that a school employee might be a lesbian, then it was a simple next step for people to notice that these women might be lesbians.

Sometimes the terror of being found out pushes closeted and ambivalent gay men or lesbians to act out public hostility toward homosexuality, so as to persuade heterosexual society that they themselves couldn't possibly be homosexual, or to distract everyone from noticing or questioning their own lifestyle. For example, as director of the FBI, J. Edgar Hoover viciously persecuted gay men and lesbians, while at the same time allegedly carrying on a long-term intimate relationship with a man.[30] Some closeted legislators vote against gay rights legislation to keep suspicion from themselves. There is guilt by association when it comes to sexual orientation in heterosexual culture, and thus as emergent bisexual persons, gay men, or lesbians, we often don't dare associate with others like ourselves.

A Moment of Switching Identity:
Arrows toward the Dominant Journey

Some gay men, lesbians, and bisexual people at this stage again try living as heterosexual people, marry, or end their same-sex sexual explorations. If I am a bisexual person, this may be a moment when I fall in love with a person of the other gender and decide or am pressured by this form of "mixed marriage" to lead a heterosexually identified life. If I am a person with strong homoerotic orientation, but still have only a very negative concept of a possible gay or lesbian identity and life, I may elect to stop acting on my homoerotic orientation, stop exploring how to live and be gay, and attempt to live an ostensibly heterosexual life, with or without heterosexual relationships or marriage. The woman I fell in love with during law school made such a choice. After a year-long relationship with one woman and then falling in love with me, she decided living life as a lesbian was too scary for her and went looking for a husband. She married, had another child, and has led an ostensibly heterosexual life for many years. Yet when we talk, she tells me her primary feelings are still for women, and she dreams of being old in the company of other women.

Entry onto the heterosexual continuum may involve the hostility stage toward lesbians and gay men, as people try to distance themselves from their gay and lesbian experiences, or people may be closer to the heterosexual transition where they feel tolerant and polite toward lesbian and gay people. If a bisexual person feels less afraid about her or his own bisexuality, then the transition to heterosexually identified bisexuality may include intellectual acceptance, tolerance, or greater understanding such as that found fairly far along in the blue section of the heterosexual journey. Some bisexual people who marry continue nonetheless to spend time with and devote energy to their gay or lesbian friends and causes.

More Life In and Out of the Closet

Just as there is no single all-encompassing and accurate definition of *lesbian* or *gay man* or *bisexual person*, there is no one story that accurately reflects all of our experiences of coming out and figuring out how to live our lives. Some of us greet our internal coming out with joy, as mentioned earlier. For these people, there may well still be a period of bargaining and closeting vis-a-vis family or in other settings, as we take slow steps in constructing our newfound identity and discovering what it means to our lives.

Our stories are profoundly affected by the age at which we come out. For the bisexual person, gay man, or lesbian who comes out either to the self or others when in college, there may be a period of very up-front gayness supported by a small bisexual, gay, or lesbian peer group existing in the relative safety of the college community. While a person will probably experience taunts and other antigay responses from some peers, college is a time when career and adult family roles are not jeopardized by one's bisexuality or gayness. Many college students manage to delay coming out to parents until their financial dependence is over; they thus delay dealing with family reactions while at the same time accelerating the need to separate from "home" in order to keep the emotional distance their closet requires. Other students come out to parents or their parents become aware of their orientation. Major disruptions of relationships occur in a minority of situations, but a significant proportion of students report feeling some role reversal as they help "take care of" their parents for a while after coming out; others report long periods of parental silence and denial, a kind of uneasy calm. All these possibilities involve students who are precipitated into self-reliance and separation from family sooner than they otherwise might be. Most campuses do not provide targeted counseling or support programs for their emerging gay, lesbian, and bisexual students, leaving them to rely on peers for help when needed.

In addition, on most campuses, academic and career advisers, either through obliviousness or cowardice, are unlikely to push a college student to explore the implications of gayness or bisexuality for his or her career plans. The gay man applying to law school may not get honest advice from the prelaw adviser when he says he wants to write in his application essay that his experience of being gay has propelled him toward a legal career because he has become fascinated by the role of law in regulating social change and enforcing civil rights.

The young lesbian who declares an education major and is preparing to teach in the public schools probably never discusses with her adviser how her sexual orientation relates to her career plans. Only later, when she confronts the problem of having to become closeted in order to get and keep a job, does this period of protected, relatively open, exploration of identity end.

Another possible initial response to coming out is the plunge into "the life," with no looking back. This immersion is depicted in the early blue section of the chart and described in the next chapter. Convinced that everything is inevitably lost from prior life, some of us jump headlong into our gayness, clinging to it as to a life ring as we feel ourselves forever cut off from all prior relationships and roles. This experience of discontinuity may be a motif of many lesbian and gay life stories, and the flexibility, adaptability, and self-reliance it breeds are reported personality traits of many gay, lesbian, and bisexual people.[31]

Pressures to Change: Entering the Transition

For many of us who have tried to remain invisible, anger at having to live this double life eventually intrudes, the stress caused by the fragility of the veil is no longer bearable, or our own need for honesty and personal integrity requires change. Invisibility becomes overwhelming, and the need to figure out more about how to live and be gay calls us onward. The transition away from collusion and subordination begins now. The burden of isolation born of being unable to risk exploring fully what a lesbian or gay identity could mean, as well as the isolation of not sharing with family and friends the person loved the most, of not building a fulfilling social life, of keeping secret personal searching and important discoveries, have become too heavy. Many lesbians, bisexual people, and gay men constantly constrain their own lives in order to take care of the heterosexual people in their lives, avoiding any conversation or conduct that would make heterosexual people uncomfortable. We do this even though it may involve lying or going places alone or with a friend of the other sex instead of one's lover, being separated from one's lover at holidays, going to the hospital alone, even at times dying without one's friends or loved ones around. Such constraint blocks construction of fully realized lesbian or gay identity for many people.

AIDS is one of the most recent reasons why gay and bisexual men have felt unwilling and have often been unable to continue living lives of this kind of subordination. The constantly repeated occasions for grief with which many gay men and lesbians live due to the deaths of so many loved ones make it almost impossible for many of us to function in heterosexually dominated work settings, family gatherings, and community organizations and keep these AIDS-related, overwhelming emotional and physical realities of our lives hidden. HIV positivity and AIDS have also forced many men out of their closets as they've had to disclose their health status to family and employers. The overt hostile responses of many heterosexual people to the increased visibility of gay men that has come with AIDS has also propelled many of us to new political awareness, rage, and determination to live more honestly and visibly in the world.

The isolation and pain of hiding eventually become untenable. When we can no longer live rejecting ourselves and limiting our interactions with others, we are close to entering the transition. The questions at this point near the end of the orange section and just before entering the transition are often, "**Can I like myself as a gay, lesbian, or bisexual person**?" and "How can I live and be lesbian, gay, or bisexual?" It is time to attempt construction of a healthy sexual identity.

Another way we may question now is to ask ourselves, "Who am I and who can I become as a gay, lesbian, or lesbian/gay-identified bisexual person?" The themes for this period include a continuation of the **coming out/dual life** issues. I need to talk so I may **test whom can I tell.** In addition to this need to speak, even an inability to remain silent any longer, there is a need for experiences from which I can learn. Since speaking is often so dangerous in the heterosexual contexts to which I have been tied, and since I need experiences with gay and lesbian people, at this point in my journey I actively go looking for other such people.

This is the moment we are most likely to **leave** our **home community**. Such a leaving is especially frequent among people from rural areas and for some people of color. Although we are ready to search for other bisexual, lesbian, or gay people and to try living our developing identity as lesbian, gay, or bisexual people, we may not be ready to risk our relationships with family, old friends, neighborhood, or cultural community. In addition, it often seems easier to find gay, lesbian, and bisexual people's gathering places and welcoming institutions in large cities.

Therefore, we may move to a larger or different city, or spend time in a neighboring town or a different part of our own city. We split our lives geographically in order to act out our emergent bisexual, gay, or lesbian identity without letting anyone "at home" really see and know. Sometimes I will also try to talk with a few of the heterosexual people most important to me, a close friend, a sibling, a parent. If I am bisexual I may still be keeping that part quiet, afraid of losing the emerging sense of belonging I just glimpse as possible within lesbian and gay communities.

The other theme that begins now is the **search for communities** of lesbian and gay people. Despite my continuing terror of doing so, I know I need to interact with people among whom I can figure out what it means to be myself as a lesbian or gay man of color, or as a white lesbian or gay man.

I am in search of some sense of "collective self" and some history, as Joan Nestle puts it:

> We need to know that we are not accidental, that our culture has grown
> and changed with the currents of time, that we, like others, have a social
> history comprised of individual lives, community struggles, and customs of
> language, dress, and behavior—in short, that we have the story of a people
> to tell. To live with history is to have a memory not just of our own lives
> but of the lives of others, people we have never met but whose voices and
> actions connect us to our collective selves.[32]

This search for community has often been particularly difficult for people of color because of the continuing racism of many people in white gay and lesbian communities. Hemphill states, "The post Stonewall white gay community of the 1980's was not seriously concerned with the existence of black gay men except as sexual objects. . . . Coming out of the closet to confront sexual oppression has not necessarily given white males the motivation or insight to transcend their racist conditioning. . . . There was no gay community for black men to come home to in the 1980's."[33]

If I am a person of color, I may have difficulty finding, or may not right away feel ready to find, lesbians, gay men, and bisexual people from my own culture and other cultures of color with whom to explore the meaning of my color and orientation together, as indivisible aspects of who I am.[34] Many gay men, lesbians, and gay/lesbian-identified bisexual people of color begin this part of the journey participating in white-dominated gay and lesbian communities. It is only later that they succeed in finding, or feel ready to participate in, lesbian and gay communities of color. What a person of color does, if anything, to seek out other gay people of color and when, has much to do with what point the person has reached in racial identity development.[35]

The process of identity development, whether for subordinant races or sexualities, is a process that

> must be undertaken by people who must embrace negative or stigmatized
> identities. This process moves gradually from a rejected and denied self-
> image to the embracing of an identity that is finally accepted as positive.
> Both models describe one or several stages of intense confusion and at least

one stage of complete separatism from and rejection of the dominant society. The final stage for both models implies acceptance of one's own identity, a committed attitude against oppression, and an ability to synthesize the best values of both perspectives and to communicate with members of the dominant groups.[36]

For many people of color, this process necessarily involves finding a community or group of gay/lesbian people of color as the context for coming out. Such a group or community is almost always sufficiently removed from the home community to permit coming out without coming out at home until considerably later.[37] One such organization was begun in 1976 in New York City. Created by African-American lesbians, the group's statement reads:

> The official name of this organization is the Third World Gay Women's Organization. We call ourselves the Salsa-Soul Sisters. We came into being because there was no other organization that we knew of in the New York area, existing for or dealing with the serious needs of third world gay women. We started by searching out each other, because of the strong needs we have in common, and to grow to understand the ways in which we differ.
>
> Our immediate aim is to provide a place where third world gay sisters can meet other gay sisters, other than in bars.
>
> We hope to become an organization of third world gay women who feel joy as well as pride in being able to say, "we did it ourselves." Meaning, we started, formed, maintained, and governed an organization that is helpful and inspiring to third world gay women. We share in the strengthening and productivity of the whole gay community.[38]

Today, in Boston, there exist Queer Asian Pacific Alliance, an organization of Asian-American lesbians, gay men, and bisexual people, and Girlfriends, a lesbians and bisexual women-of-color network. In New York, a bimonthly newsmagazine titled *Colorlife* is published. In California two organizations of South Asian gay and lesbian people publish newsletters which are mailed home to India and other countries, and Arab-American lesbians, bisexual people, and gay men have networks and groups, as do Asian-Americans. Large urban areas are most likely to have such groups and media.

On the sexual orientation diagram, the end of the orange section may also involve experimentation and sexual **promiscuity** or a period of determined **monogamy.** In important ways this place on the journey is like a delayed early adolescence. It takes place whenever the person reaches this stage, whether during actual middle or late adolescence or during early, middle, or late adulthood.

Beginning to develop my gay, lesbian, or bisexual identity and leaving my home community often also involves feelings of **estrangement from my religious institution**, community, or tradition. Many bisexual, lesbian, and gay people have been taught in such institutions that same-sex sexual behavior is sinful. Now when I am ready to live a full life as a lesbian, gay, or bisexual person I am also likely to feel least welcome in many churches and synagogues. So long as I was just thinking about all this I could avoid or delay an actual confrontation with my religious tradition. If my denomination is one that condemns same-sex sexual behavior, such as orthodox Judaism, Catholicism, and most evangelical protestant groups, in order to love my gay or lesbian self I now have to reject or reinterpret the condemnatory doctrines, distance myself from that tradition, or seek out a more welcoming spiritual home.

Even if I come from a religious tradition that is tolerant, the frequent emphasis on and sanctification of heterosexual unions may serve as a frequent reminder of my otherness. Many deeply religious lesbian, gay, and bisexual people at this stage of the journey stop attending worship services and instead find more individual ways of continuing to live spiritual lives or simply live separated even from such individual practice. If the individual, community, and institutional aspects of religious life had been important in the past, such estrangement can cause a deep loneliness and grief.

I may seem to avoid such a break by speaking about my emergent identity with my clergyperson. Sometimes I am heard and welcomed, often I am pitied, prayed for, or condemned. Some of us quickly find new spiritual homes in welcoming congregations of our own denomination, such as with "more light" Presbyterians, an "open and affirming" United Church of Christ congregation, or a Reconstructionist Jewish Havurah. Alternatively, we may find a gay/lesbian friendly denomination such as the Unitarian Universalists, or we may seek out one of the denominations which primarily serve lesbian and gay people. These include among others the protestant Metropolitan Community Churches (MCC) and the mostly African American Unity Fellowship Churches.

Despite the spread of such supportive religious communities, for many of us institutional religious ties as well as private spiritual life may suffer for a while now. This is in part because, as we live more developed lesbian or gay lives, we are also more aware of increasingly vocal religiously based rejections of us, and continuing refusals on the part of many major denominations to ordain gay, lesbian, or bisexual clergy, or to sanctify our committed relationships.

The social skills heterosexual children need are acquired during preadolescence and adolescence, but the many lesbian, gay, and bisexual people who do not come out during junior and senior high school have to acquire the necessary skills later in life. How do I, as a woman, ask a woman out on a date anyway? Do we date or do I just invite her home with me to begin with? If we go out to the movies, who pays? How do I cope with seeing her with another woman the night after we were out together? I was twenty-eight years old and figuring out these things that most ninth graders have already figured out. And I did just what a ninth grader on a first date does: I faked it, pretended I'd done this many times before, played it cool.

At this point I may want to talk about my bisexual, lesbian, or gay identity and yet I am terrified of doing so. The spilling over of tension born of attempts to live a dual life may mean that defensive emotions are brought to each interaction with a heterosexual person about my orientation. I seem to turn each discussion into a confrontation. I often **demand acceptance** unequivocally from family, friends, acquaintances, the world. I may feel easily infuriated or deeply disappointed when even well-meaning people in their responses to my disclosures betray ignorance or ambivalence or awkwardness about my sexual orientation or identity.

Also at this point, I frequently feel overwhelming **anger at heterosexual privilege** in all its manifestations: at the economic benefits available to heterosexual people through marriage; at a straight person's right to hold hands in public with a lover; at the family recognition given to a sibling's grief during a divorce. If I am bisexual I may also feel furious at the biphobia of some gay and lesbian people, and feel jealous of the extensive political and cultural institutions that exist for gay and lesbian people but within which I feel the need to hide my bisexuality.

I am often in a very reactive posture now. I do not yet have a comfortable sense of how I want to present myself as a lesbian or gay man, but I cannot stand the isolation both from straight family and friends and from gay and lesbian people, isolation which has been the result of my closeted life. I can't keep quiet with all the straight people in my life anymore, so I feel my membership and safety in relationships, communities, organizations, and my family may be in jeopardy. I may not yet feel a real sense of belonging in any part of the lesbian or gay communities which I've begun exploring. Something has to change. I enter the transition with much conflicting emotion and lots of energy.

To Live, To Love

5

Transitions for Gay Men, Lesbians, and Gay/Lesbian-Identified Bisexual People

H E A T H E R   W I S H I K

The move into gay, lesbian, or bisexual identity* may involve what the majority culture views as **flamboyant appearance and manner**. As a gay man I may find myself comfortable being a **"queen"** or "SNAP! queen."[1] As a lesbian I may further develop or adopt for the first time a **butch** or **femme** sensibility through dress, physical carriage, and in my intimate relationships emotionally and sexually.[2] As a gay man I may wear six earrings at a time and a Queer Nation T-shirt. As a lesbian I may wear labrys earrings and lots of political buttons declaring my dykehood.

Flamboyance is relative: as a gay male investment adviser I may be most comfortable continuing to lift weights and dressing in pin-striped suits for work, but my socks may get a shade brighter, and when I'm relaxing with friends I wear my button-fly jeans with one button open. As a lesbian attorney I may continue to wear skirts and stockings to court; what's changed is the new ring on my ring finger that my girlfriend gave me and that I now dare to wear to work.

I'm trying on what it means to be lesbian or gay, looking for a version that fits me and that is comfortable given my own sense of gender, and the heterosexual, lesbian, and gay communities I am choosing to move in and out of, or feel the need to stay in contact with. I may also be trying to act as "in your face" to the heterosexual world and as obviously gay or lesbian to the gay and lesbian worlds as I can, all at once.

---

*The transition journey for bisexual people who at this stage identify as bisexual is discussed in chapter 6.

103

I've decided I'm going to try to be a great gay man, lesbian, queen, dyke, whatever. I've decided to figure out how to be me, all of me, but the ways in which I explore continue to be affected profoundly by the standards of both heterosexual dominance and the mores of the lesbian and gay communities to which I have access. And often the bravest among us are the most obvious, the ones who make room for the rest of us, the ones who take most of the homophobic heat. Although not everyone at the Stonewall Inn was in drag in 1969, some were:

> You see, it was queens, in high heels and chiffon, who fought cops for Stonewall; sissies who had bottles and billy clubs wailed at and on them as they marched down city streets for "our" rights. It was drag queens who patrolled the docks and piers with straight razors, fighting and dying at the hands of joyriding homophobes. . . . Yes, we shimmer in the glitter of expensive fashions, but we also get down and dirty for the cause, allowing our other brothers—who aren't ready to make "the statement" yet, or who can't be identified as queer "Uptown"—to lead reasonably comfortable lives enjoying gay rights, the pride parades, the bars, parks, baths and movies. . . . Before you turn your head, remember that our true heroes were proud queens who died for your right not to be a queen. . . .[3]

Appreciation for the most visible among us even made it into a recent Ann Landers column:

> Dear Ann Landers:
>
> This letter is for "Sabotaged in Calgary," who expressed misgivings about the flagrant behavior of some homosexuals, saying they damaged the image of all gays.
>
> . . . I've never worn women's clothes and I do not frequent gay bars, but as a safely closeted gay man in America, I give credit to those who are putting themselves on the line in the fight for gay rights.
>
> The legitimate heroes in my book are the pioneer drag queens who rioted in the Stonewall bar in New York in 1969 and rebelled against prejudice and discrimination. This so-called segment of "lunatic fringe" is not blocking progress, Ann, it is promoting acceptance and understanding.
>
> One of Them
> in Lawrence, Kansas

I was unprepared for the blizzard of letters in support of the bizarre paraders. Keep reading.

> Dear Ann:
>
> I have a message for the gay male who signed his letter "Sabotaged in Calgary." He was critical of extremists in the gay community who dress . . . and march in gay parades.

. . . I'd like to say something to "Sabotaged" and other gays who think like he does. If you want a different image of gays, get out of your closet and present it. Until you do, be thankful that the "kooks" are out there, because they are the ones who are taking it on the chin for the rest of us. Those "limp-wristed sisters" have real guts. They have gained for all homosexuals the few rights we have today.

Just for the record, Ann, if you saw me, you wouldn't guess in a million years.

A Lesbian in St. Louis[4]

Flamboyance, promiscuity, mannerisms and costuming, butch/femme and other role behaviors in and outside of sexual encounters, and a variety of same-sex relationships all can be a part of this initial immersion into gay and lesbian life. Some of this behavior may turn out to be an experiment or a way to shore up my still incomplete and insecure gay or lesbian identity or my still-to-be-expanded understanding of my gender identity—behaviors I will discard or "tone down" later. Some behaviors which may support aspects of my emerging lesbian or gay identity and my sense of gender and thus feel deeply satisfying and important, may become a part of me for the long term. Some of this may involve finding a centered, grounded, defiant, and resistant way to hold fiercely to my sense of self in the world, to perfect a way of loving, to do what feels natural.[5] Some behaviors may be manifestations of my continuing internalized homophobia or some as-yet-unhealed hurt from early abuse which will feel less necessary later as more healing takes place and a more positive internal identity emerges.

The particulars of costume and mannerism vary by historical moment, ethnicity, and race. Describing mainly white gay males in San Francisco in the 1980s, Richard Rodriguez has located important meaning in some frequently stereotyped kinds of gestures: "The impulse is not to create but to re-create, to sham, to convert, to sauce, to rouge, to fragrance, to prettify. No effect is too small or too ephemeral to be snatched away from nature, to be ushered toward the perfection of artificiality."[6] Marlon Riggs describes the depth of meaning contained in contemporary black gay male mannerisms, despite the frequent caricature of such mannerisms by what he calls "Hollywood's Black Pack" of heterosexual male filmmakers and entertainers:

Within the black gay community, for example, the SNAP! contains a multiplicity of coded meanings: as in—SNAP!—'Got your point!' Or—SNAP!—'Don't even try it.' Or—SNAP!—'You fierce.' Or—SNAP!—'Get out my face.' Or—SNAP!—'Girlfriend, pleeeease.' The snap can be as emotionally and politically charged as a clenched fist, can punctuate debate and dialogue like an exclamation point, a comma, an ellipse, or altogether negate the need for words among those who are adept at decoding its nuanced meanings.[7]

Audre Lorde describes the scene at a lesbian bar in New York City in the 1950s:

> The Black women I usually saw around the Bag were into heavy roles and it frightened me. This was partly the fear of my own Blackness mirrored, and partly the realities of the masquerade. Their need for power and control seemed a much-too-open piece of myself, dressed in enemy clothing. They were tough in a way I felt I could never be. Even if they were not, their self-protective instincts warned them to appear that way. By white america's racist distortions of beauty, Black women playing "femme" had little chance in the Bag. There was constant competition among the butches to have the most "gorgeous femme" on their arm. And "gorgeous" was defined by a white male world's standards.[8]

Discussing lesbian butch/femme behavior, Julia Penelope tells her experience of it in the late 1950s and the 1960s:

> Whatever definitions and explanation are now offered as reasons for going back to playing roles, it is necessary to understand that those of us who chose them and lived by them manifested our choice in every sphere of our life. I wasn't a butch only in bed. I was a butch in the bar, on the street, on the dance floor, and during those solitary moments when I examined myself in the mirror. As I've learned new responses and behaviors, I've discarded the shell I inhabited as a butch. Working from the outside in, the first behaviors I dropped were the very obvious and trivial, but symbolic, external gestures: lighting another woman's cigarette, opening doors and holding them for femmes, . . . leading when I danced, . . . and maintaining that I didn't know how to cook. I strutted, swaggered, blustered, and swore, mostly to hide my insecurities, self-doubts, and lack of confidence. And, sometimes, I had to put my body on the line and fight when men or other butches called my bluff.[9]

Other women did not find femme/butch roles restrictive or something to get rid of later. Nestle has written about how complex and fulfilling these modes of living and loving have been for her and other women and about the transition from femme to sometime-butch that has come with age for her. She and Leslie Feinberg have both eloquently called for contemporary lesbians and feminists to value the women who came earlier and to recognize the fully autonomous, assertive, sexually free selves some of them created in the context of butch/femme lesbianism.[10]

Some contemporary college lesbians, bisexual people, and gay men, into what they call "gender-bending" or "gender blending," are taking the historical traditions of gay male and lesbian cross-dressing—that is, passing as the other gender or dressing as a queen, a butch, or a femme—and other defiances of gender stereotypes, and are creating their generation's versions as part of exploring their bisexual, lesbian, and gay identities. One young man who works for me wears his hair long and dyed purple. A young woman wears her hair very short, has large tatoos on her arms, and is often taken for a man on the street, even though she says she is not deliberately "passing" as a man. These young people coexist with others who appear and act in ways that are indistinguishable from their heterosexual peers, choosing to explore their bisexual, gay, and lesbian identities via relationships and group participation without gender bending or surface visibility.

Increasing Vulnerability

Many people enter the journey at this stage. Having come out to ourselves with joy and relief, we plunge directly into the "scene," the subculture, adopting some outer trappings to be sure we will be recognized by other gay men and lesbians, and feeling freer in mannerisms, language, and dress to defy the heterosexual world's rules. We are both less able and less willing to hide who we are sexually, and more emotionally ready to and needful of building a positive lesbian or gay sense of self, a sexual identity.

For all these reasons, we are now more **vulnerable** when dealing **with unaware heterosexual people, especially family**. Many of us face a rapid rude awakening at this moment, because some of our parents or siblings turn out to feel unable, at least at first, to cope with our newly emerging, increasingly visible or disclosed identity. The overriding question is Whom to tell? Particularly in white families, lesbians and gay men are often **disowned when we come out**. Regardless of culture, sometimes our newfound insistence on being our lesbian, bisexual, or gay selves is accompanied by the loss of long-term friendships, or we survive a beating after leaving a gay or lesbian bar.

My own story of this moment involves relatively mild experiences of rejection and hostility from certain family members. I felt an eagerness, hunger, and joy to be discovering myself as a lesbian and an overwhelming need to share this newfound and still very raw sense of self with my mother because I couldn't stand how distanced I felt from her while I kept my sexual identity secret. I told my sister first, who was supportive, and asked her to come with me to tell my mother, which she did. My mother's initial response was to try to be "understanding." Nonetheless, she communicated withering anger that I should have upset her with such horrible news at the "wrong moment" when she was herself still recovering from surgery, and disappointment that I should have been so "damaged" by my father (from whom she was long divorced) that I had "become unwilling" to "relate" to men.

I lived with feelings of **depression, sadness,** and **grief** for a long time after that conversation, despite my simultaneous and continuing positive emotions about my lesbianism. Many formerly married lesbians and bisexual women lose their children at this stage. Having just begun their own coming out process, they have a strong need to try lesbian relationships, spend time with other lesbians, and become involved in lesbian culture just at the moment when their ex-spouse, or soon-to-be ex-spouse, not yet used to the idea of bisexuality or lesbianism, is most likely to make it a custody issue. Women are often told by courts to be celibate, keep your lesbianism quiescent or lose your children. To be given such an ultimatum at this moment in the journey is incredibly painful since either way it means losing, delaying, or foregoing development of aspects of self.

For many gay men and lesbians, the negative real-life consequences and the emotional fragility they still feel about themselves combine and may become overwhelming. **Suicide increases again** at this stage on the continuum, as the tough realities of living as a gay, lesbian, or bisexually identified person come home to us.

Those of us who don't turn our pain inward on ourselves often find a lot of **anger surfaces** as we reach a deeper understanding of how constraining and difficult our lives have been and may well be in the future as lesbians and gay men in heterosexually dominant cultures. We recognize and feel taunted daily by the many heterosexual privileges granted by contemporary cultures. Everything from health insurance to child custody is attached to heterosexuality. Almost every product on the market is sold using heterosexual life situations as the advertising vehicle. Most heterosexual people flaunt their orientations constantly, from wedding rings and pictures of family on their desks to kisses and hand-holding on the street, in the movies, at the airport, in the hospital.

This is a period when, with anger so close to the surface, we are likely to feel and show a fair amount of emotional **pain** and also are likely to be pretty **pushy** and to **overtalk** and **overreact**. We do this with family who don't act adequately sensitive in reaction to an old friend's failure to invite our significant other to an event and as an answer to a sister's announcement of her upcoming wedding. It becomes more and more difficult to let things slide so we confront and argue, even though to do so may not always be safe or productive or tactful or loving. We are not easy to live with at this stage. The tendency to act out of anger may extend to our interactions with gay men and lesbians. Often at this moment it feels hard to respect the diversity of opinions and working styles among the gay men, lesbians, and bisexual people with whom we may be volunteering at, say, an AIDS service organization or community center. Everything feels so urgent, and every decision feels like it carries so many consequences, that we may find it hard to compromise about anything, may find it tempting to accuse people who disagree with us of putting us all in danger politically or of threatening our "community."

This period is full of contradictions. We leave our marriages and may lose our children, yet gain a profound sense of self-worth and acceptance or begin more meaningful intimate relationships than we have had before. We grieve for the limitations heterosexual dominance places on the possibilities of living as a bisexual person or gay man or lesbian, and yet feel joy for our depth of connection with other gay, bisexual, or lesbian people. We become increasingly vulnerable to the slights and rejections of family and other heterosexual people in our life and cultural community because our gay, bisexual, or lesbian identity is becoming stronger, more central, less "closetable," while our need for approval from and connection with heterosexual people and communities continues. Some of us may feel torn as various aspects of our own identity seem pitted against each other because of external messages. "Don't raise lesbian issues in the context of women's reproductive freedom battles," we are told, "it could lose some pro-choice allies." Or don't be out as a gay black man around whites because the African-American community doesn't need to give whites any more excuses for racism. Don't come out as gay because you are already "one down" as a South Asian man in the United States.

Some bisexual people who have self-identified as lesbian or gay until this point find that this is a moment of **emergent bisexual identity**. For a person who has reached a point of feeling relatively positive about the gay or lesbian aspect of self, and who has begun experiencing a sense of belonging and community with other gay men and lesbians, to have heteroerotic feelings consciously surface now can be part of allowing the whole self room to grow. It can also be terrifying, as one bisexual woman explained:

> To fall in love with a man, to be anywhere outside the center of my community, threatened my treasured sense of belonging. It confused the exhilarating feeling of pride that had blossomed when I claimed my lesbian identity. . . . All kinds of internal voices began warring . . . people will look at me, see me with a man, and they'll never know I love women. And if I truly loved women, why would I want to be with a man? Am I deserting my own feelings? I don't want to lose woman-centered culture. I haven't been a lesbian long enough. People will say I "went back to men." The lesbian community will think I've defected. I want to belong to the community. I want to belong.[11]

The Decision to Learn

With the **decision made to learn** about ourselves as gay and lesbian people comes a shift of focus. No longer is primary energy involved in seeking approval or warding off disapproval from heterosexual people and heterosexual culture. The decision to learn is born of such concerns as

— the need to strengthen and more fully develop a positive sense of self as a lesbian, gay man, or bisexual person;
— the desire to reexamine one's assumptions about the meaning of maleness and femaleness as part of an effort to construct a positive gay or lesbian identity;
— the need to know more about one's internalized homophobia, its particular manifestations based in personal history, and as determined by the wider culture;

— the need to know more about how to interact positively with and take care of oneself in interactions with family, friends, colleagues, home cultural community, and the larger society;

— the desire to figure out how to minimize the double life of being closeted in some settings and not others and how to cope better with the stresses involved in whatever double life is necessary or unavoidable;

— for bisexual people, the need to find a setting for acceptance of the whole self and to explore the meaning of bisexuality with others who so identify.*

Cultural Immersion

Surrounding the decision to learn is the seeking of **education within** our own **lesbian, gay, or bisexual communities** and an immersion in gay and lesbian culture. At this moment I may feel ravenous, propelled by a fascination with and desire to surround myself with lesbian and gay people wherever I can find them, to fill myself with information about gay and lesbian art, music, history, anything I can find and to which I can afford access.

Gay, lesbian, and bisexual cultural immersion can involve making ourselves known to lesbian and gay colleagues who are more visible than we've been, and asking to be included in social gatherings. It can mean seeking out places where we can be surrounded by other lesbian and gay people, such as gay and lesbian organizations, bars, and softball teams, or known hangouts such as piers, parks, and rest stops. Depending on our resources and educational background we may also go looking for gay/lesbian bookstores, find museum exhibits to browse, or borrow books. We may go to music festivals or a concert given by a gay or bisexual performer, or borrow recorded music by such artists from a gay or lesbian friend. We may subscribe to gay magazines and watch movies by and about gay men and lesbians.

If we have some money to spend we may vacation in Provincetown on Cape Cod, the Russian River resorts in California, Rohobeth Beach, Delaware, Ogonquit, Maine, or Fire Island in New York. Probably we will find a way to spend time with groups of other gay and lesbian people. For example, we may volunteer at an AIDS service organization. We may do all this without our families of origin or our colleagues at work having an inkling, or we may do this more openly and defiantly.

---

*The bisexual journey for some homosexually identified bisexual people departs at this point into a separate, bisexual journey (see Chapter 6) where bisexual people who have been heterosexually identified also join in creating bisexual organizations and institutions, settings in which identification as bisexual is welcomed and learning can occur. Other bisexual people depart later in the journey into such separate forums. Some homosexually identified bisexual people continue to identify as primarily gay and to live in gay or lesbian culture. Thus the continuum from this point depicts bisexual journeys both within the bottom line and separate from it; such journeys are discussed here and in chapter 6.

How do emergent bisexual people, gay men, and lesbians, ready for more interactions with their own kind, find these other people? The answer has changed over time and also depends on how old a person is when this search begins. For many years in the United States, the only places to meet other bisexual, gay, and lesbian people were private parties or bars. Tucked away in neighborhoods where powerful segments of heterosexual society would never notice them, and paying exorbitant amounts to the mob and police to avoid unannounced vice-squad raids, these bars were the small, crowded gathering places permitted to gay men and lesbians. Today in most major cities there are also high school gay/straight alliances and support groups, bathhouses, community centers, churches and synagogues, counseling centers, bisexual organizations, gay and lesbian choruses, Alcoholics Anonymous meetings, newspapers, bookstores, athletic teams, and other settings for meeting people. But for people who live outside large cities, a bar is still often the only public setting where two adult men or women can dance, hold hands, have a drink, sometimes have a sexual encounter, and be surrounded by others doing the same thing. For youth in rural areas, there still may be no gathering places, although telephone hot lines and support groups are proliferating.

Bars were one of the primary public settings in which gay and lesbian culture of the 1950s and 1960s was created, and still today they are central institutions for many lesbian and gay communities. In Chicago one bar had a smoke-free, alcohol-free, chemical-free room for a while. In Vermont one bar has nights for women only, for men only, and for both. In Hawaii there is a video bar; in Austin, Texas, there was until recently a country and western lesbian bar. The point is that today, when adults in transition decide to go find the "gay community," more often than not they end up in a bar.

This is a time when we are busy seeking an **education** about being gay and lesbian or bisexual, not from heterosexual culture where we have gotten our information before, but from **within** our **gay, lesbian and bisexual communities** or through lesbian- and gay-authored books. We look for people with whom to explore and construct our identities in positive ways, including searching for people who share our class or cultural backgrounds:

> I wanted to tell you about my visit to San Francisco, about coming together with my Latina lesbian/feminist sisters. The joy and the pain of finding each other, of realizing how long we've "done without." . . . But how perfectly wonderful to finally have a family, a community.[12]

> Gay American Indians was founded in 1975 by Randy Burns (Northern Paiute) and Barbara Cameron (Lakota Sioux) to serve the needs and interests of the gay American Indian community. We came together then to share a common identity, to give and receive emotional support, and to share our rich heritage as American Indians. . . . GAI has become an

extended family for gay Indians. . . . GAI has re-created the kinship ties of the traditional Indian family in an urban setting, and this has made all of us stronger.[13]

Out of sheer instinct, I think, I made a new year's resolution to go to a support group of queer Asian women, most of whom were lesbian but turned out to be at least bi-friendly enough for me to feel accepted, if not completely understood.[14]

The search for education within our lesbian and gay communities includes a search for information, literature, and role models from the present and in history. This is a time for lots of reading.[15] We search for the historical "truth," the retellings by current authors and scholars, retellings in which the gay and lesbian content and identities have been written back into the stories of famous and ordinary people from the past and present. As Essex Hemphill has explained, information about and contact with gay people, including people of one's own culture, are essential both for finding role models for oneself and reinforcing continuing connections with one's culture. "It is not enough to tell us that one was a brilliant poet, scientist, educator, rebel. Who did he love? It makes a difference. I can't become a whole man simply on what is fed to me: watered-down versions of black life in America. I need the ass-splitting truth to be told, so I will have something pure to emulate, a reason to remain loyal."[16]

Bisexual people at this point may feel an urgent need to find a bisexual community rather than continuing to operate within or at the margins of gay and lesbian groups. As a bisexual person I may feel increasing anger at the extensive political and cultural institutions that exist for gay and lesbian people, but within which I feel the need to hide or downplay my bisexuality, at the lack of comparably developed bisexual institutions and communities for me to grow in, and at the invisibility or rejection of bisexual people in most heterosexual contexts.

Self-Affirmation and Self-Love

All this contact with other lesbian and gay people is supporting a more inward task. It is time to **examine internalized homophobia**, that is, the ways in which I still reject or negatively judge my lesbian self or project negative feelings at other lesbians or gay men who don't fit my ideas of "acceptability." I am seeking ways to erase what's left of my internalized hatred of my own homosexuality and to replace these vestiges with a sense of wholeness, of **self-affirmation and self-love** about my lesbian or gay identity. This step also often involves dealing with internalized feelings about my race and gender, since I am working to be a whole person.

This is also a time when I am likely to make a serious commitment to deepening and sustaining friendships with lesbians if I am female or gay men if I am male. These friendship groups will now provide me sustained contact, holiday and vacation company, reliability and help in times of need, coparenting of children, love and nurture. These are roles that only family members, and select others such as mother's best friend, a best girlfriend, or an army buddy usually provide to heterosexual people.

This experience of **friends as family** characterizes many gay and lesbian people's lives, regardless of their culture of origin. The relationship skills elaborated now in building and keeping such deeply engaged friendships are important and will be useful later in our journeys.

Lesbian Separatism

For lesbians, and white lesbians in particular, this stage may involve exploring **separatism**—one way of being a lesbian in the world. Whether "cultural separatism" is chosen temporarily or for the longer term, lesbians may feel the desire or need to work, worship, and live within as many lesbian-only or woman-only settings and institutions as possible. Separatist organizations are sought partly to gain relief from male dominance which rests with particular weight on lesbians in work and family settings, but also to explore the meaning of lesbianism, free of the constraints of functioning in the presence of heterosexual or bisexual people and gay men.[17] Celebration of lesbian cultures and cultural diversity in such settings challenges a woman's ideas about femaleness as well as about what it means to be a "real" lesbian. However, separatism has been a choice both more difficult and more politically problematic for women of limited economic means or women of color to entertain. It requires resources to separate from daily interactions with majority culture, for example, by purchasing a tract of land as a lesbian-only residence or retreat. Women of color, while agreeing that lesbian psychic and sexual separateness from men is a crucial and positive aspect of lesbian identity, have also questioned whether separatism helps make any real political change, if it means ignoring in one's life and political work the issues of oppression that cross gender lines, in particular racism.[18]

Bisexual women may also participate in lesbian separatism, although separatism in the long run may become untenable for them. In the past, bisexual women seeking to learn at this stage often silenced their bisexuality in order to find acceptance within lesbian circles. Today bisexual women who identify as primarily woman-oriented are more likely to insist on their right to be part of lesbian institutions and culture while being open about their bisexuality, an insistence that is sometimes welcomed and sometimes opposed:

> So bisexuality falls outside the thick black line that marks the boundaries of
> community, and perhaps that's why it's often viewed as shaking the
> durability of a self-sufficient, woman-loving culture. But it shakes our insides
> too. It makes every one of us vulnerable to the possibility that it could
> happen to us. . . . Lesbian and gay communities, experts by experience in

113

being shunted off to the side, being denied and excluded, find it difficult to embrace our own fringes because of fear.[19]

Gay men sometimes elect their own form of separatism. In some urban areas men can choose to live with, work with, and patronize, for most social and commercial services, only other gay men. These gay neighborhoods and communities are usually mostly white, and AIDS has had a devastating effect on some of them, but many gay men from rural areas or smaller cities still feel they must move to New York City, or San Francisco, or Los Angeles in order to explore fully what it may mean to be gay.

In addition to separatism, another important change is that I can now more often **choose when to deal with heterosexism**. I am not as reactive to every incident, am not so easily hooked emotionally by media slurs, overheard jokes, or people's obliviousness. I am feeling stronger in my own identity and I pick and choose when to spend energy in response to heterosexism around me. Thus when I fill out a medical history form at a doctor's office I may decide to check off "single" rather than writing in "not applicable" or "partnered" for the marital status question. I may do this not to hide my lesbianism from this doctor but simply because I am tired and choose not to do battle this day on this front.

Gay Men and Intimacy

For **gay men**, this time may involve **explorations of intimacy** which were not as possible earlier because they require a positive sense of self and some healing from the childhood experiences of rejection many gay men have had.[20] The positive self that is now emerging may also have less need to remain guarded in relationships as well as less need for rigidity of gender identity, a rigidity that may have interfered with emotional intimacy in the past. If such old hurts and fears, including fear that true intimacy would produce a vulnerability that was "unmanly," have prevented sustained relationships, a man in this stage may finally allow himself a deep and open relationship with another man or men. He may feel positive enough about himself and his gay identity to love and be loved.

If a man already has an ongoing intimate relationship, he may explore new varieties of intimacy with friends and be more open or more personally honest. Men may become involved in gay organizations or activities now as they explore the diversity of positive gay male lifestyles and identities. AIDS has certainly helped push more men away from casual sexual encounters and toward more sustained relationships, both sexual and otherwise, and has also engendered a great deal of progay political and social service activity among gay men. Yet many gay men have throughout this century sustained long-term relationships. Such relationships are not a post-AIDS phenomenon.[21]

Bisexual men who have been gay-identified may be more open with their male friends and lovers about their continuing interest in women, or they may become involved with a lesbian or bisexual woman in having a child, while remaining primarily within gay circles.

Expanding the Meaning of Maleness and Femaleness

After making the decision to learn, lesbian, gay, and bisexual people face another major issue: expanding the meaning of maleness and femaleness. If I were a gay man who had participated in bodybuilding in order to feel male, I may now recognize and appreciate what was compulsive and what was healthy about that behavior and make choices about my desired appearance less driven by conventional ideas of maleness. As a lesbian I may discover and work through negative feelings about women who look very delicate or very solid. In relationships we may go beyond appearances, letting go of roles grounded in traditional gender ideas and individualizing our responsibilities in intimacy based on skills, desires, and needs. We feel less need to judge other lesbian and gay people based on their gender-related behavior or appearance. At the same time we give ourselves permission to explore more things we had forbidden ourselves because of gender rules we had internalized.

The Late Transition

This is another moment in the journey when a person may turn to therapy. This time the agenda is very different from what it was in the orange zone. In the orange area, therapy was a possible way of changing gay or lesbian orientation. In the blue area, after a decision to learn, therapy is a means of developing a positive bisexual, gay, or lesbian identity. As one counseling guide puts it, "It is now time to move beyond merely helping gays cope and adjust to helping them develop innovative and satisfying ways to grow as gay people."[22]

Individuals may work on changing their victim behavior patterns, finding ways of acting out of personal empowerment when faced with negative responses to their sexual orientation, and probing remaining internalized negativity about their orientation. Obviously, only therapists familiar with gay men, bisexual people, lesbians, and their struggles can be helpful in this sort of work, since it is crucial that the therapist recognize the heterosexism, biphobia, and homophobia of the context in which the bisexual person, gay man, or lesbian is struggling to develop self-esteem. Also, the therapist must be able to help persons distinguish a problem that originates with their own behavior from one that is truly external to them.

This learning process helps gay men, bisexual people, and lesbians become more aware of their choices in dealing with heterosexism. Now we can make our reactions more specific and appropriate to the situation, less angry, and more creative, yielding greater feelings of empowerment. This greater flexibility and skill in interactions with heterosexual people come in part from increasing recognition of individual diversity, both among gay men, lesbians and bisexual people, and among heterosexual people. Our **search for heterosexual approval ends**.

As we develop more self-esteem and a more grounded and complex sense of gay or lesbian identity, we often participate in attempting to bring about systemic change, including helping to **build lesbian and gay institutions**, some mostly white institutions, some institutions specifically created by and for lesbian and gay people of color, and some institutions and coalitions working to value diversity. We create health clinics and hospices where we can be cared for by professionals who themselves either are gay and lesbian or are committed and trained to both welcome us and be aware of our particular medical needs, including but not limited to needs related to AIDS.

We develop arts organizations, literary journals, and news magazines. We operate investment-advising firms and law firms catering to lesbian and gay clients. For those of us who desire an institutionally affiliated spiritual life, this is often a time of **renewed religious ties**. Gay and lesbian clergy have created religious denominations and lesbian and gay people are helping to create welcoming congregations. We operate restaurants and card shops. In some cities and towns we occupy whole neighborhoods.

We do all these things in part because heterosexual institutions exclude us or do not respond adequately to our particular needs. We also create our own institutions as a positive way of celebrating who we are. They are a means of continuing to build caring communities in which we may live, grow, and change, and of providing safe and nurturing places for ourselves where we can obtain needed services as well as the rest and spiritual renewal necessary to sustain our existence as subordinant people living in a world of heterosexual dominance.

As we deepen our sense of positive bisexual, gay, or lesbian identity, we also tend to deepen our desire for meaningful relationships and familial ties. At this stage we may **create symbols and** enact commitment **rituals** to recognize lesbian or gay identity or to honor long-term relationships. We may do this privately, as I have done with the woman with whom I have shared my life for over twelve years, or we may do so publicly in the presence of family and friends or with the help of a religious congregation.

We also may organize politically to obtain such recognition from employers or government entities. Denmark, Norway, Sweden, and the Netherlands have created legal ceremonies and a legal status for gay and lesbian couples who wish recognition similar to that available through heterosexual marriage. Increasing numbers of clergy in various religious denominations in the United States perform ceremonies honoring gay and lesbian couples, although recently several Protestant denominations and Conservative Judaism have, after periods of study, officially refused to sanction such ceremonies.

This is a time when some gay men, lesbians, and bisexual people who have not yet done so may explore issues of childbearing and raising children. If we already live with a same-sex lover who has children, this may be the first time we take on a parental role. Or we may bring the lover's children to live in our household and be out in our gayness or bisexuality with them for the first time. If we do not have children, we may seek to adopt or to create children through artificial insemination or through an alliance with a gay man or lesbian.

These choices to create families and to have children are still very risky because we do not undertake them surrounded by recognition or approval from the larger society. It is true that in several states, courts have agreed to recognize both partners in a lesbian or gay male couple as adoptive parents, reasoning that it is better for a child to have two legal parents than one. But in several cases, lesbians who helped raise a biological child of a lover have failed, after the adult relationship ended, to be recognized as a parent with visitation or custody rights. They have been told they have no recognizable legal relationship to such a child. Lesbian mothers and gay fathers who are biological parents continue to lose custody of their children in some states because they are lesbian or gay. Nonetheless, many lesbians and gay men are successfully having children, raising children, adopting children, fostering children, and increasingly are visible with those children in their communities. This reality that lesbians and gay men are parents is now entering children's literature and school diversity curricula, albeit surrounded by great controversy. For example, the book *Heather Has Two Mommies*[23] was part of the Children of the Rainbow curriculum, proposed for use in the New York City public schools, and then withdrawn.

These decisions to create family often also involve **attempts at renewed ties with** one's own birth **family and or community of origin**. The gay male couple in Vermont who invited their parents and siblings to their Quaker commitment ceremony was asking their birth families to transcend whatever hostility they had felt in the past to their sons' gay identity and to celebrate it with them. In such situations, members of birth families themselves must "come out" to strangers as family members of a gay or lesbian person.

There is nothing like a newborn to challenge the parents of a lesbian to let go of their rejection of their daughter in the process of welcoming their grandchild. But sometimes parents do not take these steps. The baby who biologically is the lover's child may not be viewed by the co-mother's parents as their grandchild. The baby who by adoption is the legal child of one woman may not seem like a "real grandchild" to the second woman's parents.

At this stage, gay or bisexual persons are strong enough to put their relationship with their birth family at risk, either coming out for the first time to siblings or parents or asking, by speaking about themselves more, that parents who have accommodated their bisexuality or gayness in limited and unspoken ways move further along. This insistence is not about the need for approval, as were some earlier attempts to discuss sexual orientation with family. This time the agenda is attachment. Such attempts to foster deeper family intimacy sometimes produce breaches in the uneasy compromise relations of the past and sometimes yield healthier and closer ties.

Similar attempts to open collegial relations or friendships which have been limited by silence about the sexual orientation of one person are typical at this time. Again, the new "comings out" are not about approval, but about contact, continuity, honesty, and care. They are a way of honoring the heterosexual people important to the gay man, bisexual person, or lesbian; a way of saying, "I care about you so deeply that I want our relationship to include your knowing who I really am."

Whether a person during this stage maintains or builds new active ties with many heterosexual people or operates mainly within lesbian, gay, and bisexual communities depends on many variables. Urban settings make possible much more separation into gay, lesbian, and bisexual institutions, gay/lesbian neighborhoods, or separate bisexual organizations than do rural settings. The rural environment also renders a gay man or lesbian who is out much more visible than he or she would be in a large city. Such heightened visibility often means an ongoing need to build strong ties to heterosexual people and institutions in order to maintain some safety. It also may mean increased isolation from other gay and lesbian people in the rural setting who are fearful of being associated with me if I am an out gay man or lesbian. Such rural isolation adds to the necessity for visiting more urban settings for contact with lesbian and gay people and communities. People of color may also feel less inclined or able to separate from their heterosexual community of color, and gay and lesbian institutions or groups created by and for people of their home cultural community may not always be available.

Another variable that may affect the degree of separation a person adopts is whether or not she or he has children. Motherhood and fatherhood complicate the lives of lesbians, bisexual people, and gay men in significant ways. Children in the household force continuing interactions with heterosexual people, families, school personnel, and other institutions. Having children may also limit a gay, bisexual, or lesbian parent's access to some lesbian and gay settings. Lesbians with male children are often prohibited from attending some lesbian cultural events with their sons, for example.

Through this later stage of transition, bisexual people, gay men, and lesbians continue to lead double lives, although the settings in which they keep their sexual orientation fully hidden may decrease and the distance between their public personas and their personal identities may narrow. Nonetheless, because of the dominant culture's obliviousness, which still often includes the assumption that everyone is heterosexual, the bisexual person, gay man, or lesbian usually must come out in every new setting if he or she wants to avoid being presumed straight. In gay and lesbian settings, bisexual people must repeatedly come out too.

I own a button that reads "Don't presume I'm straight." Sometimes I think I should probably put it on the way I do my watch, every morning of every day. Actually, I don't feel safe wearing that button at all times in all places. And sometimes I don't even feel safe hanging that button inside my house. Several years ago my house was burglarized. Such a break-in could have happened to anyone on my road. But only in my house did the burglars tear up and leave in pieces on my dresser the photograph of my young son, after they had taken the jewelry from the box where I also kept my lesbian-mother buttons. Gay men, lesbians, and bisexual people fully comfortable with themselves and their orientation, thus having "nothing to hide," continue often to need to keep their orientation quiet in order to preserve physical safety in this culture, where antigay and lesbian violence is increasing rapidly.

The late transition involves acceptance of the diversity and mutability of sexual identity, including an ability to recognize honestly one's own changing constructions and reconstructions of identity over time. It involves a readiness to learn about and value the full diversity present among gay men and lesbians. For white gay men and lesbians, if we have not yet "done our homework" about race, our attempts now to work in multicultural coalitions will require us to do so, to learn more about our whiteness as well as about how our experiences differ from those of gay and lesbian people of color. Such readiness makes it possible for some of us to do the work of **organizing and building coalitions** among gay and lesbian peoples as well as with bisexual and heterosexual people, when shared tasks and concerns make such coalitions and organizing necessary.

As lesbians and gay men we must also, before we are through the transition, come to terms with our own biphobia and with the heteroerotic behaviors, histories, feelings, and/or capacities many lesbians and gay men have, even though as lesbians and gay men we probably don't intend to act heteroerotically again. Many gay men and lesbians erase and deny their past heterosexual sexual histories and desires in the process of immersing themselves in a lesbian or gay community and in constructing their lesbian or gay identity. In some settings, men and women who were once married are viewed with disdain by other gay men and lesbians, as converts might be viewed within religious communities.

In other settings, formerly married gay men and lesbians, especially those with children, tend to be the most accepted public spokespersons to the straight world and tend to be given a disproportionate amount of attention and leadership. This causes legitimate anger from lesbian separatists, among others. At this point on the continuum, we are working together toward ways of communicating with each other that are not distorted by heterosexist norms and that make room for and value the many gay and lesbian identities we have created.

Some people who have been living as lesbians or gay men may once again begin exploring relationships with people of the other gender or may self-identify as bisexual. Some may choose to reenter heterosexual life, if a long-term relationship develops. Assuming they have resolved their internalized homophobia and fully accepted their same-sex sexual feelings, they are likely to enter a heterosexual relationship, out as a bisexual person, and to continue to support social changes that honor diversity of sexuality. Others will move at this late transition point into primary identification as a bisexual person, regardless of the sex of the person or persons with whom they are intimate. Such a move puts them onto the bisexual transition journey described in the next chapter.

The themes at the end of the lesbian and gay transition are expansion of self and comfort with diversity. As to self, we proud gay men and lesbians and homosexually identified bisexual people, people of color and white people, enter the next part of the journey loving our bodies and our full sexual identities, our maleness and femaleness in their expanded meanings, our cultural identities consciously integrated and inseparable from both. We travel toward more intense interactions with other people whether we remain primarily separatist or not, with a sense of awe and **value** for the complexity of **every person's journey** and for the courage it has taken for anyone to travel this far.

Reconstructing Identity

Transitions for Bisexual Men and Women

H EATHER W ISHIK

> There should be no
> universal map of how
> one can love or be loved
> in return.
>
> —*Cliff Arnesen,*
> *"Coming Out to Congress"*
>
> We are not fence-sitters.
> Let us strive to be
> bridge-builders.
>
> —*Amanda Udis-Kessler,*
> *"Present Tense"*

The journeys described in the prior chapter and in chapter 7 include experiences of transition that many bisexual people will find familiar.* However, there are additional aspects of the bisexual journey. For some bisexual people, regardless of prior primary identification, the decision-to-learn stage also marks their **coming out** to themselves as bisexual. This leads eventually to coming out to other people and, for some, to adopting a **primary bisexual identity**. Such a coming out marks the beginning of separation from journeying within or at the margins of lesbian/gay or straight contexts or within primary identification as gay/lesbian or straight.

Before this stage, some bisexual people already have been identifying as bisexual within gay or straight contexts, at least to themselves. The early transition may mark the point at which they decide the journey must be one which permits more open acknowledgment of their whole sexuality and that neither gay nor straight identification permits that. For some people, resistance to using labels that feel constraining continues, even as more interaction with others who call themselves bisexual helps with the further elaboration of identity.

Since the mid-1970s, but particularly since the early 1980s, organizations, networks, groups, publications, and events have emerged which can support people developing their sense of identity as bisexual. Access to such contexts for developing a positive bisexual selfhood is particularly important because neither

---

*As the lesbian author of this chapter, I have not used the first person, but rather have relied on stories by out bisexual people to illustrate the experiential realities of the bisexual transition.

literature, psychology, nor contemporary culture provides an agreed-upon meaning for the term *bisexuality*. Thus, for bisexual people, the process of building a sexual identity includes struggling with the categories and dualisms of heterosexually dominant cultures, including the "monosexual paradigm"[1] and dualisms about sexual orientation and gender. Recognition of the full range of one's erotic feelings may simply lead to profound feelings of isolation and confusion in the absence of contexts for validation of that full range.

The positive power of participating in bisexual contexts is illustrated in Indigo Som's story about her experience planning the 1990 National Bisexual Conference:

> Organizers were planning the first national bisexual conference for June. I joined the people of color caucus and for the first time felt that there was something really wonderful about being bisexual. Finally there were people like me! People who understood me exactly as myself, instead of trying to relate to only a fragmented part of me. At last I was allowed to indulge my bisexual point of view, instead of feeling like I had to squeeze into the lesbian community's margins.[2]

The almost total invisibility of bisexuality in contemporary majority culture has made it difficult for people to know that such an identity is even possible. Nate Brown explains that his first access to the idea took place when he was in his early forties: "After a few years of marriage, I happened across a classified ad for a rap group at the Bisexual Center in San Francisco. Bisexual? My vocabulary had never included that word. Not knowing what bisexual was, I put the ad aside for several months. When I happened to notice the ad again, something told me to check it out. My life was changed forever."[3]

Some bisexual people continue to find primary identification as lesbian/gay or straight most comfortable; others have a primary commitment as an out bisexual person within gay/lesbian or straight communities. Some find adopting an open bisexual identification still means journeying and doing political and community work within gay and lesbian contexts because they feel bisexual people are "a constituency within lesbian and gay liberation."[4]

Once people have **come out** to themselves as bisexual, with or without the help of other people and organizations, they still face coming out issues with those important to them. Bisexual people who have been living heterosexually identified lives will experience their first coming out to others. It can be complicated to figure out how to come out and in what settings to do so, as illustrated by the story of one previously heterosexually identified woman:

> When I came out as bisexual, I went through a physical transformation that resembled that of other women in their coming-out process. I cut my long, permed hair. I stopped shaving my legs. I gained some weight. I got rid of my makeup. I was coming out as bisexual and feminist and lesbian, all at

the same time. More accurately, I was coming into myself as feminist, out to the world as bisexual, and joining a lesbian-identified women's community centered around the college I was attending. As a bisexual person, I was very isolated; there was no bisexual community in my community.[5]

Heterosexually identified bisexual people are often already married and may have children by the time they come out. Coming out as a bisexual person during a marriage can be terrifying. The risk is **loss of** the existing **relationships** with spouse and children. The coming out process often requires, for relationships to continue, the **renegotiation of** those **relationships.** Spouses may react with fear, confusion, and anger. Media spotlighting and scapegoating of bisexual males as transmitters of AIDS to the heterosexual population have contributed to feelings of fear and hostility about bisexual people and have reinforced stereotypes about bisexual promiscuity.[6] Despite the complexities, however, many out bisexual people maintain marital relationships, both those entered into before coming out and those entered into afterward.

Some heterosexually identified bisexual people do not come out to the spouse or others during marriage, but keep their bisexual orientation and desires, and any sexual activities outside the marriage secret until the spouse dies or the marriage ends ostensibly for other reasons:

> When my wife died in 1978, I was sixty-nine years of age. I began seeking outlets in the gay community without much success. I did join Unitarian Universalists for Lesbian and Gay Concerns and here found friends with whom I could speak openly and freely. . . .
>
> As I continued with UULGC I received much support, and after an international convocation in San Diego in 1986, I felt loved enough that I decided to "come out." I first came out to my San Diego friend of fifty years whom I was visiting at the time. He was very accepting. . . . then I had dinner with a niece also living there. She was very loving and accepting. In the past I had rationalized not coming out because I had few friends in the gay and bisexual community; if I came out to straight friends and lost them I would be bereft. With these initial coming out experiences I no longer worried about this.
>
> I came home and wrote letters to my children, coming out to them. . . . I kept track until I came out to ninety-three people with 100 percent acceptance, including my children and their spouses.[7]

People who have identified as lesbian or gay face a **second coming out** when they identify as bisexual. This second coming out requires coming out to one's gay or lesbian lover, friends, and community as well as to heterosexual people or relatives of importance. "To come out as bisexual in the gay community for many means a loss of support in the face of heterosexism. This fear kept me 'in the closet' as a bisexual, because I was so fearful of losing my community, my gay community, my support system and grounding."[8]

As a bisexual person coming out in lesbian or gay settings often discovers, many in lesbian and gay communities vehemently reject bisexual people and bisexuality, both as a sexual orientation and as a sexual identity. From the bisexual person's perspective, such gay/lesbian views have been labeled biphobic:

> Acknowledging only the "heterosexual" side, bisexuals are perceived by gays as being immune from the discrimination and violence that face all sexual minorities. Our "heterosexual privilege" somehow outweighs those times we get chased from bars, beaten in parks, infected with HIV, or are rejected by our biphobic lovers. Three acquaintances have committed suicide because of the confusion and anger their bisexuality created in their lives. Obviously, biphobia has devastating consequences on the ability of bisexuals to live healthy lives.[9]

The frequent negative responses bisexual people face from gay and lesbian people have been called by at least one writer "horizontal hostility."[10]

The issue of access to heterosexual privilege is a real one for a bisexual person who has heretofore identified as lesbian or gay and is embarking on a mixed-sex relationship:

> Many people do look at me with a man and assume I'm heterosexual. . . . I can kiss my partner in public without fear of harassment. . . . But I didn't desert my own feelings. I love my partner and know I would have been short-changing myself, my capacity for a mutually fulfilling and loving relationship, if I had denied my feelings for him in favor of a fixed lesbian identity. And heterosexuality, although it does carry certain privileges, is not necessarily easy. Feminist heterosexuality isn't easy, and feminist bisexuality is yet more complex.[11]

Bisexual identification separate from gay and lesbian or heterosexual settings often involves at this stage a yearning for others, for information, for history, for gathering places, for books, and a **search for community**. Today there are bisexual networks, newspapers, and political and counseling organizations in many cities in the United States as well as a growing body of literature about bisexual experience from which people in the transition can draw support:

> We need a Bisexual Community more than ever. I don't think we should turn our backs on the lesbian and gay communities: certainly, many of us are grateful for the support and role models we found even in the most biphobic communities, but I do think it's time we stopped bothering the nice dykes and faggots with our timid pleas for validation. We need to create a bifriendly place here, and the best way to do that is to be Bisexual and proud, Bisexual and brave, Bisexual and honorable. For that, we need to find each other. Besides, some of us are out here already and we're waiting for you![12]

The rapidly emerging bisexual networks, organizations, and institutions are a contemporary phenomenon, one that may have been jump-started in part by the AIDS epidemic and the frequent scapegoating of bisexual people in connection with AIDS:

> Nowhere do we know of a bisexual community emerging in reaction to the polarization of heterosexual and homosexual people as is happening today. There are political circumstantial reasons for this, the key escalator being AIDS, which has exposed the false assumptions supporting this charade. Building bisexual community is crucial. Community gives a shared sense of pride and acceptance of the whole. It breaks down the isolation and fear, giving strength to those who come out.[13]

Initial bisexual identification sometimes includes a need to seem as acceptable as possible to both heterosexual and gay and lesbian people. Although many bisexual people are monogamous, a heterosexist stereotype of bisexual promiscuity continues and sometimes constrains people from exploring non-monogamous modes of living. "It is difficult enough to persuade people to accept us as individuals who have made a 'both/and' choice, refusing the 'either/or' pressure of our culture. To choose to be in a sexual relationship with only one gender at a time makes the 'both/and' choice a bit less apparent and therefore a bit more palatable to nonbis."[14] Others may find their initial joy at having discovered an identity that encompasses the whole self includes exploration of choices such as triangles and nonmonogomy. The move into bisexual networks helps provide diverse models of bisexual life choices.

Construction of new meaning now becomes a theme because bisexuality doesn't operate within dominant culture's given categories. Recognizing the existence of bisexuality pushes boundaries and cannot be contained in dualist thinking: "(W)e challenge many people's personal sense of what constitutes sexual identity. Whether we threaten by introducing a third category or by undermining the notion of categories altogether, we cause enough discomfort that many people deny our existence."[15] Part of the necessary construction of new meaning involves **discarding** internalized **negative stereotypes** about bisexuality, while recognizing the kernels of truth contained in them. One of the most powerful of these stereotypes, which must be dealt with in the transition to **positive bisexual identity**, is that bisexuality is just a stage in the development of sexual identity, not a sexual orientation or identity itself.

Some heterosexual, gay, and lesbian people do identify as bisexual at a stage in their own journey toward recognition of their actual orientation and construction of their sexual identity. Given that understanding, it is easy to see that some people who identify as "monosexual" have repressed their bisexuality and in the process labeled it a stage. In addition, some bisexual people experience lesbianism or gayness as a stage.[16]

None of this means bisexuality doesn't exist as a sexual identity. For some people it is a chosen identity; for others it is one dictated by a strong, perhaps biologically based, erotic orientation toward both genders and toward people regardless of gender. How to speak about this orientation is something bisexual people are still working on. New language possibilities include speaking of bisexual orientation as one of "sexual ambiguity" or "polyvalent attraction,"[17] "pansexuality" or "pansensuality."[18] Out of African and American Indian traditions of perceiving people with ambierotic desires as people possessing attributes of both genders, some people-of-color communities refer to bisexual and transgender people as "two-spirit" people.

Claiming positive identity also requires developing a sense of positive meaning for bisexuality. Bisexuality has often been discussed as merely a combination of heterosexual and homosexual desires, or as something in between these two. Building positive identity often includes a search for meaning through books, events, organizations, and sharing life stories, in order to construct a description of what bisexuality is instead of what it is not. It also includes a search for historical and contemporary role models: "There have been rare 'out' bisexual communities that we know of: The Bloomsbury group is one. . . . Because of social prejudice and outright discrimination, it's terribly difficult to compile a list of historical figures who've had significant love relationships with both genders throughout their lives."[19] This search for meaning is also an imperative for the building of community[20] and is thus a major shared task within many bisexual networks and organizations.

Now, in some cities, bisexual people are creating their own networks from which to **organize and build coalitions**, primarily with sympathetic gay and lesbian organizations although sometimes with heterosexual ones as well. In the transition, as bisexual identity feels stronger and the fear of losing the prior primary identity fades, people may choose greater involvement in specifically bisexual organizations or caucuses.

The theme of the end of the transition for bisexual people is expansion of self and comfort with diversity. Those who identify primarily as bisexual now have developed some comfort with and pride in this identity, and some skill in negotiating the transitions between gay and lesbian settings and heterosexual settings. They are taking advantage of whatever bisexual support networks, settings, or people are useful and available in the locale. An eagerness for places where everyone values the full diversity of human sexuality marks the move into the green section of the sexual orientation and identity continuum.

Questioning Assumptions, Expanding Ourselves and Relationships

Transitions for Heterosexual and Heterosexually Identified Bisexual People

CAROL PIERCE

In the late 1970s I decided that if I was to work as a professional in the area of gender issues, I needed to examine any biases I might have about human sexuality.* I attended a week-long human sexuality course that pushed every button possible, but in a way that kept my defenses low and enabled me to learn. The section on homosexuality was interesting but not very personal at first. However, the course was being taught in a city with large gay/lesbian communities at the time of their gay pride parade. We all went. Having held public office and wanting to keep my options open for returning, I was suddenly terrified of being caught on national television watching the parade. My visceral fears of guilt by association were intense. Later I was embarrassed enough about my reaction that it made me thoughtful. I was terrified of voters' reaction to my being associated with homosexual people. I didn't want to react that way, but I couldn't take a chance. I was being pulled into the transition. About that time I also had someone close to me come out. I found myself dealing with the transition whether I liked it or not.

The action of subordinants moving into the transition is what forces dominants to move. Nothing has so powerful an effect on a dominant person as a

---

*Whereas in chapter 3, the terms *heterosexual* and *heterosexually identified people* covered many who would later identify as bisexual, lesbian, or gay, in this chapter we assume more specific identification with these terms. Many who have identified as straight are now clearer about their orientation and have or are about to enter the gay, lesbian, or primary bisexual journeys. Therefore, in chapter 7, although shifting journeys continue to occur particularly in the early transition, more and more of those who identify with the heterosexual or heterosexually identified bisexual journey clearly understand and identify with their declared orientation.

subordinant who does not accept subordinance and has blossomed, comfortable with her or his identity. The marchers in the gay pride parade were certainly proud of their identity. Lesbian, gay, and bisexual people speaking to us directly and self-confidently about themselves evoke emotional responses that as heterosexual people we do not expect. We are thrust into a personal journey where we can no longer remain part of an oblivious, silent group. We have our own work to do.

Here in the early transition, some who until now have identified as straight let themselves become more aware of a wider sense of their own orientation. As discussed in chapters 3 through 6, the process of questioning our sexual identity happens in many places on the continuum. Here again, as some look at their own homophobic and biphobic reactions, they realize they served as a cover for their real identity. Some who switch to the lesbian or gay journey here to test their sense of orientation may return later to the heterosexual journey as a heterosexually identified bisexual person. Finding the space and support to think this option through is difficult in a heterosexist world that perceives sexuality in the early orange section as centered in heterosexuality, or in the late orange section as bipolar, that is, either heterosexual or homosexual, an either/or frame of reference. Straight people entering the transition tend to think in terms of gradations of sexual orientation from straight to bisexual to gay or lesbian.* It seems like a major step to include the possibility of bisexuality in this way. This concept can feel as threatening as moving to a bipolar definition was in the late orange section, particularly if we are acknowledging our own bisexuality. To name ourselves as bisexual takes courage. We need time to answer such questions as Do I want to be known as bisexual, or do I remain quiet about this part of myself? Am I a heterosexually or homosexually identified bisexual person or primarily bisexually identified? If so, what does that mean? How do I find someone to talk to about this?

The Effect of Previous Work on Gender and Race

Many people approach this transition based on the work they have already done on other "isms," which is helpful in many ways as a model for exploring a new one. Each "ism" has important differences, however, so having done work on race, gender, class, physical ability, or any other issue of cultural dominance and subordinance *is not a substitute for doing one's work on heterosexism.*

For instance, if we have been thoughtful about the dominance and subordinance of gender and/or race, the idea of identifying with dominance or subordinance is not new, and it is perceived as important. We have learned to acknowledge our impact as dominant or subordinant. How we respond to admitting heterosexual dominance depends on whether we have experienced roles of domi-

---

*Cultural patterns of thought encourage thinking in terms of gradations of sexualities. Later in our journey we will see the inadequacy of such a frame of reference.

128

nance and/or subordinance on gender and race. Identifying as dominant may be new to straight women of color because of the double subordinance of gender and race. In fact, Makeda Silvera says, "heterosexual privilege is the *only* privilege women of color have access to."[1] The experience of being dominant by gender or color may or may not be familiar to straight white women and straight men of color, depending on whether they have left their issues of subordinance to explore ways in which they carry dominance in society. If they have explored such issues, they will find it easier to identify with dominance here. Reluctance to do this usually comes from the clarity and urgency one feels from being subordinant and the fear that attention will be taken away from the issues of one's subordinant group. Jewelle Gomez reports:

> I think it's even more dangerous for people of color to embrace homophobia than it is for whites to embrace racism, simply because we're embattled psychologically and economically as an ethnic group. We leave ourselves in a very weakened position if we allow the system to pit us against each other. I also think it renders Black people politically smug. That's the thing about homophobia, racism, anti-Semitism, any of the "isms"—once you embrace those you tend to become smug.[2]

Awareness of the various combinations of dominance and subordinance which an individual carries and of their effect on one's beliefs and actions is important. Straight white men, of course, are reminded again of their privileges, likely bringing feelings of "Will this never end?"

If a person dominant in gender and/or race has experienced previous journeys of appreciative discovery and growth, this transition will likely be anticipated in that light. If not, the residue of resistance from dealing with gender or race may be enlarged here. The crucial ingredients are: Have we grasped the idea that there exist many ways for dominance and subordinance to manifest themselves? *And* when we are part of the dominant group, do we understand that *we* have to work to see how we benefit from and are hurt by this dominance and collude to keep it alive?

This chapter assumes that a minimum of previous work has been done on such issues, particularly on gender. Those who have much insight into these issues will be affirmed for their work. However, understanding the ways in which gender issues and heterosexism intersect may be new, and such intersection is important for everyone.

One final word of caution as we enter the transition. It is important to remind ourselves once again that we and others are doing the best we can from our own life experience. We must not be such harsh judges of our own behavior that guilt and self-flagellation get in the way of our journeys. We need to remember to see our behavior as data, as information about ourselves to be aware of, considered, and talked about with others who are also on this journey, so that we have the courage to take risks to do things differently. Self-judgment enlarges guilt to the point that it interferes with thinking clearly about the effects of our actions and the ways we want to change.

Entering the Transition

The words *I* and *we* are used in different ways as we enter the transition. It was important in chapter 3 consciously to ask heterosexual readers to think in terms of *we* in order to heighten awareness of belonging to the dominant group and the ways this is different from belonging to the subordinant group. This awareness facilitates our *conscious identification* with dominance, rather than unconscious participation in oblivious heterosexism.

At the same time though, the dominance of oblivious heterosexism also supports a *we* feeling where dominants assume subordinants are grateful to be included in how dominants perceive and feel about the world. Dominants often use *we* irresponsibly to include subordinants in their view and experience of the world. As long as I can justify my actions by what the majority do and say, and particularly by what respected leaders do and say, I can sustain an illusion that all is well and that I, in particular, am a good person.

To move into the transition requires that I now separate myself from the crowd and individualize myself on a journey where the only person I can be responsible for is myself. The transition demands a willingness to

— acknowledge the person I have been as a heterosexual;
— look at how I am living out my heterosexuality, or my heterosexually identified bisexuality;
— admit to myself my fears about and resistance to sexual orientation and sexual identity issues as well as to gender issues;
— leave what has been comfortable and explore my inner thoughts and what may be my personal need to be homophobic and biphobic; and
— **see my culture as heterosexist with dominance patterns.**

The journey is now a personal one and demands speaking in *I* as well as *we*.*

Usually, I (speaking to heterosexual experience) am drawn into the transition when **someone close to me comes out as lesbian, gay, or bisexual**. The emotion of this disclosure sets me reeling. Without such visceral impact, my acceptance of homosexuality and bisexuality stays quietly intellectual. For years, unbe-

---

*The *I* and *me* used in this chapter refer to myself, Carol Pierce, as the straight author. However, I would like you, the heterosexual and heterosexually identified bisexual reader, to read the *I* as if it applies to yourself. *We* need to agree to do this in order to bring the issues to a more personal level. *I* is interspersed with *we*, *our*, and *us* in order to generalize to typical straight and straight-identified bisexual experience. Resistance often emerges when we are asked to identify with a dominant group. If you feel such resistance, be aware of whether your response is an emotional one, particularly anger. Think about why your emotions are stirred.

known to me, gay men, lesbians, and bisexual people have been interacting with me. They may include a mother or father, son or daughter, husband or wife, a close friend, relative, or co-worker. I am shocked. I have questions such as, "How could I not have known? Is she or he sure? Would he or she like to talk to a counselor? How could you do this to me now?" It always feels like the wrong time for someone to bring up or make such a disclosure. Someone is getting married, leaving for school, going on an important trip; we're celebrating a holiday; your Dad is tired tonight; this is not a convenient time to hear about this!

I am apt to bombard the person with questions to "help" her or him rethink the absurdity of such an identification. A typical sarcastic question is, "Have you ever kissed someone of the same sex?" (Of course, as a heterosexual person, it didn't take a kiss to know I was attracted to the other sex.) I am thrown back in my journey often to hostility and fear, because I am facing **personal involvement**, not just theoretical involvement. My resistance is up.

My **emotions are intense and scary**. My confusion is real. Everything I have ever heard about homosexuality is present in my consciousness. The reality of homosexuality is close and intimate. Some of my emotions come from my terror of visualizing same-sex acts. It was bad enough to have to consider homosexual strangers being sexual, but now my imagination has to deal with known loved ones and friends "doing it."

I need to release myself from such emotional responses by desensitizing myself to my visualizations. What is, just is. This orientation and identity are not me and require nothing of me but acceptance of what is natural for bisexual people, gay men, and lesbians. I pass through stages of shock, disbelief, and sorrow before I come to such acceptance. The shock and disbelief are part of getting past my overactive imagination coupled with some voyeurism. My sorrow at first is directed at feeling sorry for someone "like that." In time I see that my sorrow is more likely my feeling sorry for myself that *I* have to change.

In my shock and disbelief I not only question the person, hoping this coming out is all a mistake, but I face the fact that I may have to walk down the street with someone who is known to others as homosexual or bisexual, and thus be suspected of being homosexual myself—**guilt by association**. Will the hostility, violence, joking, and avoidance of lesbian, gay, and bisexual people that I have participated in with others, either actively or through my silence, now be turned on me? What will I tell friends? How will I react and interact with someone who is out, when I have *always* felt uncomfortable in the presence of homosexual and bisexual people? Dealing with my guilt-by-association fears continues throughout the transition. The shunning of bisexual people, gay men, and lesbians has been so complete that my reputation seems on the line if I am seen in their company. In fact, I am now dealing with my own coming out. To the extent that someone close to me is out, I am now required to be out as a parent, daughter, son, sister, brother, cousin, or friend of a gay, lesbian or bisexual person. I cannot out them, but where and how they are out, outs me as relative, colleague, or friend.

As threatening as it is to find that someone close to me is a bisexual person, gay man, or lesbian, it may be just as threatening to realize that **someone of the same sex is or could be attracted to me**. My fear is that if a lesbian or gay man is attracted to me (I still perceive bisexuals as either gay or lesbian), I must be homosexual or at least bisexual. My reaction is likely one of panic, because I haven't yet learned that we who haven't thought through our sexual orientation are the ones who are threatened. My fear of homosexual and bisexual people is that "they" will switch me, that "they" can control who I am.

As I move into the transition, I am more aware when a lesbian or gay person is attracted to me. It is harder to dismiss and forget as I have done in the past. If I as a heterosexual woman think about it, I can probably remember times when this occurred and how quickly I brushed it aside and denied it was happening. Now when it happens, I still don't want to acknowledge or think about the possibility. I haven't the slightest idea what to do or what is expected of me. The realization that this is possible can be terrifying.

Straight men and women are not attracted to every member of the other sex; each of us usually experiences sexual chemistry with only a few people. So it is with lesbians, gay men, and bisexual people. Occasionally a straight woman may be attracted to an individual gay man, or a straight man to a lesbian, finding their interest unreturned. It is the same with gay men or lesbians being attracted to straight people, although many gay and lesbian friends tell me that they really are not much attracted to straight people.

Straight men and women need to become aware in the early transition of their tendency to overreact to the approach of a lesbian, bisexual person, or gay man. We project individual instances of same-sex attraction to us onto all gay and lesbian people, indiscriminately believing they are attracted to everyone of the same sex and that bisexual people are attracted to everyone of both sexes—the prowler image.

Although many same-sex childhood experiences are pleasurable and mutual, if we had one or more abusive same-sex sexual experiences when we were in an earlier place on the continuum, particularly in childhood, it is likely to be remembered for the terror and anger that it brought. At the time, we either made a scene or, more likely, ran from the incident with deep feelings of guilt for participating. Now we need to reflect on any feelings of secrecy or shame and what our reactions were and their lingering effect. Do our unresolved feelings about childhood same-sex experiences support current fears of bisexuality and homosexuality?

In the transition we need to be aware of what supports childhood and adult fears. Do we avoid hearing or doing things that might heal childhood trauma and our general fears of homosexuality? Do we seek friends and counselors with whom to talk? Books, movies, and television programs also have much to offer. We need to rethink what we are willing to watch, talk about, and read and how to see or hear what is presented.

For instance, commercial movies traditionally play on our fear of same-sex attraction. Where homosexuality is implied or directly brought into the story line, the emphasis is usually on the terror the straight person feels on being approached by a gay or lesbian person, and the flight into mental stress, illness, or violence of a gay man trying to come to terms with his identity.

Most movies have left us with the impression that homosexuals are usually male, become mentally ill when they discover their homosexuality, and randomly stalk heterosexuals. The Italian movie *Basileus Quartet*[3] illustrates the terror of a young straight man when he is approached by an older gay man, who is eventually institutionalized as sick because of his homosexuality. Do we sympathize with the straight man's discomfort or with the gay man as unduly judged sick? Are we so uncomfortable with homosexuality that our own fears cause us to justify the straight man's behavior rather than see the horror of a life lost because of our cultural terror of homosexuality? Common sense has yet to tell us that, for bisexual people, lesbians, and gay men, sexuality "has its own regulatory principles, its own rhythm of expression and containment, arousal and satiety, just as for straight people."[4]

Lesbians are found less often in movie story lines. However, the movie of D. H. Lawrence's short story "The Fox"[5] depicts violence in a lesbian relationship when a straight man enters the scene and takes one partner away. What is our reaction? Are we happy he entered the story? Do we perceive one woman as bisexual or as "saved"?

Straight people in the orange section of the continuum habitually condemn and avoid movies that have gay or lesbian characters. As we become more tolerant near the end of the orange section, we assume such movies may be all right for lesbian, gay, and bisexual people, but we would have no interest in seeing them. Actually, many movies with gay, lesbian, and bisexual characters are meant for straight people. The sensitive story lines about the reality of lesbian, bisexual, and gay life are what *we* need to see. They bring us into the transition. Many such movies are too painful for lesbian, gay, and bisexual people to watch because of their vivid portrayal of the everyday pain of being gay, lesbian, and bisexual. Such movies include *Oscar Wilde, Oranges Are Not the Only Fruit,* and *A Special Day.*[6] These are movies for us—straight people. Thankfully, more movies are being produced that not only share the pain of bisexual, lesbian, and gay male life but celebrate the naturalness of it. Movies that depict in more balanced ways the reality of gay life, as well as show appreciation and comfort with it, are *A Torch Song Trilogy, Desert Hearts,* E. M. Forster's *Maurice, Philadelphia, Go Fish, And the Band Played On, The Wedding Banquet,* and *Tales of the City.*[7] *Victor/Victoria*[8] is a comedy that highlights many of the stereotypes straight people have about gay men and *The Adventures of Priscilla, Queen of the Desert*[9] speaks to stereotypes about cross-dressing. Independent film-makers and mainline Hollywood studios are increasingly producing movies and TV programs with gay, lesbian, and bisexual themes. Opportunities for straight people to enjoy and better understand the life and times of the lesbian, bisexual, and gay person and community are expanding.

Who Am I?

Several types of experience may force me to think about who I am sexually. These may include having someone close to me come out as lesbian, gay, or bisexual; only partially understanding same-sex sexual experiences of childhood, adolescence, or adulthood; and discovering or remembering that someone of the same gender is or was attracted to me. Or perhaps I am allowing my feelings of attraction to others of the same gender to surface. Such memories and the emotions attached to them make me face the hard question: **What is my sexual orientation?**

The time has come to think through and reflect on what I missed doing in my growing-up years—consciously addressing the question of my sexual orientation and identity. How do I know I am heterosexual? Did I ever *decide* I was heterosexual? Am I denying my homosexuality or bisexuality because of cultural heterosexism? These questions can no longer be avoided. I think back to my first experiences of sexual and emotional attraction. Was it to those of the same gender or to those of the other gender or both? How did I really feel? Did I really want the sexual and/or affectionate or intimately emotional relationships I have had? Who or what do I, or have I, avoided in relationships? Most people confirm their heterosexuality through this exploration. Some, however, find they must consider whether they are gay, lesbian, or bisexual people. Some of us rather quickly discover by ourselves who we are, once we are open to reflecting on our core sexual self. Others of us take time, even years, and may seek professional help.

We may come to the conclusion that we might well have chosen a different sexual identity, but for the cultural messages that encouraged our heterosexual one. It does not mean we are unhappy or would like to live differently now. We are just aware of the influence that heterosexual culture has had on us. This is a different feeling from the person who has clear biological messages about their orientation. For them, orientation and identity do not feel like matters of choice. They just are.

For some answering the question, Who am I? brings a shift in identity. The lines on the sexual orientation continuum show this as a major place of **emergent bisexual identity**. Previously identified heterosexuals reconsider their sexual identity and may even shift identity. I am not suggesting that sexual orientation changes as a matter of mere choice: for most people, what changes is the capacity to know the self and thus to adopt an identity consistent with the sexual orientation that may have heretofore been denied. It is a great relief for previously identified straight people to acknowledge what has been felt, suspected, or buried—that they are lesbian, gay, or heterosexually- or gay/lesbian-oriented bisexual people. Their journey is not the heterosexual one.

Michael Brewer describes part of his journey of knowing, as he grew up, that he was bisexual, and of entering a heterosexual marriage and still coping with his bisexuality.

Although my wife had talked about my sexuality before our relationship, and had met my gay and bisexual friends, she had yet to deal with the reality of my sexual feelings. I realized that bisexuality means non-monogamy to me. At first I had anonymous encounters or dishonest short-term ones. They left me with feelings of self-loathing and revulsion. The pressure built until I had to pour all my pent-up feelings to my wife. She was shocked that I could be going through so much inner turmoil without sharing it with her or showing it to her. She didn't know what a consummate actor I could be.

I found the Pacific Center in Berkeley, where they have a weekly support group for married gay and bi men. With her encouragement I began to attend. Most of the men in this group were older and divorced or in the process of divorcing. However, I did meet a man my age who was married and trying to make it work. A relationship developed between us and a friendship grew between our wives. It was not easy for any of us. My wife and I went through many traumas and sleepless nights coming to terms with my bisexuality. I experienced feelings of guilt and other emotional issues. Together we all learned that although a relationship is built on a deep and spiritual foundation, sex is still an issue and can be filled with strong emotions. It proved too much for my boyfriend and his wife; their marriage ended. He wanted me to end mine and go away with him. I couldn't. I knew that the woman I was with was my life partner. . . .

Today I live a very full life. My wife and I are happy to be raising our baby girl. I have a relationship with a bisexual man who is supportive of my chosen lifestyle. He and my wife are friends. I feel freed of my own bondage, and this has freed me creatively.[10]

Some who find it difficult to identify as gay or lesbian at this point, despite discovery of strong homoerotic feelings and/or an emotional affinity with homo-sexuality, may find it safer to identify as bisexual rather than immediately shifting to gay or lesbian. Others may for a while feel that discovery or acknowledgment of homoerotic or affectionate feelings means they must be gay or lesbian, but they will later come to recognize a continuing heterosexual attraction and will choose a primary bisexual identity after a period of identifying as lesbian or gay. Some people may come home to themselves as gay or lesbian and enter the journey that identity involves.

Our feelings of gender affinity which are related to our sexual orientation as well as our cultural and familial backgrounds and experiences have many facets. Intellectually, we may identify with the same or the other gender. However, we may also have an emotional feeling toward one gender or the other which may or may not coincide with our genital or erotic orientation. For instance, I, a woman, may be genitally aroused by men but still have a strong emotional attachment and/or intellectual comfort with women. I seek and value women's company and could spend much, if not all my time with them. However, I do not have an erotic pull toward them. Or I could be erotically oriented toward women but have a great emotional attachment and comfort with men. These feelings also could be true for men.

Whatever I determine about my sexual orientation or gender affinity, I need to think through its meaning in relation to others as well as for myself. For instance, if I am a straight person, what do I do when someone of the same gender shows an intimate interest in me? Handling same-sex advances depends on what I decide about my sexual orientation. If I decide I am heterosexual, I may have some learning to do about not being offended if others of my gender are attracted to me and tell me so. That is their prerogative. However, I have the right to say, "Thanks for the compliment, but I am not interested," just as I do with unwanted heterosexual attraction. I need to learn that my heterosexual orientation is not threatened by such approaches. I also need to understand that most gay men and lesbians are rarely attracted to straight people, and I need to avoid testing this through flirting with them or feeling offended by their lack of sexual response to me.

If I revise my identity, then many concerns about who I have been and the commitments I have made will arise. If I decide I am bisexual, I will have questions about how this change affects present commitments and whether my orientation is more toward heterosexuality or gay/lesbian sexuality. Again, the continuum shows arrows in the early transition, reaching toward the lesbian, gay, and bisexual journeys, as a time when some people decide the heterosexual journey is not for them.

Making a Decision to Learn

Entering the transition is uncomfortable and never occurs at a time that feels convenient. Issues of sexuality and gender which I have put off all my life now need to be addressed. I am flooded with questions. With whom do I talk? What is it I want to talk about? What do I do with feelings of terror that come over me? I will calm down when I **make a decision** that *I* have much **to learn**. The transition is a time of learning to be comfortable with myself in a new way and comfortable with the variety of sexualities I have screened out of my life. To decide I am a learner acknowledges that I have acted as if my truth were everyone's truth, when I didn't even know very much about myself.

My fears have kept me from asking questions and listening to those who are different from me. I have acted like a dominant because I have kept the illusion that I always know all there is to know and have nothing to learn. I may even be acting like a dominant if I hide my bisexuality from myself and/or others. Making a decision to learn means learning first of all about myself, about who I am *and* the impact of my behavior on others. I do this in part by becoming aware of the diversity of experiences of which I have previously been oblivious.

The decision that I have much to learn takes the attention off the gay, lesbian, or bisexual person if I am straight, and puts it on me. *I* need to learn.

Making this decision anchors me in the transition. The intensity of emotional discomfort that draws me into the transition keeps cycling me back into the fear and hostility of the orange section until I decide I have much to learn. My task becomes clearer, and I calm down as I accept what I need to do—learn about myself, *which includes understanding my effect on others*. It is not enough that my intentions are good. I must understand the impact of my behavior.

Language and Humor

One of the first things I must do in learning about myself is **examine my language and humor**. My vocabulary reflects my fears and discomforts. Are words such as *gender, sex, sexuality, homosexuality, heterosexuality, bisexuality, lesbian*, and *gay* uncomfortable to use? Learning to use these appropriately and comfortably takes time and practice. I need to become aware of parallel terms, such as *heterosexual, homosexual*, and *bisexual*; or *lesbian, gay, straight*, and *bi* or *bisexual*.

If I say *gay man*, then I may try to say *lesbian woman*. However, many lesbians consider the phrase *lesbian woman* redundant. Lesbians are women. In this case I just say lesbian. Some lesbians call themselves gay, some don't. I need to feel comfortable enough to ask how individual gay, lesbian, and bisexual people wish to refer to their sexual identity, and then I need to speak consistently with what has been requested. In this book we use the term *gay* or *gay man* to refer to a homoerotically-identified man and the term lesbian (without adding woman) to refer to a woman-identified woman. We do this to distinguish as clearly as possible the male and female experiences of homoerotic identity.

To say the word *lesbian* in a conversation with a lesbian usually feels like a put-down at first to a straight person. This is because *I* think it is a put-down. My assumption, that is, what I project onto the woman, is that it is bad and that therefore she will feel hurt by its use. These are my fears. I now assume lesbians are proud of their lesbianism. I have to learn to ask if a gay man, lesbian, or bisexual person is comfortable with my language and not to be affronted if different terms are requested. Those who come from any subordinance need to be listened to when they state how they wish to be addressed. It is important that I not be defensive or overapologetic if something different is asked for. I can't know how everyone wishes to be addressed. I do need to be comfortable asking.

Use of the word *them* is particularly offensive to bisexual, lesbian, and gay people. In oblivious heterosexism I am afraid to use words referring to sexual orientation. Here, a euphemism for gay, lesbian and bisexual people is *them*. In the orange section my discomfort with homosexuality stopped me from saying directly what I meant, keeping a veil of ambiguity in my conversation. Using *them* supports ambiguity so that I can later hedge or deny what I said or meant.

I now use the words *they* and *them* after I have directly referred to whom I am talking about. For example, I might say, "My *bisexual, gay*, and *lesbian friends* have added immeasurably to my self-awareness as a heterosexual woman. *They* are to be commended for their patience in my learning. I share with *them* the concerns of cultural heterosexism."

Phrases used out of the blue, such as, "You know what *they* are like," with a nonverbal expression of disgust, carry assumed references as to who "they" are. The reference is implied, fostering a shared bond between heterosexual people that excludes and denigrates bisexual people, lesbian, and gay people.

The words *heterosexism*, *homophobia*, and *biphobia* need to be understood and used appropriately. I am learning not to be defensive when someone tells me that something I have done is homophobic. The emotional load I carry about my actions being named in such a way needs to be looked at. Can I hear this as information to be thought about and learned from, rather than responded to out of my guilt in such an emotional way that I am seen as defensive?

Another typical issue of language is to complain about things which are trivial (to me), such as *gay* being taken away from the English language so it can no longer be safely used to describe joyfulness. All language is constantly evolving. Change in usage often reflects those slang and code words used to substitute for things we are afraid to say forthrightly. It doesn't do much good to be angry about "good words taken away from us." Besides, I can still choose to have *gay* mean merry at times and expect others to accept this meaning.

Those who carry any subordinance have said much in recent years about dominants' use of humor. One group after another has called attention to the politics of humor, the messages that put-downs carry. I, when I am the dominant, usually find how dependent I am on humor—that is, jokes and snide and offhand remarks—for maintaining dominance. As my self-awareness of homophobic reactions increases, I begin to see how I have learned to cover up *my* discomfort about homosexuality and bisexuality with such quick reactions as changing the conversation, leaving the room, avoiding people and situations, *and* with remarks that humorously discount lesbians, bisexual people, and gay men. Such joking creates a hostile climate for them while calling attention to how smart I am. I relieve my discomfort at the cost of another's comfort. Now I need to become aware of why I am uncomfortable and deal with it as my problem. If offhand remarks and jokes using words such as *fag*, *faggot*, *fairy*, *dyke*, *limp wrist*, and *effeminate* make others uncomfortable, what is my stake in using them?

Fears and Resistance

How I react when a lesbian, gay, or bisexual person asks me to change my language tells much about my resistance. Dominants use such resistance as a cover for needing to control the ways lesbian, gay, and bisexual people are defined and regarded. I have probably often stated, or thought, that my language is alright because I didn't intend it to offend. Dominants as a group excuse themselves from changing their behavior or language by saying no offense was *intended*. Now this can no longer be an excuse. If my language is offensive, I need to acknowledge it and be responsible for the *impact* of what I say. Looking at my language tells much about my fears. It is often the first place my resistance to change shows up. Language is a good place to begin **exploring both my fears and my resistance** to bisexuality and homosexuality.

In the orange section, straight men as a group fear and resist both gay men and lesbians. However, fear is a more common reaction to gay men and resistance a more common reaction to lesbians. Briefly, fear of gay and bisexual men involves issues of same-sex intimacy; resistance to lesbians involves male response to women acting outside of male control.

Boys are taught to shun close physical contact with other boys unless it has the brusqueness of athletic exuberance. Straight men learn that any behavior that even hints of intimacy with another man is to be avoided. Gay men are feared in part because they represent a wider *range* of acceptable masculine expression than one is comfortable openly acknowledging. This is true in many cultures. Most men, while growing up, knew that too close a friendship with another boy or walking a certain way was punished by fights, exclusion, and name-calling. Now straight men are being asked to look at how such painful encounters affected them. Were parts of themselves buried and hidden?

Looking back to men's same-sex incidents in childhood often means bringing up memories of **violent childhood experiences**.* Straight men need to deal with such experiences in order to listen to gay men and lesbians without bias and hear what they are saying. These experiences likely involved being violated by a trusted adult of the same sex or participating in a group experience that hurt someone, whether yourself or another. Much resistance by straight men to dealing with male homosexuality is buried in confusing, violent memories. Such experiences are often understood to have been incidents of homosexual violation, although most experiences between an adult and a young child should be seen as pedophilia and incest. Pedophiles live almost exclusively as male adult heterosexuals with a primary erotic obsession with children. Pedophilia with a boy should not be confused with an expression of homosexuality. Seduction of young girls is often named more correctly in this culture as rape or incest. Pedophilia involves sexual dysfunction which is enacted through sexual abuse of a child, male or female.

It is not fear so much as resistance that arises in straight men when dealing with lesbians. Straight men in the orange section are uncomfortable in the presence of lesbians because lesbians do not accept the male control over them that straight women often allow. Because of sexism, heterosexual women, particularly white middle-class heterosexual women, grow up learning that dominant men can be controlled by deference. Heterosexual men's and women's strong desire to be liked by the other gender encourages these women to do much caretaking and

---

*For women, childhood sexual abuse is more likely heterosexual, though not always.

protecting of men and their emotions. Women who do this as an automatic reaction also use it as a way to control men. It prevents men from dealing with the consequences of their actions. Straight men learn to rely on this affirmation (often unwarranted) and feel women who do not do this are hostile and unwomanly. A straight man learns he can manipulate a woman who gives unwarranted affection when he is angry, feels hurt, or is emotionally distant with her.

White cultural heterosexual norms for typical ways men and women interact set the standard for how lesbians, gay men, and bisexual people are heard and perceived. Lesbians are often felt by straight men to be more hostile, angry, and aggressive than straight women because lesbians tend to be more direct, do not offer men unconditional emotional support, and therefore can't be controlled in the same ways. Lesbians cause straight men to look in more profound ways at their cultural need to dominate women. Politically, lesbians are often out front in addressing sexism, because they are less dependent on men emotionally, physically, and financially.

Heterosexist men view lesbians as a challenge sexually and politically. The often-heard degrading phrase "she just needs a good lay" is a challenge that a "good" rape would cure her and, of course, keep her under male control. Men who find it hard to listen to straight women find it even harder to hear lesbians. For example, a man's wrath can be tapped at a deeper level if he finds his wife coming out as lesbian than if she leaves him for another man, because he assumes men have access, and a right, to control women that another woman does not have. His maleness is challenged.

We need, also, to distinguish the fears of straight women from their resistance. Our fears of homosexuality most likely are tapped when we realize another woman is attracted to us or when a family member suddenly comes out. Our resistance is aroused when we are asked to be inclusive of bisexual, gay, and lesbian people and/or supportive of lesbian, gay, and bisexual causes. We are generally less fearful of gay men than lesbians. Our fears of same-sex sexuality cause us to avoid lesbian friendships. The thought of being intimate with another woman or being included in a group of lesbian couples can be distressing. This emotional reaction comes from our assumption that all lesbians are attracted to all women and expect to have constant intimate relationships—the prowler image. Coming out of the orange section, I assume I will be pressured to be one of "them." We do not remember at these moments that our heterosexual orientation does not mean we are attracted to all men and want intimacy with every man we meet. In fact, we probably avoid men to whom we are attracted at least as often as we get up the courage to speak with them.

My resistance and some terror arise with lesbians' directness on women's issues. I want to go more slowly, in other words, be more protective of men. Going slowly usually means addressing straight women's issues first if I am a white woman and people-of-color issues first if I am a person of color, because they seem less threatening and more important than issues of sexual orientation. Besides, if I am too friendly to lesbian concerns, I will be expected to support them publicly. This brings out guilt-by-association fears. I say, "If we could just solve straight women's issues or issues of race first, then we will support lesbian issues. If we take on lesbian issues now, all will be lost." Of course, such separation puts all issues of subordinance in competition with each other.

Women's issues include the fact that male-dominated culture makes rules for how *all* women are supposed to be, that is, whether women can be assertive, have choices, exert control over their bodies, feel comfortable with their body weight, control where they go and what they do, *and* live outside the sexual domination of men, including being lesbian.

Straight women want the subject of sexual domination by men to be talked about in a positive manner. We want the focus of male/female sexuality to be on how we can be trusting, intimate, and loving. We do not want the subject to be directly male sexual domination, because we fear hurting men's egos and feelings. Lesbians are more willing to name the issue without fencing: men's need to retain sexual domination over women. Straight women want limits on the issues. Our need for excessive approval from men, coming from our socialization as subordinate to men,[11] is mixed with our heterosexual orientation. We want to be liked by men as a group generally as well as by special men. We want to deal with homosexuality and bisexuality in as indirect a manner as possible so that *we* can be as comfortable as possible during any discussion.

Gay men may raise women's resistance because they are unavailable—"a good man wasted." Anger rather than fear is tapped. In people-of-color communities, such as those of African heritage, where a high proportion of the men are in prison, die in drug wars, join the military, or perhaps are involved in interracial relationships, gay men of color can raise straight women of color's anger as another group of unavailable men.

A white woman who is attracted to a gay man can be just as displeased by his lack of response. As a straight woman in white culture, I can't control gay men the way I learned to control white heterosexual men. They don't respond as much to my manipulative behavior.

On the other hand, gay men and straight women are often close friends. Initially I may or may not be sexually attracted to a gay man, but if his gayness is acknowledged and I am accepting, a friendship can develop that does not have the tensions of sexual attraction. This can be a relief from heterosexual male/female friendships, where such tensions go unstated and get in the way of friendship and working relationships.

A fear of gay or bisexual men occurs when a straight woman finds that the gay man is someone close, such as her son or husband. If it is a woman's husband who reveals he is bisexual or gay, the woman often experiences strong feelings of rejection and anger. "How could he do this to me and want to be 'that way'!" The intense work of coming to accept his new identity is long and painful. Though she feels betrayed after what has been lived together, she may also have wondered at

141

times about their relationship. He may not have always responded as she had wished, which caused her confusion. She will need to find support from others for dealing with these changes. She cannot expect to have the support from her spouse that she would like. He is busy dealing with his new identity. (This is also true for a straight man whose wife "suddenly" identifies as lesbian or bisexual.) It is hard to let go of the relationship because she hasn't changed and he has. She still loves him. It is an emotionally unilateral situation, similar to a marriage of straight partners when the husband leaves his wife or the wife leaves her husband.

There may be more women who marry as straight and then re-identify as lesbian or bisexual than gay men who first marry as straight. Women's desire for children and their learned dependency on men (a characteristic of many cultures) encourage heterosexual marriage. However, many gay and bisexual men may also marry because they desire children or the "safety" of heterosexually identified life.[12]

When a husband reveals to his wife that he is gay or bisexual, the wife is apt to experience a release of antigay emotions, pushing her back into the orange section, even if she had been well into the transition on this continuum in relation to others. Today's AIDS-related fears may exacerbate this negative reaction. She feels a breach of trust; she is angry at him for not knowing his own identity and for having duped her into a marriage he now may want to leave. She may question her own sexuality, asking such questions as, "Why was I attracted to someone who is gay?" and "Am I a lesbian because I was attracted to a man who turned out to be homosexual? What does this say about me?" These feelings are also true for a husband who finds that his wife identifies as lesbian or bisexual. He may act out by trying to get custody of children when his wife reveals her lesbianism, before, during, or after the divorce.

The straight spouse of the newly identified lesbian or gay man is almost always without support. The lesbian, gay man, or bisexual person has often, though not always, begun a relationship with another partner or found a lesbian, gay, or bisexual community. However, the straight spouse is left alone. Often that spouse's first reaction is, "There is no way I am going to talk about this with anyone else." The secrecy and shame of that person's situation and the anger it arouses combine to cause intense aloneness just when finding support is important.

Jean Gochros speaks to the difficulty straight spouses have in finding such support.[13] She introduces her chapter in *Homophobia: How We All Pay the Price* with several quotes.

My husband's coming out of his closet. Now I'm the one who's in it!

My in-laws are ashamed of him and won't speak to me. They say I caused his homosexuality. I not only lost my husband, I lost my whole close family.[14]

She later says:

> Prior to disclosure, [homophobia] may create guilt and fear, damaging straight partners' self-esteem as they helplessly try to grapple with undefined problems. Following disclosure, it stigmatizes straight partners, creating self-doubt and guilt, loss of self-identity and self-trust. Whether because of anticipated or actual homophobic and sexist reactions from others, straight partners become isolated, forced into a closet within a closet. They become increasingly confused and depressed and either have no access to or are afraid to join a support system.[15]

The spouse needs support on two levels: he or she must deal not only with his or her own homophobia or biphobia but with the change or loss of the marriage relationship. A straight spouse may also be co-parenting children who are adjusting to a parent's gay or lesbian identity becoming known. He or she may have to do this while still feeling uncomfortable, hurt, and angry about the situation.

One final word about fears and resistance is important. Where children are concerned, a mother's or father's worst fears and resistance take over. Having a son or daughter who comes out feels to many parents like a personal violation. Talking with other parents of lesbians, gay males, and bisexual people helps one to face guilt and fears. As a parent, I cannot control my son's or daughter's sexual orientation. I can only control whether she or he is able to tell me about it.

Growing Comfortable with Homosexuality and Bisexuality

Comfort grows as I learn to **talk with and ask questions of lesbians, gay men, and bisexual people** about themselves. Getting over the fear of asking questions is an important step. Those who have been culturally dominant always need to do much listening and asking questions rather than telling. My projections onto bisexual, gay, and lesbian people, for example my assumption that I know how they feel, need to be checked out. As I begin to ask questions and listen more, I may find that I ask the same questions many times and do not act on or incorporate what I hear into my conversations. One would think either I didn't believe the person or I am too dense to understand. Actually, this is more a sign of puzzlement and struggle to align what I hear with what I already know. A change in perception is being asked of me. As I become aware of this, I need to acknowledge to the gay, lesbian, or bisexual person that I have heard him or her say this before but that it is taking awhile to penetrate my old habits of thinking. My resistance shows up as not remembering, reinterpreting, or simplifying what is said.

I personally found this true as I was enlarging my understanding of the range of sexual orientation. As I moved into the transition, I listened to friends who said they had always felt gay or lesbian from earliest childhood. In my eagerness to say the right thing, I viewed homosexuality as inherent, even though some people talked about it more developmentally. I assumed this just meant homosexual orientation took some people a long time to know. Sooner or later everyone would admit that they knew all along they were homosexual or bisexual.

Actually, I now find there seem to be as many ways to come to accept one's homosexuality or bisexuality as there are people who go through this transition. Some may feel that they knew all along but had not admitted their orientation to themselves; others may feel that their homosexual orientation is not obvious in hindsight. And there may be any number of variations between these positions. The important thing for me is that I realize how easily I make assumptions that define for others how they experience themselves. Everyone needs to be free to decide for themselves, without interference, such personal things as what their sexual orientation is and how it became clear. I am acting dominant as long as I assume how individual homosexual and bisexual people, as well as heterosexuals, know their sexual orientation.

Earlier on the continuum, while I was still an oblivious heterosexual, I thought I had made great progress by agreeing that there were two sexual orientations, heterosexual *and* homosexual. If someone referred to her or himself as bisexual, I knew intellectually what that meant. Yet when I talked about homosexuality and heterosexuality, I never included bisexuality in my references. Sexual orientation meant to me either inherent homosexuality or heterosexuality. I didn't want to expend energy dealing with subtlety or complexity. Of course attention to complexity is how I show that I understand the range of lesbian, gay, bisexual, and heterosexual experiences and that I am beginning to behave in ways consistent with my beliefs. I now hear more variety and try to express this understanding of sexual orientation and identity.

My first conversations in which I tried to be open were often awkward and reflected my need to stay in control and be protective of myself and others I see as persecuted. When I was feeling inadequate, confused, and embarrassed talking about homosexuality, I covered it up by being nice and by projecting onto the lesbian, gay, or bisexual person that she or he was inadequate, confused, and embarrassed. At this point on the continuum, I have not had much experience knowing gay, lesbian, or bisexual people who are comfortable with and loving toward themselves. My homophobic behavior has been too obvious for many bisexual people, lesbians, or gay men to be out in my presence. African-American culture is often more tolerant. Being in the life usually isn't talked about, even though family and friends may know and will keep the lesbian, gay man, or bisexual person within family and social circles.

When someone has shared that she or he is lesbian or gay, an often-heard response is, "Yes, I know that ten percent of the population is homosexual"—an intellectual conversation stopper. Or a straight woman may say to a gay man, "Wonderful, I find that the most exciting men are gay!" It is unclear what value this statement holds for a gay man; it is also not necessarily true. However, it is a remark typical for some straight women who are just beginning to move into the transition who want to show they think gay men are okay. Of course it is also a protective statement that assumes the gay man has problems and needs to be told how wonderful he is—better even than a straight man. The woman is trying to build up the gay man's ego, as she is used to doing for straight men. She assumes that he "probably doesn't like himself"—a projection and put-down. Both these comments imply hope that sharing facts or opinions about homosexuality will facilitate conversation. Of course, both take the attention away from the gay, lesbian, or bisexual person and put it on the heterosexual person as smart. The straight person stays in control, rather than allowing the bisexual person, gay man, or lesbian to say more about himself or herself. A better response might be, "Thank you for telling me that," and then waiting to see if the other person has more to say; or one might ask what it is like to be bisexual, gay, or lesbian in the office, family, social group, or whatever situation one is in.

I know my comfort with the diversity of orientation and identities is growing when

— I am interested in her or his coming out stories without making judgments;
— I am as sympathetic to bisexual, lesbian, and gay people having problems in relationships as I am to heterosexual people;
— I talk with him or her about as many subjects as I do with heterosexual friends, without always assuming sexuality will be the center of the conversation.

My open attitude with gay, lesbian, and bisexual people promotes a climate of self-acceptance for homosexuality and bisexuality. If I am still holding back feelings toward my own orientation, moving toward a lesbian, gay, or bisexual identity may be less traumatic at this point on the continuum. Whether I move to an early part of the gay male, lesbian, or bisexual journey or shift to a place more parallel to the one I am leaving on the heterosexual journey in the transition, such as to the bisexual journey, depends on where those close to me are. If they have joined me on the heterosexual journey this far, my new identification will be less jarring than if I have been alone. However, the impact of identifying a change in one's sexual identity is always there, and others will react to the news from a variety of places on this continuum.

Continuing on the heterosexual journey, I am tempted to assume that my learning will come from lesbians, bisexual, and gay people. It is important to find other heterosexual and heterosexually oriented bisexual friends with whom to do much of my learning. I am not just learning about homosexuality and bisexuality, but about heterosexuality, especially my own. I come from oblivious heterosexism. Until I understand what it means to be heterosexual, I cannot parallel homosexual and bisexual people in conversations about sexual orientation, that is, we cannot affect each other or share similar or differing experiences. When someone describes being homosexual or bisexual, can I describe being heterosexual in terms other than being normal?

I also need other heterosexual people to talk with about my fears, clumsiness, and guilt for past experiences and behavior as well as our shared heterosexuality.

To expect lesbians, gay men, and bisexual people to hear my stories of homophobia and biphobia puts a grave burden on those who have carried the weight of my (and others') hostility and discounting. Expecting them now to take care of me when they are the ones who have suffered through my insensitivity is too much to ask. It is with those who identify as heterosexual that I need to share my frustrations with my behavior and personal learning. Gay men, lesbian, and bisexual people prefer to learn that I am no longer homophobic by my actions and language, not by long stories that ask for sympathy for who I have been and what I have done. Only in a close friendship, where the need to share my prior actions has been welcomed, is such sharing appropriate.

What I might do is acknowledge what I have done and ask if my bisexual, gay, or lesbian friend needs to say anything to me. I would like to know if I in any way still discount her or his presence, distort the meaning of her or his actions, lack inclusiveness, or speak disparagingly of her or him. I do not want to do this any more, though I must not place my lesbian, gay, and bisexual friends in the role of being responsible for correcting or changing my behavior. That is my responsibility.

Expanding the Meaning of Maleness and Femaleness

Expanding the meaning of maleness and femaleness is a major theme of the transition. The heterosexual dominance of society, which serves to reinforce and support male dominance and female subordination, creates unnatural boundaries between women and between men. Culturally cultivated homophobic and biphobic fears have helped reinforce hard boundaries for what is appropriately male and female. One fear apparently is that masculinity will be lost and everyone will become homosexual. A related fear is that men will become feminine, depending on the culture. For example, the fear within Mexican culture is not that men might be gay—bisexuality can be accommodated within masculinity. The fear is that men will become feminine.[16] These fears for men underlie both men's and women's thoughts and actions in the transition.

Traditional Western sex roles firmly lock masculinity and femininity into separate spheres. Masculine and feminine are considered hierarchically ordered polar opposites. When we move away from this polarity to thinking in terms of partnership and collegiality, feminine and masculine are considered complementary, but also as existing within both men and women. When we move to valuing a diversity of sexualities, we are apt to think that the masculine and feminine become blurred because our comfort is based on limited definitions. Definitions with clear lines separating masculine from feminine focus our attention away from diversity and self-definition and the variety of human experience. The transition asks that we become comfortable with more ambiguity about boundaries of female and male, femininity and masculinity.

Cornel West speaks of the problem of self-image for black men:

The prevailing cultural crisis of many black men is the limited stylistic options of self-image and resistance in a culture obsessed with sex yet fearful of black sexuality.

> This situation is even bleaker for most black gay men who reject the major stylistic option of black machismo identity, yet who are marginalized in white America and penalized in black America for doing so. In their efforts to be themselves, they are told they are not really "black men," not machismo-identified. Black gay men are often the brunt of talented black comics. . . . Yet behind the laughs lurks a black tragedy of major proportions: the refusal of white and black America to entertain seriously new stylistic options for black men caught in the deadly endeavor of rejecting black machismo identities.[17]

The issues we must address on this journey are not limited to a masculine/feminine frame of reference, however. *Much of the hard work of boundary setting for men and women comes between men and between women.* Men, historically dominant, have many ways of sanctioning each other for breaking the code of traditional Western masculinity. Masculinity has meant identifying with strength and power, avoiding anything seemingly feminine, and being in control of women and other men who break the code of masculinity. White women's subordination is enforced by separating them from each other and fostering competition between them for the approval and attention of men. They have to work hard to know themselves, trust each other, and rethink the assigned and assumed boundaries between them. In contrast, women of color often maintain closer relationships with each other within their culture than white women do within the individualism of white culture. However, black women often carry the obligation to teach black boys to be tough, that is, manly; such toughness is needed by most black men for survival. Girls are taught to be autonomous but still are presumed to have relationships with men. In Asian cultures where tradition assumes women will marry between the ages of eighteen and twenty-five, mothers focus their daughters on preparing for the event all during childhood. These examples of typical ways for women to act in different cultures may change as racism and sexism lessen. What we have yet to examine is the unspoken cultural assumption that all this behavior is intended to insure that only heterosexual liaisons are made.

The question straight men and women must answer is, "How have I been affected by my acceptance of gender boundaries?" It is easy for heterosexist men and women to collude to keep unnecessary limits on masculinity and femininity when a range of relationships between women and between men is not valued. The merging of compulsory heterosexuality with a history of sexist limitations on women and men limits the range of relationships all women and men have with each other. Lesbians, bisexual people, and gay men in particular seem to us outside the scope of acceptable friendships.

When heterosexual relationships are viewed as central, it is easy to give diminished attention to same-sex relationships, except for a few special ones.

When I discount giving time and attention to those in general cultural groupings similar to myself, I discount myself.

In *Living in the Light*, Shakti Gawain and Laurel King state,

> For some people, being in a close, intense relationship with a person or persons of the same sex is the most powerful mirroring process they can find. Two women, for example, often seem to find a depth of connection with each other that they don't find with a man. . . . They totally reflect and support each other in becoming whole and balanced.
>
> A man sometimes seems to find a matching male intensity with another man—an ability to go all out that he wouldn't find with a woman.[18]

Men's fear of close same-sex relationships comes from their heterosexist learning that intimacy, sensuousness, and sexuality are feminine attributes. These traits are particularly frightening when found in men. A man who expects to find these only in or from women is often confused or terrified when another man has any or all of these attributes. Maleness is limited by such fears. In order to expand the meaning of maleness and femaleness, straight heterosexist men need to be able to separate intimacy, sensuality, and sexuality so that their fears do not cause them to project onto others more than what is meant. If they do this work first with heterosexual women, they will be helped to do the work of this transition, which is not to project their sexual fears onto gay men or assume unwanted sexual intimacy with lesbians. Straight people, both male and female, need to learn to be comfortable with intimacy with the same as well as the other sex, *without assuming sexuality*. We need to be able to feel and observe sensuality in others *without assuming seductive intent*. Latin and African-American cultures give men and women more freedom to be seductive without sexual intent than do Anglo, Asian, or Middle Eastern cultures. The fun of being seductive must always focus on the other gender in a heterosexist environment.

Our fears of same-sex sexuality are likely based on our experiences of heterosexual advances, as well as our imagined, *not necessarily real*, experiences of advances from gay men, lesbians, and bisexual people. Heterosexist women are uncomfortable with women making advances because traditionally that is something only men should do. When in the orange section of this continuum, another reason we may be embarrassed by a woman's advances is that we are used to feeling protected and a bit helpless in "advance" situations. It doesn't seem right to feel this way with another woman.

As a straight woman, I have learned to defer to a man approaching me. I assume that this is necessary where sexual attraction is to be acknowledged. Similarly, straight men are uncomfortable when men act in ways prescribed for women. For instance, women have carried the responsibility for saying yes or no to sexual advances. Things feel out of control when one man approaches another and the one approached has not learned to handle this situation.

When boundaries for what is acceptable in maleness and femaleness are changed or are more fluid, homophobic and biphobic fears are apt to be raised for both straight men and straight women for some time as we move into the transition. We too easily go back to our unfounded fears of the orange section where we inappropriately imagine that gay men, lesbians, and bisexual people are ready to make sexual overtures.

Compulsory heterosexists see gay men, lesbians, and bisexual people as the sum of what they do in bed, not as people or a group of people who have a variety of ways of experiencing life which adds new dimensions to maleness and femaleness. Bisexual people, gay men, and lesbians become "not male" and "not female" when the expressions of maleness and femaleness are strictly confined. Bisexual people's comfort with attraction to both genders particularly challenges straight people's requirement that the other sex is a love *object*. Bisexual people live with a fluidity of roles that is outside our experience as straight people. This fluidity often erases artificial boundaries between the genders which support objectifying the other sex as a love object. Maleness and femaleness must no longer be defined through someone else being the "other," that is, what we should not be. Our need for strict boundaries for femaleness and maleness has for too long supported us in using gay men and lesbians to show the limits of these definitions. Concepts of gender should not be based on negative notions of what we should not be, but on a refreshing excitement for who we are in our diversity. The pressure to examine issues of gender continues to build.

A Midtransition Check

It is helpful to do a midtransition check. In this transition I am simultaneously doing many things:

— taking the initiative to conquer my fear of homosexuality by thoughtfully looking at where my aversion comes from—perhaps from my religion, parents' cautioning remarks, attitudes of friends, frightening childhood experiences, and the pressure of a peer group's hostile bantering;
— seeking out contact with gay men, lesbians, and bisexual people with whom I have been uncomfortable for conversation on any subject, particularly where I might have the opportunity to learn something from them (something as innocuous as where a good restaurant is or how something works). I begin to perceive them as present in the environment;
— becoming more aware of my development as a straight male or female, and understanding that that is a specific form of human development;
— deciding I will be open to the idea that I have much to learn about being heterosexual from interacting with those of my gender; and
— becoming comfortable with the idea of bisexuality, which means acknowledging biphobia as I begin to understand the diversity of human sexuality.

Other things I need to pay attention to are how competition plays out in same-sex relationships; whether I appreciate differences in relationships as much as commonalities; how and what I have to learn from bisexual people, gay men, and lesbians and their relationships; how I can be more sensitive to and inclusive of sexual diversity; and how I handle myself publicly on the issues of homosexuality and bisexuality. Am I comfortable in the company of gay men, lesbians, and bisexual people? Am I trustworthy? Will I keep their confidences? Am I overreacting in my eagerness to do it "right" by boldly entering lesbian, bisexual, and gay activities and communities without sensitivity to the fact that I am joining their culture, *not* bringing mine?

There will be a time during the transition when I feel resistant to dealing with these issues. This resistance is tied to the pain of acknowledging my past actions. The farther I go on my journey, the more painful it can be to live with who I was. Somehow we must each make our own peace with the guilt of our past so that it does not prevent us from moving along our journeys.

Same-Gender Straight Relationships

In order to expand the meaning of maleness and femaleness, we need to **relook at same-gender relationships**, particularly male and heterosexual ones. The male journey[19] to self-understanding needs to be taken in the presence of other men and the female journey in the presence of other women. Leading up to making a decision to learn in the transition or perhaps here in midtransition, men who have always felt at odds with cultural definitions of maleness may want to learn more about the gay male journey. This means reading, watching movies, and listening to gay men talk about themselves. For most, this will only confirm their heterosexuality and bring personal comfort for who they are.

Because of men's experiences in the orange section, the journey in the transition is about grief—grief for the lost parts of themselves covered up and denied by the fear of violence or the experience of it. Heterosexist men confined together produce fears of violence in each other. In the early orange section, control is exerted through physical strength by deciding who will be brutalized. The most frequent victims are men who occupy the margins of acceptable maleness: men who are "too gentle," "too colorful," "too graceful." Heterosexist men's ritualized places, such as the military, prisons, hunting camps, and truck stops, have always supported this sort of control. In the late orange section of the continuum, men who have physical strength or the power to buy it, assume dominance and control over violent men in the early orange section. They take responsibility for restraining brutality in institutions where they have a stake, such as in business, and political, religious, and educational institutions. Nonetheless, heterosexual men's continuing fear of allying with gay men is in part the fear of being beaten up for showing aspects of their self that don't fit traditional maleness.

It is not just physical violence that is feared and experienced. Men in the orange section do not exhibit colleagueship or shared power when dealing with each other. When mutual empowerment is never considered, psychic violence is done, burying much of a person's humanness. In the transition grief for what is undeveloped and/or lost because of such brutalization supports recovery.

An equal fear for straight men can be gentleness that seemingly violates the hard boundary between men. Gentleness and close connections are associated with gay men, which means being non-male. To feel connected and to talk about a relationship means letting go of control over boundaries and being a quiet, empathetic listener. A real fear of many straight men is that having such a conversation with another man, particularly a gay man, might reveal things about the straight man that he has hidden or buried, which means feeling out of control and hence effeminate.

Traditionally, straight men are allowed or expected (often reluctantly) to talk about relationships only with women, especially a spouse or lover. Since women carry the responsibility for initiating the conversation, talking about relationships is associated with women, intimacy, and therefore, with being sexual. *Maleness has meant expecting to talk with special women about having shared, close relationships and never to talk with men about having such a relationship*. Where this is true, the result is emotional dependency on women. A more self-sufficient emotional life allows more satisfying relationships with men and hence an affirmation of maleness that is not dependent on emotional distance from other men.

Expanding the meaning of maleness and femaleness does not refer just to straight/gay, lesbian, or bisexual relationships. One of the characteristics of dominance and subordinance is that *subordinants never feel safe until dominants look at the relationships between them*. Straight men need to look at their relationships with each other. As long as they have a hierarchy based on "masculinity," men who "appear" gay will always be at the bottom of the hierarchy and lesbians will represent a challenge to "acceptable femininity."

If straight men want to develop relationships with gay men, they have to be aware of how pecking-order issues make it unsafe for gay men to take risks. The same is true for straight women. Gay men and lesbians are aware of how straight men and women relate. What they observe determines the risks they will take in the presence of straight men.

Straight women who have not dealt with their gender issues with men keep lesbians and gay men at risk by giving automatic deference to dominant, straight men. They collude with straight men to stay dominant by carrying high approval needs from them and, at best, are oblivious to heterosexism.

Learning from same gender non-sexual straight relationships then, means straight men look at their relationships, and straight women look at theirs. A collegial approach and the valuing of diversity are basic ingredients to the quality of these relationships. Questions straight men and women need to ask of these relationships are:

— How much or how little is one-upmanship a part of the relationship? Is competition a constant undercurrent?

— Do we learn from and value each other's ideas and resources?

— Is the relationship one where we feel free to share our feelings and live the emotions that are created?

These same questions apply to the relationships between straight women and men. Lesbians and those gay and bisexual men who have some insight into male/female issues are aware of the gender dynamics in straight male/female relationships. Men and women who collude to keep gender dominance and subordinance alive in their relationships will exclude, or at best tolerate, lesbian, gay, and bisexual people.

Competition and Valuing Differences

Competition can be healthy or unhealthy. We have little awareness of how it affects us because it is so much a part of us. The competitive norms of white, dominant culture, based on heavy individualism and expansionist desires which all cultures are caught up in, need to be understood in the context of heterosexism. A tennis match is a form of competition based on skill; winning and losing is clear. The competition inherent in acting dominant and subordinant, however, is emotionally destructive to both. This competition invades our life in ways we do not recognize. Dominants act as if they have already won. Subordinants are supposed to act as if they have already lost. Until we question these roles, we are unaware of participating in a culture where the norm is to feel competitive.

One way competition gets played out in heterosexist society is that heterosexual people feel they are better than bisexual people, lesbians, and gay men— more righteous. Heterosexual people act as if they have already won. The questions we must ask ourselves are, Can I allow people to be different? What is my stake in having everyone be like me? How am I threatened by difference? Do I have a need to feel superior or "normal" compared to those declared "lesser"? The transition is a time to look inward and answer these questions for ourselves. It is only when I feel noncompetitive that I can value diversity. This means finding common interests around which to bond and feel inclusive of others.

Dominants make their views and experiences of race, culture, gender, and sexual orientation exclusive, competitive categories. Those who act dominant in any of these categories lack experience in feeling inclusive in that category. For instance, could we bond as a group of parents belonging to different genders, cultures, races, and sexual orientations? Would our status as parents hold us together while we explored the different experiences we share because of race, culture, gender, *and* sexual orientation?

We are asked in the transition to give up the values of heterosexist culture, which devalues differences. The need to be competitive and exclusive, that is, to feel superior to homosexual and bisexual people, must be eliminated if heterosexist bonding is to give way to valuing the contributions and diversity that lesbians, gay men, and bisexual people bring to friendships and work groups.

Learning from Gay Men, Lesbians, and Bisexual People

Straight women and men have much to **learn from lesbians, gay men, and bisexual people**. This learning will happen as we become comfortable with expanding the boundaries of maleness and femaleness.

One area in which straight women have difficulty learning from lesbians is women's issues. White feminism is recovering from excluding two major groups of women—lesbians and women of color. As a straight feminist I assume that because I am heterosexual, I know more about men than lesbians do. In some ways this is true, but I can also lack insight because I am so close to specific men as well as to men in general, that I am apt to be protective.

When I do not seek lesbians to work with on women's issues, I am missing a viewpoint and vital support. Notice I did not say, "when I do not let lesbians work with me." I need to be aware that there are times when I think I am cooperating but my language and behavior say something else; for example, my expectation that lesbians will join with me in what I have defined as "the work." We need a mutual feeling of joining together. I need to build relationships with lesbians so that *I* can be trusted to work on women's issues with them. I need lesbian theory, cultural perspectives, and worldview to enlarge my vision of women's issues as well as other societal concerns.

Heterosexist women perceive lesbians as outside the system and therefore inadequate to deal with it. We must remember that the experience of subordinance is to perceive and know things dominants don't, because subordinance creates and permits insights into dominant behavior of which dominants are unaware. Lesbians have a cultural view and theoretical frame of reference that comes out of their own experience. I have much to learn from lesbians about feminist theory and women's issues *because of my lack of insight as a heterosexual dominant.*

If I am a white straight woman, I need to be aware of how my unacknowledged racism supports listening only to white lesbians, thereby supporting racism in the lesbian community. As stated earlier, lesbians sometimes say things to men more clearly than I do because of my heterosexual need to be liked by men in general and/or to be protective of them. Women of color often speak with more directness than white women. We may fear that lesbians of color will say things too clearly and hence threaten our ways of controlling and manipulating straight white men. Working with lesbians forces us to face unacknowledged and often painful aspects of our relationships with straight men.[20] Straight women cannot afford to compete with lesbians about who will control the work in society that deals with sexism. We must work together. All insights are needed.

Lesbians also push us to understand our own orientation. As our distasteful emotional biases toward homosexuality and bisexuality are dispelled, choice suddenly looms up. We are forced to consider our own orientation and the reasons we identify with heterosexuality. We are faced with the question of our sexual identity: "Who am *I*?"

What I, a heterosexual woman, have to learn from some gay men, particularly those well into the transition, is comfort with a broader range of male expression. I often say to straight men that I would like them to be more expressive and in touch with their emotions. Gay men often test my real feelings about this topic. Unconsciously I may feel a gay man does not measure up to the old standards of maleness to which I still obviously cling. He may not "let me" be a little helpless and manipulative, or I may still require some machoness for a man to be masculine. I may find I talk a good line but am not entirely comfortable with men who enjoy my company without responding to or putting up with my feminine manipulation. I may have much to learn about close friendships with males which do not include playing sexual games.

Straight men would do well to ask the question "What do I have to learn from lesbians and gay men?" People or groups whom we intensely dislike often represent something we avoid in ourselves. Straight men can learn from lesbians to not always expect women to take care of them emotionally and through homemaking support. White straight women's need for approval and their reliance on empowerment from straight men interfere with being direct on this issue with men. Straight men can learn from lesbians to deal directly with women without relying on heterosexual seduction. Comfort with friendships with all women is increased and widened in scope when directness is facilitated in interactions.

In the transition, the presence of lesbians and gay men who are out and comfortable with themselves give straight people (particularly men) permission and safety to deal with a wide range of physically or sexually abusive childhood experiences. Experiences with pedophiles and/or incestuous relationships can no longer be forgotten. What is buried starts to emerge, sometimes in images, dreams, and forgotten relationships. Finding a way to understand what happened and to deal with the feelings of terror and violated trust is crucial. Gay men and lesbians who have dealt with their violent experiences can often lend straight men and women support and understanding for what happened. Some straight men and women report that it is easier to discuss same-sex and other kinds of abuse with gay male and lesbian friends because they are less likely to greet such disclosures with disbelief or denial and more likely to respond empathetically to the hurt and the healing needed to feel good about oneself physically and sexually after abuse. Such empathy grows from the experiences of homophobia. Since sexual violence is endemic in sexist and heterosexist culture, it is important to find places to go to remember and heal childhood abuse. Lesbians and gay men, who have moved well into the transition and beyond, not only speak outside the milieu of heterosexist culture but act outside it as well.

As straight women and men, we are being pulled about here on the continuum to answer more deeply such questions as "Who am I?" and "What is my sexual orientation?" In those cultures where girls have been permitted freer, closer relationships with other girls, knowledge of one's sexual orientation may be clearer at an earlier age. It may also be that the need to define oneself as clearly heterosexual or lesbian is less important. Freedom to explore close relationships, whether sexual or not, creates a less polarizing environment for sexual orientation. In those cultures where there is tight control over childhood experience, along with a highly individualized tone to the culture, emotions around feelings of sexuality are less explored.

Straight white women have often had this experience. In our adult years we may turn to the safety of same-gender relationships to do our exploring. We often seek lesbian friendships to help us. Dominants, however, have a habit of taking from subordinants what they want and then leaving. We may be somewhat blithe in the relationships we form with lesbians, expecting that we can try some things and leave. We do not always stop to think we are returning to the safety of the straight world, especially when things get uncomfortable for us. This, of course, means abruptly leaving bonds we have made with lesbians. We enter a friendship or relationship saying we are there to stay and pledging fidelity, only to leave when a male relationship comes along. Since we were teenagers, we have used our girlfriends and women friends in this way—both heterosexual and lesbian.

Now as adult women, we need to be aware of whether we are using lesbians solely for our own needs, that is, whether we are in the relationship merely to learn about or heal ourselves. When we are in crisis, for example, when someone of the other sex hurts us, do we use lesbians and gay men for healing? Many gay men and lesbians become fearful of and angry about straight men and women using them in this way, particularly if there is no acknowledgment of their help.

Beginning a friendship or relationship of warmth and intimacy should not be taken lightly. Heterosexist culture supports entering relationships for reasons of ownership or dependency on another. Heterosexist relationships are not viewed as something to work on, where the goal is truly understanding one another over time. A relationship is something that just is; it is not expected to be a process of growth and change for the partners. Heterosexist people often enter relationships they would not enter if they knew themselves better. In such relationships they project their wants and needs onto others. Others are used for their own desires, not in the context of each person's needs. We often learn about our misuse of friendships when we blithely enter and soon leave one with a lesbian or gay man. When heterosexual and heterosexually identified bisexual people take the option of returning to the "accepted" world again, leaving what was pledged as a long-term relationship, we disregard the fact that sexual orientation is not something entered and left at will, even though we were testing for our sexual identity.

Bisexual people can do the same thing as straight people in acting out "comings and goings" with lesbians and gay men, that is, assuming heterosexual privilege. How to honor one's own decision to be a heterosexually identified bisexual person without abusing the possibility of heterosexual privilege takes much thought and clarity with others about who one is. Our insensitivity to the inability of lesbian and gay people to enter the safety of the heterosexual world is painful to them. Our actions are never just personal decisions, but set in the climate of cultural heterosexism.

At times of prolonged gender segregation, when a straight man has no female companionship, such as during military duty, incarceration, or shorter separations such as a hunting trip, he may feel free to engage in sexual activity with other men. He may not feel particularly uncomfortable or guilty about such same-sex behavior, but this is probably because he does not think of it as a homosexual relationship.[21] The behavior has no name. His conscious or subconscious assumption becomes that the nature of same-sex relationships (homosexuality) is temporary. When a heterosexual relationship is possible, the straight man assumes he will return to "normal," that is, to a heterosexual relationship. His expectations of moving on quickly may be disrespectful of the emotions and attachment of the gay or bisexual man who may be involved.

The expectation by straight men and women that they are able to enter the gay, lesbian, and bisexual communities secretly and temporarily without identifying with them can be thoughtless and even abusive. We need to be clear about our motives and whether we are using "others" for our own ends without sharing the consequences of living as bisexual, lesbian, or gay. To lesbians and gay men, straight women and men and some bisexual people are unreliable in a crisis. We leave. Gay baiting is the crisis that makes us leave the fastest. We fear for our safety and fade into the background, choosing the route of joining the oppressor by our silence.

We cannot avoid taking our tentative first steps in understanding who we are by reaching out to those whom we have excluded because of our fears—lesbians, gay men, and bisexual people. We need to be clear, though, about what we are doing and not rush in with blithe assurances of always being available. Unfortunately, learning about ourselves and our homophobia involves making mistakes, such as being insensitive and unclear about what we are doing. Being vulnerable and willing to take risks to learn about ourselves in relationships is never easy.

It is important that straight people learn from gay men, lesbians, and bisexual people about the coming out process, that is, about defining one's own orientation. We need to experience our own growth process, to ask ourselves "Who am I? What is my sexual orientation and the identity I want to have?" When we are impelled into the transition, we ask the question "What *is* my orientation? Am I really heterosexual?" "What has it meant and what does it mean to me to be heterosexual?" Listening to stories of how bisexual people, lesbians, and gay men take on their identity provides glimpses of the variety of ways one comes to know one's sexual orientation and how one develops a sexual identity. This focus is very different from surreptitiously using gay, lesbian, and bisexual people for our own needs.

Inclusiveness

Changing the environment from one of open hostility to covert rejection in the orange section, then to **inclusiveness** in the transition, is central to our journey. As I listen and ask questions, the climate of acceptance of bisexual, gay, and lesbian people expands. I learn what it takes for individual bisexual people, gay men, and lesbians to feel comfortable. Whether they are known openly or quietly within a work situation or social group, they need the respect and acknowledgment that everyone does. This includes accepting their ideas and building on their statements, asking their opinions, confronting them as I do others, and asking them to join me for lunch and other informal activities.

My sense of inclusiveness is important, whether or not I know lesbians, bisexual people, and gay men are actually present. The climate needs to be accepting *at all times* because most gay men, lesbians, and bisexual people are unrecognized in groups and organizations. My commitment to inclusively support same-sex relationships means paying attention to such things as

— making sure banter and jokes are free of homophobic language;
— comfortably referring to lesbian, gay male, and bisexual needs and rights when making policy and setting procedures;
— speaking of gay men, lesbians, and bisexual people generally as friends, though not in a way that highlights their sexuality or outs them;
— showing public support for causes such as gay, lesbian, and bisexual rights and AIDS concerns;
— reading fiction and nonfiction books and magazines about a variety of sexualities, and not hiding them, but comfortably having them visible in my home; and
— showing as much sympathy for bisexual people, lesbians, and gay men upon their loss of a partner as I do with straight people.

There is another important step. Most of what has been said so far speaks to ridding myself of homophobic and biphobic ways. My next step is to be able to converse with someone, whatever his or her sexual identity, about who they are *and who I am* in a friendly way. Can I intelligently and sensitively take the initiative, if appropriate, in talking with a lesbian, bisexual person, or gay man about his or her life and interests as I share mine? If direct references to sexual identity come up, do I know myself well enough to share mine and its implications for my life in a casually comfortable way? Can I refer to myself as heterosexual when my actions and ideas reflect this orientation?

Public Demeanor

I need to be **trusted by bisexual people, lesbians, and gay men not to identify them in public places**, independent of whether they have at another time publicly identified themselves. For me to talk about someone else's sexual orientation puts them at grave risk. Our culture is too violently homophobic to take away from individual gay men, lesbians, and bisexual people control over where they are known. While some present themselves in a public way in groups or public demonstrations, they may still need to be closeted in other places to avoid violence, ostracism, discrimination, and hostility.

It is a matter of trust that, in public situations, I not share the identity of friends. It is important that I make a conscious decision not to talk about others' sexual orientation or identity. Even among my closest friends whom I trust not to be homophobic and biphobic, I need to use caution in discussing others' sexual orientation or identity. To disclose someone's sexual identity means that I have increased the number of people who know and that the information has gone beyond my ability to honor confidentiality.

If someone has publicly identified as lesbian, gay male, or bisexual, such as when addressing gay, bisexual, or lesbian concerns, I may share with close friends that person's identity and my appreciation for her or his work. If I were walking casually down the street or sitting in a restaurant with that person, however, I would not refer to her or his sexual identity because random public violence is too prevalent. Even writing a check to someone showing the purpose of the check is for a gay cause can put a gay or lesbian person at risk of being outed at their bank. I find that once I know someone is bisexual, gay, or lesbian and I have become comfortable with it, I must pay constant attention to avoid casually referring to their identity with others. This is probably one of the most difficult things to incorporate into my life. I begin to appreciate the energy that lesbians, bisexual people, and gay men have put into hiding their identities and the effects of living a double life.

Accepting a Range of Sexualities

My comfort with varying sexual orientations and identities comes from recognizing a range of sexual experience and forms of desire. For me, sexuality is no longer an either/or issue. As stated in chapter 2, we can have a heteroerotic, homoerotic, ambierotic, or autoerotic orientation. Because straight people have viewed their heterosexual orientation as not just central to the human experience but morally exclusive—the only way to be—one way to think about the range of sexual identity is to picture bisexuality at the center, with heterosexuality expanding out one way and homosexuality the other, with graduations in between. Such a linear image is not only limiting, but inaccurate and inadequate. Ambisexuality and also autoeroticism are just what they are, not central to other orientations. As a first image (and one given to us by Kinsey)[22], putting bisexuality "in the middle" forced me to forego the feeling that my heterosexual orientation is central to all others or exclusively right. A vision for the green section, (Where the Journeys Lead) is that we are all simply ourselves; we have no need to define ourselves in relation to others on a continuum of sexualities.

I know *I* decide my sexual identity based on self-knowledge, that is, how I feel toward the same sex and the other sex, and I can't be seduced into it. I can be seduced into behaving a certain way at a particular time, but this does not determine my orientation. As a heterosexual person I have asked the question of gay men, lesbians, and bisexual people, "Who or what made you gay, lesbian, or bisexual?" Such a question no longer concerns me, though I may be interested if someone wishes to talk about it. I had never thought to ask a heterosexual person, "Who or what made you heterosexual?" I now see that sexual identity is not what you do to me; it is how I give meaning to my inner orientation and how I decide to identify. I could identify as gay, lesbian, heterosexual, or bisexual, choosing to be lesbian- or gay-identified or heterosexually identified in my bisexuality. I could be actively sexual or celibate in my behavior. These are culturally mediated personal choices. Of course if this is true for me, then it is true for others.

My acknowledgment and understanding of bisexuality are clearer. I understand bisexuality as a reasonable choice for sexual identity for people of ambisexual orientation, allowing me to be more emotionally accepting of friends and relatives who may move between different sexual identities at various times in their lives. I can read and appreciate Ann Fox's description of her experience as a bisexual woman.

> College was an intense time of growth, of coming into my independence from family and establishing myself as a vibrant and sexual being. As a seventeen-year-old freshman, I had a hunger for life even more powerful than my thirst for knowledge. I shared these years with my college roommate, and she became my best friend. The passion we shared for adventure and experience gave rise to feelings of closeness and love, and that love spilled over, under, and through the fence of social acceptability that women are supposed to wrap around our feelings for other women. I couldn't deny that I was in love with her and didn't understand why I should even try.
>
> Since that time, I have loved other women. I have loved women in the same deep and romantic ways that I have loved some of the men in my life. I have loved them as friends, as lovers, and as possible life partners. For me, there has never been a question as to whether my feelings for women were more or less real than my emotional ties to men. They are simply (and complexly) different. I can no more deny the depth of my ability to love people of both genders than I could the fact of being, myself, a woman.[23]

Fox may have always felt this clear about her sexual identity, or, as many bisexual people do, she may have tried a straight and then a lesbian identity several times before deciding on a bisexual identity. Earlier Michael Brewer was quoted relating how he knew he was bisexual but wanted a heterosexual lifetime relationship that would still honor his same-sex orientation (see 134).

When accepting a variety of sexual identities, I need to **recognize that lesbian, gay, and bisexual experiences vary, ranging from loving relationships to violent, brutal ones**, just as heterosexual relationships do. All relationships can get into trouble, regardless of sexual orientation. Everyone needs understanding friends and relatives who are supportive both of hanging in at times and working things out, and of getting out of the relationship when that needs to happen. Can we, as heterosexuals, truly be supportive of gay male, bisexual, and lesbian friends, instead of communicating the feeling that having the relationship *at all* is the problem?

A major block to my appreciation of the range of relationships one finds among bisexual people, gay men, and lesbians is the narrowness of my experience with bisexuality and homosexuality. Questions about normality and legality still publicly surround these sexual orientations. Heterosexist culture forces or at least supports me in believing same-sex acts are unnatural. Therefore, voyeurism is my only tool for understanding same-sex or bisexual orientations.

Over the years I have wondered about same-sex sex and bisexuality. Whether an occasional thought or a habitual prurient interest, this has been a form of voyeurism, particularly if my interest resulted in snickering and derision of the act, followed by "going back for more." This behavior from the orange section needs careful attention now in the transition. If I am to hear lesbian, gay, and bisexual people tell their stories, sex acts are not what I am interested in; they are personal and private. What I am interested in is sharing stories that answer the questions in chapter 1, such as How do I know I am heterosexual, gay, lesbian, or bisexual? What has this meant to my life? The transition becomes a time when I learn I have a story of my own to tell. If stories about our most personal selves are told only by one group of people (bisexual, gay, and lesbian), with silence coming from the other group (heterosexual), voyeurism is encouraged. So, the question is, *What is my story as a heterosexual person?*

My knowledge of gay, lesbian, and bisexual life has been limited to homophobic people's crushing condemnation of homosexuality or obscene references to it, or I have been deeply influenced by those gay men and lesbians who, reacting strongly to compulsory heterosexuality, are flamboyant and angry. As straight people, we must understand this behavior for what it often is—an attempt to shake us out of our insensitivity to compulsory heterosexuality and move us along in our understanding of the gay, lesbian, and bisexual journeys. Such behavior is not necessarily an end or goal for lesbians, bisexual people, or gay men. As more lesbians, gay males, and bisexual people of all cultures find it safe to come out, my role models enlarge and change for gay men, lesbians, and bisexual people. My goal now is to know enough about other people's journeys so that not only do I make correct assumptions about the meaning and normality of their behavior, but we mutually facilitate each other on our journeys; and I am clear enough about my story to share it.

Whether the reader is a white heterosexual person or a heterosexual person of color, accepting a range of sexualities means understanding them in the *context of a specific culture*. How and when racism and heterosexism intersect is particularly important to understand. bell hooks describes the effect of assuming heterosexism and racism are the same.

Often black people, especially non-gay folks, become enraged when they hear a white person who is gay suggest that homosexuality is synonymous with the suffering people experience as a consequence of racial exploitation and oppression. The need to make gay experience and black experience of oppression synonymous seems to be one that surfaces much more in the minds of white people. Too often, it is seen as a way of minimizing or diminishing the particular problems people of color face in a white-supremacist society, especially the problems encountered because one does not have white skin. Many of us have been in discussions where a non-white person—a black person—struggles to explain to white folks that while we can acknowledge that gay people of all colors are harassed and suffer exploitation and domination, we also recognize that there is a significant difference that arises because of the visibility of dark skin. Often homophobic attacks on gay people occur in situations where knowledge of sexual preference is indicated or established—outside of gay bars, for example. While it in no way lessens the severity of such suffering for gay people, or the fear that it causes, it does mean that in a given situation the apparatus of protection and survival may be simply not identifying as gay.

In contrast, most people of color have no choice. No one can hide, change, or mask dark skin color. White people, gay and straight, could show greater understanding of the impact of racial oppression on people of color by not attempting to make these oppressions synonymous, but rather by showing the ways they are linked and yet differ. Concurrently, the attempt by white people to make synonymous experience of homophobic aggression with racial oppression deflects attention away from the particular dual dilemma that non-white gay people face, as individuals who confront both racism and homophobia.[24]

It is important to read about and listen to the many culturally and politically influential people who were and are lesbian, gay, or bisexual, appreciating their accomplishments and cultural referents rather than dwelling on their sexuality as scandalous.[25] Such stories expand our understanding of cultural contexts.

Being More Public

Solidarity in public meetings and parades means that I do not think about or worry that someone might think I am lesbian or gay based on my association with lesbians and gay men. In the 1960s, long hair for white men and unisex clothing for men and women generally became public statements of disengagement from the cultural norms of white male superiority and power. This behavior brought derision because sexist people need to know immediately who is male and who is female. The question had to be asked why we needed to know a person's gender unless we wanted to treat men and women differently, that is, as dominants and subordinants, or unless we wanted to keep interactions sexualized between men and women.

As we deal with our fears of publicly associating with bisexual people, lesbians, and gay men, we have to ask a similar question: Why is it important to sort people out into heterosexual, homosexual, and bisexual categories? In reality, this information is needed only when we choose to view homosexuality and bisexuality judgmentally, as evil or sick, and our homophobic and biphobic fears bring such discomfort that we need to avoid all known contact. In other words, we want to stay dominant and assume that heterosexism is normal.

Solidarity in public is a very real and present concern for family members of lesbians, bisexual people, and gay men. In the transition, gay, lesbian, and bisexual people create ceremonies to symbolize and acknowledge commitments. Invitations to participate force us to make decisions about whether and how we will be a part of such celebrations. Will we continue to hide and avoid acknowledging what is true or will we proudly participate? A growing ability to include new partners and friends in family gatherings and to welcome additions to both casual and formal occasions suggests we are now well through the transition.

Each step of becoming more public causes us to be aware of the vestiges of discomfort still with us. Just when we think we've done it all, something else jolts us. We attend or even march in a gay pride parade and think, "Well, this is okay; I can do this and feel all right." But then we find ourselves in a small group where most people are gay or lesbian, and we panic for a bit. Or we accept a cousin's orientation as bisexual but panic when our sister identifies as lesbian, saying to ourselves, "Is everyone in this family homosexual?" We overreact because of the closeness of the person and a flash feeling that we are the ones who are different.

If we accept lesbian, gay, and bisexual relationships as loving, then we need to accept expressions of these relationships in public in the same way we accept heterosexual people being loving in public. It is time to stop flinching when our gay brother brings home his partner and they sit together on the couch touching, one with an arm around the other. It is time to assume our lesbian friends will automatically bring their partners to our parties and dance together in the same way heterosexual couples do. If we are upset, it is our job to deal with our reaction and not take it out on the bisexual person, gay man, or lesbian.

Marching in parades, joining demonstrations, and being inclusive of lesbian, gay male, and bisexual family members and friends are public affirmations of comfort with homosexuality and bisexuality, but they are, at the same time, comfort with *my* heterosexual orientation and identity. Others' perceptions do not change or throw into question my orientation or identity. Their hatreds and fears no longer control me. This is a personal journey only I can make for myself.

Joining bisexual people, gays, and lesbians at public events is one way to experience their culture. Another way is joining them in their more private activities, that is, being **willing to enter lesbian, gay, and bisexual culture**. Earlier in the transition we may have had the opportunity of attending a party or other gathering where we were the only heterosexual person or one of few. Often we handled our first such experiences by gathering up our courage and burying our fears and discomfort. We were watchful and very dependent on others making us feel at ease. As an overreaction to our defensiveness and guilt in the late orange section, we may even have been a bit forward about how we entered lesbian, gay, and bisexual community life. In our eagerness to seem accepting, we assumed we were always welcome. Our willingness to enter bisexual, gay, and lesbian culture now is more judicious. We are not there to prove anything. We have learned how to participate where appropriate in these cultures, and our behavior is not that of a dominant asking others to join their ways.

An example of the way we kept the culture ours (heterosexist) in the mid-orange section—particularly the section from **gay jokes and pejoratives** to **nervousness around "them"**—was related to me by a lesbian friend. Province-town on Cape Cod is known as a gay town, friendly to everyone. My friend and her partner were dining on the deck of a restaurant with a view of the ocean. The majority of the diners seemed to be gay and lesbian with some heterosexual diners. However, one group of obviously heterosexual men and women spent the evening talking loudly enough for everyone in the dining room to hear. Their stories and behavior emphasized flirting, sexuality, and gender roles between men and women. At one point one man said he had a male secretary for a week and couldn't stand him so he fired him.

While the loud talkers were carrying on, another heterosexual couple walked out on a pier that was central to everyone's view of the ocean panorama and started making love. Their public, heavy petting was their statement of feeling free to be in someone's face (actually many people's) about making sure heterosexual behavior was dominant and known. Everyone could not help but be drawn into their exhibition of heterosexual culture.

This is called staking out heterosexist turf, that is making sure that one is not a part of gay and lesbian culture, even though in the minority. Such staking out is meant to intimidate any who are not straight. Of course, if a gay man or lesbian showed such staking out on heterosexual turf, retaliatory violence would likely be immediate. I find many heterosexual people rude in ways that few lesbian, gay, and bisexual people ever would be, even if they felt safe enough from intimidation. The straight people participating in the two above examples have little or no awareness of the deep anxiety and guilt they feel about associating themselves with homosexuality, only the "fun" they think they are having—*in order to stay comfortable.*

We have seen how in the transition straight men and women begin dealing with their fears of guilt by association. Now, near the end of the transition, we are aware of the importance of separating heterosexual culture from heterosexist culture. We are beginning to recognize what makes a culture heterosexist, such as staking out our turf and assuming male/female pairing in our language, stories, advertisements, definitions of family, insurance policies, social gatherings, media events, political candidates, and religious beliefs. Hopefully, we may be trusted enough to be included in gay, lesbian, or bisexual gatherings, that is, we know how to comfortably enter their culture.

The skill dominants always need to learn is how and when it is appropriate to enter another culture without assuming others will adjust to them. We also know there are times when those of another culture, such as bisexual people, lesbians, and gay men, like to be among themselves. We are not offended by such requests.

My Part in Heterosexist Culture

Now I am more aware of culturally informed homophobia and biphobia, from the ever-present reality of random violence in public areas, to the notion that homosexuality is an illness, to the covert hostility of oblivious heterosexism. As I acknowledge my journey and see others acting out compulsory heterosexuality, I now see how I participate in it by the signals I give, such as

— not just refraining from laughter at homophobic remarks and jokes, but failing to call attention to their inappropriateness;
— avoiding references to homosexuality and bisexuality even when appropriate, that is, not saying the words;
— assuming there is no culturally imposed damage to lesbians, gay men, and bisexual people because of heterosexism;
— discounting lesbians in women's culture, gay men in men's culture, and bisexual people in heterosexual culture;
— not trying to understand the multicultural complexities of gay, lesbian, and bisexual life;
— detaching myself from known or suspected lesbian, gay male, and bisexual people in groups; and
— making myself acceptable in the work environment by taking on mannerisms as a professional woman or man that overaccentuate femininity and masculinity.

This last issue is not only a sexist issue, but a heterosexist one as well. For instance, the way straight women wear makeup and high heels, that is, dress in a feminine manner, can set up a climate emphasizing a heterosexist culture of teasing and suggestiveness. Heterosexual women who participate in this climate are often deemed acceptable, which means lesbians are not. Lesbians have often been referred to as "women in sensible shoes." As more comfortable shoe styles have become available and are eagerly worn by straight women, this stereotype is fading. Although not all lesbians shun makeup and high heels, lesbian theory and understanding of femininity support a naturalness of style and an acknowledgment that much of the history of feminine adornment is based on men's control of women. Straight women who accept men's need to control them are encouraged to be seductive in their dress and manner.

Another way a heterosexist climate is created is by straight people leaving known bisexual people, lesbians, and gay men out of informal communication systems and, hence, organizational power. Lesbians have often separated themselves from sexist bantering and teasing, which has the effect of putting them outside the informal communication system—a painful consequence. Heterosexist men sustain such a climate by making themselves the center of attention through their mannerisms of taking up space with their physical stance and posturing, holding the conversation to their opinions and interests, assuming dominant power, and relying on humor to cover their discomfort. Homophobic straight people leave gay men out of the informal communication system because gay men expand the boundaries of maleness beyond straight peoples' comfort. Straight women who have high needs for indiscriminate approval from straight men collude to produce a heterosexist atmosphere by supporting the suggestive bantering and teasing which form a basis of comfort for sexist men.

I have now spent enough time in the transition to be aware of some ways my behavior supports cultural homophobia. My willingness to drop these behaviors and assume ones more inclusive of gay men, bisexual people, and lesbians, along with developing an understanding of my heterosexuality, is the finishing work of the transition. I am now dealing openly with heterosexual people who are at earlier places on the continuum, calling attention to the effects of their behavior. I must choose where and how I do this, as lesbians, bisexual people and gay men do, because I understand the ever-present danger of violence from people still on the early part of the continuum. However, in many places where I am known as heterosexual, I can help change the climate by speaking up when gay men, lesbians, and bisexual people would be in jeopardy. I am not embarrassed to *publicly* support lesbian, gay, and bisexual issues. My taking on other heterosexual people carries a powerful impact and relieves the gay male, lesbian, and bisexual person from seeming hostile by always having to call attention to his or her concerns.

By taking the initiative to learn about our heterosexuality as a diversity, rather than obliviously assuming it is the standard, and by showing interest in the complexities of experience of those whose diversity has been maligned, we set the course for finishing the work of the transition. We **value everyone's journey**; therefore we assume a **commitment to relationship building** with those who represent a diversity of sexualities. Such understanding and insight are not tasks that are accomplished and then put aside. They represent a process of ongoing awareness which always keeps part of us in the transition.

As we move into chapter 8, "Where the Journeys Lead: Imagining the Possible," we are ready for a vision of possibilities.

Where The Journeys Lead

Life is not easy, but it's simple.
—*Susan Taylor*

Imagining the Possible

HEATHER WISHIK AND CAROL PIERCE

Valuing a **diversity of relationships and sexualities** (the green section of the sexual orientation and identity continuum) is a vision, one some people can imagine but which few of us actually live out at this time. The foundation for the vision is built on our experiences of self-defining our sexual identity, including a redefinition of the meaning of gender, and of learning to respect other peoples' journeys of self-definition.

What is valued in the green section is diversity, not sameness (the frequent meaning of the word equality today), not commonality, tolerance, or integration based on a dominant standard. Valuing diversity is a stance where there is no set norm against which to evaluate all comers. Instead, we recognize the powerful gift given to everyone when everyone's experiences, background, point of view, skills, and ways of being are welcomed and available in interactions both at work and in more personal relationships.

The journeys of understanding mapped and discussed here do not end: they are lifelong for individuals, perpetual for organizations. However, we do have a glimpse of what organizations or groups would feel like, individual behavior would look like, and operative conceptual frameworks might include if people had travelled the journeys mapped by the orange and blue sections of the graphic. Thus, the green section is not a place but a description of processes at work and of some of the conditions we might strive for.

Many of us indulge in wishful thinking sometimes. Such thinking about culture change regarding diversity sometimes includes imagining that when we all "get it" relations between and among us will be calm, easy, predictable. In fact, when people genuinely commit to valuing differences, interactions become more emotion filled, less predictable, more varied, and less orderly. What is simple about being in groups where we are each and all valued is that underlying commitment, the core value that every one of us brings resources to the table and must be treated in a way that welcomes full presence. Living this way doesn't, however, feel easy. The responsibilities involved challenge every person accustomed to less fully engaged and truthful interactions.

In the midst of a larger culture which does not yet value sexual diversity, maintaining the deep commitment necessary to interact in the ways required to do so is not easy for organizations or for individuals. However, people and groups are beginning nonetheless to work from such a sense of commitment, to feel their way through what it requires to live with the actual diversity of human sexualities and relationships.

In this chapter we will try to give examples of what some of the necessary processes and conditions for working together are. But first, a parable here to remind each of us how volatile and dangerous these times are, how far from valuing sexual diversity we in the United States still are. The parable also is an expression of our deep concern about the drive to find biological markers for some types of sexual orientation, a drive coming from both heterosexual and lesbian/gay/bisexual quarters.

We are concerned that the emphasis on locating biological causation for exclusive homoerotic desire will function to devalue or erase emergent understandings about the core life task for everyone of sexual identity development, and may diminish the visibility of the immense range of desires many people are capable of feeling. We also fear the political uses to which such data may be put if it is available before most people in this country and the world have travelled further on the journeys of understanding mapped here. We see the predominant United States culture as on the top line of the continuum in the red section, with most heterosexual people's attitudes ranging from the point under denial that is named contagion to the points after oblivious heterosexism designated politeness and tolerance. Some people are still in the ostracism stage where anti-gay violence is acceptable. Some people, most often close colleagues or family members of a lesbian or gay man who has come out, are well on their transition journey, exploring their own sense of orientation and identity, talking and asking questions, re-looking at their same gender relationships. In other words, as a whole, heterosexual people in the United States have not reached the point of really deciding to learn about these issues of human sexual diversity.

This means we feel some urgency as we encourage heterosexual people to read, to ask questions, to look at our own sense of orientation. There is some urgency as we encourage gay, bisexual, and lesbian people to seek each other out, to learn how to love ourselves, to gain strength enough to insist on living our lives fully, including coming out, being visible to key heterosexual people in our lives.

In order to illustrate all these concerns, and to give readers a context in which to consider committing themselves to the wonderful and invigorating complexity of trying to live with the full diversity of sexualities and relationships, we provide the following parable. It was inspired by the example of Derek Bell's story "The Space Traders"[1] and by the play "Twilight of the Golds" which was produced on Broadway during 1993.

The Haves and the Have-Nots: A Parable—*Heather Wishik*

The plane ride was long, we had been delayed and I, usually unable to sleep on planes, had dozed off. I awoke, not in my tenth row seat but seated on a city park bench on a leaf strewn fall day. There were a few people resting on other benches, their belongings in carts close by.

"Are you listening?"

I turned to my right. A woman, at least I thought it was a woman, whom I was sure had not been there a moment before, was seated next to me. Her voice was Lauren Bacall deep, her hair grey. "My name is unimportant," she said before I could ask. "Think of me, if you like, as all the woman-identified-women and all the man-loving men of the past rolled into one presence."

As I stared at her face I saw some of my favorites pass by—Anna Freud, Jimmy Baldwin, John Singer Sargent, E.R., Bessie Smith in her evening gown—their features like shadows hovering, shape changing one into the next on this person's face.

"May I call you Audre?"

She smiled knowingly. "Of course. Audre Lorde was one of the fiercest of us all. I'll answer to the call of her name with pleasure. And now, I have something to tell you, something you must listen to with your heart and your head and know you must remember it all."

For the next long while—what seemed a long while anyway—Audre spoke, telling me this story:

There has been a change on this planet, a change going to begin showing itself very soon. We have chosen you, and don't be asking who we is, chosen you to know about the change now so you can prepare for it with the others you know are ready to help. Listen well for I am telling you this from the time after the change took place, but you are hearing it before it starts.

One morning people awoke all over the globe to find some people had new markings on their bodies. Almost square splotches, about an inch across, scattered all over the body, and in a contrasting hue to a person's skin. Darker splotches if a person was light, lighter splotches if a person was dark.

Some people had a few marks—others had over a hundred—and some had none at all. The first lady had 23, the president had 150, their son had none. Sixty

169

percent of the women in the military had many marks, and 75% of the men did. Sixty percent of Catholic priests had more than 20 marks. In the world population one in 25 people, or 4%, had no marks at all, although another one in 7, or 14% had fewer than 10 marks.

The morning the marks appeared there was panic as fear of a new infectious plague spread. Doctors, hospitals, healers, wise elders, and clergy were inundated with people demanding explanations.

Stigmata, some clergy named the marks, and declared them a divine sign. The medical profession could find no signs of infection. Certain healers smiled, suggesting more would become clear soon, it was not good to rush to judgment. By the first evening newscasters were reporting babies born that day were both marked and unmarked—some were haves and some have-nots.

Within the first 24 hours lesbian, bisexual, and gay people around the world figured it out. People who experienced exclusively homoerotic desires had no marks, and those people whose desires were predominantly homoerotic had only a few; everyone else was significantly marked.

In one region of South Africa witchcraft was blamed and have-nots were by the second morning being chased from their homes. By the third day Moslem purists in Saudi Arabia had begun strip searching people: have-nots were arrested. In Los Angeles groups of young skin-heads were also strip searching people without visible splotches on their faces or hands: have-nots were beaten and left naked in the streets. In Israel Orthodox youth drove apparently mark-free men away from prayers at the wailing wall, yelling at them in Hebrew that they were unclean. By the end of the week the world understood that gay and lesbian people, and predominantly homoerotic bisexual people, were the have-nots.

In the United States, in addition to ongoing panic about contagion and a cynicism about whether or not health professionals and the government were telling the whole story, people in communities large and small started clamoring for exclusion from schools of unmarked teachers and children, because they were viewed as potentially contagious, because they were bad influences on others, were immoral, or were seen as designated by the divine as lacking holiness. Street violence and discrimination spread quickly. The president declared a national emergency, called up the Army Reserves to help quell the violence, and opened closed military bases as places of refuge for persecuted have-nots. Unmarked parents of young children, and parents of unmarked young children, sought safety on the bases first. Unmarked people who were poor or homeless also quickly moved to the bases. Some more affluent have-nots used make up or tattoos to pass as haves. The Army Reserves quickly assigned the have-nots among the soldiers to guard the bases, since their presence on the streets was simply causing more violence than it was worth.

By the third week the United Nations Security Council passed a resolution calling on member nations to guarantee human rights regardless of the presence or absence of the stigmata. The European Community, most of Eastern, Central, and Southern Africa, New Zealand and Australia, Thailand and Hong Kong adopted such laws quickly, despite calls from the Pope and Moslem leaders not to do so.

In the United States senators from North Carolina, New Hampshire, and Indiana led the fight in Congress to terminate eligibility for military service and federal employment for have-nots. The bill passed after the have-nots in Congress, 17 in the Senate, 62 in the House, left the joint session en masse in protest. The legislation's preamble stated that the change involving the markings was not yet fully understood, that unmarked people were understood to be homosexual, that the biological differentiation suggested homosexuals might possess other biological differences besides being unmarked that were potentially dangerous or contagious to heterosexual people, that exposing children to people possessing homosexual inclinations was not consistent with the public policy and values of the majority of citizens, and that the markings were a gift of clarity to be acted on appropriately, through quarantine or separation in employment, education, public accommodations, etc. In arguing for passage the Senator from North Carolina said:

"These stigmata are like the blood of the lamb painted on the door frames of Jewish homes in ancient Egypt. No harm shall come to those who bear the marks but those without will face their proper fate." Although some Senators objected to the religious nature of the debate, a majority of those voting agreed that public safety required separation of the haves and have-nots until the situation was better understood, however long that took.

In delivery rooms mothers stopped asking "is it a boy or a girl" and started asking "is the baby a have or a have-not?" Scientists debated how many marks were required to qualify a person as a have; most advocated a 1/16th rule. The maximum marks found were 160. Therefore, persons having at least 1/16th that many, or a minimum of 10, qualified as a have. A person with 9 or fewer marks was a have-not.

In countries like China, where strict family size limitation was required, or like Romania where economic distress had already caused a pattern of child abandonment, or India where prenatal sex selection was already being practiced, birthing clinics began filling with abandoned have-not babies as marked parents, terrified of the social consequences to the rest of the family, chose not to keep their have-not newborns. United States adoption agencies, for the first time in decades, had access to numerous otherwise healthy newborns free for adoption.

For months violence continued to sweep the globe in waves. In the countries which adopted separation policies families were split apart unless have-not members managed to pass or marked family members elected to move with their have-not relatives to the camps, bases, and other settlements set up for have-nots. In the United States the hitherto liberal president folded in the face of public pressure and agreed that all have-nots would be interned. The round ups began. Resister groups formed: some have-not members passed as marked and others went underground, hoping to maintain their mobility and to help nurture a coalition of marked allies in order to provide whatever aid it might be possible to gather. However, very few marked people were willing to risk their freedom in the struggle. The staunchest allies were, predictably, marked parents and marked adult children of have-nots.

At about the same time as the internment orders were being carried out, medical research determined that no simple prenatal screening was possible because the marks didn't develop until the last few weeks of gestation. Congress was already in an uproar over the data being presented to them about the percentages of have-not men and women who were biological parents of children and/or were or had been in heterosexual marriages. The House voted that the relatively minor surgery of vasectomy was a minimally intrusive way of trying to prevent have-not babies from being born pending further research to determine what if any genetic processes were at work, and the Senate quickly passed a similar measure. All have-not men who were in heterosexual marriages or who were already fathers were told to report for sterilization, with the promise that new technology would permit reversal should the research discover that have-not status was not genetically linked to the father. Have-not women in marriages were not required to submit to sterilization but were urged to use contraception until further notice, and have-not men and women were barred from participating in artificial insemination.

Because contagion was still considered a possibility, pregnant women were put into isolation as soon as labor commenced and no fathers or other relatives were permitted into delivery rooms. After a baby emerged and was checked for marks, mothers of have-not babies were urged to release them immediately for adoption into have-not families. If the mother refused, she was put into a segregated ward for have-not babies. That is, the mother's identity followed that of her child—she was treated as if she were a have-not if her baby was a have-not and she chose to keep it. Meanwhile, federal money was allocated for drug and genetic research aimed at assuring that fetuses developed marks, and for continuing the search for genetic markers that would predict which fetuses would be born have-nots.

The prediction was that eventually a gene would be located that caused have-not fetal development. Scientists hoped a drug for men could be developed. The drug would target sperm that carried homoerotic orientation and kill those sperm, or would prevent sperm from attaching to an ovum which carried homoerotic orientation. Researchers predicted success within a decade.

The most immediate crisis, after the waves of initial violence stopped, was how to organize the millions of people interned. Have-nots and their loyal family members in every repressive country had to be provided with social services, including care for abandoned have-not babies, and with access to education, work, and recreation. In the United States the Supreme Court upheld the internment on the grounds that domestic tranquility required it. The Court also decided the government had a right to decide that have-nots, because it was "clear" they had a "biological defect," were not similarly situated to other citizens and could, therefore, be treated differently. The Court, making an analogy to resident aliens, said have-nots could constitutionally be treated as people toward whom the state had a duty of care but who were not on an equal footing with the haves who were full citizens. Immigration laws and visa requirements were adapted for consistency with the separation and internment policy, meaning effectively that no foreign travelers who were have-nots were welcome in the United States.

The internment lasted for five years, during which time medical researchers reassured everyone that contagion was not involved, and that no other discernable physical differences which could pose a threat to haves were associated with have-not status. Then small groups of have-nots were relocated to specific neighborhoods in cities, and were provided separate facilities for transportation, separate sections of workplaces to work in, and other forms of accommodation were made to their slow re-entry into the newly constructed apartheid-like U.S. society.

Audre's voice stopped and she stared at me. "You get the whole story? Remember every word? I'm only telling it once."

I was shaking my head. "Why? Why would people react to the biological proof with such rejection? Shouldn't it be the opposite—if orientation is really biological doesn't that make it simpler for many people to accept us as fully human?"

Audre chuckled deep in her chest. "You should know better by now, with all you've done and learned. There is nothing like a biological difference to bring out the worst in people. Look at the way women have been talked about for having periods, and surely you recall all the nonsense the minute those British doctors published papers saying PMS really existed. People love to believe biology is destiny. And what about all those damned reports about intelligence: IQ tests supposedly proved stupidity and brilliance were both inherited, and racially linked, they said. Remember?"

"Listen. After this change comes people won't know if biology really has anything to do with forms of desire, other than that certain desires will be linked to skin markings. We still won't know what causes desire; we'll just know who feels what and how strongly. The lines will be easier to draw, the differences will seem more real. The bigots who denied our existence before will clap hands and say I told you so, these 'homosexuals' are out of favor with the divine. How will they explain newborns, you ask? Come on, silly, original sin of course. And the squishy middle, the ones who never cared much about us, they along with the liberals always back away from biology. After all, biology is 'real proof' to them since they can't hang on to what they can't see. They don't believe in anything strongly enough to do that."

I still had trouble absorbing how bad the story sounded. "But why so few hetero allies, why not liberals who get it that the biological link just means we are all humans, born with a variety of desires? Why make us pathological?"

"Heather, Heather, I have not got all day. Your job is to figure out how to do something about this, not question whether or not my story will happen if you don't. Liberals will cave to massive vehemence and compromise away all our rights in the name of protecting us. Look at 'don't ask, don't tell.' Nuff said. With gay, lesbian, and our kind of bisexually oriented people only 16 to 18 percent, it will be easy to make us the not o.k. ones, the newest social scapegoat. The sudden onset of the change will leave people fearful that some kind of contagion caused it. People will say that the recent increased tolerance of gay and lesbian people spread our existence. After all, 16–18% have-nots is going to seem like a lot to people who read the magazine reports saying we were only 2% of the population. Remember those cover stories throwing all those stats around based on identity only, instead of based on core desires? We will be viewed as dangerous, as capable of erasing a person's marks through too much contact, as capable of causing unborn babies to become have-nots."

"So what am I supposed to do?" I wasn't feeling very powerful, just sad.

"Figure out what has to happen so when this change comes at least some people won't react the way I told you they will if you don't do something."

"Tall order, Audre. This is complicated. Do I have to take on the whole world?"

"Start here in the United States. We are talking to key people in other places. You will not be the only one working on this." She reached over to me and I noticed her skin was thin, papery like a very old person's. Her hand rested on my hand for a moment. "There is no time for worrying. Remember what I've told you. Remember."

I looked down at my hands, wondering what I could do. "What about getting the people you are telling together," I asked, looking up toward her, but she was gone. And I was back in the tenth row as we began descending toward Boston. My ears popped all the way down, my eyes were heavy, and I didn't have any idea what time it was, but I remembered every word Audre had said.

Living to Value Us All

The above parable is a reminder to us about how much there is to do if human sexual diversity is to be valued—not tolerated, not accepted, but valued. Too many people in the world still think homoerotic desire is a proper ground for persecution, a form of desire which should be eradicated, an evil. Children are being hospitalized by parents for treatment by therapists who claim to be able to change orientation. A majority of the Democratically controlled Senate thought it was good public policy in 1994 to prohibit public schools from providing positive support services to bisexual, lesbian, and gay youth or even from referring such youth to support services outside of school. Gay men are being murdered by teen age boys all over the country.

We cannot be complacent about the hate that continues to infect our communities. But hate is not the only problem. Tolerance which takes the form of

174

requiring gay, lesbian, and bisexual people to stay silent, or acceptance which takes the form of permitting us at the workplace but requiring our partners to remain invisible, doesn't help build community.

The parable gives us a glimpse of a time when clearly there would be no neutral ground on this issue, when non-action would be collusion in the violation of someone. We believe that silence in the face of current conditions about sexual orientation is also collusion in continuing things as they are. We know it is difficult for many well meaning heterosexual people to see this as collusion when they have no immediate contact with violent gay bashings or any real awareness of the costs of their own heterosexism to themselves, their children, their families. It is also difficult for some bisexual, lesbian, and gay people to know in their hearts that continued closeting is collusion in the status quo, difficult to know this in the face of the real risks that can accompany coming out.

We want to imagine how people might be with one another, to get to know each other, build trust, and in the process transcend the deeply problematic cultural views about sexual orientation and identity with which we've grown up in this country. We want to imagine how we could prevent such a cataclysm of hate from occurring should we face a more possible change, such as a prenatal test for supposed genetic markers allegedly predictive of primary homoerotic desire.

How might people treat each other, what might their processes, commitments, values, and understandings be? We believe that the prior chapters help tell what learnings people might need in order to move toward valuing each other in the way we imagine possible. These chapters make it clear that we believe heterosexual people must construct self-consciously their own sexual identities, must come to know clearly their own stories of discovery of orientation. Lesbian, bisexual, and gay people must continue to work together to construct healthy sexual identities, but also must sometimes interact with heterosexual people, telling the truth of our stories and our complex identity journeys. Assuming people have done these things, how would our organizations, our interactions in groups, be described? What follows is a discussion of what is depicted in the green part of the chart.

Imagine the group is a group of families joined by their membership in a faith community, or as neighbors in a building or block, or as employees in a unit of a large corporation, along with their families. The group has been told about the coming earthly change, and has decided to make a commitment to work together to build a community where everyone is able to be safe, loved, welcomed, and fully, authentically present and participatory. Such a community would have the key characteristics of any healthy community. Richard Orange says these include: *membership*, being known in a context and having a role and place; a sense of *common bond* that brings members together and holds them together over time; an experience of *safe harbor*, a place of refuge where one can be oneself and tell the truth; a place where every member exercises *leadership*, meaning responsibility, accountability, and direction; where everyone understands the responsibility for open *communication* and that silence is not acceptable; where a sense of *spirituality*, that is, a knowing there are things larger than the self and community involved, helps guide the community and its members; and where members demonstrate *commitment* to the community's nourishment and survival over time.[2]

In addition, this group of families who are striving to demonstrate that it is possible to form a community where human sexual diversity is valued, would have some other characteristics. First, as the community members work together they will **consider process openly.** This means the who, what, when, where, or why of how things happen. People work on how they work together in order for each to be able to be fully present and valued. This involves much listening and asking of questions about what people mean and what people need. Ongoing development of explicit ground rules and norms, that is, continuing explicit discussion of emergent group culture, will support this.

One norm important at the outset will be that of greater emotional involvement. **Emotions** need to be **more available** rather than consciously kept walled off from interactions. Emotional responses will be valued as important information. One of the key reasons why this will need to be a norm is that people are attempting to be known in aspects of identity not usually made fully visible to non-intimates, as well as because deep feelings which make the self difficult to reveal without accompanying emotion are often attached to one's current sense of sexual identity and gender identity. Some of these deep feelings come from one's past history of struggle associated with developing one's current sexual identity. If these two characteristics were operating and we were to spy on our neighborhood group, what would one of their gatherings sound like?

Imagine a group of adults who have agreed to develop educational programs for the children of the community. As we listen in on one of their gatherings, one member is tearfully telling the story of a high school friend who committed suicide because he was gay. The group takes the time to hear the story and supports the expression of emotion. They know that the decision whether or not to include suicide prevention information with children needed to be made in the context of the real experiences of suicides linked to identity development. The tearfully told story was a resource, necessary information presented in a necessarily compelling way, for the group in making its decisions. It was also necessary for the teller to speak the story, and feel safe enough to express the emotions linked to the remembering and retelling, in order for him to be a part of the group's work, for him to be known to the group in context, and for him to know the group as a safe harbor for expression of his ideas and opinions.

Another thing we would find in these gatherings is that all individuals would be encouraged to articulate to themselves and the group, using whatever media worked best, their unique and complex **self-defined** and constructed **sexual identity** intertwined with their sense of gender identity, including selectively telling about the formative experiences which helped them put these aspects of identity together. People might develop together ways of diagramming the complex interplay between the specifics of gender identity of both the self and of the people for whom desire has been felt over the life course, and of the person's capacities for forms of desire that are gender linked and that seem not to be gender linked. In other words, the group's understandings about the categories of sexual and gender identity would be much more multivariant than they are in present discourse and telling each other about identity would be expected.

Thus, the actual **diversity of sexual identities** would be visible in each group. In addition, the meanings for **maleness and femaleness** would be **expanded** by welcoming each individual's understanding of gender and by seeing the actual variability of gender identity as another resource for the community. This expansion is something the group quickly concludes that children will need to know about, as models for their own full and free gender development, unhampered by the currently tight boxes of acceptable maleness and femaleness in which boys and girls are asked to fit themselves.

Each new subgroup in the community, as people work together or get to know each other, would take time to bear witness for these tellings of individual journeys. Such time is a tangible way in which a **commitment to relationship building** would be practiced. **Colleagueship would be valued** and relationships in the group would be characterized by a desire to **live in equity,** meaning:

— relationships characterized by shared responsibility for the care of the relationship;
— commitment to regular feedback;
— valuing both process and task;
— flexibility,
— connection of feelings and intellect;
— growing accustomed to wide swings of emotion or the constant engagement of emotion;
— increasing skill at simultaneous presence as an autonomous self and as a relational or connected self, including managing one's boundaries to permit both connectedness and maintenance of self-differentiation.

Relationship building is a key skill, as is listening, for building a healthy community. The commitment made both by telling one's own identity development story and in listening to those of other group members is an example of how a group could practice both skills.

The group working on an educational plan for the community's children might want advice from other organizational members. The issue of what children should be told about sexuality is a volatile one for many people, including those in our hypothetical organization. In the face of the parable's predicted drastic world change, members might be feeling some urgency, fear, anger, desire to protect, and other emotions in relation to the children and what they would need to know.

The group might ask existing resource groups and networks to meet and discuss the question of what the children ought to be told. Thus, an existing African American group and other culture specific groups might meet, a gay men's support group might meet, a Bible study group might meet, a women's group might meet. **Support systems and networks, reflecting** the **diversity and commonalities** of experience, belief, or identity, that people needed and which served to provide even safer harbors, would be valued as providing nourishment and additional ways in which members of the larger group could continue to work well together. This understanding would be a part of our hypothetical group's commitment to building themselves into an **open and affirming organization,** and to figuring out how to build such organizations elsewhere in the larger community.

If we go back to our small group working on an educational plan, members will undoubtedly want to tell each other about the kinds of families and committed relationships which exist among them, and find ways to show the children how the idea of **family** is being **redefined** by this community, redefined to include families of choice as well as of blood, families of children and two mothers or two fathers, families of groups of adults and no children. In addition, **definitions of committed relationships** between two adults will **broaden** to include asexual companionship, sexual life partners of the same sex, heterosexual life partnerships, friendships lived as centrally important in people's lives, and other forms. Such redefinitions will feel urgent to our group given that many children may face adoption or family disruption after the change Audre predicted, but they are important parts of valuing sexual diversity whether or not such a change were to take place. In such a setting the sense of possible **intimacy** also **expands,** intimacy for example between friends of the same sex and of different sexes. The community is likely to want children to learn to value their same sex friendships and the close emotional and affectionate support possible in them. They might also want children to value the mentoring relationships they may find in their lives and the passionate though asexual attention given and received in such relationships, as well as other forms of intimacy too often avoided through homophobic fear today.

If this hypothetical community is to prepare itself and its children for the change, by trying to create a place where the full diversity of relationships and sexualities are really valued, everyone will need to be **loving one's own body and sexuality,** meaning a deep treasuring and valuing of the self, physically, intimately. This will be a real shift from the effects of dominance and subordinance on attitudes toward the body and toward sexuality. For heterosexual people a healing, involving a recognition and knowing about our full range of physical feelings, those present and those possible, needs to take place. Knowing desires may exist without being acted on, knowing acknowledging such desires can bring closeness rather than terror, will be important. For lesbians, gay men, and bisexual people, the healing will bring comfort in the body, a love for its disobedient

178

survival, and an admiration for that inner knowing strong enough to have surfaced despite the massive denial and repression to which we have been subjected by heterosexist culture. In addition, gay men, lesbians, and bisexual people can come to accept and value the full range of feelings that exist in some of us, including whatever feelings of intimacy or desire across gender lines some of us have had or continue to have.

All these characteristics mean that our small task group will exist and do its work in ways quite different from most small groups of today. The work it sets out to do will be understood to be deeply personal, the relationships it needs to build in order to do its work will engage members more deeply, meanings will shift and expand. Each person will be asking themselves "what do I want, what am I feeling, what is this relationship really about, what is this situation or problem really about, what part of my self and experience need to be known in order to do this work, what assumptions and categories need to be stated explicitly and reassessed, what are the implications systemically for the personal stories we are telling each other as we work?" These questions are never settled but are constantly reopened, making relationships, definitions of work and tasks constant only in their capacity to change, and making understandings of self and sexuality an ongoing discovery that is central to the elaboration of both collegiality and intimacy, as well as to social change.

Our capacity to value a diversity of relationships and sexualities will grow in depth and wisdom if we are willing to create communities where we can be fully known to one another in our wondrous and shifting complexity. We hope a world-wide change, such as the violence the parable predicts, will not be necessary, that we can begin telling ourselves and each other our fuller stories, stories we believe can help free us to join together in travelling the journeys mapped and described here.

Appendix A

Definitions and Categories

HEATHER WISHIK

Common language is essential if we are to understand one another while we explore sexual orientation and identity issues. This appendix clarifies how we use several key concepts throughout this book. It is important to remember that language has been and continues to be used to distort and deny much having to do with sexual orientation and identity.

We believe that contemporary, Western, heterosexually dominated cultures have often used the labels homosexual, lesbian, and gay to signify people who engage in specified sexual behaviors. This collapse of all the possible meanings of being gay or lesbian into a focus on sexual behavior only, has resulted in a habitual response to hearing the words homosexual, lesbian, or gay. For most English-speaking, heterosexual adults today, hearing the words homosexual, lesbian, gay, or bisexual or hearing someone come out as lesbian, gay, or bisexual sets off mental images of two men engaged in anal penetration, two women engaged in oral sex, or a person engaging in both these behaviors in rapid, repeated succession. This seldom admitted but almost universal internal voyeuristic response to a person's self identification as lesbian or gay is not surprising since, until recently, we have had no concept for understanding the words gay or lesbian other than as a declaration that one engages in such sexual behaviors. There is no comparable, genitally focused, internal mental response to a person's revelation of heterosexuality via an engagement or wedding ring, or other statement.

In addition, a culturally obsessive discussion occurs around the topic of causation of sexual orientation. One of the first questions always asked by the media and in community or organizational settings when sexual orientation comes up is What causes people to be gay or lesbian? We note that the question of what causes heterosexuality or a generic inquiry about causes of sexual orientation are much less often posed outside academic circles. We think such causation inquiry is profoundly beside the point, but it is also a symptom of a problem inherent in modern compulsory heterosexuality. People are usually prevented from a conscious examination and construction of a heterosexual identity in the context of knowledge of all the possible identities. Thus, many heterosexually identified people feel deeply tentative about their orientation and identity. They want proof—a way of knowing they are not gay or lesbian (and are heterosexual). This is one basis, we believe, for the obsession with causation and desire for biological explanations.

What really matters to us is to understand how categories describing human sexual diversity are used to oppress, to create dominance and subordinance, and how we can all learn to transcend the limits of this use of these categories. Nonetheless, answers to the causation questions are used by heterosexual, gay, lesbian, and bisexual people to justify everything from maintaining the status quo to supporting substantial social change; from gay bashing, imprisonment, and religious condemnation to gay civil rights laws, ordination, and marriage.

Whether sexual orientation and gender are biological or socially constructed is an ongoing debate between broader positions labeled essentialism and social constructionism. In gay and lesbian history, the debate also concerns whether lesbians and gay men have existed throughout history, although not always so labeled, or have existed only in the last hundred years, as the identity and lifestyle of lesbian and gay man have become socially possible (see Appendix C).

Over the last twenty-five years, the categories lesbian, bisexual, and gay have been given a second level of meaning within gay and lesbian circles in addition to that relating to sexual behaviors. The newer layer of meaning, which we name sexual identity, is one of socially constructed experiences of identity and of membership in groups (gay men, lesbians, bisexual people) with aspects of their own cultures. A third layer of meaning has emerged more recently which is named sexual orientation. This layer has to do with what many people, particularly heterosexual and gay men, report as a core knowledge from early childhood about the nature of their sexual inclinations and capacities—whether they are homoerotic or heteroerotic.

These reports of deeply felt knowing about the self, beginning as young as two, three, or four years of age, have led to assumptions that some portion of the group of factors which may lead to a person's adult sexual identity and behaviors may be set early in life or may be innate. Some preliminary research has begun to suggest that biological factors may be contributing to some people's felt homoerotic orientation. (See Appendix C for more about these studies.)

Whether this third layer—orientation—exists at all, separate from identity and behavior, is still highly contested. To add to the confusion, the phrase *sexual orientation* is popularly used to mean a person's sense of sexual identity and preferred sexual behaviors, or to mean all three concepts—orientation, identity, and behavior. In addition, the phrase *sexual identity* is sometimes used to mean a person's gender identity, that is, a person's sense of maleness or femaleness, instead of his or her sense of gayness, bi-ness, or straightness. Both because of these linguistic confusions and the emergent multiple layers of meaning around the categories represented by the words we have, we include some working definitions.

As is evident from the definitions below, we have taken an approach which straddles the essentialist and the social constructionist positions by separating orientation from identity and both from behavior. While we do not know what percentage of people experience an early and strongly directed sense of sexual orientation that is narrowly heteroerotic or homoerotic, we grant that such experience is true for some people and that an increasingly credible explanation for some of these reported experiences is that some biological factors are somehow at work. Such people, nonetheless, still face the life task of constructing a culturally conceivable sexual identity.

We also grant that for some people their inmost sense of erotic capacities and inclinations is more open-textured or ambisexual. Thus, for them, whatever may be innate about sexual orientation, if anything, contributes no more than open possibilities within which they develop or "try on" one or more culturally conceivable sexual identities during their lives. We suggest that most if not all aspects of gender, gender identity, and sexual identity are culturally mediated and individually constructed.

This position presents some language problems. For example, we use the phrases *same sex* and *other sex* to represent a person's biological sex. This phrasing assumes there are two exclusive biological sexes, but we know this is not as true as we are often led to believe. We also know that gender identity can be a blend of what is defined by heteropatriarchal cultures as two separate genders. Expansion of the culturally constructed ideas of gender and of the individually internalized gender identities which flow therefrom is explicitly important and necessary in the journeys this book describes.

Sexual Orientation: Sexual orientation is a term used to describe a person's inmost or core sense of predisposition, capacity, or inclination to enjoy types of erotic and/or emotional or affectional desire, intimacy, or sexual interactions.

Sometimes this sense of predisposition or capacity is very specific, sometimes very broad. A person may feel strongly or exclusively heteroerotic or homoerotic, or more or less ambierotic. Some people are first aware of their orientation at a very early age.

We do not know what causes sexual orientation as defined here. We do know that humans have manifested homoerotic and heteroerotic desires throughout all cultures and times. An increasing number of studies suggest that for at least some portion of the population, sexual orientation may be a biologically based predisposition involving genetics, prenatal hormones, or some combination of these.

183

If a biologically based predisposition does exist, it could contribute to a person's most deeply felt sense of self as a sexual being by helping to determine the angle or direction of a person's erotic or emotional sensibilities. Orientation, as a form of biological predisposition, would be beyond a person's conscious capacity to change, whether it were directed exclusively or predominantly toward persons of the same sex or the other sex, toward persons of any sex, or toward erotic experiences with one's own body separate from relationships or interactions with anyone else (what might be termed an autoerotic orientation).

We are not talking about more extreme patterns of sexual desire or interpersonal behavior which may develop through a combination of heteropatriarchal cultural messages taken to a pathological extreme and/or through childhood trauma, abuse, neglect, or other developmental events. Thus, sexual desires deeply linked to imbalances of power and anomalies viewed today as pathological (such as pedophilia, the desire for adult sexual contact with young children) are not sexual orientations in this definition. Yet the line between sickness and normality in sexual behavior is a culturally determined one: adult male sexual initiation of pubertal boys is and has been viewed as appropriate and sacred in many cultures. Nonetheless, for the purposes of this book, sexual orientation does not include pedophilia. Sexual orientation as used herein is a phrase that applies to a person's capacity for or direction of erotic, affectional, and/or emotional desire. Sexual orientation probably includes infinite variations and may be bipolar—a degree of attraction to males and masculinity and a degree of attraction to females and femininity—in many combinations, the most familiar of which currently are called heterosexual, homosexual, bisexual or ambisexual, and autosexual.

Sexual Behavior: How a person acts sexually/erotically. Both the sexual/erotic conduct a person engages in and the sexual/erotic conduct a person desires and/or fantasizes about are sexual behaviors.

Sexual behaviors include actions in which people engage involving sexual and relational intimacy with themselves and others and behaviors designed to produce erotic pleasure. They include costuming, gesturing, and other social behaviors which signal sexual interest and desired behavior toward others; they also signal gender identity. Sexual behaviors signal gender identity because, in modern heterosexually dominated cultures, gender identity is definitionally heterosexual.

Sexual behaviors are culturally mediated. From the form of kisses, to the prevalent types of genital contact, to the meaning given the colors of certain flowers, cultures and subcultures, varying with time, define what sexual behaviors are encouraged under what circumstances, which actions are viewed as erotic and which disgusting, and what categories of acts are considered taboo.

Thus the sexual and/or erotic behaviors a person engages in at various points in life may have little to do with the erotic desires flowing from that person's sexual orientation, especially if the person's sexual orientation involves desires that are culturally condemned or repressed. The capacity to engage in sexual behaviors is not, for many people, limited to those behaviors consistent with their dominant sexual orientation: some gay men are capable of having heterosexual intercourse, for example.

Sexual behaviors may change over time as persons shift their own sexual identity and/or understanding of their sexual orientation, or modify their definitions of gender, or decide for social, political, or psychological reasons to alter behavior, or decide to rebel against, transcend, or accede to cultural pressures.

Sexual Identity: Sexual identity is a term for the ways in which a person living in her or his particular cultural and historical context experiences, makes sense of, labels, and lives out her or his own combination of sexual orientation, biological sex, and gender.

Sexual identity is developed and elaborated over time and involves culturally available choices about behaviors, language, and meaning. The opportunity consciously to develop one or more healthy, self-affirming, adult sexual identities is profoundly affected by one's family of origin, childhood religious context, and home culture. As one matures, access to resources supportive of such development, including other people, can be crucial.

Sexual identity affects how persons understand their biological sex and construct their gender identity and how they understand and interact with persons of the same and other sex. Sexual identity involves consequences for and choices about emotional attachments and social, cultural, and political involvements.

In present culture, sexual identity may also be a label people impose on an individual, based on that person's appearance, interests, and behaviors (sexual and otherwise). For our purposes, sexual identity is not simply an externally imposed label; it is an identity claimed and constructed by the individual about her or himself from what it is possible to claim in the person's culture. Clearly external labels affect what the individual, particularly in childhood, can and does know and feel about the self. Whether or not accurate, these external labels may be internalized as true for long periods in a person's life.

Sexual identity often changes over time as a person's understanding of his or her own behaviors and/or orientation changes. It can also be changed by an individual in response to cultural norm shifts, political events, and migration from culture to culture, or between subcultures within a culture.

Let us take, for example, a woman who has the capacity for erotic intimacy with both men and women. She has a predominantly but not exclusively homo-erotic sexual orientation. Early in her life she does not take seriously her feelings toward women, in part as a result of cultural repression (heterosexism) and in part as a result of her own misunderstanding of the meaning of her capacity for heteroerotic and homoerotic enjoyment. That is, she thinks she can't possibly be a lesbian since she can have orgasms with men. She has never heard of ambisexuality as an orientation or bisexuality as a possible identity. She might marry early in life and identify as and behave as a heterosexual woman. After learning more about lesbianism and feminism, and after persistently experiencing erotic desire toward women, she might later in life decide to identify as a lesbian or as a bisexual woman. As a second example, a man with an ambisexual orientation might identify as gay while in a relationship with a man and later identify as heterosexual while in a relationship with a woman. It is also possible that this man would identify as bisexual throughout this whole period.

The available conceptions of sexual identity are in part determined culturally. For example, in contemporary Western culture we have terms for people who are presumed to be sexual exclusively with persons of their own sex and for people who are presumed to be sexual exclusively with people of the other sex (homosexual, heterosexual; gay/lesbian and straight). We have a catch-all for people who, during their lives, have or desire erotic experiences with persons of both the same and the other sex (bisexual, bi). All three of these conceptions are inadequate and confusing. The behavioral, political, and cultural differences between someone who identifies as gay and someone who identifies as bisexual are not defined accurately by the terms. In addition, identifying as a homosexual is not the same as identifying as lesbian or gay, and this difference in meaning has been true since the late 1960s.* That is, possible sexual identities are deeply tied to cultural/ historical moments and age cohorts.[1]

The inadequacy of the available terms for sexual orientation and identity is in part a consequence of the cultural need, in heterosexually dominated culture, to define the majority as exclusively heteroerotic and to deny the frequency of ambisexual capacities in humankind. In addition, we do not have terms for a person who is, for example, autosexual, that is, oriented and preferring to be sexual with his or her own body, not sexual with another person's body. The three-part conception of sexual orientation and identity current in Western culture is not an adequate description of the varieties of sexual orientation present in humans; the list of three possible sexual identities is also too short.

Sexual identity is not just about sexual behaviors. Many lesbians, for instance, say their lesbianism means they are woman-identified. This description may mean they have worked to construct a sense of empowered woman-self. Sometimes heterosexual women also call this construction of positive woman's identity a woman-identified perspective.

Lesbians may mean by *woman-identified* that they prefer to spend time with other woman-identified women as friends and acquaintances, prefer to immerse themselves in women's music and art, prefer to engage in sports with women and in political work with woman-identified women as well as often being erotically oriented toward or sexually desiring women. Boston marriage,[2] the nineteenth-century New England term for romantic friendships between women, only some

---

*Identity constructs change in cultures over time. Gay identity is a more self-affirming visible and political identity than the 1950's construct, homosexual, usually involves.

of which were genitally or otherwise physically sexual, is an example in recent history in this country of a time when being woman-identified was recognized, named, and accommodated culturally, at least as a positive stage prior to marrying a man.

Sex: A person's sex is his or her biological status based on a set of primary sex characteristics which are usually either male or female.[3]

Primary sex characteristics include the internal reproductive organs and external genitalia. Secondary sex characteristics include those that usually develop during puberty, but they are more variable across races and within sexes than are primary sex characteristics. Facial hair, female breast development, and the lower male vocal range are all secondary sex characteristics.

The presence of a set of primary sex characteristics depends on a combination of chromosomes and hormones, including the array of X and Y or X and X chromosomes. In particular these characteristics depend on the presence or absence of a certain gene usually found on the Y chromosome but sometimes attached to the X, and on both prenatal exposure to androgens and progestins and the body's capacity to produce and absorb testosterone, estrogen, progesterone, and androgen. The influence of hormones prenatally is not yet fully understood, nor is the interaction between environmental demands, hypothalamic sensitivity, and the production and metabolization of sex hormones.[4]

Most biological females—persons with the reproductive organs and genitalia of females—also have two X chromosomes. Most biological males have one X and one Y, but there are males who have two X's, with a bit of Y attached to one X. Some babies are born with X and Y chromosomes but without the ability to produce sufficient androgen; there are females with an X and Y but without the crucial bit of Y, and others with only an X.

Since the midpoint of this century, in Western countries, persons of ambiguous sex based on reproductive organs and external genitalia often have received early medical intervention to assign a clear sex. Others whose external genitalia appear clearly male or female at birth are treated with hormones at puberty when secondary sex characteristics which usually develop at this time fail to appear, causing discovery of a hormonal or chromosomal anomaly. Such treatments at birth render external appearances clearly male or female; treatments at puberty usually result in secondary sex characteristics consistent with the external genitalia, although some of these persons may be sterile because of the absence of developed internal reproductive organs. Such surgical and hormonal interventions may result in sex assignment that does not correspond to the chromosomal evidence.

Sex Identity: A person's sex identity is his or her "acceptance of membership in a particular sex category."[5]

Sex identity usually but not always corresponds to biological sex. For example, some people do not accept that they are male even though their bodies possess the primary sex characteristics of males. Such people are called transsexuals in contemporary Western cultures.*

Gender and Gender Identity: Gender is the culturally constructed definition of man and woman, including a person's social status as either a woman or man, girl or boy. Gender identity is also the culturally constructed definition of man and woman as internalized and adopted by the individual and lived through actions, behaviors, and values which combine as gender roles, masculinity and femininity, maleness and femaleness, or as a transgender identity.[6]

Gender identity is constructed from the gender socialization experienced throughout life, beginning with birth, and from the self-definition of man and woman, maleness and femaleness developed within the cultural-political context of a person's time and place, culture and class, religion, ethnicity, physical ability, and sexual orientation. In this sense it may be most accurate to speak of the existence of many gender identities.

In contemporary Western cultures, gender meanings include defining "real" men and women as heterosexual. Thus, sexual orientation and identity become aspects of gender definition and of a culture's gender systems. In contemporary western cultures people who are other than exclusively heterosexual "become"

---

*Transsexualism is understood by many in the medical and psychological professions to be an issue of sex identity, that is, a person feels like a man born in a woman's body. However, some commentators have suggested that transsexualism may at least sometimes be instead an issue of gender identity. That is, the rigidity of the dominant cultural constructions of gender, the social status and meanings ascribed to being a man or woman, may for some transsexual people be the source of their conviction that their biological sex does not correspond to "who they are." Their internalized sense of social status and meaning related to their biological sex profoundly does not match the culture's construction of the gender associated with that biological sex. Whether a transsexual person experiences the dissonance as one between sex and sex identity or between sex and gender identity, he or she may adopt a gender role belonging to the sex different from the biological one. When the dissonance is profound, some transsexual people alter their bodies hormonally and/or surgically, a process known as sex change. Dominant Western culture is still ambivalent about whether sex change is possible. For example, a male-to-female transsexual in Britain has been denied by both British and European Community courts the right to change the gender on her birth certificate, a change necessary to permit her legally to marry a man in Britain.

This book treats transsexualism as a phenomenon separate from sexual orientation and sexual identity. It is nonetheless a condition that may make it particularly difficult for a person to sort out his or her sexual orientation and sexual identity, given heterosexually dominated culture's definitions. For example, a male-to-female transsexual before surgery may find men erotically attractive and thus be labeled by others as gay, although he will not necessarily self-identify in this way. After surgery she will be labeled by others as heterosexual if she continues to be involved sexually with men. Another male-to-female transsexual before surgery may find women erotically attractive but may identify herself as heterosexual, believing such attraction to women has to do with her desire herself to become biologically a woman. She may expect that after surgery she will experience erotic attraction to men, only to discover that she continues to be erotically oriented to women. She may then attempt to come out as a lesbian and seek inclusion in lesbian communities, an attempt that may be greeted with hostility by many lesbians who believe that the behaviors and personality traits produced by socialization as a male with male privileges don't disappear with a sex change operation and that, therefore, male-to-female transsexuals do not belong in women-only spaces.

people of ambiguous gender, by definition.* This is why reexamination of the meaning of gender, and of one's own gender identity, is required as part of the sexual orientation and identity journeys described here.

Combining the Concepts

Sex is initially biological and is usually set at birth, or shortly thereafter through medical intervention. **Sex identity** is the very early internalized recognition of one's biological sex as true or not. **Gender identity** is a culturally mediated individual journey. Gender identity can thus change over time. This does not usually mean that a man will conclude at some point in his life that he is a woman. Instead, what being male means to an individual man may change over time, and this change in some dimensions of that man's gender identity may lead to changes in attitude and behavior which are essential to his journey about sexual orientation and identity.

Sexual orientation may be both biologically influenced and culturally constructed or mediated, or it may be completely an artifact of culture. It may involve a biologically constructed range of possibilities which are given meaning and forms of expression through culture, for example. As a predisposition for core desires, it is often experienced as inalterable by conscious manipulation. There is probably a greater variety of sexual orientations than is usually acknowledged as possible, and there are probably more people with expansive sexual orientations, that is, a range of erotic capacity and inclination, than is generally believed to exist today. **Sexual behaviors** are culturally situated and learned. Patterns of interaction and meanings ascribed to them differ depending on the culture and the era as well as on the individual's gender and the roles ascribed by the particular era and culture to that gender. Sexual behaviors can be tried out, adopted, abandoned, altered; they are subject to conscious choice and modification, cultural encouragement and repression.

Sexual identity is the cluster of meanings an individual gives to the combination of his or her own gender, sexual orientation, and sexual/erotic behaviors and desires. It too is culturally mediated and can be changed by the individual and the culture over time. The capacity to know the self in these regards may be limited by cultural repression and sexual abuse experiences as well as internalized gender-identity constraints. The journey to self-knowledge about sexual orientation, behavior, and identity is one that takes courage and a willingness constantly to push outward from the meanings learned and available in one's own particular era, culture, and situation.

---

*See Chapter 2 and Appendix C regarding forms of same-sex behavior in other times and cultures consistent with the gender system.

Aspects of Sexual and Gender Identity

People's sexual and gender identities affect them and are lived in many ways. In particular, we live out such identities through our physical desires, our emotional commitments and affinities, and our intellectual and political stances (identity politics). It is possible for a man to feel erotically oriented toward men but emotionally oriented toward women. In such a situation, the man may choose to build an intimate, long-term relationship with a male partner, while nonetheless acknowledging that in doing so he misses intimacy with women, relations he found emotionally satisfying. It is possible for a woman to feel erotically oriented toward men and emotionally oriented toward women. In this case she may marry, but the most important ongoing friendships in her life are with women. A woman may feel erotically and emotionally oriented toward women, and thus live as a lesbian in her personal and social life, but be intellectually and politically engaged by ideas, activities, and forms of professional relationship which have been culturally labeled male.

All of these examples suggest that the cultural limitations on gender roles and behavior create stresses for people as they try to live out their full identities in relationship with others. What the man who elects to live in a relationship with a man and forego intimacy with women may miss emotionally might be possible with a man if male/female socialization changed and more men were more skilled at the deeper emotional intimacy usually labeled female. On the other hand, it may be that sexual orientation is more complex than we have heretofore acknowledged and that it encompasses multiple variables of erotic and emotional or affiliative desires as well as dual axes of attraction, one for each gender, and these variables may not all be directed the same way in any one individual.

APPENDIX B

Childhood Experiences

HEATHER WISHIK

This book and the sexual orientation graphic describe journeys of attitude, awareness, self-identification, and behavior as they are experienced by late adolescents and adults, although more and more people travel portions of this journey during early and middle adolescence.[1] Awareness of sexual orientation and construction of gender and sexual identities do not just begin at a person's eighteenth birthday. Children, too, acquire attitudes and develop behaviors relating to gender identity and sexual orientation, and most begin construction of their sexual identity before adulthood.[2]

People today are more likely to begin articulating their sexual identity during childhood than were children a decade or two or three ago. While the proportion of young children conscious of homoerotic or heteroerotic feelings and fantasies may not have changed, the context in which such awareness occurs has changed drastically. Children are more likely than ever before to see on television or in print media real or fictional lesbian, bisexual, and gay people, or hear talk about a sexual orientation other than heterosexual from parents, teachers, or schoolmates. There used to be almost total silence about alternatives to heterosexuality, combined with epithets. Now in many children's experiences there exists a range of negative, stereotyped, and more accurate depictions of the fact that some people are gay, lesbian, or bisexual. Media images include, for example, talk shows and the "Men and Books" SNAP! queens of the Fox network television show "In Living Color," a show many seventh graders list as their favorite, and the lesbian character played by Sandra Bernhard on ABC's "Roseanne." Sexual orientation is still never mentioned in the curricula of most schools, but this too is changing, more often in private than in public schools.*

At a private school in Massachusetts, I spent an hour talking about homophobia with four seventh grade classes as part of a social studies curriculum about prejudice. These are some of the comments the students wrote afterward:

Good that our school let a lesbian come and talk.

I was really surprised when she said that most crimes committed against gays or lesbians were done by high school students.

The presentation was completely different than I thought it would be. I expected an embarrassed woman admitting she was gay as if she was an alcoholic! It was actually just her discussing what homophobia was, and describing what had happened to her because of it.

I do not think we need people to come speak to us about this kind of stuff. I think we all know about this.

I hate gays and lesbians. I thought it was a positive experience but I don't know why she made it seem like I couldn't hold grudges.

I couldn't believe someone could be so open about being a lesbo.

I agree with everything she said and I think there is no reason to be afraid of homosexuals.

The following is a brief description of some of what has been hypothesized, surmised, or reported retrospectively about childhood experiences of sexual identity construction as well as some of the things young people today are telling us about their experiences. As will rapidly become clear, the childhood process of gender-identity construction is usually deeply intertwined with the child's emergent awareness of sexuality and sexual orientation, although the relationship between gender and sexual-identity development takes many forms.

---

*In New England The Gay and Lesbian School Teachers Network (GLSTN), an organization begun by independent school teachers, held its fourth annual conference near Boston and attracted public school principals and teachers in substantial numbers. In Massachusetts, a report compiled by the Governor's Commission on Gay and Lesbian Youth has spurred schools to provide support services and to increase the curricular visibility of gay, lesbian, and bisexual people. Most recently, Massachusetts adopted legislation protecting gay and lesbian youths' right to equal educational access. See Massachusetts Governor's Commission on Gay and Lesbian Youth, "Making Schools Safe for Gay and Lesbian Youth," Boston, February 25, 1993; Don Aucoin, "Weld Signs Gay Student Rights Law," *Boston Globe*, December 11, 1993.

At birth, children have no information or attitudes about the meaning of gender, let alone about sexualities. Almost from birth, however, children in modern Western cultures are taught about maleness and femaleness. From blue and pink disposable diapers, blankets, and clothing to adult approval and disapproval, infants are given information about "appropriate" gender behavior.

By the time children are two or three years of age, they have fully internalized the implications of stereotyped gender roles, incorporating gender-specific life stories into their play, fantasies, and dreams. Thus the three-year-old white boy tells his mother that he wants to grow up to be a knight who rides on horses to adventure. When mother says this sounds like fun and she'd like to do this too, he vehemently insists that "girls cannot ride horses and have adventures." When mother indicates disappointment that she might be restricted to a life without adventure, the boy says, "Don't worry Mom, I'd love and marry you anyway."[3]

Acquiring information about maleness and femaleness, and asking questions about what is male and what is female, occupy young children through the preschool years. These are also years when children first learn about reproduction, through birth of a sibling, contact with animals, school lessons, or parental behavior and explanations. These are also years in which many children explore autoerotic feelings.

By age four or five, some children are already manifesting behaviors that don't fit the gender stereotypes they have learned. Adults may label such behaviors in girls "tomboyism" and in boys "sissy" behavior. These gender-bending children may show interest in activities typical of the other gender or dislike of activities typical of their own gender. This may involve things many parents will tolerate—boys who like the color pink and stuffed animals, and girls who like tree climbing and playing ball. Or it may involve behaviors, such as a boy insistent on wearing girl's clothes, that push the limits of parental comfort and garner for the child punishment, prohibition, referral to therapy, or other discouraging responses.

Gender-bending behavior does not necessarily signal that a child's sexual orientation is homoerotic, although parental response to gender bending is often based on such an assumption. It is also true that many gay men, lesbians, and bisexual adults report they behaved as children in gender-traditional ways, even as some of them were conscious quite early of having homo-aesthetic and/or homoerotic feelings. In fact, some lesbian and gay adults report that extreme gender conformity was a central part of their adolescent closet.

Based on interview data, it seems apparent that many boys who eventually mature to identify as gay have erotic feelings about males, including their fathers, very early in life.[4] This may also be true of boys who as adults identify as bisexual.

According to the theories of psychiatrist Richard Isay, such early same-sex feelings sometimes provoke hostility and rejection from a father who doesn't understand his son's attempts at intimacy with him. Also, such a boy may try to imitate his mother in an attempt to win or win back the affection of his father. This exacerbates the paternal rejection as the father comes to view his as-yet-unacknowledged gay or bisexual son as a sissy, which quickly leads to concerns that the son is gay. Such early concern about a son's sexual orientation may lead to pressure on the boy to become more manly. Sometimes this includes physical beatings or increased pressure to prove manliness and heterosexuality through sports and, later on, dating. A mother too may pressure a young boy who fails to act gender appropriate. This early articulation of parental anxiety about the son's sexual orientation may give the boy language and categories, albeit with negative connotations, which enable him to recognize his own gayness quite early, sometimes even before school experiences with peers' use of epithets like *faggot*.

The motif of paternal rejection characterizes, according to Isay, many a gay man's early childhood. Dominant culture, including psychiatry, has for much of this century blamed overinvolvement of the mother for a gay male's sexual orientation. In fact, parents don't determine sexual orientation, and the appearance of closeness between a gay man and his mother during childhood may be a function of both paternal rejection and the boy's response to it, rather than maternal overprotection.[5]

Some girls who feel erotic desire for females and the mother early in life do experience maternal rejection or hostility.

> I was four or five when I heard the song, "The Girl That I Marry." . . . I pondered what the girl *I* would marry would be like. One afternoon, when the song was playing on the radio, I informed my mother, solemnly, that the girl I married would be just like her.
>
> She was not flattered. In fact, she seemed disturbed. She said: "Girls can't marry girls. Only boys can marry girls."[6]

Other girls may simply experience their mothers' distancing, a common experience for all daughters. That is, a mother often withdraws nurturing earlier from daughters than from sons as part of teaching girls to provide nurturing rather than to expect it.[7] A lesbian child's desires for maternal intimacy may not be differentiated by her mother from a straight daughter's desires, since both are often weaned from nurturance early enough to protest.

If a lesbian tries to act like Daddy, she is probably labeled a tomboy, a label mainly descriptive of physical competence and assertiveness. It does not carry the exclusively derogatory connotations that sissy does for a boy, nor is *tomboy* always equated with *lesbian*, in the same way *sissy* is tightly associated with *fairy* and *faggot* for boys.

It may be true that tomboys spend less time with traditional mothers than do girls who are happy to engage in traditional female behaviors such as cooking and sewing. Nonetheless, such girls probably do not face a second round of maternal rejection comparable to what gay boys experience with their fathers. In fact, many

194

tomboys garner admiration from their mothers, who wish they had been as assertive as their daughters are able to be. Girls who are conscious early of erotic desire toward women do not typically experience early parental or social recognition that they may be lesbian, which might explain the delay many girls experience in recognizing their lesbianism. Some data about coming out to the self suggest that boys tend to do so several years earlier than do girls.

Gilbert Herdt and Andrew Boxer have described the prepubertal, early childhood stages of sexual-identity development this way: "The first experiences are concerned with early development from birth to puberty. Desire is here based in aesthetic feelings and responses that are neither purely of the body nor of the culture. They are not discretely 'erotic.' Yet these early experiences are more strongly influenced by intrinsic desires and feelings than later ones."[8] The authors define what they mean by intrinsic desires in explaining their view of sexual-identity development processes.

> These processes begin, we think, with a given, perhaps a biologically grounded, form of "desire." . . . Desires, we believe, originate from within the nature of the person, as a state of being and adaptation. We think of these elements as "internal" in the sense of the potentials of being a person; however, desires interact with cultural experiences and social learning . . . yet the earliest desires, we believe, are ontologically prior to and directive of all later cultural learning and teaching, especially after the entry of the child into school and diverse peer groups; subsequent socially learned desires build upon them. It is fruitless to search for "nature/nurture" dichotomies here.[9]

These early experiences of desire become permeated by cultural constructs by the time a child goes to school.

Modern culture's polarization of appropriate gender behavior has lessened somewhat for children. For example, girls are now allowed to be athletic and feminine. Nonetheless, the range of acceptable gender behavior often continues to be quite narrow within a child's peer group, particularly for boys. In some cultures the boy who wears red shoes to kindergarten will be asked by his male peers why he is wearing "girl" shoes or may be called sissy or faggot; or the new sixth grader in town who comes to the first day of school wearing a brightly colored jacket hears the word *fag* tossed at him.[10]

The epithets relating to sexual orientation enter the child's vocabulary by school age. These words may be heard without any associated meaning other than disobedience to proper gender behavior, or they may be understood as the derogatory label for the sense of differentness the boy or girl feels about himself or herself.

> I was eleven years old when I was first called "faggot," and although I was ignorant of the total meaning of the word, I was irate, to say the least. Growing up black, and effeminate or androgynous, was no easy

achievement. . . . In retrospect, . . . I think the cruelest part of being labeled "queer" or "sissy" is the lack of explanation about the meanings of those words. I wanted to understand the totality of my supposed "perversion"; I could count on any and everyone to spit the word faggot at me, but there was no one able to go further and say that along with the daily anguish of disapproving sneers and catcalls, there would also be the love of a man. A black man. If someone had told me then what I now know about being a faggot, I would have gladly withstood the name-calling.[11]

Some school-age children sense feelings they know may be different from those of others. The girl at age five who likes to sit in front of the kindergarten teacher during story time so she can look up the teacher's skirt at teacher's thighs and the darkness above her thighs is beginning to feel erotic interest in someone of the same sex. She enjoys the feeling she gets but already knows she must not say anything about it to anyone.[12]

By third grade she is fascinated by her teacher's large breasts and smooth legs. Her teacher's body makes the girl want to be close and to touch. Again, the girl knows she must not tell anyone or do anything obvious about these feelings. Instead, she tries to be a good student, one the teacher will want to hug. By this stage the girl senses that other girls probably don't feel this way about the teacher. If she is a secure child, she doesn't worry too much about her own otherness. If she is less secure or lives in a family with traditional gender-role expectations or conservative religious attitudes about sexual desire, she may begin to believe there is something wrong with her or that her feelings are sinful.

Thus by the time they reach elementary-school age, two groups of children are beginning to struggle with cultural limitations regarding gender. One group is tussling with the narrowness of acceptable gender behavior but is not experiencing any aesthetic or erotic sensations other than autosexual or heterosexual ones. Another group includes both gender conformists and gender-benders who are experiencing same-sex aesthetic fascination and/or erotic feelings, either exclusively or simultaneously with heteroerotic interest. Many children experience neither of these struggles, behaving through these years within the gender and sexual orientation expectations of their families, churches, schools, and peer groups.

Until recently almost all elementary-school-age children in Western culture were taught to assume everyone is heterosexual. This assumption is still built into most of the media, curriculum materials, and church and family information school-age children receive. If any information about bisexuality or homosexuality was made available, it undoubtedly described such orientation as bad or sinful, and that it involved not being a real boy or a real girl. A boy who can't throw a ball is a faggot or fairy; a girl who always wears jeans and climbs trees is a tomboy; a homo is a man who might bother a boy in a public rest room, someone to watch out for and run away from; a dyke or lesbo is a woman who looks like a man or who wants to be a man.[13] The degree of absence of information and role models varies depending on the person's culture.

> I felt immensely alienated from myself as a child and as a young adult. I didn't feel I truly fit in the black community because I was different and I knew it. . . . There was no black gay community. No support. Nothing. Even today a number of black gay children grow up not having anybody to look to. What information and images they get are all derogatory put-downs.[14]

> These are some of the stories I must tell you. . . . This will cause many things to happen. One is to help ensure that young women of colour know a simple and powerful fact: lesbians of colour exist. I was alone for many years and had no knowledge of this phenomenon called lesbianism. And some people think it only happened years ago, and that I am too young to have experienced this, and I say, no, for a girl who grew up in a working-class Lebanese extended family in a factory city, I was not too young.[15]

Invisibility, homophobic taunts, and adult silence about lesbian, gay, and bisexual people leave children to figure out the meaning of their "differentness" themselves. This childhood atmosphere means the very personal and private process of lesbian/gay identity development is, according to theorist Anthony D'Augelli, "conditioned by fear and shame."

> Even in early childhood, one learns that such an identity is problematic. Homophobic comments are routine in elementary schools, and exploration of same-sex physical and emotional closeness is severely punished by parents and others as soon as it appears. . . . The "hidden curriculum" of heterosexism is taught to all, even those children who as adults will self-identify as lesbian, gay, and bisexual. In contrast to other groups, lesbians, gay men, and bisexual people have grown up absorbing a destructive mythology before they appreciate that it is meant for them. Homophobia at such an early age is unusually resistant to change. . .[16]

Some kids think they must really be the other sex. Julia Penelope, recalling her thoughts at age five, says: "Well, if girls couldn't marry girls, if only boys could marry girls, I figured I must be a boy. I'd been offered no alternatives so I had to be one or the other. Of course, my genitals certainly identified me as a girl, so I figured that God had made a mistake in my construction and I must be a boy *inside*. My insides just didn't match up with my outsides."[17]

A combination of increased visibility of gay and lesbian people of many cultures, gay and lesbian publishing and film making, and more public information, plus dialogue and education about AIDS in the early grades, means that increasing numbers of young children are being taught, or are acquiring information, about the existence of gay men, lesbians, and homosexuality. There is still practically no information about bisexual people and bisexuality available to children. For those children who do acquire information about lesbians and gay men, it is often simply to learn that "gay men get AIDS and die." Such partial information translates into playground taunts and games. Instead of yelling that a certain disliked child has "cooties," the epithet now is "ooh, he has AIDS." The riddle on the playground is no longer a knock-knock joke. It is "Do you know what *gay* means?" Answer: "Got AIDS yet?"

For children experiencing same-sex erotic desires, such information is both helpful and hurtful. They are more likely today than ever before to know that some adults have same-sex feelings too, that they are not the only ones in the world who feel as they do. Their school library is more likely today to have a book presenting homosexuality as an alternative lifestyle rather than as an illness. But children are also likely to be haunted by the fear that if they kiss someone of the same sex they will die of AIDS. That is, they may think the inevitable life story for someone who is sexual with a person of the same sex includes early death from a terrible illness. And since the media have been ineffective at differentiating between gay men and lesbians regarding the incidence of AIDS, children of both sexes may be haunted by such fears. In addition, the continuing invisibility of bisexuality in the literature available to children means they are still learning the either/or attitude of heterosexual culture about sexual orientation and thus trying to fit their own experiences into one of two categories. Many bisexual people report concluding in young adolescence that they must be gay, based on their same-sex erotic feelings; many other bisexual people report concluding at that age that they couldn't be gay because they had sexual feelings toward the other sex too.

Cultural messages about lesbians and gay men have impact on how children give meaning to their early sexual experiences. Many children interact sexually with kids of their own sex, although boys probably do more of this than do girls in contemporary Western cultures. However, whether or not a preadolescent or adolescent has such encounters or feelings, heterosexual culture encourages the person to view them as aberrational, childish, developmental, or by some other label that permits the experiences to remain isolated and ungeneralized. For example, the school counselor to whom one teen boy went during junior high to talk about his homosexual feelings told him that "youngsters often go through a homosexual phase and that he could still grow up straight, marry, and have a family."[18]

Some children experience abusive same-sex sexual encounters with adults or older teens, although children, and females in particular, are much more likely to be abused by heterosexual men or male pedophiles than by gay men or lesbians. Nonetheless, the ten-year-old boy who is intimidated into sexual encounters with older boys at boarding school will have a tendency to bury the memory for a long time, and bury along with it his own recognition that he may have had or currently has same-sex feelings. And the eleven-year-old runaway who was raped by a truck driver is likely to assume that the man was gay and may identify gay men as dangerous and hateful throughout his life, unless he is able to recognize that his abuser was probably a heterosexually identified pedophile.*

Preadolescence brings with it increasing pressure to conform to traditional gender roles and to heterosexuality. This is true in part because contemporary Western educational systems deny the existence of preadolescent sexuality and, by silence, condemn children to the tyranny of their peer group.[19] Most teens simply assume their own heterosexuality as the culture assumes it for them. Sexual development doesn't include, for most children, a chance to ask themselves what their sexual orientation might be. This means that for those kids who find themselves able to conform to the heavy pressure brought to bear on them to explore and develop heterosexually, there may be a long delay in recognizing they are capable of other kinds of feelings, if they are.

Those children who have trouble conforming, because they are developmentally slow to move into puberty, because they have sexual/emotional feelings for persons of the same sex, or because they are simply interested in activities not typical of their gender or cannot behave in enough gender-appropriate ways, are all punished with increasing severity for nonconformity. Epithets, social ostracism by peers, criticism from teachers, and increasing hostility from parents are all forms this punishment takes. At the extremes, boys are beaten up by fathers to toughen them, or beaten or raped by heterosexual male peers or adults for being "fags." One gay man who grew up in a rural environment reports that "I learned what it 'meant' to be 'homosexual' from heterosexual men. They forced me as a teenager to give them blow jobs because they told me that was what I as a 'fairy' liked to do."[20]

One young gay man reports that in junior high,

> because he didn't conform to the local macho standards of dress and behavior, he was challenged to fistfights daily. Once in biology lab classmates threw frogs that they had been dissecting at him. Another time, after a water-polo game, a student held him under water so long that he almost drowned. [He] grew depressed, got erratic grades and became rebellious. His weight shot up . . . and he quarreled constantly with [his mother].[21]

---

*The authors accept two concepts about sexual relations involving adults and children. First, that in contemporary Western cultures (and in many other cultures) it is an abuse of adult power in almost every circumstance. Some interactions between a sixteen- or seventeen-year-old with a young adult may be the possible exception. Second, that *most* adults who seek out children for sexual relations do so in response to deep psychological urges which constitute a sexual dysfunction called pedophilia. We also grant that in some times and in some contemporary cultures, adult sexual initiation of and ongoing relations with pubertal children was or is the norm and may be experienced positively by some but not all children in such cultures. In particular, some male-to-male adult/adolescent culturally contextualized initiation practices may be experienced as positive or nurturing, but child brides given to mature adult males do not usually have such positive experiences and are more likely to experience their circumstances as abuse, rape, and imprisonment.

Girls may be beaten or raped by fathers to teach them the right sexual feelings or by peers to make them "real women." They may be kicked out of their homes as well. One sixteen-year-old whose father discovered her love letters to and from another girl was taken by him into the field in back of her home, severely beaten, and told never to come home again. She was left outdoors at dusk with only the clothes she was wearing. She slept outdoors for several days until she lied about her age and got herself into the military. Another girl at seventeen was shoved across the kitchen into the refrigerator by her father. She left home and lived with a high school teacher.[22]

Gay and lesbian teens are more likely today than ever before in history to be aware of their homoerotic feelings and to give meaning to them by deciding such feelings indicate they are homosexual:

(O)ver the last decade Gay America has become more visible, often in a positive light as it took care of its sick and dying. Gay characters now show up on television and in the movies, such as the recent "Longtime Companion," the first feature film about AIDS in the gay community. News reports proliferate about the gay-rights movement, the phenomena of gay surrogate parenting and adoption, and about prominent figures who are homosexual—all of them, from congressmen to local AIDS volunteers, providing high-profile role models and raising the expectations of gay youth.[23]

Nonetheless, an examination of the literature about gay and lesbian adolescents has shown that certain powerful preconceptions continue to have profound impact on the process of becoming gay experienced by youth. These are:

First, people assume that the youths are heterosexual: everyone should be straight growing up. Second, adolescent homosexuals privately experience isolation; they feel stigmatized (internal homophobia) because they desire the same sex. Third, to express their desires erotically, homosexuals must act or dress like the opposite sex, being gender reversed in self-identity and behavior. Finally, anyone who has homoerotic desires must be like everyone else who has them, thus conforming to the stereotyped symbolic images of "homosexuality" in the social imagination . . . that oppresses homosexuals.[24]

In college contexts I see evidence of these assumptions as they impact the coming out processes of individual students. Regarding stigma, one gay man told a coming out support group that "every morning the first word I hear in my head as I wake up is 'gay, gay, gay.' Is there ever going to be a day when that stops?" A young lesbian has shifted from experimenting with wearing neckties to experimenting with growing her nails long as she sorts the aspects of gender identity which feel linked to her identification as lesbian. One young man not yet able to

200

name a sexual identity but consciously questioning is often told by gay, lesbian, and bisexual peers that they have assumed he is gay based on his "effeminate" physical appearance. Another young man tentatively identifying as "sexually diverse" talks about his aversion to gay men who are very effeminate and his concern that if he is gay he has to act that way. A bisexual woman speaks about how threatened her parents feel about the possibility of her ending her long-term relationship with a man, an ending she feels the need for in order to explore her feelings for women before making a more permanent relational choice.

Although youth are coming out earlier, this does not mean that early identification as lesbian, gay, or bisexual occurs in a supportive or safe peer or school environment for most adolescents. After coming out at his public high school, "I had food thrown at me in the cafeteria and someone hit me in the back of the head with a coke," one seventeen-year-old reported; an eighteen-year-old tells of repeatedly being called faggot and having "male students blow kisses at him."[25] These are the mild stories. The journalist Neil Miller reports that in public high schools "antigay comments are common currency long after ethnic and racial slurs have been deemed unacceptable; cautious administrators and school boards often discourage open discussion that might create a more accepting atmosphere."[26] Miller goes on to report that "one teacher in a white-collar Boston suburb described attitudes prevailing at her school this way: 'We counsel gay students not to come out. They'd get killed. At our school, male students get harassed just for being in drama or chorus.' "[27]

Most violent gay bashing is perpetrated by male adolescents. The tension of and peer pressure surrounding sexual identity and gender development, together with adult silence about lesbians and gay people, or overt adult homophobia, help produce such acting out. Near Boston three high school girls followed an out lesbian off the school bus and beat her up. When the school's response was a three-day suspension, viewed by the students as a slap on the wrist, the message to the other kids was clear: it is basically okay to beat up a queer. The unwillingness of most teachers to intervene when teens use antigay slurs has permitted a climate of intimidation and harassment to flourish in high schools. Within the high school peer group, it becomes a badge of courage to bad mouth or harass someone viewed as gay. Shoring up masculinity by bashing gay men has become an acceptable recreational activity in some high school and young adult male groups. In 1994 proposed federal legislation would have required schools to remain silent about sexual orientation or condemn everything but heterosexuality. Federal funds would have been cut off from any school which presented non-judgmental information about the existence of gay, lesbian, and bisexual people, or offered support or referral services for lesbian, bisexual, or gay students.[28]

Access to positive, diverse models of what it might mean to be gay is crucial if teens are to survive without acting out violently against others or themselves. The vast majority of visible gay and lesbian people in the media and working as spokespersons in political and AIDS contexts have been white. Although African-American lesbians have been publishing and speaking about their experiences as lesbians of color for almost two decades,[29] lesbians from other cultural backgrounds have more rarely published and organized until recently.[30] Besides James Baldwin and a few others, African- American gay men have just begun to speak, make films about, and publish out of their black gay viewpoints.[31] This is not to suggest that lesbians and gay men of color have not existed or published, but only that they have rarely published work dealing explicitly with their sexual orientation until recently, making it difficult for young people in particular to find in the media or in the library any accurate information about gay and lesbian people of color. What one does see almost exclusively are portrayals of stereotyped queens by such African-American male comics and filmmakers as Keenan Wynans and Eddie Murphy.

Essex Hemphill tells how, during adolescence he spent a month in the library reading everything he could find about homosexuality. He says, "If anything, I could have concluded that homosexuality was peculiar to white people, and my conclusion would have been supported by the deliberate lack of evidence concerning black men and homosexual desire.[32] Hemphill goes on to speak eloquently of all the ways his adolescence would have been different if there had been available to him a black gay anthology such as Joseph Beam's *In the Life*.[33]

The continuing relative invisibility of bisexuality means that some teens experiencing same-sex feelings assume these feelings indicate they must live exclusively gay lives, when actually their own orientation leaves them choices about which sexual identity to adopt. Teens who adopt a gay or lesbian identity early on may later in young adulthood reexamine and acknowledge their heteroerotic feelings and desires and the range of identities available. Teens with access to support groups about sexual identity are usually more aware of this range of possibilities because such groups tend to be inclusive of bisexual and transgender teens.

In my recent experiences working with college freshmen and sophomores I see a significant number of both men and women who initially come out as bisexual after high school years which included fairly extensive heterosexual romantic relationships. Older adolescents, at least in college, seem more aware of the possibility of bisexual identity. While the earlier psychiatric assumption—that bisexuality is a phase on the way to acknowledging, or a form of denying gay or lesbian sexual orientation—has proved inaccurate, it is unclear what proportion of adolescents will retain their bisexual identification after they explore more fully their homoerotic feelings. It is possible that for some of today's late adolescents, bisexual identity serves as a means of maintaining continuity with and acknowledgment of past heteroerotic experiences. In early college years such continuity is important psychologically because teens are separating from home and family. The students who are identifying as bisexual may include some who will continue to elaborate a bisexual identity and others who feel unready to adopt a gay or lesbian sexual identity, identities which feel more separate from a prior heterosexually identified self.

The college students I see who are identifying as gay or lesbian, in contrast with those identifying as bisexual, are for the most part students who, during earlier adolescence, were more aware that they had homoerotic feelings. These students often are not ready or able until the college years to give meaning to their homoerotic feelings in terms of a sense of sexual identity.

More lesbian and gay teens are coming out at a time when physical violence and verbal abuse against gay and lesbian people are at an all time high in this society,[34] and when substance abuse among teens is rampant. The implications are obvious. All but a lucky few gay and lesbian teens are children at profound risk.[35] Daniel Lader, the "gay poster child" whom *Newsweek* spotlighted in its Summer/Fall 1990 special issue about teens, has the exceptional mother who responded supportively when he came out to her at age fifteen. That she was able to find him a community-based counseling group for gay teens is also exceptional and has everything to do with their residence in the San Francisco area.[36] Such non-school-based support groups also exist in Chicago and a few other large cities.

Most lesbian and gay teens are socially isolated within their peer groups and families, with virtually no supportive services available to them through school guidance offices or other agencies. One of the few exceptions is the Philadelphia public schools, which has initiated a program of sex education that includes information about homosexuality, guest speakers who are gay and lesbian, and lesbian and gay staff who help train teachers and counselors.[37] The New York public school system has a separate school for some gay teens which is operated in conjunction with the Hetrick-Martin Institute, a support services organization for gay and lesbian youth. In Chicago, the Horizons Center runs a support group for teens.

In New England the school-based formation of support groups for students occurred first in private preparatory schools such as Phillips Andover and Concord Academy. The public schools lag behind, but by 1994 thirty public school groups existed. Such groups are often called some variation on Gay/Straight Alliance, to make it safer for students to participate without their sexual orientation or identity being known to the entire school. In addition, lesbian and gay private school teachers and coaches are increasingly coming out.

Nonetheless, most teens, regardless of orientation, have little or no access to accurate information about homosexuality or to adults who can serve as positive role models or accepting counselors.* These youths also have little chance to learn

---

*Social services for lesbian and gay teens, for the most part privately funded and operated, are proliferating, particularly, but not exclusively, in urban areas. They include hotlines, support groups, counselors, lending libraries, and other services. The Massachusetts Department of Health is developing a statewide program to train youth as peer educators about sexual orientation and homophobia.

relationship skills. In the words of one teen, "You miss out on dating. . . . You feel socially retarded."[38] Gay and lesbian teens lack social selves growing up,[39] and their isolation and experiences of abuse often create patterns of emotional dependency which bode ill for the success of their attempts at intimacy when they finally occur.[40] In my work with college students I see some students who, as a result of their emergent lesbian or gay sexual identity, had no real opportunities to explore romantic or intimate relationships during junior high and high school. Many of these same students, constrained by confusion, low self-esteem, and the need to hide homoerotic feelings, also had few friends of either gender. These students arrive at college markedly more inept and inexperienced socially than their heterosexual age peers. They are also engaged in additional tasks on top of the ordinary ones of adolescence. These tasks include having to transcend the negative cultural assumptions and stereotypes about homosexuality (working with their internalized homophobia) and giving up "previously internalized heterosocial life goals," a process that may involve a kind of "grief work."[41] These youths are also the first generation coming out in the context of AIDS.

For some of these students, college is the first time they have experienced a peer group of gay, bisexual, and lesbian friends, which feels both terrifying and crucial. They are terrified of rejection by the group that feels like the only possible place of belonging after many years of social isolation. They are ambivalent about membership in the group given their continuing internalized sense of stigma attached to being lesbian, gay, or bisexual. As a result, some students keep a distance from even these peers. Others plunge for a while into activity with such a group to the exclusion of, and sometimes to the jeopardy of, school work. Ineptitude and inexperience with one-on-one relationships, a fragile, rarely disclosed, and untested sense of gay, lesbian, or bisexual identity, and the perceived inability to call on a parent for advice or solace also suggest the need for considerable college-based adult and peer support when problems such as rejection by a heterosexual roommate occur.

In addition to dealing with social isolation and peer hostility, gay and lesbian youth often deal with either keeping secret their orientation from their parents or their parents' reactions to their orientation. Recent research suggests, and my work with college students confirms, that most youth today have a strong desire to tell their parents about their emerging sexual identity and do so hoping for acceptance.[42] As the process of coming out occurs at earlier ages, the likelihood increases that parents will become aware of their child's nonheterosexual sexual identity while the child is still living at home, or at least while the child is still financially and psychologically dependent. Thus, for an adolescent, the physical and psychological risks of coming out to parents are greater than they are likely to be for older adults. It is worth noting that many people in earlier age cohorts often simply did not come out to parents and suffered the psychosocial consequences of keeping their sexual identities hidden from families throughout their adult lives.[43]

Most youths hide their homoerotic feelings from parents as well as friends, and "learning to hide" has been proposed as a theme of the young person's experience of emergent gay or lesbian identity.[44] First disclosures to friends occur at a mean age of sixteen.[45] Disclosure to parents tends to come later than disclosure to a friend and tends to be experienced as difficult.[46]

In a study of lesbian- and gay-identified youth in Chicago ranging in age from fourteen to twenty-one, the authors found that parental awareness happens most often in one of two ways: the parents find out themselves or through another person, or the youth directly discloses his or her orientation. The latter is more common.[47] Children facing prejudice based on an aspect of identity, such as race or religion, usually have parents who share the same aspect of identity and have experience with the associated social consequences. Not only do lesbian, bisexual, and gay children and their parents not have this common identity or type of experience, but parental reactions often reproduce the prejudices of the larger society at least for a while.

A relatively small but significant percentage of youth experience a major breach in the parent-child relationship as a result of coming out. In the Chicago study, of 202 youth, 7 were at the time of the interview living in shelters after being thrown out of their parental homes.[48] In another study, one sixteen-year-old girl had recently been sent by her parents to a residential treatment facility where she was subjected to aversion therapy to "cure her" of her lesbianism.[49]

The gender dynamics of the parent-child transitions after a child discloses his or her sexual identity are complex. In addition to finding that both girls and boys come out directly to mothers more often than to fathers, Boxer, Cook, and Herdt's study shows the father-daughter relationship is the most likely to experience negative change as a result of the child's coming out. This is only a correlational result, and the research group has not yet examined causes.[50] One theorist discusses issues particular to mothers and daughters who are experiencing coming out transitions, including the mothers' grief response as they let go of the belief they will always be the primary female in their daughter's life, an expectation they do not hold for sons.[51] Another researcher found parents have greater difficulty accepting a lesbian daughter than a gay son, and related this to their disappointment about expectations that the daughter would bear children.[52]

It should be no surprise that recent federally commissioned research suggests that youth exploring sexual-identity issues constitute 20 to 30 percent of all completed youth suicides.[53] Such kids are also one of the most likely groups of teens to be homeless, since they are at risk not only of being kicked out of the house but of running away. They are also at risk of poor performance in school, dropping out, and of becoming substance abusers.

Sexual identity conflicts are exacerbated for youths of color, who face issues of discrimination based on their race and culture as well as their sexual orientation. They deal with negative attitudes toward sexual orientation issues from both the dominant culture and their home communities. Coming out means risking loss of access to their own culture, if their families, neighborhoods, and/or peers reject them for being lesbian or gay, or feeling they must isolate themselves from their home community for a while.[54]

One study of youth of color in Toronto found that the process of coming out to parents involves alienating changes in a child's relationship to the ethnic community, including choosing not to be involved in cultural activities in an attempt to protect the family from shame.[55]

All of these problems have to do with dominant society's attitudes about homosexuality and the continuing refusal to provide children with access to accurate and nonjudgmental information about sexuality in all its forms. These are not, in other words, problems inherent to sexuality or homosexuality.

Teens who are in the process of coming out to themselves as lesbian and gay are not the only ones at risk. Teens who are, as far as they are aware, heterosexual but who rebel against traditional gender roles also face problems of self-esteem and familial and social rejection.

The boy who is not athletic in high school, is interested in studying, and tries to be profeminist in his attitudes and treatment of young women faces taunts from both peers and adult men; he is a "nerd," "wimp," "mamma's boy," "fag." When he sits at a sidewalk cafe across from a construction site and does not try to grab the female runner's behind as she jogs by him, despite the urging of the construction workers watching, he is taunted and sits enraged at men and what being male means today. When his father treats the waitress in the restaurant to leers, the boy stares at the tablecloth, feeling both embarrassed by and rejecting of his dad.[56]

Such nonconforming heterosexual kids under pressure from peers sometimes engage in premature heterosexual sexual activity in order to get the pressure to lift, or join in antigay taunts or bashing, to obtain relief. They may also believe their peers' taunts and think that their gender nonconformity does mean they are or may be lesbian or gay. These children are another group at risk of suicide.

In other words, issues of sexual orientation and gender are intertwined from birth for children. The development of attitudes and the access to information about lesbians, gay men, and bisexual people, identities, and lifestyles take place in the context of learning about proper gender behavior and roles. The lessons of youth about sexual orientation are sources of distress for almost all young people, those on the way to heterosexual identity as well as those on the way to or those who have already discovered bisexual, gay, or lesbian identity. The lessons about gender are also both stressful and constraining for many children regardless of orientation. So long as families and educators fail to provide children with support for seeing gender and sexual identity as flexible and varied, as aspects of self to be explored, discovered, and elaborated, children will be tyrannized by childhood oversimplification of adult and media messages about traditional gender roles and presumptive heterosexuality. By our silence we condemn most lesbian, gay, and bisexual, as well as heterosexual children to beginning their adult journeys, if they survive to begin them, in the most troubled stages, the orange section of compulsory heterosexuality. As Anthony D'Augelli has pointed out, such childhoods are the situation out of which adult gay men, lesbians, and bisexual people develop great powers of "performance in a wide range of social settings."

> This ability to act in differentiated ways—to manipulate one's development—is at the core of lesbian, gay, and bisexual life.
> But this power to self-create is also rooted in context. Lesbians and gay men shape their own development out of necessity, due to a heterosexist culture which provides no routine socialization for them.[57]

APPENDIX C

An Overview of Scholarship about Sexual Orientation

HEATHER WISHIK

Scholarship about heterosexuality has often called itself scholarship about human sexuality or sexuality. Rarely has it positioned itself in an explicit context of diverse sexualities and made clear its incompleteness. This is changing. The latest edition of Masters & Johnson's work has been retitled *Heterosexuality*.[1] What follows is an overview of work about sexual orientation with a focus on orientations other than heterosexual. Nonetheless, we believe it is crucial that we see many questions needing further scholarly attention to be ones that probe the construction of compulsory heterosexuality and describe all available sexual identities in relation to whatever the culturally dominant sexuality, if any, was and in relation to the gender system at hand in the cultures and periods under study.

History

According to historians George Chauncey, Martin Duberman, and Martha Vicinus, until the 1980s, research on the history and incidence of homosexuality had been difficult to pursue because such work faced the real risk of government censorship and lacked academic sponsorship.* Work by late nineteenth-century scholars, including studies by John Addington Symonds and Havelock Ellis, had been suppressed by the British government. The Berlin-based Institute for Sex Research, founded in 1919 by German homosexual intellectuals, was the site in

---

*The views and information in this chapter were culled from many sources. The authors do not necessarily agree with each viewpoint. This summary is provided so that readers may have access in an introductory form to some of the work done by various important thinkers.

1933 of the first large-scale book burning by the Nazis, who torched the entire institute library. And in the 1950s most of the Kinsey Institute's funding was withdrawn in reaction to its findings about the high incidence of same-sex sexual behavior. The birth of social history and women's history as well as the growth of political activism around the issue of sexual orientation have combined recently to make it possible for historians to work creatively in researching and theorizing about homosexuality through time and across cultures. The work is being done both by activists who have carried on a great deal of the archival work and by professional historians.[2]

Historians of human sexuality disagree about whether the categories and identities heterosexual, homosexual, and bisexual are modern phenomena or ones that persist through time and across cultures, albeit described by various terms and referring to varying categories of behavior and social identities. This disagreement is often labeled as one between essentialism and social constructionism.[3] Historians also disagree about how various sexual behaviors relate to one another, given that different eras and cultures assign diverse meanings to each behavior. They also disagree about whether there are any universal characteristics of heterosexual, homosexual, and bisexual people across time and culture. Jonathan Ned Katz, a social constructionist looking at Eurocentric cultures, explains:

> the traditional concept of homosexuality . . . is so profoundly ahistorical that the very existence of Gay history may be met with disbelief. The common image of the homosexual has been a figure divorced from any temporal-social context. The concept of homosexuality must be historicized. Ancient Greek pederasty, contemporary homosexual "marriages," and lesbian-feminist partnerships all differ radically. Beyond the most obvious fact that homosexual relations involve persons of the same gender, and include feelings as well as acts, there is no such thing as homosexuality in general, only particular historical forms of homosexuality. There is no evidence for the assumption that certain traits have universally characterized homosexual (or heterosexual) relations throughout history. The problem of the historical researcher is thus to study and establish the character and meaning of each varied manifestation of same-sex relations within a specific time and society. The term "situational homosexuality" has been applied to same-sex relations within prison and other particular institutional settings. The term is fallacious if it implies that there is some "true" homosexuality which is *not* situated. All homosexuality is situational, influenced and given meaning and character by its location in time and social space. Future research and analysis must focus as much on this conditioning situation as on the same-sex relations occurring within it.[4]

Another social constructionist, historian Robert Padguy, explains his view as follows:

"Homosexual" and "heterosexual" *behavior* may be universal; homosexual and heterosexual *identity* and *consciousness* are modern realities. . . . To "commit" a homosexual act is one thing; to *be* a homosexual is something entirely different. . . . This conversion of acts into roles/personalities, and ultimately into entire subcultures, cannot be said to have been accomplished before at least the seventeenth century, and as a firm belief and more or less close approximation of reality, the late nineteenth century. What we call homosexuality (in the sense of the distinguishing traits of homosexuals), for example, was not considered a unified set of acts, much less a set of qualities defining particular persons, in pre-capitalist societies.[5]

Padguy may be incorrect that it is only a late nineteenth-century capitalist phenomenon to assign a group of acts and qualities to people who are homoerotic in inclination. While homosexual behavior undoubtedly occurred without formal ritualization or social recognition in many early noncapitalist cultures, there also existed a variety of culturally formalized homoerotic traditions. Some of these may have been primarily systems for permitting people to adopt cross-gender identities. The homoerotic opportunities were perhaps a secondary aspect of institutionalized cross-gender roles, as in some American Indian tribal berdache traditions.[6] These tribal traditions included the possibility of same-sex marriages or sexual relationships between a cross-gender adult and an adult of the same sex who did not behave across gender.[7]

Preservation of the gender system in this way is one non-Western, pre-nineteenth-century example of a coherent social accommodation of both cross-gender desire and homoeroticism. In some of the African and Indian tribal traditions, such people were viewed as having extra spiritual power because of their access to the qualities of both genders. They sometimes took on spiritual roles, as in the Hausa tribe, where the bori were a spiritual cult that involved women and men who cross-dressed, some of whom were involved in homoerotic sexuality.[8]

It is also true that many non-Western, pre-nineteenth-century societies, including, for example, the Japanese, incorporated homosexual behaviors quite formally while not assigning a unified set of traits to a person based on the desire for or involvement in such behaviors. Adult samurai warriors during the fifteenth and sixteenth centuries acted as mentors to adolescent boys in training to be samurai. Such mentoring included sexual relations and love letters, paintings about such relations, poetry, and other rituals. This tradition, incorporating male homoerotic relations between an adult and an adolescent as a developmental part of training for adulthood, is similar in many ways to the Greek male citizen's ritualized relations with adolescent boys.[9]

Audre Lorde has reported that among the Fon of Dahomey, West Africa, twelve forms of socially recognized marriage still exist today, including marriage between two women, called "giving the goat to the buck." In such marriages, one of the two women may bear children who are then treated as members of the other woman's blood line. Some of these women are sexually intimate and some are not.[10]

211

As for the existence of bisexuality, or its invisibility, this too has been said to vary with time and place in culture. Charles Henri Ford, one of the Americans living in exile in Paris who formed a circle around Gertrude Stein, has asserted that

> the clear distinctions we presently experience between gay and straight worlds did not exist back then. Many people moved casually between the gay and straight worlds and felt they belonged to both. They did not feel they had to choose or declare undying loyalty for one or the other group. In fact, some of these artists now claimed as gay, such as Djuna Barnes, refused that label for themselves, and were more comfortable with no label or, if with any label at all, bisexual. As Ford says, "They're always referring to Djuna now as a lesbian, but . . . she had many lovers, male and female."[11]

John Boswell, on the other hand, believed that homosexuality existed as both a behavioral reality and an intellectual category for human experience throughout Western history at least as far back as Aristophanes.[12] Boswell rejects the polarization inherent in labeling historical theories essentialist or social constructionist. Claiming a continuing agnosticism "about the origins and etiology of human sexuality," Boswell nevertheless claims as a basic supposition of his historical work that "gay persons have been widely and identifiably present in Western society at least since Greco-Roman times."[13] Boswell recently defined gay persons as "those whose erotic interest is predominantly directed toward their own gender (i.e., regardless of how conscious they are of this as a distinguishing characteristic)."[14] He also suggests that throughout Middle Eastern and Western history, three major theories of sexuality, or sexual taxonomies, have existed, although one or another has dominated at various times. According to Type A theories, all humans are polymorphously sexual, that is, capable of erotic and sexual interaction with either gender. Type B theories posit two or more sexual categories, usually but not always based on sexual object choice, to which all humans belong. The most common form of Type B taxonomy assumes that humans are heterosexual, homosexual, and bisexual, but that not all societies allow expression of all varieties of erotic disposition. Type C theories consider one type of sexual response normal (or "natural" or "moral" or all three) and all other variants abnormal ("unnatural," "immoral").[15] Boswell provides numerous examples from classical and medieval Islamic, Greek, and Roman texts to support his view that Type B taxonomy existed, that is, that some writers understood humans to be divided into predominantly homosexual, heterosexual, and bisexual groups, and that such awareness included recognition of an erotic preference, often lifelong, which was of natural origin, or was a matter of "innate character (or a mythic prehistory)."[16]

Vern Bullough is more vehement: "Homosexuality has always been with us; it has been a constant in history, and its presence is clear."[17]

The issue, however, remains how one understands the anthropological evidence from many cultures of a wide variety of male-to-male sexual behavior. This evidence includes the post-Kinsey study of 76 societies by Ford and Beach,[18] who found that in 47 of the 76 societies there was some form of socially accepted same-sex sexual behavior. As David Fernbach points out, these traditions, in about 30 cultures studied, most commonly take the form of a "berdache" tradition where some men live as women. The second most common form, found in 13 societies, is that of married adult males having sex with male children or adolescents. Most rare, and found in only 3 societies in the Ford and Beach study, is mutual masturbation between adult males, a practice viewed in those societies as a practice secondary to heterosexual relations.[19]

Fernbach interprets this evidence as consistent with a gender system involving male dominance and views it as different from the meaning of being gay in modern Western cultures, where gay means sexual relations between (adult) males on an equal basis. He also points out that there are today what he calls "forms of homosexuality that are consistent with the gender system" in Western societies. These include male-to-male sexual behavior in prisons, behavior viewed as a substitute for temporarily unavailable heterosexual relations and characterized by the pairing of a dominant male with a subordinant male.[20]

Michel Foucault and Daniel Halperin believe that the description of human sexuality as homosexual and heterosexual is a modern conceptualization less than a hundred years old, preceded by very different ideas about human sexual behavior which did not divide people into polarized personality types.[21]

Halperin suggests that pre-twentieth-century Western understandings about, and rules for, acceptable sexual behavior were most often organized in one of two ways: by social status, as in Greece where male citizens were allowed to desire sex with all political subordinates, including women, foreigners, and younger males; or by gender, as in nineteenth-century Europe where same-sex erotic desire was viewed as gender "inversion" or disobedience, as was the desire to wear cross-gender clothing or to behave in ways atypical of one's own gender (a woman with political ambition, for example).[22] Carroll Smith-Rosenberg and Lillian Faderman, in their works about female-to-female relationships, make similar points about the gender-defining nature of nineteenth-century Western acceptance of ostensibly nongenital but nonetheless intense sensuality between women.[23] More recently Faderman has explicitly sided with the social constructionist point of view. Not only is she convinced that few women are, in her words, "born different," but, in addition to her belief in the rarity of truly biological lesbian sexual orientation, Faderman thinks the development of a lesbian sexual identity is a twentieth-century phenomenon:

> Before women could live as lesbians the society in which they lived had to evolve to accommodate, however grudgingly, the possibility of lesbianism— the conception needed to be formulated; urbanization and its relative anonymity and population abundance were important; it was necessary that institutions be established where they could meet women with similar

interests; it was helpful that the country enjoyed sufficient population growth so that pressure to procreate was not overwhelming; it was also helpful that the issues of sexuality and sexual freedom became increasingly open; it was most crucial that women have the opportunity for economic self-sufficiency that would free them from the constant surveillance of family. The possibility of life as a lesbian had to be socially constructed in order for women to be able to choose such a life. Thus it was not until our century that such a choice became viable for significant numbers of women.[24]

Julia Penelope explicitly takes Faderman to task for, among other things, suggesting that women born lesbian are "genetically and hormonally abnormal."[25] Penelope agrees that naming love between women as lesbian is a modern phenomenon, but rejects the notion that the existence of such love, women who desired it, and women who lived it out in some conscious way are also modern social constructions. Penelope grants the distinction between orientation, which she thinks is for her innate, and identity, which she describes as changeable, including describing her own adoption of the identities queer and gay before coming to a lesbian identity. However, when taking on the essentialist-versus-constructionist debate, she does not seem to distinguish clearly between sexual orientation and sexual identity, merging the two into sexual identity:

> Given my brief history and the fact that I'm quite sure I have always been a Lesbian, it should be clear that I'm among those cast in the "essentialist" role in "post-modern" debates. I do believe that my own Lesbianism is innate; I was *born* a Lesbian. I don't understand why so many of the popular theories of our day describe essentialism and social constructionism as necessarily opposing accounts of sexual identity. . . . Judging from my own experience, both accounts of Lesbian identity are accurate. It is not an either/or situation. I was born a Lesbian in a specific social and historical context. . . . I believe there have been Lesbians "like" me (but also "not like" me) throughout history, even though they could not have called themselves "Lesbians," and even though their experience and interpretations of them were shaped by their own historical, economic and cultural contexts.[26]

Penelope also rejects Faderman's assertion that society constructed "lesbian identity." Penelope points out that women who wanted to love women

> didn't wait around for someone to establish "institutions" where they could meet—they created them for themselves; . . . and while it has been easier in the twentieth century for women to find ways of living independently, others in the past also managed it, choosing to live as priestesses, nuns, prostitutes, or, having rejected such occupations, cross-dressed so they could work as men and make a livable wage. . . . society did not "construct" their identity; it has merely provided, in the twentieth century, conditions that make it easier for us to act on that identity.[27]

Paula Allen Gunn, in her writings about lesbians in American Indian tribal cultures, suggests there probably existed women who "dealt exclusively with" other women, including sexually, but believes that in understanding the meaning of their existence, it is crucial that we recognize the historical and cultural specificity of ideas about the existence of homosexuality and the important connections between the construction of those ideas and gender roles:

> Lesbianism and homosexuality were probably commonplace among old Indians. But the word *lesbian*, when applied to traditional Indian culture, does not have the same meaning that it conveys today. The concepts are so dissimilar as to make ludicrous attempts to relate the long-ago women who dealt exclusively with women on sexual-emotional and spiritual bases to modern women who have in common erotic attraction for other women.
>
> This is not to make light of the modern lesbian, but rather to convey some sense of the enormity of the cultural gulf that we must confront and come to terms with when examining any phenomenon related to the American Indian. . . .
>
> Spheres of influence and activity in American Indian cultures were largely divided between the sexes. . . . in terms of any real sense of community, there were women and there were men.
>
> In such circumstances, lesbianism and homosexuality were probably commonplace. Indeed, same-sex relationships may have been the norm for primary pair bonding. Families did not consist of traditional nuclear units in any sense. There were clans and bands or villages, but the primary personal unit tended to include members of one's own sex rather than members of the opposite sex.[28]

As mentioned earlier in this appendix, there has been considerable historical writing about American Indian berdache and hwame traditions. Some nonnative commentators have viewed the existence of such roles and traditions as evidence of American Indians' historical acceptance of bisexuality and/or homosexuality. Gay and lesbian American Indian commentators caution against applying contemporary labels and the worldview they carry to such a historically and culturally distant context; at the same time they celebrate the historical evidence of American Indian openness regarding varieties of human sexuality.[29]

In Halperin's terms, berdache-type traditions, which have been found on every continent, not simply among American Indians, are examples of social rules for acceptable sexual behavior organized by gender. Men who were sexual with other men did so only so long as one of the men socially "became" a woman.[30] Fernbach has suggested that men who dressed as women in berdache tradition may be more akin to the contemporary male-to-female transsexual than to today's gay man.[31]

The word *homosexual* was first used in the English language in 1892; the word *heterosexual* followed eight years later.[32] The new words not only gave new names to old ideas, but also may have signaled shifts in Western culture in the socially ascribed meanings and significance given to the sex of the person who was the object of another's sexual desires.[33] The new language may also have been a signal that Western cultures had begun to adopt a new, idealized heterosexual model for male/female intimate relationships, "one in which eroticism was defined as central and legitimate."[34]

The modernity of the idea that the gender of the object of erotic desire is central to both a person's sexuality and personality is surprising because the concept is so accepted today. Whether the idea is accurate or not—that is, whether one believes people are born with or develop in early childhood a "sexual orientation" (an inclination, which may vary in strength or exclusivity, to find a particular sex erotically worthy of desire), which then constitutes a central factor in personality, and that this would be true regardless of the extant cultural attitudes—it seems important to understand the idea's modernity.

This modernity reminds us that our assumptions about sexuality, both the aspects of behavior that count as important sexually and the implications for personality and lifestyle that sexual behaviors entail, are neither universal constants present in all human societies nor unchanging scientific truths, but instead are historically and culturally specific social constructions, albeit ones which may share similarities, as Boswell believes, with categories used throughout much of history in many cultures.

In this regard it is worth noting an example of a religious approach to sexual orientation which continues today to view same-sex conduct as violating proper gender roles while carrying no necessary implications for personality. The Catholic church's contemporary view is that all sexual activity other than potentially procreative sex between spouses is sin.[35] This view does not, however, necessarily entail the assumption that personalities are of three types—heterosexual, homosexual, and bisexual—although the church now recognizes the existence of several human sexual orientations, given from birth by God, meaning, as we do, the direction of a person's primary erotic inclination, response, and desire. The Catholic church does not label persons whose erotic desires involve members of their own sex sinners, unless such persons act on their desires, thus committing a sin. People born gay are, therefore, assumed to be in all respects like anyone born heterosexual, except that the person's desired sexual behaviors are prohibited and celibacy is, therefore, the only moral choice.

Psychology

The transformation of secular, modern Western attitudes from viewing same-sex erotic desire or activity as one of many possible deviations from appropriate gender roles to viewing such desire or activity as also a marker of a distinct personality type occurred at least in large part at the behest of the newly emerging profession of psychiatry.[36]

Freud's ideas about sexual development, and his assertion that sexual desires had a central organizing role in personality development and adult personality, certainly were influential in the development of twentieth-century ideas about sexuality and sexual orientation. Interestingly, Freud thought all people were bisexual, meaning that men and women have the psychological, erotic, and biological characteristics and capacities of both sexes. Freud suggested that males and females shift back and forth during maturation through stages in which their own gender, or their capacity for feelings and behaviors belonging to the other gender, is dominant. He viewed homosexuality as a form of arrested development: in the normal person, homoeroticism is a stage that eventually gives way to heterosexuality. Freud did not view homosexuality as neurosis, nor did he believe therapy could change sexual orientation. He believed homosexual people could be otherwise "normal" psychologically.[37]

Freud labeled female disobedience to traditional gender role behavior, including female homoerotic inclinations, as penis envy.[38] Interestingly, although this idea "stuck" for a long time within the psychiatric profession, it was not the only one emergent at the time. According to Lillian Faderman, Alfred Adler, Freud's contemporary, gave a very different explanation for lesbianism: "lesbianism is for some women a means of protest over being accorded an inferior position in society."[39] As Faderman points out, this explanation is similar to that of twentieth-century radical feminist theory, discussed later in this chapter.

Other psychoanalytic thinkers rejected not only Freud's assumption that everyone is bisexual but his views about libido, or sexual energy, as a force in personality. These experts believed that male homosexuality was an "adaptation" to poor parenting, including the combination of a distant father and an overinvolved mother. Female homosexuality, by contrast, was in part believed to result from a father's overinvolvement in his daughter's intellectual education and from paternal pressure on a daughter to develop a traditionally male career. Thus, homosexuality was viewed as a curable mental deviation, illness, or neurosis.[40] It is this latter view which still informs much of popular culture's treatment of homosexuality, despite the fact that most members of the psychiatric and psychological professions, including the professional societies in the United States, stopped designating homosexual orientation as a disease or mental illness in the early 1970s.[41]

The diagnostic manual used by U.S. psychologists (DSM III) no longer lists homosexuality per se as a condition. Although some psychological studies of gay people have reported higher than average amounts of stress, anxiety, or depression, when such studies are probed carefully, often the substance of the reported problem is coping with rejection of gayness by society and one's family. Other studies have found gay men and lesbians identical psychologically to heterosexual adults.[42]

In the last decade, psychological research and theoretical work about lesbian and gay male identity have proliferated. Much of this work, published in the

Journal of Homosexuality, has been produced by gay and lesbian psychologists, sociologists, and other gay and lesbian research professionals. The several themes that emerge from this work include the need to examine the "life course" experiences of people who identify as lesbian or gay and the significance of a person's age group on how the life course looks. The latter is because of the power of the cultural/political context to affect the social and psychological consequences of identifying as lesbian or gay. Another theme is recognizing the impact on the possible life courses of gay men created by the emergence of visible gay culture nationally, that is, the existence of political events, community service institutions, athletic and artistic groups, and so on, outside of the largest urban, gay male "satellite communities."[43]

In addition, these researchers are less interested in the causes of homosexuality, the focus of earlier psychological work, and more interested in how people experience identification as lesbian or gay and what factors impact the qualities and contexts of that experience, the mental health of people so identifying, and the methods which yield positive results in therapeutic work with such people. The first age group of people who have been politically, proudly out as lesbians and gay men since the explosion of American gay and lesbian culture after the Stonewall Riot of 1969 is now in middle or early old age. AIDS is also a group-defining event, as is the new prominence of lesbian and gay civil rights on the national political agenda. Shared identity as a gay man or lesbian now depends not only on sexual behavior, but also on participation in a cultural identity that is less isolated and boundaried and increasingly diffused into the larger culture. All this means an expansion of available social roles, including profound shifts in definitions of family, new community formation, and changing opportunities to consolidate and elaborate gay and lesbian identity.[44]

Research and writing about lesbian psychologies have included examination of developmental issues, identity issues in the context of cultural identities, issues of identity formation in the context of heterosexual assumptions about life course, the diversity of women's sexual identities, bisexual identity as it has unique meanings for women, women's socialization as it affects lesbian couple relationships, and the impact of race and culture differences on lesbian couples. Also, lesbian experiences of aging, eating and weight problems, alcoholism, incest history, and internalized homophobia are not the same as the experiences of heterosexual women or of gay men, and an emerging literature deals with these kinds of issues. Unique aspects of mother-daughter relations for lesbians, the psychosocial stresses experienced by lesbians creating families with children, and the child-rearing styles, attitudes, and experiences of lesbians, including how these differ by race, have also been the subject of recent literature. There is also a growing body of literature discussing how all these developmental and psychosocial factors affect lesbians' interactions with one another as well as attempts by lesbians to function together as communities, political and cultural groups, or in institutions.[45] Again, the focus is no longer on the "causes" of lesbianism but rather on the experiences of women who identify as lesbian or bisexual and the contextual factors which affect and construct those experiences.

In past psychiatric and psychological research as well as in popular literature, bisexuality was often viewed as a form of homosexuality: as a stage on the way to fully developed homosexuality, as a defense against identification as homosexual or heterosexual, as confusion, or as retarded sexual development.[46] Little research focused exclusively on bisexuality until the last decade, despite the fact that higher numbers of people engage in bisexual behaviors than in exclusively homosexual behaviors.

The research that does exist uses the word *bisexuality* in several ways. Kinsey and other early researchers used it purely to refer to persons who engage in sexual behaviors with both men and women, regardless of their own sense of orientation or identity. This focus on genitality rather than sexuality added to confusion about the term's meaning. More recent researchers tend to use *bisexuality* to refer to persons whose sense of their sexual orientation and their self-defined sexual identity includes eroticizing both sexes. This use of the term *bisexual* includes the recognition that some people who eroticize both sexes self-identify as essentially heterosexual or homosexual.[47] Additionally, some people who have exclusively heterosexual experiences self-identify as bisexual.[48] Current theorists also recognize the social pressures that have existed and continue to exist to discourage self-identification as bisexual, including in the recent past gay/lesbian community "pressure to identify with one or the other side" and the negative conceptualizations of bisexuality in the media.[49]

One of the most complex attempts at definition has been developed by Fritz Klein and colleagues, who use the Klein Sexual Orientation Grid, a measure of seven variables reported by subjects in terms of their past, present, and ideal life. The variables include sexual attraction, behavior, fantasies, emotional and social preferences, self-identification, and lifestyle. Klein concludes that sexual identity is for all people what he calls "multi-variate and dynamic" and that no clear definitions of *bisexual*, *homosexual*, or *heterosexual* now exist.[50] More recently, Robert Berkey Brandon and colleagues have developed a sexuality scale that recognizes six possible types of bisexuality, and which takes into account changes over time in both desires and behavior, thus creating such labels as *concurrent* and *sequential* bisexuality.[51]

Gary Zinik has reviewed the research literature about bisexuality and suggests that two major psychological theories about the nature of bisexuality characterize the current scholarly debate.

The conflict model views bisexuality as inherently characterized by conflict, confusion, ambivalence, and the inability to decide one's sexual preference. The alternative view is the flexibility model. This view explains bisexuality as characterized by cognitive and interpersonal flexibility and, for some people, the desire for personal growth and fulfillment. The conflict model portrays bisexuals as anxious "fence-sitters," while the flexibility model describes bisexuals as experiencing the "best of both worlds".[52]

As Zinik explains, the theorists from the 1950s through the 1970s often adopted the conflict model, which assumes sexual orientation is dichotomous. The model has embedded in it the notion that men and women are "opposite" sexes and that "eroticizing one sex precludes eroticizing the other."[53] This model then posits that anyone claiming bisexuality is confused, in a transitional stage masking their true orientation, or in denial about their true orientation, which is usually presumed to be homosexual. The latter presumption is based on "the *one drop* notion of homosexuality which states that since homosexuality is not something one would choose voluntarily in this culture in light of the social costs involved, the slightest evidence of it must indicate a deep, predispositional feature of the individual."[54]

More recent clinical research adopts the flexibility model. This model suggests that

> bisexuality is characterized as the coexistence of heteroerotic and homoerotic feelings and behaviors, and an integration of homosexual and heterosexual identities. . . . Such dual experience may require a form of perceptual/cognitive flexibility that allows one to "see" seemingly opposite sexual objects as erotic and arousing. Qualities such as androgeny (sex-role flexibility) and interpersonal flexibility would aid such individuals in conducting sexually and emotionally intimate relationships in a comfortable manner.[55]

Zinik points out that the flexibility model involves both/and thinking and sees the sexes not as opposites but as "variations on a theme."[56] This model agrees that bisexuality may sometimes but not always involve confusion and ambivalence, that is, it is not inherently problematic, but rather may be seen as "successful adjustment to a dual homosexual and heterosexual preference."[57]

In addition to definitional changes in the clinical literature, recent research has begun to collect some developmental information about bisexuality. The evidence to date suggests that most bisexual people identify as heterosexual first and that in their twenties and thirties they first experience homosexual erotic interest. In addition, many adults who identify as bisexual report so identifying over a long period of time, and self-esteem increases with the length of time a person has so identified. Experiences of conflict and confusion occur most often after the initial discovery of "dual erotic interests."[58] In terms of psychological adjustment, several studies have found no variation among heterosexual, homosexual, and bisexual subjects regarding anxiety, depression, and hostility.[59]

In general, there is in psychology a trend toward developmental theories about sexual identity. These theories recognize that typically a child adolescent or adult goes through a period of presumed heterosexual identity; before any other identity can coalesce that heterosexual identity has to be let go. These theories also recognize the fluidity of sexual identity over a full life course but Anthony D'Augelli points out certain life stages support or restrict identity modification more than other stages.[60]

Frequency

How many people are oriented heterosexual, bisexual, gay, or lesbian in our culture is a question that, in the 1990s, has taken on a life of its own. In 1993 the Alan Guttmacher Institute published the results of face-to-face interviews with American men about their sexual behavior. The study, designed to look at the frequency of condom use, reported that 2.5 percent of respondents claimed to engage exclusively or predominantly in homoerotic behavior and that 1 percent self-identified as gay. The study design has been criticized, however, calling into question the accuracy of these numbers.[61] A University of Hawaii study reports that about 5 percent of the population is gay. The Kinsey Institute work on *sexual behavior* still constitutes the largest sample of data specifically gathered to answer the question of frequency of homoerotic behavior. The first Kinsey studies from the early 1950s, which only look at white people, the second Kinsey study from the late 1970s, and the newest from the late 1980s confirm that a persistent minority of men and women in the United States participate exclusively in homoerotic sexual behavior, and that a larger minority participate primarily in homoerotic sexual behavior. This group, made up of those either exclusively or primarily homoerotic in behavior, constitutes about 13 percent of males and half that percentage of females. In addition, the original Kinsey studies suggest that bisexual behavior is widespread, defining bisexuals to include those persons who have equal sexual contacts with both sexes and those who have primary contact with one sex but significant contacts with the other during adulthood. Not counting those persons who are exclusively or primarily homoerotic, 37 percent of men and 13 percent of women reported same-sex sexual contacts to the point of orgasm after adolescence.[62]

Other data include a 1927 article reporting a survey of married and unmarried women which found that 18.4 percent of unmarried and 16 percent of married women had had homoerotic experiences. In 1976, 10 percent of the Hite Report's respondents identified themselves as lesbians.[63] Since the 1970s, several other scales for measuring sexual identity have been developed, including the previously mentioned Klein Sexual Orientation Grid, which attempts to measure fantasies and attitudes in addition to orgasms.[64]

It is the Kinsey data about reported behavior which yield the frequently articulated estimate that 10 percent of the population is homosexually oriented. There is, however a difference between orientation, identity, and behavior. Some people who are homoerotically oriented may never behave homoerotically, choosing either celibacy or heterosexual conduct. It is also possible, at least theoretically, that some who behave primarily homoerotically may not be so oriented. One can imagine a man who spent most of his teen and adult years in prison, for example, reporting almost exclusive homoerotic behavior, but this might not indicate anything about the full range of his erotic inclinations. Thus, the extrapolation from Kinsey data about behavior to incidence of sexual orientation is an estimate based on an imperfect analogy. There is also no obvious statistical link between behavior and identity. It is likely that, using the 10 percent figure, the proportion of adults whose primary sexual behaviors are homoerotic is underestimated; if the 10 percent figure is understood to mean adults who are exclusively homoerotic in their adult behavior, however, the percentage may well be too high. And the number has no relationship to how many people self-identify as lesbian, gay, or bisexual.

Causation

Attitudes about sexual orientation include assumptions about its etiology and variety; such assumptions carry political implications. If one believes that sexual orientation is a matter of reversible personal choice, for example, then one is less likely to designate discrimination based on sexual orientation a civil rights issue than if orientation is a characteristic of birth like sex or race, even though this is not the only analysis consistent with constitutional civil rights analyses and traditions. If one believes that all people are polymorphously sexually oriented (bisexual) and that culture is what polarizes their behavior, sense of identity, lifestyle, and therefore, their assumptions about sexual orientation, then one may be more likely to encourage social and political changes that assume heterosexual people, lesbians, and gay men are fundamentally alike. Policies responsive to the particular needs and concerns of each group may be viewed as transitional necessities, given culturally imposed polarization behavior and sense of identity.

If one believes most humans are either heterosexual, gay, or lesbian and/or that each orientation includes distinct personality characteristics or life story implications, then one might advocate policies which recognize and address such diversity. If one believes that gay male homoerotic orientation differs causally as well as behaviorally from lesbianism, then social and political agendas which treat gay men and lesbians as fundamentally the same will not make sense.

There is at present no scientific agreement about the origins of human sexual orientation. In the vacuum created by this lack of agreement, theories abound to which political baggage attaches. Five groups of theories are current: the psychological, the hormonal, the genetic, the sociobiological, and the lesbian feminist. The distinction between psychological and biological theories is sometimes not clear or useful. Simon LeVay, a neurobiologist, has said

> You shouldn't draw such a distinction between biological and psychological
> mechanisms. . . . What people are really getting at is the difference between
> innately determined mechanisms and culturally determined mechanisms,

but people screw that up and say that's the difference between biology and psychology. It isn't. It's two different approaches for looking at the same thing: the mind. Biologists look at it from the bottom up, from the level of synapses and molecules, and psychologists are looking at it from the top down, at behavior and such.[65]

As discussed earlier, psychologists have believed homosexuality to be a form of arrested development, a form of neurotic adaptation to abnormal parenting, or more recently, simply a normal variation of human development carrying no necessary implications for mental health. Bisexuality, on the other hand, has been presumed universal or a form of arrested development, and currently, simply a type of human development.

In addition to developmental psychology's explanations for sexual orientation, there are numerous biological theories to explain why some people mature with predominantly homoerotic, heteroerotic, or bisexual desires. These include the genetics, social biology, and hormone theories.

The genetics theories are based on twin, adoption, nuclear family, and DNA studies. In July 1993, Dean Hamer and colleagues from the National Institutes of Health published a report of their study on the role of genetics in male sexual orientation. In their sample, which included 122 self-identified gay men and their families, Hamer et al. found "increased rates of same-sex orientation . . . in the maternal uncles and male cousins . . . but not in their fathers or paternal relatives."[66] In DNA studies on the forty families in their sample in which there were two gay brothers and no known nonmaternally linked gay relatives, Hamer et al. found a shared, unique marker on the tip of the long arm of the X chromosome in 64 percent of the pairs of brothers. Because male fetuses receive X chromosomes from their mothers, the results suggest that there is maternal transmission of some types of male homosexuality. The linkage analysis suggests, according to the article, that the results warrant "a statistical confidence level of more than 99 percent that at least one subtype of male sexual orientation is genetically influenced."[67]

The DNA study is the most recent in a spate of studies reported in the last couple of years which attempt to examine genetic sources of homosexuality. One group of studies has focused on twins, both identical and fraternal, and non-genetically related adopted siblings. J. Michael Bailey, Richard Pillard, and co-researchers have found that 56 percent of the time, if one identical male twin is gay, the other is also. The figure is 48 percent for lesbians. Among fraternal twins, 16 percent of lesbians' twins are also lesbian and 22 percent of gay men's twins are also gay. Six percent of adopted sisters of lesbians and 11 percent of adopted brothers of gay men are also lesbian or gay.[68]

Because 100 percent of identical twins do not identify as gay, some analyses have suggested that genetics must play a part in only some cases or be only one of several factors that contribute to sexual orientation. However, none of these critiques make clear distinctions between orientation and identity or take into account explicitly the social pressures against lesbian and gay identification. It is possible, therefore, that the study results are lower than the actual incidence of homoerotic orientation in twins; it is also possible that genetics is only one of several factors contributing to sexual orientation. However, in comparing hypotheses about gay men and lesbians, Michael Bailey states, "There's a widespread feeling among lesbians and others that female sexual orientation is more socially influenced than is male behavior, that it's more a political decision and a chosen behavior. But we now think it's substantially if not completely innate."[69]

Anatomical studies of the brain are another recent development in investigating biological bases or corollaries of homosexuality. These studies include 1990 findings that "a cluster of cells in the human brain called the suprachiasmatic nucleus," which regulates daily rhythms, was "nearly twice as large in homosexual men as it was in heterosexual men," and a 1992 report that a portion of the hypothalamus, called the third interstitial nuclei of the anterior hypothalamus, was twice as large in heterosexual as in homosexual men.[70] These recent findings are based on small samples and have yet to be shown to be causes, not effects. However, they must be seen against a background of increased understanding of the processes of gender differentiation, as they occur anatomically in fetal brains.

The hormonal theories include recent work by Richard Pillard and James Weinrich, who suggest that gay men may have received insufficient amounts of "Mullerian inhibiting hormone or a substance analogous to it," which results in a failure of the brain to "defeminize" from its "default" organization, "thereby creating what Pillard calls 'psychosexual androgyny.' " In this view, gay men are basically masculine males with female aspects, including perhaps certain cognitive abilities and emotional sensibilities. Lesbians could be understood as women who have some biologically masculine aspects.[71] These theories are not yet supported by hormone studies. Sometimes cited in support, however, are behavioral studies which try to link early cross-gender behavior in boys with adult bisexual and gay identities, such as those by Richard Green.[72] Studies and theories which combine gender behavior or deviance with sexual orientation categories and look for biological antecedents of both have been heavily criticized, in part because the sociocultural influences on gender and its definition are so strong and complex and gender definitions are so variable among cultures.[73] An additional theory from sociobiology is relevant. Assuming human reproduction is the evolutionary goal which helps determine the selection of many human characteristics, sociobiologists suggest that male promiscuity and female selectivity are probably biologically beneficial but that these tendencies are moderated by each other in heterosexual relations. In homosexual relations, no such moderation occurs: therefore, gay men will be much more promiscuous than lesbians, lesbians will be more monogamous than heterosexual women, and gay men will be more promiscuous than heterosexual men, and all of this is believed caused by evolution.[74]

Earlier hormone theorists suggest that sex is chromosomally based and that sexual orientation is governed by a combination of sex chromosomes, prenatal and perhaps postnatal exposure to sex hormones (notably androgens and estrogens), and some childhood environmental factors having to do with sex assignment. John Money in the United States and Gunter Dorner in West Germany have engaged in hormone research on animals and with humans born with hormonal anomalies and are the main proponents of prenatal hormone theories about sexual orientation.[75] Since it is impossible experimentally to manipulate hormone levels prenatally in human fetuses, research on rats has been used to suggest that homosexual orientation is related to prenatal exposure to higher-than-usual androgen and estrogen levels and that a combination of the levels of such prenatal exposure to hormones with gender socialization produces one's sexual orientation. The social biologists, looking through a Darwinian lens, try to explain why the human species developed to include people of various sexual orientations. Such Darwinian explanations use principals of evolutionary selection to suggest reasons for genetically determined or socially adaptive variety in sexual orientation: balanced superior heterozygote fitness, kin selection, and parental manipulation.[76] (A heterozygote is a zygote or the organism that develops from a cell characterized by its genetic constitution and subsequent development, which has a group of possible mutational genes at one or more loci.)

Briefly, the theory says a species may be stronger if it consists of individuals who carry varied genetic traits which, when mixed in particular combinations, yield superior adaptability to some conditions, even though other combinations may yield less adaptable individuals. An explanatory analogy sometimes is made to sickle cell anemia genes: with one such gene a person is resistant to malaria; with two a person is seriously ill, yet the gene persists in the species even if all the people with two genes die, because the adaptation available from having one gene is so beneficial.[77]

Social biologists suggest that if sexual orientation is genetic, it may be associated with some adaptive quality as yet unknown and only available if an individual has one gene of each of two types. If the heterosexual gene is dominant in persons with one such gene, and such people have some sort of beneficial adaptive quality, then persons with two homosexual genes will continue to appear in the species and the homosexual gene will persist as well, even if people with two homosexual genes never reproduce. Although this theory is not new, no genetic research has yet revealed recognizable genetic differences associated with sexual orientation, although some twin studies suggest there may be genetic links and other studies are preliminarily suggesting possible anatomical correlations to sexual orientation.[78]

Kin-selection theory says that there are situations in which it is more beneficial for some individuals, who for whatever reason are not as likely to succeed in reproduction as are others, to further their own presumed evolutionary/biological need to reproduce by giving aid to genetically similar siblings and foregoing attempts at reproduction themselves. Parental manipulation theory is related: if parents can encourage one or more offspring to aid their siblings instead of reproducing themselves, then the reproducing siblings may have more offspring and a net increase in reproduction may occur.[79]

Mildred Dickemann has recently used Darwinian behavioral theory to suggest that part of managing reproduction in response to environmental conditions includes the development of variants of male and female gender roles and behaviors. These variants are developed supposedly through parental coercion and individual choices. Rejecting genetic explanations, Dickemann talks about European historical evidence for gradations of gender behavior, particularly for male subgenders, culturally supported, some of which include bisexual or primarily homoerotic sexuality. Dickemann's theory, which sees homoerotic behavior as a secondary characteristic of traditions whose primary function was to create and institutionalize alternate gender behaviors, is similar to Harriet Whitehead's interpretation of American Indian berdache traditions.[80]

One example Dickemann gives concerns patrilineal inheritance in high-status families. She suggests that sons other than the first are "cadet sons" who experience delayed marriage and, therefore, pose a threat to female chastity, which is valued due to patrilineal dependance on identifiable heirs. Dickemann says these sons are problematic to the family and society and have often been encouraged to become religious celibates or to spend their time with other similar males, to go on crusades or join conquests, exploratory expeditions, or military forces. To parents, cadet sons are lower-investment, higher-risk offspring who are insurance against the death of the first son. By birth order they are assigned roles which at times "were characterized by bisexuality or even preferential homosexuality, as in the religious elite in the court of Charlemagne, or probably the Knights Templars."[81] Dickemann finds a similar pattern "among agrarian feudal and monarchical societies in China, Japan, North India, and the Middle East where patrilineal inheritance resulted in intense paternity concern, with the seclusion . . . of women" also marked. In these cultures she finds man/boy love the ideal in both court and religious settings.[82] Dickemann's life history theories are similar to kin-selection and parental manipulation theories in that all three assume sexual orientation is a matter of choice and/or parental/social control.

Lesbian and Feminist Theories about Sexual Orientation, Lesbianism, and Bisexuality

Beginning with Simone de Beauvoir in 1949 and escalating with the emergence of radical feminist theory in the 1960s, feminist and womanist writings in the United States, Britain, France, and throughout Western Europe have included analysis of the politics of sexuality and sexual orientation.

> Beauvoir observed that often women choose to become lesbians . . . when
> they simply want liberty and decline to abdicate in favor of another human

being as the heterosexual relationship generally demands of females. . . . Beauvoir further points out that most little girls feel outraged at their lack of privilege, at the limitations imposed on them by their sex. The real question is not why some females refuse to accept those limitations (i.e., become lesbians), but rather why most do accept them and become wives. Women conform through docility and timidity, Beauvoir believes, but when their ego sense is too strong or their ambitions too absorbing or the compensations offered by society for being the second sex too inadequate, they refuse to conform and they choose lesbianism.[83]

Lesbian-feminist theory has particularly focused on the meanings, causes, history, and practice of lesbianism in "heteropatriarchy." These theories have supported many women in their positive experiences of the coming out process.

As discussed earlier in this chapter, beginning in the late nineteenth century, psychological and biological theories about sexuality, including homosexuality, have shared an approach that can be termed essentialism, "the view that sexuality or sexual practice is 'an essence,' 'a part of human nature' or 'inherent.' . . . In other words, the sexual is viewed as having to do with a permanent characteristic which is grounded in one's biological make-up. It is fixed and unchanging. . . . The social construction of sexuality is ruled out."[84] By contrast, some feminist theories suggest that both gender and sexuality, including what we call sexual orientation, are socially constructed and that heterosexuality in particular is a core institution of the pervasive male dominance called patriarchy.

> Sexuality is to feminism what work is to Marxism: that which is most one's own, yet most taken away. . . .
>
> The molding, direction, and expression of sexuality organizes society into two sexes—women and men—which division underlies the totality of sexual relations. . . . As the organized expropriation of the work of some for the benefit of others defines a class—workers—the organized expropriation of the sexuality of some for the use of others defines the sex, woman. Heterosexuality is its structure, gender and family its congealed forms, sex roles its qualities generalized to social persona, reproduction its consequence, and control its issue.[85]

For some theorists, lesbianism is a choice to refuse to be oppressed in the way women usually are; it is rebellion against the ordinary power relations in patriarchal capitalism; it is an affirmation of a woman's freedom; it is a redefinition of what it is to be a woman. One early article titled "The Woman Identified Woman" explained it:

> What is a Lesbian? A Lesbian is the rage of all women condensed to the point of explosion. She is the woman who, often beginning at an extremely early age, acts in accordance with her inner compulsion to be a more

complete and more free human being than her society—perhaps then, certainly later—cares to allow her. . . . She may not be fully conscious of the political implications of what for her began as personal necessity, but on some level she has not been able to accept the limitations and oppression laid on her by the most basic role of her society—the female role.[86]

One core insight of early radical feminism is that the personal is political. In Western culture, where homosexuality is "consistently personalized, privatized and individualized,"[87] this early feminist insight helped spark some early, male-dominated gay liberation movement groups. These groups were, at least in part, attempts at consciousness with an agenda that was homophile in the sense of affirming homosexuality as a form of human sexuality just as worthy as heterosexuality. Lesbian feminism went further in suggesting that heterosexuality was an oppressive institution and that lesbianism was both a matter of personal inclination and "a specific challenge to sex relations"[88] as constructed in patriarchy, and in this sense a political act. Some gay male theorists, including David Fernbach, then picked up on this insight that modern lesbian and gay male identity may be, at their core, challenges to society's gender system.[89]

Early lesbian feminism's notion of the political lesbian suggested that at least some women "became lesbians in order to make a political statement."[90] Yet clearly some women called themselves lesbian before such political consciousness emerged or so early in their own lives that their coming out preceded political consciousness. Such experiences are not necessarily inconsistent with the idea of political lesbianism, however, although within lesbian circles there was in the 1970s considerable discussion of whether women who knew early in their lives that they were lesbian were the "real" lesbians and women who came to their lesbianism through feminism or after heterosexual marriages were not.[91]

As Beauvoir said, even little girls rebel against their lack of privilege. Lillian Faderman, in looking historically at female romantic friendships of the seventeenth through nineteenth centuries, suggests that while a woman who spent years of her life emotionally, and sometimes physically, intimate with another woman would not have talked about their involvement as rejection of patriarchy, many such women in fact were seeking a kind of autonomy and nurturance unavailable in their cultures from relationships with men.[92]

There is a second feminist explanation for lesbianism other than the chosen political rebellion theory, although at times it overlaps with the first. Adrienne Rich, among others, has suggested that because women are the original source of nurturance for children and because human females originally lived in female bands where their primary adult bonding was woman-to-woman, a hypothesis that all women are basically woman-identified, or at least on a lesbian continuum, is possible. She points out that the species' need for occasional sexual contact with males for the purpose of reproduction does not inevitably carry with it any need to structure long-term primary relationships with individual males or to focus romance, nurturance, intimacy, and desire toward males.[93] Rich then quotes Susan Cabin, who has written:

> patriarchy becomes possible when the original female band, which includes children but ejects adolescent males, becomes invaded and outnumbered by males; that not patriarchal marriage but the rape of the mother by the son, becomes the first act of male domination. The entering wedge, or leverage, which allows this to happen is not just a simple change in sex ratios; it is also the mother-child bond, manipulated by the adolescent males in order to remain within the matrix past the age of exclusion. Maternal affection is used to establish male right of sexual access, which, however, must ever after be held by force (or through control of consciousness).[94]

Rich then suggests that historically there exist many forms of "woman-identified experience," of "primary intensity between and among women," and that perhaps all women

> exist on a lesbian continuum . . . whether we identify ourselves as lesbian or not. [Such a possibility] allows us to connect aspects of woman-identification as diverse as the impudent, intimate girl-friendships of eight or nine year olds and the banding together of those women of the twelfth and fifteenth centuries known as Beguines . . . who managed—until the Church forced them to disperse—to live independent both of marriage and of conventional restrictions . . . to the more celebrated "lesbians" of the women's school around Sappho of the seventh century B.C. with the secret sororities and economic networks reported among African women; and with the Chinese marriage resistance sisterhoods . . . the only women in China who were not footbound . . . to disparate individual instances of marriage resistance: for example, the type of autonomy claimed by Emily Dickinson . . . [and] the strategies available to Zora Neal Hurston.
>   If we think of heterosexuality as the "natural" emotional and sensual inclination for all women, lives such as these are seen as deviant, as pathological, or as emotionally and sensually deprived. Or . . . they are banalized as "life-styles." . . . But when we turn the lens of vision and consider the degree to which, and the methods whereby, heterosexual "preference" has actually been imposed on women, not only can we understand differently the meaning of individual lives and work, but we can begin to recognize a central fact of women's history: that women have always resisted male tyranny. . . . And we can connect these rebellions and the necessity for them with the physical passion of woman for woman which is central to lesbian existence: the erotic sensuality which has been, precisely, the most violently erased fact of female experience.[95]

Rich also suggests that lesbian experience is not the same as gay male experience and that equating the two erases female reality. Rather, women stigmatized as lesbian have been, to Rich, part of "the complex continuum of female resistance to enslavement" and should not be separated from such female tradition and differences, including women's relative lack of economic and cultural status vis-a-vis men. She also alleges that the anonymous sex and pederasty in which some gay men participate do not interest lesbians, and that there are differences in the quality of male-to-male and female-to-female relationships. All these are Rich's additional reasons for rejecting a joint label encompassing gay men and lesbians and equating them.[96]

In addition to theorizing about the social construction of sexuality, the oppressive nature of institutionalized heterosexuality, and the chosen, politically rebellious nature of some lesbianism, lesbian feminists have explored definitions of lesbianism and rejected psychiatry's emphasis on genital sexual behavior as a proper locus of definition, a locus which lesbian feminists see as a male viewpoint. As Judy Grahn has put it, "Men who are obsessed with sex are convinced that lesbians are obsessed with sex. Actually, like any other woman, lesbians are obsessed with love and fidelity. They're also strongly interested in independence and having a life work to do."[97] Lesbian feminists, including Mary Daly and others, view friendship as a primary element of female erotic attachment, "a sensual attachment to a kindred spirit, with the potential of getting back as much as is given,"[98] and a relationship whose strength is measured by "the level of intimacy, uniqueness and equality that can be achieved by two women,"[99] rather than by sexual activity.

The presence of political theories surrounding the social definition of lesbianism and the permeation of such theories into individual women's understandings about their own sexuality are somewhat unique. Gay men in the United States have not, to nearly as great an extent, developed such political theory, although in Germany, beginning in the late 1800s, there was considerable theorizing, research, and publishing about gay male sexuality. This activity was halted by the Nazis. In the United States, gay men have organized and sought an end to antigay discrimination through legal and political channels since the late 1950s and early 1960s, when they organized to repeal sodomy and overbroad solicitation laws. During the last decade since AIDS, however, gay men have articulated political theories about homosexuality and its social status, sometimes borrowing from and building on feminist ideas and sometimes ignoring or urging suppression of some of feminist theory in the name of a continuing quest for legal change in the form of gay civil rights.

As discussed earlier, some feminist theories state that lesbianism can be a choice motivated by a desire to reject or avoid the disadvantages of female status in patriarchy. These theories also suggest that because more women than men may be born ambisexual, women have more opportunity to make a choice. In the last decade these theories have been greeted with hostility by some politically organized gay men and some of the lesbians who work with them. Within the nationally led and state-based gay and lesbian civil rights campaigns, it has often been politically useful to claim that homosexuality, male and female, is *always* a matter of birth or unchangeable inner identity in order to make analogies to the civil rights protection accorded matters of gender and race.

In the process, the implications of the insights of early radical feminists and subsequent lesbian theories are rarely included in such organized political analysis and planning, but often have been relegated to lesbian-separatist dialogue and institutions. In addition, bisexuality often has been relegated to invisibility in the gay civil rights struggle, since many bisexual people refuse to define their sexual orientation or identity as purely a matter of birth orientation.

Lesbian-feminist separatism's theories have also been and continue to be used to reject bisexuality. Some lesbians, including some who work or are friends with men, continue to advocate sexual separatism as the preferred feminist conduct, rendering bisexuality along with heterosexuality "politically incorrect" for feminists.[100]

Some feminist theorists have begun more recently to write and theorize about bisexuality itself. As Elizabeth Reba Weise explains, bisexual feminist theorists

> are excited about the possibilities of a bisexuality informed by the understanding that sex and gender are classifications by which women are oppressed and restricted. We see bisexuality calling into question many of the fundamental assumptions of our culture: the duality of gender; the necessity of bipolar relationships; the nature of desire; the demand for either/or sexualities; and the seventies' gay and lesbian model of bisexuality as a stage in working through false consciousness before finally arriving at one's "true" orientation. . . . A bisexual-feminist perspective embraces the reality that sexuality can be a fluid and changeable part of being human. It rejects the dichotomization of politics and desire. . . . To be bisexual-feminist women means to live an intensely examined life. . . . In these writings, and in our lives, we are rejecting the rule set out for us, the rule that says "Choose only one." We are redefining the world and demanding to be accepted on our own terms. We are creating a place to come home to.[101]

Several central themes are emerging in bisexual feminist writings. One is a rejection of sexuality as static, tied to the sex of the person with whom one is in current relationship. Another is a rejection of dichotomous thinking. A third is an emergent hypothesis that women, perhaps more often than men, may possess a diffuse or nonexclusive potential sexuality.[102] Although the idea of a "polymorphous" sexuality is not new, and has been posited as essentially human by post-Freudian thinkers such as Herbert Marcuse, current French feminists writing about female sexuality and bisexuality in particular seem to be suggesting that female anatomy permits a more open sexuality. "Woman has sex organs just about everywhere," Luce Iraguay has said.[103]

Helene Cixous defines bisexuality as follows: "Bisexuality—that is to say the location within oneself of the presence of both sexes, evident and insistent in different ways according to the individual, the nonexclusion of difference or of a sex, and starting with this 'permission' one gives oneself, the multiplication of the effects of desire's inscription on every part of the body and the other body . . . [it] does not annihilate differences but cheers them on, pursues them, adds more."[104]

In an attempt to speak to questions of definition and causation, Dvora Zipkin lists several of her conclusions:

1) our sexual identity, although a very personal choice, is at the same time a very public and political statement and may mean very different things to different people;

2) sexual identity can—and does—change over time, as we, ourselves change;

3) our sexual identity may not necessarily be the same as our sexual behavior;

4) bisexuality is itself fluid—there is no one way to be "bi" (that is, it may mean different things to different people and may include preferences);

5) pressures from and influences of our communities may contribute to changes in our sexual identity;

6) many bisexual women share a general sense of not belonging to either the lesbian or heterosexual world; we may even feel like impostors;

7) support, validation and affirmation for who we are and who we choose to be, whether from writings, groups or individuals, is vital both for maintaining a healthy and self-accepting identity as bisexual women and for promoting a healthy acceptance by others; and

8) our stories as bisexual women are as unique and varied as we are.[105]

Bisexual feminist theorists are also trying to articulate what is feminist about bisexuality, in part in response to the legacy of lesbian-feminist articulations of what is feminist about lesbianism. For example, Margaret Lihee Choe states,

bisexuality has come to symbolize much more than sex in the feminist context in which we now speak. Bisexuality could even be seen to be lesbianism of post-feminism. Feminist bisexuality is a statement that says: "Loving women now is a given; we know we love women, we know we want to be with women; and now we're strong enough to love men. On our terms." In choosing a lover I use my own standards and reject dichotomization. As an Asian (formerly oriental) I've seen the necessity of taking control of my racial identity. As a bisexual feminist I seek to take control of my sexual pleasure.

Feminist bisexuality is still an individually forged identity. As such it is problematic, for identity is that which makes one recognizable to one's self and to others. My not being black or white in America may make bisexuality easier. One could even say that bisexuals are the Asians of sexual America: you're not one or the other, so you're overlooked.[106]

Amanda Udis-Kessler posits that bisexual feminists bring their experience of relationships with women to their relationships with men, permitting them to recognize subtle patterns of dominance which heterosexual women might not see as clearly. At the same time, because bisexual women are at times in relationship with men, their attempts to change the structures of sexism have direct impact on individual men. Udis-Kessler states, "Understandings that enable us to make changes in patterns of heterosexual intimacy, household division of labor, child care and childrearing, male-female communication patterns, money management and the like, may then become more accessible to heterosexual feminists and play a role in ending the reproduction of sexism that goes well beyond merely those women who identify as bi-feminists."[107]

Karin Baker takes the analysis one step further. She suggests that bisexual people, when they relate sexually to people of the same sex, challenge compulsory heterosexuality and share this challenge with feminists, lesbians, and gay men. But bisexual people go further, Baker believes, than do lesbians and gay men, because bisexual people refuse to limit their sexuality to one sex; this refusal, Baker sees, is a subversion of the dual gender system. "Lesbian and gay relationships challenge gender by avoiding traditional gender roles. However, lesbian and gay sexuality is based on attraction to a specific gender to the same degree that heterosexuality is. By definition, heterosexuality and homosexuality rely equally on a strictly defined gender system . . . in many cases . . . bisexual people recognize that most, if not all, of what they find attractive in another has little to do with gender."[108] Baker posits that part of what is politically important about bisexuality is its rejection of compulsory monosexuality.[109]

Concluding Thoughts

Combine the fact that no single scientific theory about what produces particular sexual orientation is accepted as correct and the historical and political insights of Katz, Halperin, Faderman, Rich et al. and we come up with the notion that sexual orientation as a central basis for constructing a personal sexual identity may well be a modern Western cultural construction. One possible conclusion that follows is that biological causation research may be beside the point and doomed to failure if sexual orientation as we presently understand it is purely a cultural artifact.

We, the authors, assume there probably are biological factors involved for some people in producing the predominant angle of direction for their erotic desires, but whether such sources cause a pattern of behavior we would recognize as heterosexual, lesbian, gay male, or bisexual is a very different question. There may well be developmental or familial influences on erotic inclination and behavior, but the relationship of these sources to the collection of behaviors that constitute heterosexuality, bisexuality, or homosexuality is also not clear. What is most clear to us is that cultural, political, and social norms affect, if not construct, sexual behavior, attitudes, and sense of self-identity as well as defining the idea of sexuality itself. It is also clear to us that the compulsory heterosexuality of modern Western cultures is part of the modern sex/gender system and causes much social and individual damage and that there are lessons to be learned from other cultural traditions, including American Indian tribal traditions, which included more flexible gender categories, and more recognition of the gifts of homoerotic identity and sexuality.

This continuum and book and the workshops conducted using them are intended to help people probe their own attitudes about sexual orientation and sexual identity and to expand their capacity to work with others in ways that recognize and value sexual diversity, while letting go of their own attachment to roles of dominance and subordinance. For these purposes it may be the better part of valor simply to put the issues of causation and historical continuity or discontinuity on the shelf.

Two understandings or working assumptions which grow out of the attempts to understand the psychology and causation of sexual orientation will nonetheless be helpful in this work. The first is that, at least in modern Western societies, *sexual orientation*, in the sense of the most deeply felt direction or directions of erotic inclination, no matter what its cause, tends for most, but not all people, to be persistent throughout one's adulthood and nonresponsive to personal or therapeutic attempts to alter it, regardless of the sexual identity one constructs or the behaviors and lifestyles in which one engages. It is also true that many people change their *sexual identity* and *behaviors* one or more times during their lives, and others go through some or all of life unclear about their sexual orientation and without consciously constructing a sexual identity. In other words, heterosexually dominant societies make it very difficult for individuals to accept any orientation or identity other than heterosexuality.

The second insight is that the attitudes, behaviors, lifestyles, and senses of personal identity which surround sexual orientation and sexuality are social constructs, constructs related in large part to social constructions of gender, constructs that can be understood, examined, and changed at the individual and group levels. This continuum and book attempt both to provide accurate information about sexual orientations and sexual identities and to assist people in understanding the origins and evolution of attitudes about sexual orientation and identity so that we all, regardless of culture, orientation, or identity, might learn better how to live and work together.

Notes

Chapter 1

1. Gilbert Herdt and Andrew M. Boxer, "Introduction: Culture, History, and Life Course of Gay Men," in Gilbert Herdt, ed., *Gay Culture in America* (Boston: Beacon Press, 1992), 19.

2. Andrew M. Boxer and Bertram J. Cohler, "The Life Course of Gay and Lesbian Youth: An Immodest Proposal for the Study of Lives," in Gilbert Herdt, ed., *Gay and Lesbian Youth* (New York: Harrington Park Press, 1989), 315–43.

3. *My Bodyguard*, Tony Bill, director, 20th Century Fox, 1980.

Chapter 2

1. Adrienne Rich, "Compulsory Heterosexuality and Lesbian Existence," *Signs: A Journal of Women in Culture and Society* 5, no. 4 (Summer 1980): 631–60; also published in Trudy Darty and Sandee Potter, eds., *Women-Identified Women* (Palo Alto, CA: Mayfield Publishing, 1984), 119–48; see esp. p. 124. See also Appendix A in this volume for a review of the modernity of contemporary language for, and concepts about, sexual orientations.

2. The term *compulsory heterosexuality* is Adrienne Rich's, in "Compulsory Heterosexuality."

3. Michael Ruse, *Homosexuality* (Oxford: Basil Blackwell, 1990), 3–8, referring to A. C. Kinsey et al., *Sexual Behavior in the Human Male* (Philadelphia: W. B. Saunders, 1948); and idem, *Sexual Behavior in the Human Female* (Philadelphia: W. B. Saunders, 1953).

4. See Amanda Udis-Kessler, "Notes on the Kinsey Scale and Other Measures of Sexuality," in Elizabeth Reba Weise, ed., *Closer to Home: Bisexuality and Feminism* (Seattle: Seal Press, 1992), 311–18, for a discussion and critique of several sexuality scales, including Kinsey's.

5. Cross-dressing is a phenomenon that has occurred in many cultures and throughout human history. Heterosexually dominant cultures have sometimes honored cross-dressing by including it as part of respected rituals and forms of artistic expression, as in some forms of Chinese and Japanese theater. Heterosexually dominant cultures have also viewed cross-dressing as criminal and a sign of sickness. For example, in Europe and the United States over the last couple of hundred years, male cross-dressing has been treated harshly by the legal system. At other times, or in certain situations, cross-dressing, particularly by women, has simply been accepted as the only practical way to dress, as in the rural Yankee attitude toward farm women wearing male attire when working in the fields. Historically, cross-dressing combined with passing as men have served as means for women to escape gender-role limitations and barriers to autonomy. In some American Indian tribes, male cross-dressing in particular was part of an established tradition of gender-blending of persons involved with some of the tasks of both sexes; these persons were often healers or spiritually important members of their bands. See Midnight Sun, "Sex/Gender Systems in Native North America," in Will Roscoe, ed., *Living the Spirit: A Gay American Indian Anthology* (New York: St. Martin's Press, 1988), 32–47.

In contemporary Western culture, deliberate cross-dressing, rather than a relatively unisex or more traditional male or female appearance, can be adopted by gay men and lesbians for many reasons. These include everything from occasional feminist refusal to be thrown off balance by high heels and have one's skin irritated by stockings and makeup; to a feminist choice to pass as male in order to avoid the sexual harassment and violence to which women are subjected; to a gay male insistence on expanding the definition of maleness to include pleasure in adornment with a wide range of colors and textures; to participation in the African-American gay male cultural events and institutions centered around voguing; to adoption of a "butch" identity as part of the construction of one's lesbian sexuality. There are also straight people who cross-dress—men who enjoy wearing women's clothes occasionally or frequently, in private or under their outer attire or more publicly, and women who are most comfortable dressed in ways that cause misidentification of them as male. Some public cross-dressing is labeled transvestitism, a term sloppily used in contemporary culture but intended to describe people who dress in ways that involve a gender role different from both their biological sex and their internalized gender identity; for example, a biological man who identifies as male but dresses and acts periodically as a women. See Holly Devor, *Gender Blending: Confronting the Limits of Duality* (Bloomington: Indiana University Press, 1989), esp. 19–20. In a world less attached to polarized definitions of female and male, we would be less able to speak about cross-dressing since there would be fewer rules of appearance tied to biological gender. For a discussion of transsexualism see Appendix A, footnote on page 188.

6. Julia Penelope, *Call Me Lesbian: Lesbian Lives, Lesbian Theory* (Freedom, CA: Crossing Press, 1992), 78.

7. Tomas Almaguer, "Chicano Men: A Cartography of Homosexual Identity and Behavior," in Henry Abelove, Michele A. Barale, and David M. Halperin, eds., *The Lesbian and Gay Studies Reader* (New York: Routledge, 1993), 255, 258, 262.

8. Cherríe Moraga, *Living in the War Years: Lo que nunca paso por sus labios* (Boston: South End Press, 1983), 50–124.

9. Joseph Beam, *In the Life: A Black Gay Anthology* (Boston: Alyson Publications, 1986).

10. Gloria Wekker, "Matiism and Black Lesbianism: Two Idealtypical Expressions of Female Homosexuality in Black Communities in the Diaspora," in J. DeCecco and J. Elia, eds., *If You Seduce a Straight Person Can You Make Them Gay?* (Binghamton, NY: Harrington Park Press, 1993), 145, 146–52; also Audre Lorde, "Scratching the Surface: Some Notes on Barriers to Women and Loving," in *Sister Outsider: Essays and Speeches* (Trumansburg, NY: Crossing Press, 1984), 45–52.

11. Interview with Zelda, an African-American woman minister, August 1993, by Heather Wishik. For further description of the particular risks associated with coming out which people of color face, especially the issue of loss of home/cultural community, see Essex Hemphill, "Introduction," in Essex Hemphill, ed., *Brother to Brother: New Writings by Black Gay Men* (Boston: Alyson Publications, 1991), xvii–xviii; also see Makeda Silvera, "Introduction," in Makeda Silvera, ed., *Piece of My Heart: A Lesbian of Colour Anthology* (Toronto: Sister Vision Press, 1991), xiv; and bell hooks, "homophobia in black communities," in *Talking Back: thinking feminist, thinking black* (Boston: South End Press, 1989), 120–26.

12. Almaguer, "Chicano Men," 262.

13. *Tongues Untied,* Marlon Riggs, director and producer, 1989 (film).

14. Nice Rodriguez, "Straight People, Wild Ducks, and Salmon," in Silvera, *Piece of My Heart,* 204–9.

Chapter 3

1. Martin Hoffman, *The Gay World* (New York: Basic Books, 1968), 32–33.

2. Ron Simmons, "Some Thoughts on the Challenges Facing Black Gay Intellectuals," in Hemphill, *Brother to Brother,* 211.

3. Jewelle L. Gomez and Barbara Smith, "Taking the Home out of Homophobia: Black Lesbian Health," in Silvera, *Piece of My Heart,* 41.

4. _____ "Lesbians of Colour: Loving and Struggling, A Conversation Between Three Lesbians of Colour," in Silvera, *Piece of My Heart,* 162.

5. Richard A. Isay, *Being Homosexual: Gay Men and Their Development* (New York: Avon, 1989), 81, 128.

6. Isaac Julien and Kobena Mercer, "True Confessions: A Discourse on Images of Black Male Sexuality," in Hemphill, *Brother to Brother,* 170–71.

7. When the Allies liberated the Nazi concentration camps at the end of World War II, they kept the gay men imprisoned, believing this population had been justifiably incarcerated. See Erwin J. Haeberle, "Swastika, Pink Triangle, and Yellow Star" in Martin B. Duberman, Martha Vicinis, and George Chauncy, Jr., *Hidden from History: Reclaiming the Gay and Lesbian Past* (New York: New American Library, 1989), 373; and Richard Plant, *The Pink Triangle* (New York: Henry Holt, 1986), 181.

8. See National Gay and Lesbian Task Force, "Anti-Gay Violence, Victimization, and Defamation, 1988" and subsequent years (NGLTF, 1517 U Street NW, Washington, DC 20009). Recent studies by the National Gay and Lesbian Task Force and testimony in Congress in support of the recently passed Hate Crimes Statistics Act both indicate that in this country, antigay and lesbian violence increased dramatically during the 1980s, since the AIDS epidemic surfaced in the United States.

9. Carmen Vazquez, "Appearances," in Warren J. Blumenfeld, *Homophobia: How We All Pay the Price* (Boston: Beacon Press, 1991), 157–58.

10. Michelle M. Benecke and Kirsten S. Dodge, "Lesbian Baiting as Sexual Harassment: Women in the Military," in Blumenfeld, *Homophobia,* 168.

11. Brian McNaught, lecture, University of Vermont, 1990.

12. Brian McNaught, *On Being Gay* (New York: St. Martin's Press, 1988), 22.

13. Letha Scanzoni and Virginia Ramey Mollenkott, *Is the Homosexual My Neighbor? Another Christian View* (New York: Harper and Row, 1978). Several mainline Christian denominations have moved toward welcoming gay, lesbian, and bisex-

ual people into their congregations, e.g. The United Churches of Christ and the Presbyterians. The Unitarian Universalists have been leaders in welcoming gay, lesbian, and bisexual people as have the Reform and Reconstructionist Movements of Judaism.

14. McNaught lecture, University of Vermont, 1990.

15. Kinsey et al., *Sexual Behavior in the Human Male*, 650.

16. See "Citizen Cohn," Frank Pierson, director, HBO video, 1992.

17. Vynnie Hale, kick-off rally for The New Hampshire Coalition to End Discrimination, Manchester, NH, November 10, 1993.

18. Richard Green, "Sexual Identity of 37 Children Raised by Homosexual or Transsexual Parents," *American Journal of Psychiatry* 135(6): 692–97. See also the extensive review of studies about children of gay and lesbian parents: Charles J. Patterson, "Children of Gay and Lesbian Parents," *Child Development* 63 (October 1992): 1025–42.

19. Conversation with an African-American gay man, May 1993.

Chapter 4

1. Adrienne Rich, "Foreword," in Julia Penelope and Susan Wolfe, eds., *The Coming Out Stories* (Watertown, MA: Persephone Press, 1979), xii; reprinted as *The Original Coming Out Stories* (Freedom, CA: Crossing Press, 1989).

2. Beth Brant, "Reclamation: A Lesbian Indian Story," in Darty and Potter, *Women-Identified Women*, 97.

3. See, for example, Penelope and Wolfe, *Coming Out Stories*.

4. Penelope, *Call Me Lesbian*, 35.

5. Conversation with A. N., November 19, 1993, Boston.

6. Penelope, *Call Me Lesbian*, 36.

7. Joseph Beam, "Brother to Brother," in Beam, *In the Life*, 231.

8. Silvera, *Piece of My Heart*, xv, 162, 163, 167; Hemphill, "Introduction," in *Brother to Brother*, xvii–xviii. Darryl K. Loiacano, "Gay Identity Issues Among Black Americans: Racism, Homophobia, and the Need for Validation," *Journal of Counseling and Development* 68 (1989): 21–25.

9. Audre Lorde, *Zami: A New Spelling of My Name* (Watertown, MA: Persephone Press, 1982), 224.

10. Hemphill, "Introduction," in *Brother to Brother*, xxii.

11. Lillian Faderman, *Odd Girls and Twilight Lovers: A History of Lesbian Life in Twentieth-Century America* (New York: Penguin, 1992), 75.

12. Conversation with Robyn Ochs, November 1993, Boston.

13. Penelope, *Call Me Lesbian*, 6.

14. Andrew Boxer and Gilbert Herdt, *Children of Horizons* (Boston: Beacon Press, 1993), 203–206.

15. Charles Harpe, "At 36," in Hemphill, *Brother to Brother*, 54.

16. Maurice Hoo, "Speech Impediments," *Witness Aloud: Lesbian, Gay, and Bisexual Asian/Pacific American Writings* 2 (Spring/Summer 1993): 107–12, 108.

17. Bobbie Griffith. See B. Jaye Miller, "From Silence to Suicide: Measuring a Mother's Loss," in Blumenfeld, *Homophobia*, 79–94.

18. Isay, *Being Homosexual*, 68–73.

19. Esther Rothblum, "Introduction: Lesbianism as a Model of a Positive Lifestyle for Women," in Esther Rothblum and Ellen Cole, eds., *Loving Boldly: Issues Facing Lesbians* (Binghamton, NY: Harrington Park Press, 1989), 7, 8.

20. Sexual orientation "deprogramming" is still the goal of some programs operated in religious and in pseudopsychiatric contexts. The National Center for Lesbian Rights reported in 1992 that it assisted an adolescent lesbian from California who had escaped from a so-called sexual orientation treatment center in Utah. The young woman had been sent there pursuant to an Individual Educational Plan (IEP) developed by her school and mother in response to the girl's lesbianism. Her tuition was paid by the school district. (Liz Hendrickson, "Dear Friend of NCLR," National Center for Lesbian Rights, San Francisco, December 1992.) A Protestant minister reported to this author in 1992 that his denomination offered him access to a "Christian counseling program" designed to change his sexual orientation from gay to straight.

21. Penelope, *Call Me Lesbian*, 43.

22. Beth Brant reports that a 1975 reading of a love poem to a woman by Audre Lorde generated her recognition of her own lesbianism. Brant, "Reclamation," 97.

23. Joan Nestle, *A Restricted Country* (Ithaca, NY: Firebrand Books, 1987), 100–109.

24. Richard Rodriguez, "Late Victorians: San Francisco, AIDS and Homosexual Stereotypes," *Harper's*, October 1990, pp. 57–86, quote at 59–60.

25. M. Owlfeather (Shoshone-Metis/Cree), "Children of Grandmother Moon," in Roscoe, *Living the Spirit*, 100.

26. Hemphill, "Introduction," in *Brother to Brother*, xxviii.

27. Conversation with Asian gay man, Boston, January 1993.

28. Rodriguez, "Late Victorians," 58.

29. Cheryl Clarke, "Saying the Least Said, Telling the Least Told: The Voices of Black Lesbian Writers," in Silvera, *Piece of My Heart*, 172–73.

30. PBS Frontline, "The Secret File on J. Edgar Hoover," February 9, 1993.

31. Boxer and Herdt, *Children of Horizons*, 205, 206.

32. Nestle, *Restricted Country*, 110.

33. Hemphill, "Introduction," in *Brother to Brother*, xviii–xix.

34. C. Allyson Lee, "An Asian Lesbian's Struggle," in Silvera, *Piece of My Heart*, 116–18, includes discussion of Lee's early resistance to Chinese culture, what she calls her "sinophobia," and her later readiness for and seeking contact with Asian lesbians. Lee also discusses what she calls the "Asianophile" phenomenon among white lesbians, that is, white women feeling attracted to Chinese and other Asian women because they are Asian.

35. Racial identity development has been described as a developmental process by several theorists. Several researchers who study lesbians and gay men of color have noted similarities between the developmental stages of minority identity development models and models of sexual identity development. Several of these researchers have also noted the interdependence of positive sexual identity development and positive minority identity development. See C. S. Chan, "Issues of Identity Development among Asian-American Lesbians and Gay Men," *Journal of Counseling and Development* 68 (1) (1989): 16–20; O. M. Espin, "Issues of Identity in the Psychology of Latina Lesbians," in Boston Lesbian Psychologies Collective, ed., *Lesbian Psychologies: Explorations and Challenges* (Urbana: University of Illinois Press, 1987), 35–51; Loiacano, "Gay Identity Issues among Black Americans," 24. The two schemes often compared are that by Cass about sexual identity (identity confusion, identity comparison, identity tolerance, identity acceptance, identity price, and identity synthesis) and that by Atkinson, Morten, and Sue about Minority Identity Development (conformity, dissonance, resistance, and immersion, introspection, synergic articulation, and awareness). V. C. Cass, "Homosexual Identity Formation: A Theoretical Model," *Journal of Homosexuality* 4 (1979): 219–

35; D. R. Atkinson, G. Morten, and D. W. Sue, *Counseling American Minorities* (Dubuque, Iowa: Brown, 1979).

36. Espin, "Issues of Identity in the Psychology of Latina Lesbians," 39, discussing the Cass and Atkinson, Morten, and Sue models.

37. C. S. Chan, "Issues of Identity Development among Asian-American Lesbians and Gay Men," 16–20, citing W. S. Wooden, H. Kawasaki and R. Mayeda "Lifestyles and Identity Maintenance among Gay Japanese-American Males," *Alternative Lifestyles* 5 (1983): 236–43.

38. Nestle, *Restricted Country*, 185–86.

Chapter 5

1. Marlon Riggs, "Black Macho Revisited: Reflections of a SNAP! Queen," in Hemphill, *Brother to Brother*, 253–57.

2. Joan Nestle, ed., *The Persistent Desire: A Femme-Butch Reader* (Boston: Alyson Publications, 1992); Penelope, *Call Me Lesbian*, esp. 1–16; Faderman, *Odd Girls and Twilight Lovers*, esp. chap. 7, 159–87.

3. Reginald T. Jackson, "The Absence of Fear: An Open Letter to a Brother," in Hemphill, *Brother to Brother*, 209–10.

4. Ann Landers, "Praise for Participants in Gay Parades," *Boston Globe*, January 4, 1993, p. 34.

5. Nestle, *Restricted Country*, 103.

6. Rodriguez, "Late Victorians," 60.

7. Riggs, "Black Macho Revisited," 255.

8. Lorde, *Zami*, 224.

9. Penelope, *Call Me Lesbian*, 11; for another, more positive view of butch/femme roles and identities, see Nestle, *Persistent Desire*.

10. Nestle, *Restricted Country*, 100–119, 131–33 and Leslie Feinberg, *Stone Butch Blues* (Boston: Alyson Publications, 1994).

11. Ruth Gibian, "Refusing Certainty: Toward a Bisexuality of Wholeness," in Weise, *Closer to Home*, 10–11.

12. Mirtha Quintanales, "I Paid Very Hard for My Immigrant Ignorance," in Cherríe Moraga and Gloria Anzaldúa, eds., *This Bridge Called My Back: Writings By Radical Women of Color* (Watertown, MA: Persephone Press, 1981), 150.

13. Randy Burns, "Preface," in Roscoe, *Living the Spirit*, 3–4.

14. Indigo Som, "The Queer Kitchen," in Silvera, *Piece of My Heart*, 145.

15. Heterosexual culture has rendered invisible the existence of lesbians and gay men in

history as well as demanding invisibility from us most of the time today. How many of us, when we read in school the poems of Walt Whitman and Langston Hughes, great American poets, one white, one black, were told they were both gay or bisexual? In school we may have read something about Greek "customs" regarding men and youths, but little else makes it into the curricula. Adult historical literature also hides much. For example, biographers and those in control of the estates of prominent people have sometimes attempted to mask the bisexual, gay, or lesbian relationships, behaviors, and identities of such people or to delay disclosure and control the contexts in which they are identified as bisexual or gay. See, for example, Essex Hemphill, "Undressing Icons," in Hemphill, *Brother to Brother*, 181–83, regarding the Langston Hughes estate; and Doris Faber, *The Life of Lorena Hickok: E.R.'s Friend* (New York: William Morrow, 1980), 5–7 and 329–32, regarding attempts to manage disclosures about Eleanor Roosevelt's lesbian relationships.

16. Hemphill, "Introduction," in *Brother to Brother*, xxix.

17. Separatism is also a political position and epistemological stance, a commitment to trying to understand the world from a position as outside of "heteropatriarchy" as possible. Julia Penelope, using *HP* to stand for "heteropatriarchal core beliefs" and "heteropatriarchy," has explained separatism: "Separatist Lesbians think of ourselves as living outside HP society (although this is seldom true). Accepting the HP description of Lesbians as outcasts, we have chosen to stand in an antagonistic position to the HP, and it's Separatists who identify ourselves as Lesbians first and last. Whether never-het or ex-het, Separatists put our Lesbian selves first politically. The essential ingredient of Separatist politics is a rejection of everything vital to the structure of HP which requires that all assumptions be challenged and examined. . . . If we're going to change ourselves and unlearn HP's version of reality, then we're committed to examining our feelings and finding out why we have them and where they originate in our experience." Penelope, *Call Me Lesbian*, 93.

18. Barbara Smith and Beverly Smith, "Across the Kitchen Table: A Sister-to-Sister Dialogue," in Moraga and Anzaldúa, *This Bridge Called My Back*, 121–22.

19. Gibian, "Refusing Certainty," 10–11.

20. Isay, *Being Homosexual*, 85, 92.

21. David P. McWhirter and Andrew M. Mattison, *The Male Couple: How Relationships Develop* (Englewood Cliffs, NJ: Prentice-Hall, 1984).

22. A. Elfin Moses and Robert O. Hawkins, Jr., *Counseling Lesbian Women and Gay Men: A Life Issues Approach* (Columbus, OH: Merrill Publishing, 1986), 215.

23. Leslea Newman, *Heather Has Two Mommies* (New York: In Other Words Press, 1989).

Chapter 6

1. Brenda Marie Blasingame, "The Roots of Biphobia: Racism and Internalized Heterosexism," in Weise, *Closer to Home*, 48.

2. Som, "Queer Kitchen," 145.

3. Nate Brown, "A Gift to Myself," in Loraine Hutchins and Lani Kaahumanu, eds., *Bi Any Other Name: Bisexual People Speak Out* (Boston: Alyson Publications, 1991), 65.

4. Rebecca Shuster, "Beyond Defense," in Hutchins and Kaahumanu, *Bi Any Other Name*, 269.

5. Vashti Zabatinsky, "Some Thoughts on Power, Gender, Body Image and Sex in the Life of One Bisexual Lesbian Feminist," in Weise, *Closer to Home*, 142.

6. Michael Ambrosino, "Choosing Not To," in Hutchins and Kaahumanu, *Bi Any Other Name*, 348; for a group of articles about issues facing bisexual men and women in marriages, including spousal reactions to their coming out, see Fritz Klein and Timothy J. Wolf, *Two Lives to Lead: Bisexuality in Men and Women* (Binghamton, NY: Harrington Press, 1985), 87–222.

7. Cornelius Utz, "Ninety-three People = 100% Acceptance," in Hutchins and Kaahumanu, *Bi Any Other Name*, 23–24.

8. Blasingame, "Roots of Biphobia," 53.

9. Ambrosino, "Choosing Not To," 346.

10. Blasingame, "Roots of Biphobia," 48. Blasingame has also pointed out, as has bisexual theorist Amanda Udis-Kessler, that for white gay men in particular, who in white culture tend not to gain "root identity" through ethnic identity, the gay community has often served as the "key to their personal identity" in the way an ethnic community often has served people of color. The norms established in the white gay male community until recently defined, and sometimes today still define, bisexual people as "not queer." These definitional boundaries for defining the

white gay male community may be more rigid than were past understandings about gay and bisexual lives within some communities of color, where people's relationships tended to be known but not discussed or labeled in order to maintain the sense of community belonging and mutual responsibility. Blasingame, "Roots of Biphobia," 51. This insight about the gay community being the source of a root sense of identity for white gay men is important in understanding just how devastating the loss of hundreds of thousands of members of that community to AIDS has been to the survivors.

11. Gibian, "Refusing Certainty," 12.

12. Elise Krueger, 1988 letter quoted by Lani Kaahumanu, "Overview," in Hutchins and Kaahumanu, *Bi Any Other Name*, 129.

13. Kaahumanu, "Overview," 129.

14. Lenore Norrgard, "Can Bisexuals Be Monogamous?" in Hutchins and Kaahumanu, *Bi Any Other Name*, 282.

15. Lisa Orlando, "Loving Whom We Choose," in Hutchins and Kaahumanu, *Bi Any Other Name*, 228.

16. Ibid., 224, 226, 229.

17. Kathleen Bennett, "Feminist Bisexuality: A Both/And Option for an Either/Or World," in Weise, *Closer to Home*, 216.

18. Paula C. Rust, "Who Are We and Where Do We Go from Here? Conceptualizing Bisexuality," in Weise, *Closer to Home*, 300–301.

19. Kaahumanu, "Overview," 128.

20. Rust, "Who Are We and Where Do We Go from Here?" 294.

Chapter 7

1. Silvera, *Piece of My Heart*, 25.

2. Gomez and Smith, "Taking the Home Out of Homophobia," 40.

3. *Basileus Quartet*, Fabrio Carpi, director, La Rai Radio Television Italiana, 1984.

4. Starhawk, *Dreaming the Dark* (Boston: Beacon Press, 1982), 150.

5. *The Fox*, Mark Rydell, director, Claridge Pictures, 1968.

6. *Oscar Wilde*, Gregory Ratoff, director, Warner Brothers, 1960; *Oranges Are Not the Only Fruit*, Beeban Kidron, director, BBC Lionheart Television, 1989; *A Special Day*, Ettore Scola, director, Canafox Films, Montreal, 1977.

7. *A Torch Song Trilogy*, Paul Bogard, director, New Line Cinema, 1988; *Desert Hearts*, Donna Deitch, director, Samuel Goldwyn, 1986; *Maurice*,

James Ivory, director, Merchant Ivory Films, 1987. *Philadelphia*, Jonathan Demme, director, Columbia Tristar, 1994; *Go Fish*, Rosh Troche, director, Can I Watch Pictures Company, 1994; *And the Band Played On*, Roger Spottiswoode, director, HBO Home Video, 1994; *The Wedding Banquet*, Ang Lee, director, Samuel Goldwyn, 1993. *Tales of the City*, Alastair Reid, director, Working Title/Propaganda Productions and Channel 4, BBC, 1994, distributed by Poly Gram Video.

8. *Victor/Victoria*, Blake Edwards, director, MGM/UA, 1982.

9. *Priscilla, Queen of The Desert*, Stephen Elliot, director, Gramercy Films, 1994.

10. Michael Brewer, "Two-Way Closet," in Hutchins and Kaahumanu, *Bi Any Other Name*, 142–43.

11. Carol Pierce, *"Women and Victim Behavior"* (Laconia, NH: New Dynamics Publications, 1991).

12. In some cultures many heterosexually identified men have pre-marital sexual relations with other men and some also have ongoing sexual relations with other men after marriage. For example, see J. M. Carrier, "Mexican Male Bisexuality," in Klein and Wolf, *Two Lives to Lead*, 75–85.

13. Jean S. Gochros, "Homophobia, Homosexuality, and Heterosexual Marriage," in Blumenfeld, *Homophobia*, 131–53.

14. Ibid., 152.

15. Ibid.

16. Carrier, "Mexican Male Bisexuality," 75–85.

17. Cornel West, *Race Matters* (Boston: Beacon Press, 1993), 89.

18. Shakti Gawain and Laurel King, *Living in the Light* (San Rafael, CA: New World Library, 1986), 59–60.

19. Carol Pierce, David Wagner, and Bill Page, *The Male/Female Continuum: Paths to Colleagueship* (Laconia, NH: New Dynamics Publications, 1994), esp. "Men and Dominance," 16–22, and "Men In Transition," 37–45.

20. Ibid., 23–28.

21. This is true for not only some white men, but also for some men of color. See Carrier's discussion of Mexican men in "Mexican Male Bisexuality."

22. For other scales that give a wider variety of images, see Udis-Kessler, "Notes on the Kinsey Scale and Other Measures of Sexuality," 311–18.

23. Ann Fox, "Development of a Bisexual Identity," in Hutchins and Kaahumanu, *Bi Any Other Name*, 29.

24. bell hooks, *Talking Back: thinking feminist, thinking black* (Boston: South End Press, 1989), 125. hooks speaks for all people of color.

25. See Thomas Cowan, *Gay Men and Women Who Enriched the World* (New Canaan, CT: Mulvey Books, 1988).

Chapter 8

1. Derek Bell. *Faces at the Bottom of the Well: The Permanence of Racism,* (New York: Basic Books, 1992).

2. Richard Orange, an organization development consultant and New Dynamics partner, developed this list of necessary characteristics of community.

Appendix A

1. Andrew M. Boxer, Judith A. Cook, and Gilbert Herdt, "Double Jeopardy: Identity Transitions and Parent-Child Relations among Gay and Lesbian Youth," in Karl Pillemer and Kathleen McCartney, eds., *Parent-Child Relations Throughout Life* (Hillsdale, NJ: Lawrence Erlbaum Associates, 1991), 60–63.

2. Faderman, "Odd girls," 15; See also Lillian Faderman, *Surpassing the Love of Men: Romantic Friendship and Love Between Women From the Renaissance to the Present* (New York: William Morrow, 1981).

3. Devor, *Gender Blending*, vii.

4. Ibid., 2–19.

5. Ibid.

6. Ibid., vii.

Appendix B

1. Boxer and Herdt, *Children of Horizons,* 6.

2. Most of the information we have about lesbian, gay, and bisexual people's childhoods is based on accounts told as memories by adults. The construction of sexual identity is a long-term life process which is understood differently at different life stages. Childhood stories told in adulthood are necessarily interpreted from the adult vantage point at the moment the story is told. The story might differ if told another year. It is difficult for an adult accurately to reconstruct the meaning of childhood experiences as the child understood them. Thus, with the exception of some small studies of particular populations of children, such as the studies by Richard Green of sissy boys, there has until recently been little longitudinal data tracking from some point in childhood forward the experience of coming out to oneself and constructing a sexual identity. This deficit in research data is beginning to be remedied by studies such as those conducted with gay and lesbian adolescents in Chicago by Andrew Boxer and colleagues from the Evelyn Hooker Center for Gay and Lesbian Mental Health. Such research was simply not possible until there existed support services for gay and lesbian adolescents where they could make themselves visible to adults and thus available for participation in research. See generally Boxer and Herdt, *Children of Horizons.*

3. Conversation with Martha Rich, March 1990, Hanover, NH.

4. Isay, *Being Homosexual*, esp. 19.

5. Ibid. No comparable interview data about lesbians or bisexual women are known to the authors. However, many researchers and theorists hypothesize that a somewhat smaller percentage of lesbians are oriented toward women from birth. Two explanations exist for this hypothesis. First, women may be more likely to be born ambisexual and less frequently born with a polarized sexual orientation. See, for example, Eridani, "Is Sexual Orientation a Secondary Sex Characteristic?" in Weise, *Closer To Home*, 173–76. Second, in addition to birth-based sexual orientation, there is a cultural incentive to be woman-identified in cultures that subordinate women. This leads to the suggestion that some percentage of adult lesbians are lesbian-identified by choice rather than by sexual orientation; that is, some are heterosexual or ambisexual by orientation but lesbian-identified by choice out of a desire to escape heterosexual female subordinance and/or out of a political decision to identify with women-identified women as a rejection of patriarchy. This is probably not true as frequently for gay and bisexual men because there is no comparable social incentive to escape heterosexuality.

6. Penelope, *Call Me Lesbian*, 18.

7. Adrienne Rich, *Of Woman Born* (New York: W. W. Norton, 1976), esp. chap. 9, 218–55.

8. Boxer and Herdt, *Children of Horizons*, 179.

9. Ibid.

10. James N. Baker, "Coming Out Now," in "The New Teens: What Makes Them Different," *Newsweek* Special Edition (Summer/Fall 1990): 60.

11. Jackson, "Absence of Fear," in Hemphill, *Brother to Brother*, 207.

12. Conversation with white lesbian, June 1990, Vermont.

13. Devor, *Gender Blending*, 99.

14. Ron Simmons, "Tongues Untied: An Interview with Marlon Riggs," in Hemphill, *Brother to Brother*, 191–92.

15. Joanne Kadi, "A Lesbian Love Letter: This Is the Letter I Wish Someone Had Written for Me When I Was a Young Woman," in Silvera, *Piece of My Heart*, 103–4.

16. Anthony R. D'Augelli. "Identity Development and Sexual Orientation: Toward a Model of Lesbian, Gay, and Bisexual Development," in E. J. Trickett, R. Watts, and D. Berman, eds., *Human Diversity: Perspectives on People in Context*. (San Francisco: Jossey-Bass, 1994), 4–5.

17. Penelope, *Call Me Lesbian*, 18.

18. Baker, "Coming Out Now," 60–61.

19. Simon Watney, "School's Out," in Diana Fuss, ed., *Inside/Out: Lesbian Theories, Gay Theories* (New York: Routledge, 1991), 397.

20. Conversation with white gay man, June 1991, Vermont.

21. Baker, "Coming Out Now," 60.

22. Conversations with lesbians, 1980 and 1982, Vermont.

23. Baker, "Coming Out Now," 60.

24. Herdt and Boxer, "Introduction," in *Gay Culture in America*, 7, 8.

25. Diego Ribadeneira, "Going to School on Bias," *Boston Globe*, December 12, 1992, pp. 49, 52.

26. Neil Miller, "Sex Education," *Boston Globe Sunday Magazine*, November 8, 1992, pp. 15, 32.

27. Ibid., 32.

28. *Bay Windows*, "Kennedy Tries to Block Helms," August 5–10, 1994, 1.

29. See, for example, the writings of Audre Lorde, Barbara Smith, Cheryl Clarke, and Jewelle Gomez.

30. Silvera, "Introduction," in *Piece of My Heart*, esp. xiii. See also Moraga and Anzaldúa, *This Bridge Called My Back*.

31. See, for example, in addition to Hemphill, *Brother to Brother*; Beam, *In the Life*; Martin Humphries, *Tongues Untied* (London: Gay Men's Press, 1987); and video documentaries "Tongues Untied," by Marlon Riggs, 1989, and "Looking for Langston," by Isaac Julien, 1989. See also Simmons, "Tongues Untied: An Interview with Marlon Riggs," 190.

32. Hemphill, "Introduction," in *Brother to Brother*, xv–xvi.

33. Ibid., xvi.

34. NGLTF, "Anti-Gay Violence, Victimization, and Defamation Report, 1988."

35. Remafedi, Gary, J. A. Farrow, and R. W. Deisher, "Risk Factors for Attempted Suicide in Gay and Bisexual Youth," *Pediatrics*, 87 (1991): 869–875; also published in Gary Remafedi, ed., *Death By Denial: Studies of Suicide in Gay and Lesbian Teenagers* (Boston: Alyson Publications, 1994).

36. Baker, "Coming Out Now," 61.

37. Report on National Public Radio, "All Things Considered," June 26, 1990.

38. Baker, "Coming Out Now," 61.

39. The concept of social self and its absence for lesbians in culture are discussed in Sarah Hoaglund, *Lesbian Ethics: Toward New Value* (Palo Alto, CA: Institute of Lesbian Studies, 1988), 145, 296.

40. Paul Gibson, "Gay Male and Lesbian Youth Suicide," from U.S. Department of Health and Human Services, Report of the Secretary's Task Force on Youth Suicide, in Remafedi, *Death by Denial*, 50, 51.

41. Herdt and Boxer, "Introduction," in *Gay Culture in America*, 18.

42. Boxer, Cook, and Herdt, "Double Jeopardy," 59, 61.

43. Ibid., 61–62.

44. A. D. Martin, "Learning to Hide: The Socialization of the Gay Adolescent," *Adolescent Psychiatry* 10 (1988): 52–65.

45. Andrew M. Boxer and Judith A. Cook, "Developmental Discontinuities in the Transition to Gay and Lesbian Adult Roles: A Study of Homosexual Youth," cited in Boxer, Cook, and Herdt, "Double Jeopardy," 63.

46. Boxer, Cook, and Herdt, "Double Jeopardy," 85–86.

47. Ibid., 70–71.

48. Ibid., 76–77.

49. National Center for Lesbian Rights, "15th Anniversary Report," San Francisco, 1992. Forty percent of homeless youth in a 1994 Boston survey identified as gay or lesbian. Warren Blumenfeld. Introduction to *Out: Gay and Lesbian Youth*, David Adkin, director, National Film board of Canada, 1994, delivered August 14, 1994, Boston Museum of Fine Arts.

50. Boxer, Cook, and Herdt, "Double Jeopardy," 81, 87.

51. Sherry Zitter, "Coming Out to Mom: Theoretical Aspects of the Mother-Daughter Process," in Boston Lesbian Psychologies Collective, *Lesbian Psychologies*, 177.

52. A. Muller, *Parents Matter* (New York: Naiad Press, 1988).

53. Gibson, "Gay Male and Lesbian Youth Suicide"; also cited in Baker, "Coming Out Now," 60.

54. Lee, "An Asian Lesbian's Struggle," 116; Beam, "Brother to Brother," 231; see also Gibson, "Gay Male and Lesbian Youth Suicide"; hooks, *Talking Back*, 120–26; Simmons, "Thoughts on the Challenges facing Black Gay Intellectuals," 211–28.

55. B. Tremble, M. Schneider, and C. Appathurai, "Growing up Gay or Lesbian in a Multicultural Context," *Journal of Homosexuality* 17, nos. 1–2 (1989): 253–67.

56. Experience reported by sixteen-year-old boy in a story published in *The Phoenix*, Franklin High School, Seattle, Washington, Spring 1990.

57. D'Augelli, "Identity Development", 16.

Appendix C

1. William Masters and Virginia Johnson, *Heterosexuality* (New York: HarperCollins, 1994).

2. George Chauncey, Jr., Martin B. Duberman, and Martha Vicinus, "Introduction," in Duberman, Vicinus, and Chauncey, *Hidden from History*, 1–2.

3. Shane Phalen, *Identity Politics: Lesbian Feminism and the Limits of Community* (Philadelphia: Temple University Press, 1989), 124. Michel Foucault, one of the best known and most radical social constructionist historians of sexuality, posited that sex does not exist in nature except as intermingled with culture. For him there were no sexual instincts, but rather simply socioeconomically and, in Western societies, medically formulated categories or types of expression of sexuality, many of which function repressively. Commenting on a speech given by Foucault at New York University, David F. Greenberg states, "by revealing that ideas about sex were human creations, [Foucault] hoped to neutralize their power and pave the way for emancipation." Greenberg, *The Construction of Homosexuality* (Chicago: University of Chicago, 1988), 489. See also Michel Foucault, *The History of Sexuality*, 3 vols. (New York: Vintage, 1978, 1980).

4. Jonathan Katz, *Gay American History: Lesbians and Gay Men in the U.S.A.* (New York: Thomas Crowell, 1976), 6–7.

5. Robert Padguy, "Sexual Matters: Rethinking Sexuality in History," in Duberman, Vicinus, and Chauncey, *Hidden from History*, 59–60.

6. Harriet Whitehead, "The Bow and the Burden Strap: A New Look at Institutionalized Homosexuality in Native North America," in Abelove, Barale, and Halperin, *Lesbian and Gay Studies Reader*, 498–527.

7. Roscoe, *Living the Spirit*; Robert M. Baum, "Homosexuality and the Traditional Religions of the Americas and Africa," in Arlene Swidler, *Homosexuality and World Religions*, (Valley Forge, PA: Trinity Press, 1993), 12.

8. Baum, "Traditional Religions," 31.

9. David M. Halperin, *One Hundred Years of Homosexuality: And Other Essays on Greek Love*, (New York: Routledge, 1989), 54–71.

10. Audre Lorde, "Scratching the Surface," in *Sister Outsider*, 50. Here she quotes M. Herskovits, *Dahomey*, 2 vols. (Evanston, IL: Northwestern University Press, 1968), 1:320–22.

11. Kaahumanu, "Overview," in *Bi Any Other Name*, 129; quoting from Rotello, Gabriel, "Present at the Creation: C. H. Ford, author of the first Gay Novel, Talks About the Village in the '20's, Paris in the '30's, and Coming Out 40 Years Before Stonewall," *Outweek*, December 17, 1989.

12. Halperin, *One Hundred Years of Homosexuality*, 18, referring to John Boswell, "Revolutions, Universals and Sexual Categories," in Boyers and Steiner, eds., *Homosexuality: Sacrilege, Vision, Politics* (Cold Springs, NY: Salmagundi, 1982–83), 89–113.

13. Halperin, *One Hundred Years of Homosexuality*, 35.

14. Ibid.

15. Ibid., 23.

16. Ibid., 25–30.

17. Vern L. Bullough, *Homosexuality: A History of Homosexuality* (New York: 1979), 2, 62, quoted in Halperin, *One Hundred Years of Homosexuality*, 159, n. 21.

18. C. S. Ford and F. A. Beach, *Patterns of Sexual Behavior* (London: Methuen, 1970).

19. David Fernbach, *The Spiral Path: A Gay Contribution to Human Survival* (Boston: Alyson Publications, 1981), excerpted in Stephan Likosky, ed., *Coming Out: An Anthology of International Gay and Lesbian Writings* (New York: Pantheon Books, 1992), 194–96.

20. Ibid., 197–98. Modern Western societies view adult sexual relations with children, male or female, as both criminal and psychologically abnormal, labeling the desire for such behavior as pedophilia. The modernity and cultural specificity of this view are also worth noting in light of Ford and Beach's finding of widespread traditions of socially accepted adult-male-to-preadult-boy relations.

21. Halperin, *One Hundred Years of Homosexuality*, 15–18 and accompanying notes, referring

to Boswell, "Revolutions, Universals and Sexual Categories." Michel Foucault is one of the primary explicators of the social constructionist view of homosexuality. See Foucault, *History of Sexuality*, vols. 1 and 2.

22. Halperin, *One Hundred Years of Homosexuality*, 15, 16, 20–22.

23. Jonathan Katz, *Gay/Lesbian Almanac: A New Documentary* (New York: Harper and Row, 1983), 11, referring to Carroll Smith-Rosenberg, "The Female World of Love and Ritual: Relationships between Women in Nineteenth-Century America," *Signs* 1, no. 1 (Fall 1975): 1–29; and Faderman, *Surpassing the Love of Men*.

24. Faderman, *Odd Girls and Twilight Lovers*, 8–9.

25. Penelope, *Call Me Lesbian*, 21; Faderman, *Odd Girls and Twilight Lovers*, 8.

26. Penelope, *Call Me Lesbian*, 19–20.

27. Ibid., 21.

28. Paula Allen Gunn, "Beloved Women: The Lesbian in American Indian Culture," in Darty and Potter, *Women-Identified Women*, 90–91.

29. Midnight Sun, "Sex/Gender Systems in Native North America," 32–36.

30. Halperin, *One Hundred Years of Homosexuality*, 46; and David Fernbach, "The Spiral Path: A Gay Contribution to Human Survival," in Likosky, *Coming Out*, 194–95.

31. Fernbach, *The Spiral Path*, 194–95.

32. Halperin, *One Hundred Years of Homosexuality*, 15. See also Katz, *Gay/Lesbian Almanac*, 15–16.

33. Halperin, *One Hundred Years of Homosexuality*, 16.

34. Katz, *Gay/Lesbian Almanac*, 661, n. 23.

35. Michael Ruse, *Homosexuality*, (Oxford: Basil Blackwell, 1988), 183–84.

36. Halperin, *One Hundred Years of Homosexuality*, 16–18.

37. Ruse, *Homosexuality*, 21–27.

38. Faderman, *Surpassing the Love of Men*, 386, discussing Freud and Adler.

39. Ibid., quoting Alfred Adler, "Sex," in Jean Baker Miller, ed., *Psychoanalysis and Women* (London: Penguin Books, 1973).

40. Ruse, *Homosexuality*, 45–62.

41. Ibid., 203–4. Various U.S. professional associations have declined to label homosexuality an illness, including the National Association of Social Workers (1972) and the American Psychiatric Association (1973, 1987). Rothblum, "Introduction: Lesbianism as a Model," 4–5.

42. See, for example, Rothblum and Cole, *Loving Boldly*, for discussion and reviews of the psychological literature on the mental health of gay men and lesbians, including lesbian mothers; see also Gary Zinik, "Identity Conflict or Adaptive Flexibility? Bisexuality Reconsidered," in Klein and Wolf, *Two Lives to Lead*, 16–17.

43. Herdt and Boxer, "Introduction," in *Gay Culture in America*, 1, 11.

44. Ibid., 18–20.

45. See, for example, Boston Lesbian Psychologies Collective, *Lesbian Psychologies*.

46. Charles E. Hanson and Anne Evans, "Bisexuality Reconsidered: An Idea in Pursuit of a Definition," in Klein and Wolf, *Two Lives to Lead*, 2.

47. Zinik, "Identity Conflict or Adaptive Flexibility?" 8.

48. Fritz Klein, Barry Sepekoff, and Timothy Wolf, "Sexual Orientation: A Multi-Variable Dynamic Process," in Klein and Wolf, *Two Lives to Lead*, 37.

49. Hansen and Evans, "Bisexuality Reconsidered," 2; and Jay P. Paul, "Bisexuality: Reassessing Our Paradigms of Sexuality," in Klein and Wolf, *Two Lives to Lead*, 29–30.

50. Klein, Sepekoff, and Wolf, "Sexual Orientation," 38, 39, 47.

51. Robert Berkey Branden et al., "The Multidimensional Scale of Sexuality," *Journal of Homosexuality* 19, no. 4 (1990): 67-87, cited in Udis-Kessler, "Notes on the Kinsey Scale and Other Measures," 317–18.

52. Zinik, "Identity Conflict or Adaptive Flexibility?" 9.

53. Ibid., 9–10.

54. Ibid., 10.

55. Ibid., 11.

56. Ibid., 11–12.

57. Ibid., 12.

58. Ibid., 14–15.

59. Ibid., 16.

60. D'Augelli, Anthony R. "Identity Development," in E. J. Trickett, *Human Diversity*, 5, 6, 19, 25–27.

61. "Another study estimates gay population—this time it's five percent." *Bay Windows*, August 26, 1993, p. 13, reporting results of a study by Milton Diamond based on "18 studies from 1968–92 from eight countries including the United States, Japan, and England."

62. Ruse, *Homosexuality*, 3–10; Udis-Kessler, "Notes on the Kinsey Scale and Other Measures," 311–18.

63. Rothblum, "Introduction: Lesbianism as a Model," 2, 4, citing N. B. Davis, "Periodicity of Sex Desire" (1927), abstracted in *Psychological Ab-*

stracts 2 (1928): 1845; and S. Hite, *The Hite Report* (New York: Macmillan, 1976). More recently Bell, Weinberg, and Hammersmith conducted a study of about fifteen hundred men and women, two-thirds of whom were selected because they were gay, lesbian, or bisexual. The 1981 study involved conducting personal interviews and taking developmental histories. A. P. Bell, M. S. Weinberg, and S. K. Hammersmith, *Sexual Preference: Its Development in Men and Women* (Bloomington: Indiana University Press, 1981).

64. Udis-Kessler, "Notes on the Kinsey Scale and Other Measures," 313–18, discussing scales developed by Storms, Klein, and Berkey.

65. Chandler Burr, "Homosexuality and Biology" *Atlantic*, vol. 271, no. 3 (March 1993): 47–65; quote at 52.

66. D. Hamer, S. Hu, V. Magnuson, N. Hu, and A. Pattatucci, "A Linkage between DNA Markers on the X Chromosome and Male Sexual Orientation," *Science*, July 16, 1993, pp. 321–26; quote at 321.

67. Ibid., 321.

68. Michael Bailey and Richard Pillard, *Archives of General Psychiatry* 48 (1991): 1089, and 50 (1993): 217 as quoted in "Homosexuality and Biology", *Atlantic*, March 1993, 64–65.

69. Quoted by Natalie Angier, "Study Suggests Genes Sway Lesbians' Sexual Orientation," *New York Times*, March 12, 1993, section A, 11.

70. Burr, "Homosexuality and Biology," 52–53, citing the work of Dick Swaab and Simon Levay.

71. Burr, "Homosexuality and Biology," 61.

72. Ibid., 61–62.

73. Jay Paul, "Childhood Cross-Gender Behavior and Adult Homosexuality: The Resurgence of Biological Models of Sexuality," in DeCecco and Elia, *If You Seduce a Straight Person*, 41–54.

74. Ibid., 134–37.

75. Ibid., 99–112.

76. Ruse, *Homosexuality*, 131–36.

77. Ibid., 134.

78. Ibid., 133–34.

79. Ibid., 134–36.

80. Mildred Dickemann, "Reproductive Strategies and Gender Construction: An Evolutionary View of Homosexualities," in DeCecco and Elia, eds., *If You Seduce A Straight Person*, 55; Harriet Whitehead, "Bow and the Burden Strap," in Abelove, Barale, and Halperin, *The Lesbian and Gay Studies Reader*, 498–527.

81. Dickemann, "Reproductive Strategies, 60.

82. Ibid., 62.

83. Faderman, *Surpassing the Love of Men*, 386, summarizing Simone de Beauvoir, *The Second Sex* (1949; New York: Vintage Books, 1974), 456–58.

84. E. M. Ettorre, *Lesbians, Women and Society* (London: Routlege and Paul, 1980), 26.

85. Catharine A. MacKinnon, "Feminism, Marxism, Method and the State: An Agenda for Theory," *Signs: Journal of Women in Culture and Society* 7, no. 3 (Spring 1982): 515–16.

86. Rita Mae Brown, "The Woman Identified Woman," *Ladder* 14, nos. 11–12 (August-September 1970): 6, quoted in Darcy and Potter, *Women-Identified Women*, 243.

87. Ettore, *Lesbians, Women and Society*, 5.

88. Ibid., 145.

89. Fernbach, *The Spiral Path*, 198. "Gayness . . . comes into being in objective opposition to the gender system, as a deviant form and the more it escapes the vicious influences of the gendered society around it, the more it takes a form that is inherently egalitarian."

90. Ibid., 195.

91. Ibid., 195–96.

92. Faderman, *Surpassing the Love of Men*, 389–90.

93. Rich, "Compulsory Heterosexuality," 124, 133, *passim*. See also Gunn, "Beloved Women," 83–96.

94. Rich, "Compulsory Heterosexuality," 133, quoting Susan Cabin, "Lesbian Origins," Ph.D diss., Rutgers University, 1978.

95. Ibid., 136–37.

96. Ibid., 135. See also Jeannine Gramick, "Developing a Lesbian Identity," in Darcy and Potter, *Women-Identified Women*, 32. She points out that research about gay men describes an "anonymous sex" stage of coming out which her research finds is not true of lesbians, who more often "require emotional bonds before any sexual involvement is initiated."

97. Judy Grahn, "Lesbian as Bogey Woman," *Gay Women's Liberation*, January 1970; reprinted in Carol Wilson et al., eds., *Lesbians Speak Out* (Oakland, CA: Women's Press Collective, 1974), as quoted in Faderman, *Surpassing the Love of Men*, 329.

98. Faderman, *Surpassing the Love of Men*, 389–90.

99. Rothblum, "Introduction: Lesbianism as a Model," 8.

100. Orlando, "Loving Whom We Choose," 229–30.

101. Elisabeth Reba Weise, "Introduction," in Weise, *Closer to Home*, ix, xi, xv.

102. Gibian, "Refusing Certainty," 5–7.

103. Luce Iraguay, "This Sex Which Is Not One," in E. Marks and I. deCourtivron, eds., *New French Feminism*, trans. C. Reeder (New York: Schocken, 1981), 103.

104. Helene Cixous, "Sorties: Out and Out: Attacks/Ways/Out/Forays," in Catherine Belsey and Jane Moore, eds., *The Feminist Reader: Essays in Gender and the Politics of Literary Criticism* (New York: Basil Blackwell, 1989), 104; quoted in Gibian, "Refusing Certainty," 7.

105. Dvora Zipkin, "Why Bi?" in Weise, *Closer To Home*, 57–58.

106. Margaret Mihee Choe, "Our Selves, Growing Whole," in Weise, *Closer to Home*, 22–23.

107. Amanda Udis-Kessler, "Closer to Home: Bisexual Feminism and the Transformation of Hetero/sexism," in Weise, *Closer To Home*, 184.

108. Karin Baker, "Bisexual Feminist Politics: Because Bisexuality Is Not Enough," in Weise, *Closer To Home*, 259–60.

109. Ibid., 266.

Bibliography

Life Stories, Coming Out Stories

Beam, Joseph, ed. *In the Life: A Black Gay Anthology.* Boston: Alyson Publications, 1986.

Cheever, John. *The Journals of John Cheever.* New York: Knopf, 1991.

Covina, Gina, and Laurel Galana, eds. *The Lesbian Reader.* Guerneville, CA: Amazon Press, 1975.

Cowan, Thomas. *Gay Men and Women Who Enriched the World.* New York: William Mulvey, 1988.

Eichberg, Rob. *Coming Out: An Act of Love.* New York: Plume, 1991.

Fricke, Aaron. *Reflections of a Rock Lobster: A Story about Growing Up Gay.* Boston: Alyson Publications, 1981.

Gay Men's Oral History Group. *Walking after Midnight.* New York: Routledge, 1989.

Green, Michelle. *The Dream at the End of the World: Paul Bowles and the Literary Renegades of Tangier.* New York: HarperCollins, 1992.

Hemphill, Essex, ed. *Brother to Brother: New Writings by Black Gay Men.* Boston: Alyson Publications, 1991.

Hippler, Mike. *Matlovich: The Good Soldier.* Boston: Alyson Publications, 1989.

Hutchins, Loraine, and Lani Kaahumanu, eds. *Bi Any Other Name: Bisexual People Speak Out.* Boston: Alyson Publications, 1991.

Kramer, Larry. *Reports from the Holocaust: The Making of an AIDS Activist.* New York: St. Martin's Press, 1989.

Lesbian Oral History Group. *Inventing Ourselves: Lesbian Life Stories.* New York: Routledge, 1989.

Lorde, Audre. *Sister Outsider: Essays and Speeches*. Watsonville, CA: Crossing Press, 1984.

_____. *Zami: A New Spelling of My Name*. Watertown, MA: Persephone Press, 1982.

McNaught, Brian. *On Being Gay: Thoughts on Family, Faith and Love*. New York: St. Martin's Press, 1988.

Marotta, Toby. *Sons of Harvard: Gay Men from the Class of 1967*. New York: William Morrow, 1982.

Miller, Neil. *In Search of Gay America: Women and Men in a Time of Change*. New York: Harper and Row, 1989.

_____. *Out in the World*. New York: Harper and Row, 1992.

Monette, Paul. *Becoming a Man: Half a Life Story*. New York: Harcourt Brace Jovanovich, 1992.

Moraga, Cherríe. *Living in The War Years: Lo que nunca paso por sus labios*. Boston: South End Press, 1983.

Moraga, Cherríe, and Gloria Anzaldúa, eds. *This Bridge Called My Back: Writings of Radical Women of Color*. Watertown, MA: Persephone Press, 1981.

Nijinsky, Tamara. *Nijinsky Legacy*. Ed. Michel Sarda and Dounelee Ray. London: Bachman and Turner, 1990.

Penelope, Julia, and Sarah Valentine, eds. *Finding the Lesbians: Personal Accounts from Around the World*. Freedom, CA: Crossing Press, 1990.

Penelope, Julia, and Susan J. Wolfe, eds. *The Coming Out Stories*. Watertown, MA: Persephone Press, 1980. Reprinted as *The Original Coming Out Stories*. Freedom, CA: Crossing Press, 1989.

Reid, John. *The Best Little Boy in the World*. New York: Ballantine, 1986.

Roscoe, Will, ed. *Living the Spirit: A Gay American Indian Anthology*. New York: St. Martin's Press, 1988.

Silvera, Makeda, ed. *Piece of My Heart: A Lesbian of Colour Anthology*. Toronto: Sister Vision Press, 1991.

Smith, Barbara. *Home Girls: A Black Feminist Anthology*. New York: Kitchen Table: Women of Color Press, 1983.

Trujillo, Carla, ed. *Chicana Lesbians: The Girls Our Mothers Warned Us About.* Berkeley, CA: Third Woman Press, 1991.

Vega Studio's Staff. *Men of Color: An Essay on the Black Male Couple.* Sicklerville, NJ: Vega Press, 1989.

White, Edmund. *States of Desire: Travels in Gay America.* New York: E. P. Dutton, 1980.

LESBIAN/GAY THEORY

Belsey, Catherine, and Jane Moore, eds. *The Feminist Reader: Essays in Gender and the Politics of Literary Criticism.* New York: Basil Blackwell, 1989.

Blumenfeld, Warren J., ed. *Homophobia: How We All Pay the Price.* Boston: Beacon Press, 1992.

Blumenfeld, Warren J., and Diane Raymond, eds. *Looking at Gay and Lesbian Life.* Boston: Beacon Press, 1992.

Boston Lesbian Psychologies Collective, ed. *Lesbian Psychologies: Explorations and Challenges.* Urbana: University of Illinois Press, 1987.

Bunch, Charlotte, "Learning from Lesbian Separatism." In Karla Jay and Allen Young, eds. *Lavender Culture.* New York: Jove Publications, 1979.

Bunch, Charlotte, and E. Myron, eds. *Lesbianism and the Women's Movement.* Oakland, CA: Diana Press, 1975.

Collins, Patricia Hill. *Black Feminist Thought: Knowledge, Consciousness, and the Politics of Enlightenment.* New York: Routledge, Chapman and Hall, 1990.

Cruikshank, Margaret. *Lesbian Studies: Present and Future.* Old Westbury, NY: Feminist Press, 1982.

Darty, Trudy, and Sandee Potter, eds. *Women-Identified Women.* Palo Alto, CA: Mayfield, 1984.

de Beauvoir, Simone. *The Second Sex.* 1949; reprint New York: Knopf, 1993.

DeCecco, John and John P. Elia. *If You Seduce A Straight Person, Can You Make Them Gay?* Binghamton, NY: Haworth Press, 1993.

DeCecco, John, and Michael Shively, eds. *Origins of Sexuality and Homosexuality.* Binghamton, NY: Harrington Book Press, 1985.

Devor, Holly. *Gender Blending: Confronting the Limits of Duality.* Bloomington: Indiana University Press, 1989.

Ettorre, E.M. *Lesbians, Women, and Society.* London: Routledge and Kegan Paul, 1980.

Grahn, Judy. *Another Mother Tongue.* Boston: Beacon Press, 1984.

Greenberg, David. *The Construction of Homosexuality.* Chicago: University of Chicago Press, 1990.

Frye, Marilyn. *The Politics of Reality: Essays in Feminist Theory.* Trumansburg, NY: Crossing Press, 1983.

Fuss, Diana, ed. *Inside/Out: Lesbian Theories, Gay Theories.* New York: Routledge, 1991.

Herek, Gary M., and Kevin T. Berrill. *Hate Crime: Confronting Violence against Lesbians and Gay Men.* Newbury Park, CA: Sage, 1991.

Hoaglund, Sarah Lucia. *Lesbian Ethics: Toward New Value.* Palo Alto, CA: Institute of Lesbian Studies, 1988.

hooks, bell. *Feminist Theory: from margin to center.* Boston: South End Press, 1984. Esp. chap. 11, "Ending Female Sexual Oppression."

————. *Talking Back: thinking feminist, thinking black.* Boston: South End Press, 1989. Esp. chap. 17, "Homophobia in Black Communities."

Isay, Richard A. *Being Homosexual: Gay Men and Their Development..* New York: Avon, 1989.

Kirk, Marshall, and Hunter Madsen. *After the Ball: How America Will Conquer Its Fear and Hatred of Gays in the '90s.* New York: Doubleday, 1989.

Klaich, Doris. *Woman Plus Woman.* Tallahassee, FL: Naiad Press, 1989.

Likosky, Stephan. *Coming Out: An Anthology of International Gay and Lesbian Writings.* New York: Pantheon Books, 1992.

Lorde, Audre. *Sister Outsider: Essays and Speeches.* Freedom, CA: Crossing Press, 1984.

Marks, Elaine, and Isabelle deCourtivron, eds. *New French Feminism, An Anthology.* New York: Schocken, 1987.

McNaught, Brian. *On Being Gay: Thoughts on Family, Faith and Love.* New York: St. Martin's Press, 1988.

Moraga, Cherrié, and Gloria Anzaldúa, eds. *This Bridge Called My Back: Writings by Radical Women of Color.* Watertown, MA: Persephone Press, 1981.

Nestle, Joan, ed. *The Persistent Desire: A Femme-Butch Reader.* Boston: Alyson Publications, 1992.

Nestle, Joan. *A Restricted Country.* Ithaca, NY: Firebrand Books, 1987.

Penelope, Julia T. *Call Me Lesbian: Lesbian Lives, Lesbian Theory.* Freedom, CA: Crossing Press, 1992.

Phalen, Shane. *Identity Politics: Lesbian Feminism and The Limits of Community.* Philadelphia: Temple University Press, 1989.

Pharr, Suzanne. *Homophobia: A Weapon of Sexism.* Inverness, CA: Chardon Press, 1988.

Reinisch, June M. *The Kinsey Institute New Report on Sex.* New York: St. Martin's Press, 1990.

Rich, Adrienne, "Compulsory Heterosexuality and Lesbian Existence." In Trudy Darty and Sandee Potter, eds. *Women-Identified Women.* Palo Alto, CA: Mayfield, 1984.

_____. *Of Woman Born: Motherhood As Experiences and Institution.* New York: Norton, 1986.

Rothblum, Esther, and Ellen Cole, eds. *Loving Boldly: Issues Facing Lesbians.* Binghamton, NY: Harrington Park Press, 1989.

Ruse, Michael. *Homosexuality.* Oxford: Basil Blackwell, 1988.

Silvera, Makeda, ed. *Piece of My Heart: A Lesbian of Colour Anthology.* Toronto: Sister Vision Press, 1991.

Tatchell, Peter. *Europe in the Pink: Lesbian and Gay Equality in the New Europe.* London: GMP Publishers, 1992.

Tripp, C. A. *The Homosexual Matrix.* New York: Meridian, 1987.

Vida, Ginny, ed. *Our Right to Love*. Englewood Cliffs, NJ: Prentice-Hall, 1978.

Whitney, Catherine. *Uncommon Lives: Gay Men and Straight Women*. New York: New American Library, 1989.

THE WORKPLACE

McNaught, Brian. *Gay Issues in the Workplace*. New York: St. Martin's Press, 1993.

Woods, James D. and Jay H. Lucas. *The Corporate Closet: The Professional Lives of Gay Men In America*. New York: Free Press, 1993.

Repa, Barbara Kate. *Your Rights in the Workplace*. Berkeley: Nolo Press, 1993.

Wolfson, Evan. *Out on the Job, Out of a Job: A Lawyer's Overview of the Employment Rights of Lesbians and Gay Men*. New York: Lambda Legal Defense and Education Fund, 212-995-8585, 1993.

HISTORY AND GAY STUDIES

Abelove, Henry, Michele Barale, and David Halperin, eds. *The Lesbian and Gay Studies Reader*. New York: Routledge, 1993.

Blackwood, Evelyn, ed. *The Many Faces of Homosexuality: Anthropological Approaches to Homosexual Behavior*. Binghamton, NY: Harrington Park Press, 1986.

Boswell, John. *Christianity, Social Tolerance, and Homosexuality: Gay People in Western Europe from the Beginning of the Christian Era to the Fourteenth Century*. Chicago: University of Chicago Press, 1980.

D'Emilio, John. *Sexual Politics, Sexual Communities: The Making of a Homosexual Minority in the United States, 1940–1970*. Chicago: University of Chicago Press, 1983.

D'Emilio, John, and Estelle B. Freedman. *Intimate Matters: A History of Sexuality in America*. New York: Harper and Row, 1988.

Duberman, Martin B., Martha Vicinis, and George Chauncy, Jr., eds. *Hidden from History: Reclaiming the Gay and Lesbian Past*. New York: New American Library, 1989.

Faber, Doris. *The Life of Lorena Hickok: E.R.'s Friend*. New York: William Morrow, 1980. (Out of print)

Faderman, Lillian. *Odd Girls and Twilight Lovers: A History of Lesbian Life in Twentieth-Century America.* New York: Penguin Books, 1992.

_____. *Surpassing the Love of Men: Romantic Friendship and Love between Women from the Renaissance to the Present.* New York: William Morrow, 1981.

Foucault, Michel. *A History of Sexuality.* New York: Random House, 1986, 1990, 3 vols.

Gerard, Kent, and Gert Hekma, eds. *The Pursuit of Sodomy: Male Homosexuality in Renaissance and Enlightenment Europe.* Binghamton, NY: Harrington Park Press, 1989.

Greenberg, David. *The Construction of Homosexuality.* Chicago: University of Chicago Press, 1988.

Gunn, Paula Allen, "Beloved Women: The Lesbian in American Indian Culture." In Trudy Darty and Sandee Potter, eds., *Woman-Identified Women.* Palo Alto, CA: Mayfield, 1984.

Halperin, David M. *One Hundred Years of Homosexuality: And Other Essays on Greek Love.* New York: Routledge, 1989.

Herdt, Gilbert, ed. *Gay Culture in America: Essays from the Field.* Boston: Beacon Press, 1993.

Hoffman, Martin. *The Gay World.* New York: Basic Books, 1968. (Out of print)

Katz, Jonathan Ned. *Gay American History: Lesbians and Gay Men in the U.S.A.* New York: Crowell, 1976.

_____. *Gay/Lesbian Almanac: A New Documentary.* New York: Harper and Row, 1983.

Lumsden, Ian. *Homosexuality, Society and the State in Mexico.* Toronto: Canadian Gay Archives, 1991.

Marcus, Eric. *Making History: The Struggle for Gay and Lesbian Equal Rights, 1945–1990.* New York: HarperCollins, 1992.

National Gay and Lesbian Task Force, "Anti-Gay Violence, Victimization, and Defamation." (NGLTF, 1517 U Street NW.) Washington, DC, 20009, 1988 and subsequent years.

Plant, Richard. *The Pink Triangle: The Nazi War Against Homosexuals.* New York: Henry Holt, 1988.

Porter, Kevin, ed. *Between the Acts: Lives of Homosexual Men, 1885–1967.* London: Routledge, 1991.

Roberts, J. R., "Black Lesbians before 1970: A Bibliographical Essay." In Margaret Cruickshank, ed., *Lesbian Studies.* Old Westbury, NY: Feminist Press, 1982.

Rowse, A. L. *Homosexuals in History: A Study of Ambivalence in Society, Literature, and the Arts.* New York: Dorset Press, 1983.

Schmitt, Arno, and Jehoeda Sofer. *Sexuality and Eroticism among Males in Moslem Societies.* Binghamton, NY: Harrington Park Press, 1992.

Watanabe, Tsuneo, and Jun'ichi Iwata. *The Love of the Samurai: A Thousand Years of Japanese Homosexuality.* London: GMP Publications, 1989.

PSYCHOLOGY

Atkinson, D. R., G. Morten, and D. W. Sue. *Counseling American Minorities.* Dubuque, IA: Brown, 1979.

Bell, A. P., M. S. Weinberg, and S. K. Hammersmith. *Sexual Preference: Its Development in Men and Women.* Bloomington: Indiana University Press, 1981. (Out of print)

Berzon, Betty. *Positively Gay: New Approaches in Gay and Lesbian Life.* Los Angeles: Mediamix Associates, 1984.

Boston Lesbian Psychologies Collective, ed. *Lesbian Psychologies: Explorations and Challenges.* Urbana: University of Illinois Press, 1987.

Bozett, Frederick W. *Homosexuality and Family Relations.* Binghamton, NY: Haworth Press, 1990.

Coleman, Eli, ed. *Integrated Identity for Gay Men and Lesbians: Psychotherapeutic Approaches for Emotional Well-Being.* Binghamton, NY: Harrington Park Press, 1988.

DeCecco, J. P., and M. G. Shively, eds. *Origins of Sexuality and Homosexuality.* Binghamton, NY: Harrington Park Press, 1985.

Ford, Clellan S., and Frank A. Beach. *Patterns of Sexual Behavior.* Westport, CT: Greenwood Press, 1980.

Hite, Shere. *The Hite Report*. New York: Dell, 1987.

Isay, Richard A. *Being Homosexual*. New York: Avon, 1989.

Kees, Robert J. *Keys to Caring: Assisting Your Gay and Lesbian Clients*. Boston: Alyson Publications, 1990.

Kinsey, A. C., W. B. Pomeroy, E. E. Martin, and P. H. Gebhard. *Sexual Behavior in the Human Female*. Philadelphia: W. B. Saunders, 1953.

————. *Sexual Behavior in the Human Male*. Philadelphia: W. B. Saunders, 1948.

Klein, Fritz, and Timothy J. Wolf. *Two Lives to Lead: Bisexuality in Men and Women*. Binghamton, NY: Harrington Park Press, 1985.

Masters, William, and Virginia Johnson. *Heterosexuality*. New York: HarperCollins, 1994.

McWhirter, David P., and Andrew M. Mattison. *The Male Couple: How Relationships Develop*. Englewood Cliffs, NJ: Prentice-Hall, 1985.

Miller, Jean Baker, ed. *Psychoanalysis and Women*. London: Penguin Books, 1973. (Out of print)

Moses, A. Elfin, and Robert O. Hawkins, Jr. *Counseling Lesbian Women and Gay men: A Life Issues Approach*. Columbus, OH: Merrill Publishing, 1982.

Pierce, Carol, David Wagner, and Bill Page. *The Male/Female Continuum: Paths to Colleagueship*. Laconia, NH: New Dynamics Publications, 1994.

Rothblum, Esther D., and Ellen Cole, eds. *Loving Boldly: Issues Facing Lesbians*. Binghamton, NY: Harrington Park Press, 1989.

BISEXUAL PEOPLE: THEORIES, STORIES

Buck, Claire. *H.D. and Freud: Bisexuality and a Feminine Discourse*. New York: St. Martin's Press, 1991.

Faderman, Lillian. *Surpassing the Love of Men*. New York: Knopf, 1993.

Geller, Thomas, ed. *Bisexuality: A Reader and Sourcebook*. Ojai, CA: Times Change Press, 1990.

Hutchins, Loraine, and Lani Kaahumanu, eds. *Bi Any Other Name: Bisexual People Speak Out.* Boston: Alyson Publications, 1991.

Klein, Fred. *The Bisexual Option: A Concept of One Hundred Percent Intimacy.* New York: Arbor House, 1978.

Klein, Fritz, and Timothy J. Wolff, eds. *Two Lives to Lead: Bisexuality in Men and Women.* Binghamton, NY: Harrington Park Press, 1985.

Kohn, Barry, and Alice Matusow. *Barry and Alice: Portrait of a Bisexual Marriage.* Englewood Cliffs, NJ: Prentice-Hall, 1980.

McDonald, A. P. "Bisexuality: Some Comments on Research Theory." *Journal of Homosexuality* 6(3):21–35.

Ochs, Robyn, ed. *The Bisexual Resource Guide.* Boston: East Coast Bisexual Network, 1995.

Weise, Elizabeth R., ed. *Closer to Home: Bisexuality and Feminism.* Seattle: Seal Press, 1992.

Wolff, Charlotte. *Bisexuality: A Study.* London: Quartet Books, 1979.

RELIGION

Balka, Christie, and Andy Rose. *Twice Blessed: On Being Lesbian or Gay and Jewish.* Boston: Beacon Press, 1989.

Batchelor, Edward. *Homosexuality and Ethics.* New York: Pilgrim Press, 1980.

Beck, Evelyn T. *Nice Jewish Girls: A Lesbian Anthology.* Watertown, MA: Persephone Press, 1982.

Boswell, John. *Christianity, Social Tolerance, and Homosexuality: Gay People in Western Europe from the Beginning of the Christian Era to the Fourteenth Century.* Chicago: University of Chicago Press, 1980.

Boyd, Malcolm, and Nancy L. Wilson. *Amazing Grace: Stories of Lesbian and Gay Faith.* Freedom, CA: Crossing Press, 1991.

Clark, Michael. *A Place to Start.* Las Colinas, TX: Monument Press, 1989.

Curb, Rosemary. *Lesbian Nuns: Breaking Silence.* New York: Warner Books, 1985.

Fortunato, John. *Embracing the Exile: Healing Journeys of Gay Christians.* San Francisco: Harper and Row, 1985.

Freedman, Marcia. *Exile in the Promised Land.* Ithaca, NY: Firebrand Books, 1990.

Glaser, Chris. *Come Home: Reclaiming Spirituality and Community as Gay Men and Lesbians.* New York: Harper and Row, 1990.

_____. *Coming Out to God: Prayers for Lesbians and Gay Men, and Our Families and Advocates.* Westminster, KY: John Knox Press, 1991.

_____. *Uncommon Calling: A Gay Man's Struggle to Serve the Church.* San Francisco: Harper, 1988.

Gramick, Jeannine, ed. *Homosexuality in the Priesthood and the Religious Life.* New York: Crossroad Press, 1989.

Hasbany, Richard, ed. *Homosexuality and Religion.* Binghamton, NY: Haworth Press, 1990.

Heyward, Carter. *Our Passion for Justice: Images of Power, Sexuality, and Liberation.* Cleveland: Pilgrim Press, 1984.

_____. *Touching Our Strength: The Erotic as Power and the Love of God.* New York: Harper and Row, 1989.

McNeil, John J. *The Church and the Homosexual.* 3d ed. Boston: Beacon Press, 1988.

_____. *Taking a Chance on God.* Boston: Beacon Press, 1989.

Nelson, James. *Between Two Gardens: Reflections on Sexuality and Religious Experience.* Cleveland: Pilgrim Press, 1983.

_____. *Embodiment: An Approach to Sexuality and Christian Theology.* Minneapolis: Augsburg Press, 1979.

Perry, Rev. Troy, and Charles Lucas. *The Lord Is My Shepherd and He Knows I'm Gay.* Austin, TX: Liberty Press, 1987.

Scanzoni, Letha, and Virginia Ramez Mollencott. *Is the Homosexual My Neighbor? Another Christian View.* New York: Harper and Row, 1978.

Swidler, Arlene, ed. *Homosexuality and World Religions.* Valley Forge, PA: Trinity Press International, 1993.

Williams, Robert. *Just As I Am: A Practical Guide to Being Out, Proud, and Christian.* New York: Crown, 1992.

Zanotti, Barbara, ed. *A Faith of One's Own: Explorations by Catholic Lesbians.* Trumansburg, NY: Crossing Press, 1986.

LESBIAN/GAY PARENTS, PARENTS OF LESBIANS AND GAY MEN

Alpert, Harriet. *We Are Everywhere: Writings by and about Lesbian Parents.* Freedom, CA: Crossing Press, 1988.

American Psychological Association. *Lesbian Parents and Their Children: A Resource Paper for Psychologists.* Washington, D.C.: APA Public Interest Directorate, 1991. Includes annotated bibliography.

Back, Gloria. *Are You Still My Mother? Are You Still My Family?* New York: Warner Books, 1985.

Barret, Robert L., and Bryan E. Robinson. *Gay Fathers.* Lexington, MA: Lexington Books, 1990.

Borhek, Mary. *Coming Out to Parents: A Two-Way Survival Guide for Lesbians and Gay Men and Their Parents.* Cleveland: Pilgrim Press, 1983.

———. *My Son Eric.* Cleveland: Pilgrim Press, 1984.

Clark, Don. *Loving Someone Gay.* Hudson, NY: NAL/Dutton, 1978.

Cohen, Susan, and Daniel Cohen. *When Someone You Know Is Gay.* New York: Dell, 1992.

Fairchild, Betty, and Nancy Hayward. *Now That You Know: What Every Parent Should Know about Homosexuality.* New York: Harcourt Brace Jovanovich, 1979; 2d ed. 1989.

Fricke, Aaron, and Walter Fricke. *Sudden Strangers: The Story of a Gay Son and His Father.* New York: St. Martin's Press, 1991.

Griffin, Carolyn W., Marian J. Wirth, and Arthur G. Wirth. *Beyond Acceptance: Parents of Lesbians and Gays Talk about Their Experiences.* New York: St. Martin's Press, 1986.

Herdt, Gilbert, ed. *Gay and Lesbian Youth*. Binghamton, NY: Harrington Park Press, 1989.

MacPike, Loralee, ed. *There's Something I've Been Meaning to Tell You*. Tallahassee, FL: Naiad Press, 1989. Gay/lesbian parents coming out to their children.

Muller, Ann. *Parents Matter: Parents' Relationships with Lesbian Daughters and Gay Sons*. New York: Naiad Press, 1987.

Newman, Leslea. *Heather Has Two Mommies*. With illustrations by Diana Souza. New York: In Other Words Press, 1989.

Patterson, Charlotte J. "Children of Gay and Lesbian Parents." *Child Development* 63 (October 1992): 1025–42.

Pillemer, Karl, and Kathleen McCartney, eds. *Parent-Child Relations Across the Lifespan*. Hillsdale, NJ: Lawrence Erlbaum Associates, 1991.

Pollack, Sandra, and Jeanne Vaughn, eds. *Politics of the Heart: A Lesbian Parenting Anthology*. Ithaca, NY: Firebrand Books, 1987.

Rafkin, Louise, ed. *Different Daughters: A Book by Mothers of Lesbians*. Pittsburgh, PA: Cleis Press, 1990.

———. *Different Mothers: Sons and Daughters of Lesbians Talk about Their Lives*. Pittsburgh, PA: Cleis Press, 1990.

BIOLOGY

Burr, Chandler, "Homosexuality and Biology." Atlantic, March 1993, 271.

Marshall, Eliot. "Sex on the Brain." *Science* 257 (July 1992): 620–21.

Money, John. *Gay, Straight and In–between: The Sexology of Erotic Orientation*. Oxford: Oxford University Press, 1988.

Ruse, Michael. *Homosexuality*. Oxford: Basil Blackwell, 1988.

Tiefer, Leonore, "A Feminist Perspective on Sexology and Sexuality." In Marry McCanney Gergen, ed., *Feminist Thought and the Structure of Knowledge*. New York: New York University Press, 1988.

Weinrich, James D. *Sexual Landscapes: Why We Are What We Are, Why We Love Whom We Love*. New York: Scribner's Sons, 1987.

YOUTH

Alyson, Sasha, ed. *Young, Gay and Proud! For Adolescents Wondering If They Are Gay.* Boston: Alyson Publications, 1980.

Back, Gloria. *Are You Still My Mother? Are You Still My Family?* New York: Warner Books, 1985.

Bell, Ruth. *Changing Bodies, Changing Lives: A Book for Teens on Sex and Relationships.* New York: Random House, 1988.

Cohen, Susan, and Daniel Cohen. *When Someone You Know Is Gay.* New York: Dell, 1992.

Crist, Sean. *Out on Campus: A "How-to" Manual of Gay and Lesbian Campus Activism.* Bloomington, IN: Association of College Unions, Region 4, 1990.

D'Augelli, Anthony R. "Identity Development and Sexual Orientation: Toward a Model of Lesbian, Gay, and Bisexual Development," in E. J. Trickett, R. Watts, and D. Berman, eds. *Human Diversity: Perspectives on People in Context.* San Francisco: Jossey-Bass, 1994.

Donaghe, Ronald E. *Common Sons.* Austin, TX: Edward-William Publishing, 1989.

Garden, Nancy. *Annie on My Mind.* New York: Farrar, Straus, and Giroux, 1982.

Gibson, P., "Gay Male and Lesbian Youth Suicide." In *Risk Factors for Youth Suicide: Vol. 2, Report of the Secretary's Task Force on Youth Suicide.* U.S. Department of Health and Human Services, Public Health Service, Alcohol, Drug Abuse and Mental Health Administration, 1989.

Gleitzman, Morris. *Two Weeks with the Queen.* New York: Putnam, 1991.

Hanckel, Frances, and John Cunningham. *A Way of Love, a Way of Life: A Young Person's Introduction to What It Means to Be Gay.* New York: Willaim Morrow, 1979.

Harbeck, Karen M., ed. *Coming Out of the Classroom Closet: Gay and Lesbian Students, Teachers and Curricula.* Binghamton, NY: Haworth Press, 1992.

Harry, J., "Sexual Identity Issues." In *Risk Factors for Youth Suicide: Vol. 2, Report of the Secretary's Task Force on Youth Suicide.* U.S. Department of Health and Human

Services, Public Health Service, Alcohol, Drug Abuse and Mental Health Administration, 1989.

Herdt, Gilbert, ed. *Gay and Lesbian Youth*. Binghamton, NY: Harrington Park Press, 1989.

Herdt, Gilbert, and Andrew Boxer. *Children of Horizons: How Gay and Lesbian Teens Are Leading a New Way Out of the Closet*. Boston: Beacon Press, 1993.

Heron, Ann, ed. *One Teenager in Ten: Writings by Gay and Lesbian Youth*. Boston: Alyson Publications, 1983.

Heron, Ann, and Meredith Maran. *How Would You Feel if Your Dad Was Gay?* Boston: Alyson Publications, 1991.

Homes, A. M. *Jack*. New York: Macmillan, 1989.

Lipkin, Arthur. *A Staff Development Guide for Anti-Homophobia Education*. Cambridge: Harvard Graduate School of Education, 1993.

Martin, A. D. "Learning To Hide: The Socialization of the Gay Adolescent." *Annals of the American Society for Adolescent Psychiatry* 10 (1983): 652–54.

Miller, Neil. "Sex Education." *Boston Globe Magazine*, November 8, 1992.

Newman, Leslea. *Heather Has Two Mommies*. With illustrations by Diana Souza. New York: In Other Words Press, 1989.

Project 10 Handbook: Addressing Lesbian and Gay Issues in Our Schools. Los Angeles: Friends of Project 10, 1991.

Remafedi, Gary, ed. *Death by Denial: Preventing Suicide in Gay and Lesbian Teenagers*. Boston: Alyson Publications, 1994.

Remafedi, G., J. A. Farrow, and R. W. Deisher. "Risk Factors for Attempted Suicide in Gay and Bisexual Youth." *Pediatrics* 87 (1991): 869–75.

Whitlock, Katherine. *Bridges of Respect: Creating Support for Lesbian and Gay Youth*. Philadelphia: American Friends Service Committee, 1989.

Willhoite, Michael. *Daddy's Roommate*. Boston: Alyson Publications, 1990.

INDEX

Please note:

- Page numbers in **bold print** indicate words and phrases used on the continuum diagram or pages where the diagram words are described. Wording may differ in the text from the diagram in order to fit the descriptive material.
- *Italicized* page numbers indicate definitions and explanatory material.
- Index words in CAPITAL LETTERS designate subject headings.

New Dynamics is a group of organization development consultants dedicated to helping to create organizations free of bias related to culture, gender, and sexual identity.

We believe we must live and practice what we expect others to value and live.

We believe that people can create for themselves a work environment which will nourish and productively utilize their special skills, and that organizations can create for all their employees a work environment that is challenging, growth-producing, and productive.

New Dynamics has met human resources training and consulting needs of clients since 1972. We serve business, industry, human services, and educational and religious institutions.

NEW DYNAMICS Publications is a voice for women and men of diverse races, cultures, sexual identities, and callings who experience life as a creative journey. We publish those expressions of the creative search for meaning that expand our boundaries. Our publications empower people to engage in a co-creative process.

A Male/Female Continuum: Paths to Colleagueship
Carol Pierce, David Wagner, and Bill Page, second edition 1994.

Sexual Orientation and Identity:
Heterosexual, Lesbian, Gay, and Bisexual Journeys
Heather Wishik and Carol Pierce, 1995.

A Black/White Continuum in White Culture: Paths to Valuing Diversity
Linda Thomas, Ph.D. and Carol Pierce
(book forthcoming, graphic available)

Power Equity and Groups:
A Manual for Understanding Equity and Acknowledging Diversity
Carol Pierce, 1985, 1994.

For information write to: **NEW DYNAMICS Publications**
Dept AA
P. O. Box 595
Laconia, New Hampshire, 03247
Fax 603-528-7912

Authors:

Heather Wishik is an organizational consultant whose clients include corporations, universities, community groups, churches, and synagogues. She works with a diverse group of associates including, among others, the affiliated consultants of New Dynamics. Also a poet, essayist, and sculptor, Wishik served in the middle 1980's as the first lesbian liaison to the governor of Vermont from the Vermont Coalition of Lesbians and Gay Men. She has taught law and women's studies courses at several universities, and between 1992 and 1994 was the first director of the Tufts University Lesbian, Gay, & Bisexual Resource Center. A former elementary school teacher and then an attorney, her favorite professional role to date involves working with organizations on community building and colleagueship issues, including issues of race and culture, gender, sexual orientation, and equity.

Carol Pierce, author and specialist in creating diversity awareness programs, is an organization development consultant and partner in New Dynamics, an international consulting firm. She is known for her work on valuing diversity in organizations and understanding power equity in groups. She has over twenty years of experience in the field. She is the author of *Power Equity and Groups* and the co-author of *A Male/Female Continuum: Paths to Colleagueship* and the forthcoming book, *A Black/White Continuum in White Culture: Paths to Valuing Diversity.*

NOTES

NOTES

NOTES

NOTES